Lecture Notes in Computer Science 14686

The series Lecture Notes in Computer Science (LNCS), including its subseries Lecture Notes in Artificial Intelligence (LNAI) and Lecture Notes in Bioinformatics (LNBI), has established itself as a medium for the publication of new developments in computer science and information technology research, teaching, and education.

LNCS enjoys close cooperation with the computer science R & D community, the series counts many renowned academics among its volume editors and paper authors, and collaborates with prestigious societies. Its mission is to serve this international community by providing an invaluable service, mainly focused on the publication of conference and workshop proceedings and postproceedings. LNCS commenced publication in 1973.

Masaaki Kurosu · Ayako Hashizume
Editors

Human-Computer Interaction

Thematic Area, HCI 2024
Held as Part of the 26th HCI International Conference, HCII 2024
Washington, DC, USA, June 29 – July 4, 2024
Proceedings, Part III

 Springer

Editors
Masaaki Kurosu
The Open University of Japan
Chiba, Japan

Ayako Hashizume
Hosei University
Tokyo, Japan

ISSN 0302-9743   ISSN 1611-3349 (electronic)
Lecture Notes in Computer Science
ISBN 978-3-031-60427-0   ISBN 978-3-031-60428-7 (eBook)
https://doi.org/10.1007/978-3-031-60428-7

This Springer imprint is published by the registered company Springer Nature Switzerland AG
The registered company address is: Gewerbestrasse 11, 6330 Cham, Switzerland

If disposing of this product, please recycle the paper.

Foreword

This year we celebrate 40 years since the establishment of the HCI International (HCII) Conference, which has been a hub for presenting groundbreaking research and novel ideas and collaboration for people from all over the world.

The HCII conference was founded in 1984 by Prof. Gavriel Salvendy (Purdue University, USA, Tsinghua University, P.R. China, and University of Central Florida, USA) and the first event of the series, "1st USA-Japan Conference on Human-Computer Interaction", was held in Honolulu, Hawaii, USA, 18–20 August. Since then, HCI International is held jointly with several Thematic Areas and Affiliated Conferences, with each one under the auspices of a distinguished international Program Board and under one management and one registration. Twenty-six HCI International Conferences have been organized so far (every two years until 2013, and annually thereafter).

Over the years, this conference has served as a platform for scholars, researchers, industry experts and students to exchange ideas, connect, and address challenges in the ever-evolving HCI field. Throughout these 40 years, the conference has evolved itself, adapting to new technologies and emerging trends, while staying committed to its core mission of advancing knowledge and driving change.

As we celebrate this milestone anniversary, we reflect on the contributions of its founding members and appreciate the commitment of its current and past Affiliated Conference Program Board Chairs and members. We are also thankful to all past conference attendees who have shaped this community into what it is today.

The 26th International Conference on Human-Computer Interaction, HCI International 2024 (HCII 2024), was held as a 'hybrid' event at the Washington Hilton Hotel, Washington, DC, USA, during 29 June – 4 July 2024. It incorporated the 21 thematic areas and affiliated conferences listed below.

A total of 5108 individuals from academia, research institutes, industry, and government agencies from 85 countries submitted contributions, and 1271 papers and 309 posters were included in the volumes of the proceedings that were published just before the start of the conference, these are listed below. The contributions thoroughly cover the entire field of human-computer interaction, addressing major advances in knowledge and effective use of computers in a variety of application areas. These papers provide academics, researchers, engineers, scientists, practitioners and students with state-of-the-art information on the most recent advances in HCI.

The HCI International (HCII) conference also offers the option of presenting 'Late Breaking Work', and this applies both for papers and posters, with corresponding volumes of proceedings that will be published after the conference. Full papers will be included in the 'HCII 2024 - Late Breaking Papers' volumes of the proceedings to be published in the Springer LNCS series, while 'Poster Extended Abstracts' will be included as short research papers in the 'HCII 2024 - Late Breaking Posters' volumes to be published in the Springer CCIS series.

I would like to thank the Program Board Chairs and the members of the Program Boards of all thematic areas and affiliated conferences for their contribution towards the high scientific quality and overall success of the HCI International 2024 conference. Their manifold support in terms of paper reviewing (single-blind review process, with a minimum of two reviews per submission), session organization and their willingness to act as goodwill ambassadors for the conference is most highly appreciated.

This conference would not have been possible without the continuous and unwavering support and advice of Gavriel Salvendy, founder, General Chair Emeritus, and Scientific Advisor. For his outstanding efforts, I would like to express my sincere appreciation to Abbas Moallem, Communications Chair and Editor of HCI International News.

July 2024   Constantine Stephanidis

HCI International 2024 Thematic Areas
and Affiliated Conferences

- HCI: Human-Computer Interaction Thematic Area
- HIMI: Human Interface and the Management of Information Thematic Area
- EPCE: 21st International Conference on Engineering Psychology and Cognitive Ergonomics
- AC: 18th International Conference on Augmented Cognition
- UAHCI: 18th International Conference on Universal Access in Human-Computer Interaction
- CCD: 16th International Conference on Cross-Cultural Design
- SCSM: 16th International Conference on Social Computing and Social Media
- VAMR: 16th International Conference on Virtual, Augmented and Mixed Reality
- DHM: 15th International Conference on Digital Human Modeling & Applications in Health, Safety, Ergonomics & Risk Management
- DUXU: 13th International Conference on Design, User Experience and Usability
- C&C: 12th International Conference on Culture and Computing
- DAPI: 12th International Conference on Distributed, Ambient and Pervasive Interactions
- HCIBGO: 11th International Conference on HCI in Business, Government and Organizations
- LCT: 11th International Conference on Learning and Collaboration Technologies
- ITAP: 10th International Conference on Human Aspects of IT for the Aged Population
- AIS: 6th International Conference on Adaptive Instructional Systems
- HCI-CPT: 6th International Conference on HCI for Cybersecurity, Privacy and Trust
- HCI-Games: 6th International Conference on HCI in Games
- MobiTAS: 6th International Conference on HCI in Mobility, Transport and Automotive Systems
- AI-HCI: 5th International Conference on Artificial Intelligence in HCI
- MOBILE: 5th International Conference on Human-Centered Design, Operation and Evaluation of Mobile Communications

List of Conference Proceedings Volumes Appearing Before the Conference

1. LNCS 14684, Human-Computer Interaction: Part I, edited by Masaaki Kurosu and Ayako Hashizume
2. LNCS 14685, Human-Computer Interaction: Part II, edited by Masaaki Kurosu and Ayako Hashizume
3. LNCS 14686, Human-Computer Interaction: Part III, edited by Masaaki Kurosu and Ayako Hashizume
4. LNCS 14687, Human-Computer Interaction: Part IV, edited by Masaaki Kurosu and Ayako Hashizume
5. LNCS 14688, Human-Computer Interaction: Part V, edited by Masaaki Kurosu and Ayako Hashizume
6. LNCS 14689, Human Interface and the Management of Information: Part I, edited by Hirohiko Mori and Yumi Asahi
7. LNCS 14690, Human Interface and the Management of Information: Part II, edited by Hirohiko Mori and Yumi Asahi
8. LNCS 14691, Human Interface and the Management of Information: Part III, edited by Hirohiko Mori and Yumi Asahi
9. LNAI 14692, Engineering Psychology and Cognitive Ergonomics: Part I, edited by Don Harris and Wen-Chin Li
10. LNAI 14693, Engineering Psychology and Cognitive Ergonomics: Part II, edited by Don Harris and Wen-Chin Li
11. LNAI 14694, Augmented Cognition, Part I, edited by Dylan D. Schmorrow and Cali M. Fidopiastis
12. LNAI 14695, Augmented Cognition, Part II, edited by Dylan D. Schmorrow and Cali M. Fidopiastis
13. LNCS 14696, Universal Access in Human-Computer Interaction: Part I, edited by Margherita Antona and Constantine Stephanidis
14. LNCS 14697, Universal Access in Human-Computer Interaction: Part II, edited by Margherita Antona and Constantine Stephanidis
15. LNCS 14698, Universal Access in Human-Computer Interaction: Part III, edited by Margherita Antona and Constantine Stephanidis
16. LNCS 14699, Cross-Cultural Design: Part I, edited by Pei-Luen Patrick Rau
17. LNCS 14700, Cross-Cultural Design: Part II, edited by Pei-Luen Patrick Rau
18. LNCS 14701, Cross-Cultural Design: Part III, edited by Pei-Luen Patrick Rau
19. LNCS 14702, Cross-Cultural Design: Part IV, edited by Pei-Luen Patrick Rau
20. LNCS 14703, Social Computing and Social Media: Part I, edited by Adela Coman and Simona Vasilache
21. LNCS 14704, Social Computing and Social Media: Part II, edited by Adela Coman and Simona Vasilache
22. LNCS 14705, Social Computing and Social Media: Part III, edited by Adela Coman and Simona Vasilache

23. LNCS 14706, Virtual, Augmented and Mixed Reality: Part I, edited by Jessie Y. C. Chen and Gino Fragomeni
24. LNCS 14707, Virtual, Augmented and Mixed Reality: Part II, edited by Jessie Y. C. Chen and Gino Fragomeni
25. LNCS 14708, Virtual, Augmented and Mixed Reality: Part III, edited by Jessie Y. C. Chen and Gino Fragomeni
26. LNCS 14709, Digital Human Modeling and Applications in Health, Safety, Ergonomics and Risk Management: Part I, edited by Vincent G. Duffy
27. LNCS 14710, Digital Human Modeling and Applications in Health, Safety, Ergonomics and Risk Management: Part II, edited by Vincent G. Duffy
28. LNCS 14711, Digital Human Modeling and Applications in Health, Safety, Ergonomics and Risk Management: Part III, edited by Vincent G. Duffy
29. LNCS 14712, Design, User Experience, and Usability: Part I, edited by Aaron Marcus, Elizabeth Rosenzweig and Marcelo M. Soares
30. LNCS 14713, Design, User Experience, and Usability: Part II, edited by Aaron Marcus, Elizabeth Rosenzweig and Marcelo M. Soares
31. LNCS 14714, Design, User Experience, and Usability: Part III, edited by Aaron Marcus, Elizabeth Rosenzweig and Marcelo M. Soares
32. LNCS 14715, Design, User Experience, and Usability: Part IV, edited by Aaron Marcus, Elizabeth Rosenzweig and Marcelo M. Soares
33. LNCS 14716, Design, User Experience, and Usability: Part V, edited by Aaron Marcus, Elizabeth Rosenzweig and Marcelo M. Soares
34. LNCS 14717, Culture and Computing, edited by Matthias Rauterberg
35. LNCS 14718, Distributed, Ambient and Pervasive Interactions: Part I, edited by Norbert A. Streitz and Shin'ichi Konomi
36. LNCS 14719, Distributed, Ambient and Pervasive Interactions: Part II, edited by Norbert A. Streitz and Shin'ichi Konomi
37. LNCS 14720, HCI in Business, Government and Organizations: Part I, edited by Fiona Fui-Hoon Nah and Keng Leng Siau
38. LNCS 14721, HCI in Business, Government and Organizations: Part II, edited by Fiona Fui-Hoon Nah and Keng Leng Siau
39. LNCS 14722, Learning and Collaboration Technologies: Part I, edited by Panayiotis Zaphiris and Andri Ioannou
40. LNCS 14723, Learning and Collaboration Technologies: Part II, edited by Panayiotis Zaphiris and Andri Ioannou
41. LNCS 14724, Learning and Collaboration Technologies: Part III, edited by Panayiotis Zaphiris and Andri Ioannou
42. LNCS 14725, Human Aspects of IT for the Aged Population: Part I, edited by Qin Gao and Jia Zhou
43. LNCS 14726, Human Aspects of IT for the Aged Population: Part II, edited by Qin Gao and Jia Zhou
44. LNCS 14727, Adaptive Instructional System, edited by Robert A. Sottilare and Jessica Schwarz
45. LNCS 14728, HCI for Cybersecurity, Privacy and Trust: Part I, edited by Abbas Moallem
46. LNCS 14729, HCI for Cybersecurity, Privacy and Trust: Part II, edited by Abbas Moallem

47. LNCS 14730, HCI in Games: Part I, edited by Xiaowen Fang
48. LNCS 14731, HCI in Games: Part II, edited by Xiaowen Fang
49. LNCS 14732, HCI in Mobility, Transport and Automotive Systems: Part I, edited by Heidi Krömker
50. LNCS 14733, HCI in Mobility, Transport and Automotive Systems: Part II, edited by Heidi Krömker
51. LNAI 14734, Artificial Intelligence in HCI: Part I, edited by Helmut Degen and Stavroula Ntoa
52. LNAI 14735, Artificial Intelligence in HCI: Part II, edited by Helmut Degen and Stavroula Ntoa
53. LNAI 14736, Artificial Intelligence in HCI: Part III, edited by Helmut Degen and Stavroula Ntoa
54. LNCS 14737, Design, Operation and Evaluation of Mobile Communications: Part I, edited by June Wei and George Margetis
55. LNCS 14738, Design, Operation and Evaluation of Mobile Communications: Part II, edited by June Wei and George Margetis
56. CCIS 2114, HCI International 2024 Posters - Part I, edited by Constantine Stephanidis, Margherita Antona, Stavroula Ntoa and Gavriel Salvendy
57. CCIS 2115, HCI International 2024 Posters - Part II, edited by Constantine Stephanidis, Margherita Antona, Stavroula Ntoa and Gavriel Salvendy
58. CCIS 2116, HCI International 2024 Posters - Part III, edited by Constantine Stephanidis, Margherita Antona, Stavroula Ntoa and Gavriel Salvendy
59. CCIS 2117, HCI International 2024 Posters - Part IV, edited by Constantine Stephanidis, Margherita Antona, Stavroula Ntoa and Gavriel Salvendy
60. CCIS 2118, HCI International 2024 Posters - Part V, edited by Constantine Stephanidis, Margherita Antona, Stavroula Ntoa and Gavriel Salvendy
61. CCIS 2119, HCI International 2024 Posters - Part VI, edited by Constantine Stephanidis, Margherita Antona, Stavroula Ntoa and Gavriel Salvendy
62. CCIS 2120, HCI International 2024 Posters - Part VII, edited by Constantine Stephanidis, Margherita Antona, Stavroula Ntoa and Gavriel Salvendy

https://2024.hci.international/proceedings

Preface

Human-Computer Interaction is a Thematic Area of the International Conference on Human-Computer Interaction (HCII). The HCI field is today undergoing a wave of significant innovation and breakthroughs towards radically new future forms of interaction. The HCI Thematic Area constitutes a forum for scientific research and innovation in human-computer interaction, addressing challenging and innovative topics in human-computer interaction theory, methodology, and practice, including, for example, novel theoretical approaches to interaction, novel user interface concepts and technologies, novel interaction devices, UI development methods, environments and tools, multimodal user interfaces, human-robot interaction, emotions in HCI, aesthetic issues, HCI and children, evaluation methods and tools, and many others.

The HCI Thematic Area covers four major dimensions, namely theory and methodology, technology, human beings, and societal impact. The following five volumes of the HCII 2024 proceedings reflect these dimensions:

- Human-Computer Interaction - Part I, addressing topics related to HCI Theory and Design and Evaluation Methods and Tools, and Emotions in HCI;
- Human-Computer Interaction - Part II, addressing topics related to Human-Robot Interaction and Child-Computer Interaction;
- Human-Computer Interaction - Part III, addressing topics related to HCI for Mental Health and Psychological Wellbeing, and HCI in Healthcare;
- Human-Computer Interaction - Part IV, addressing topics related to HCI, Environment and Sustainability, and Design and User Experience Evaluation Case Studies;
- Human-Computer Interaction - Part V, addressing topics related to Multimodality and Natural User Interfaces, and HCI, AI, Creativity, Art and Culture.

The papers in these volumes were accepted for publication after a minimum of two single-blind reviews from the members of the HCI Program Board or, in some cases, from members of the Program Boards of other affiliated conferences. We would like to thank all of them for their invaluable contribution, support, and efforts.

July 2024

Masaaki Kurosu
Ayako Hashizume

Human-Computer Interaction Thematic Area (HCI 2024)

Program Board Chairs: **Masaaki Kurosu,** *The Open University of Japan, Japan* and **Ayako Hashizume,** *Hosei University, Japan*

- Salah Uddin Ahmed, *University of South-Eastern Norway, India*
- Jessica Barfield, *University of Tennessee, USA*
- Valdecir Becker, *Federal University of Paraiba, Brazil*
- Nimish Biloria, *University of Technology Sydney, Australia*
- Zhigang Chen, *Shanghai University, P.R. China*
- Hong Chen, *Daiichi Institute of Technology, Japan*
- Emilia Duarte, *Universidade Europeia, Portugal*
- Yu-Hsiu Hung, *National Cheng Kung University, Taiwan*
- Jun Iio, *Chuo University, Japan*
- Yi Ji, *Guangdong University of Technology, Australia*
- Hiroshi Noborio, *Osaka Electro-Communication University, Japan*
- Katsuhiko Onishi, *Osaka Electro-Communication University, Japan*
- Julio Cesar Reis, *University of Campinas, Brazil*
- Mohammad Shidujaman, *Independent University Bangladesh (IUB), Bangladesh*

The full list with the Program Board Chairs and the members of the Program Boards of all thematic areas and affiliated conferences of HCII 2024 is available online at:

http://www.hci.international/board-members-2024.php

HCI International 2025 Conference

The 27th International Conference on Human-Computer Interaction, HCI International 2025, will be held jointly with the affiliated conferences at the Swedish Exhibition & Congress Centre and Gothia Towers Hotel, Gothenburg, Sweden, June 22–27, 2025. It will cover a broad spectrum of themes related to Human-Computer Interaction, including theoretical issues, methods, tools, processes, and case studies in HCI design, as well as novel interaction techniques, interfaces, and applications. The proceedings will be published by Springer. More information will become available on the conference website: https://2025.hci.international/.

General Chair
Prof. Constantine Stephanidis
University of Crete and ICS-FORTH
Heraklion, Crete, Greece
Email: general_chair@2025.hci.international

https://2025.hci.international/

Contents – Part III

HCI for Mental Health and Psychological Wellbeing

Effect of External Characteristics of a Virtual Human Being During
the Use of a Computer-Assisted Therapy Tool 3
    Navid Ashrafi, Vanessa Neuhaus, Francesco Vona,
    Nicolina Laura Peperkorn, Youssef Shiban,
    and Jan-Niklas Voigt-Antons

My Energy to the Moon? Combining Human Energy Tracking
with Financial Chart Analysis for Advanced Desktop Work-Life Tracking 22
    Michael Fellmann, Angelina Clara Schmidt, Hannes Grunert,
    and Baidar Bukht

Overcome Psychological Alienation Through Artificial Intelligence
Painting Healing Workshops 41
    Tanhao Gao, Mengshi Yang, Jin Ning, Yue Qiao, and Hongtao Zhou

Quantification and Analysis of Stress Levels While Walking Up and Down
a Step in Real Space and VR Space Using Electrocardiogram 51
    Masanao Koeda, Yoshio Tsukuda, Katsuhiko Onishi,
    and Hiroshi Noborio

Mapping Epilepsy Monitoring Challenges for Enhanced Patient Experience 63
    Mafalda Morgado, Hande Ayanoğlu, and Rodrigo Hernández Ramírez

Exploring the Mediating Role of Smartphones Between Meaning in Life
and Well-Being 78
    Rageshwari Munderia and Rajbala Singh

Next-Gen Stress Monitoring: Social Robot and AI Integration 87
    Bhavana Nachenahalli Bhuthegowda, Akshara Pande,
    and Deepti Mishra

Open Issues in Persuasive Technologies: Six HCI Challenges for the Design
of Behavior Change Systems 99
    Amon Rapp and Arianna Boldi

iCare: Findings from the Design and Initial Evaluation of a Mental Health
App Prototype for Working-Class Women in India 117
    Jaisheen Kour Reen, Aniefiok Friday, Gerry Chan, and Rita Orji

Connecting Patients and Clinicians: Shedding Light on Functionalities
for Mental Health Apps in Depression Care 133
   Philipp Reindl-Spanner, Barbara Prommegger, Tedi Ikonomi,
   Jochen Gensichen, and Helmut Krcmar

A Study on the Effects of Experiencing a Falling Situation in Virtual
Reality on EEG and Heart Rate Variability in the Elderly 149
   Morihiro Tsujishita, Hiroshi Noborio, Katsuhiko Onishi,
   and Masanao Koeda

HCI in Healthcare

Developing Prosthetic Hand: Innovation in Hand Movement for Paralyzed
Individuals 163
   Md. Tariquzzaman Azad, Md. Farhad Hossain, Safin Rahman,
   Mohammad Shidujaman, and Mengru Xue

Study of the Effectiveness of Gamification Design Applied to Chinese
Medicine Learning App 177
   Rongrong Fu and Yongyan Guo

Accuracy Evaluation of AR Navigation in Partial Nephrectomy 194
   Toshihiro Magaribuchi, Masanao Koeda, Kimihiko Masui,
   Takashi Kobayashi, and Atsuro Sawada

An Investigation into the Rise of Wearable Technologies in the Healthcare
Sector 203
   Abhishek Sharma, Kunnumpurath Bijo, Shisir Prasad Manandhar,
   and Lakshmi Sharma

Study of a Method for Reducing VR Sickness Using the Tunnel Effect 221
   Kaito Watanabe, Katsuhiko Onishi, Masanao Koeda,
   Morihiro Tsujishita, and Hiroshi Noborio

Research on User Experience Design of Artificial Intelligence (AI)
Medical Consultation System 236
   Min Yang and Yongyan Guo

Measurement and Evaluation of Organ Shifts in Real-Life Surgery 253
   Daiki Yano, Masanao Koeda, Miho Asano, Takahiro Kunii,
   and Hiroshi Noborio

Author Index 265

HCI for Mental Health
and Psychological Wellbeing

Effect of External Characteristics of a Virtual Human Being During the Use of a Computer-Assisted Therapy Tool

Navid Ashrafi[1,2]([✉]) [ID], Vanessa Neuhaus[1], Francesco Vona[1] [ID],
Nicolina Laura Peperkorn[3] [ID], Youssef Shiban[3] [ID],
and Jan-Niklas Voigt-Antons[1] [ID]

[1] University of Applied Sciences Hamm-Lippstadt, Marker Allee 76-78,
59063 Hamm, Germany
{navid.ashrafi,francesco.vona,jan-niklas.voigt-antons}@hshl.de,
neuhausvanessa@web.de
[2] Technical University of Berlin, Straße des 17. Juni 135, 10623 Berlin, Germany
ashrafi@tu-berlin.de
[3] Private University of Applied Sciences Göttingen, Weender Landstraße 3-7,
37073 Göttingen, Germany
{shiban,peperkorn}@pfh.de

Abstract. The relevance of identification within media and its capacity to impact the user effectively has been a research focal point for years whether it is a real or fictional character. Identification in the media context shapes behavior and broadens the user's social and emotional experience. In immersive media (such as video games), virtual entities, e.g., virtual agents, avatars, or Non-Player Characters (NPCs), bridge the gap between users and the virtual realm. The sense of immersion is usually accompanied by a higher degree of identification. When using visual representations, i.e., in the form of an avatar or agent, new challenges arise concerning the visual design. In this context, media effects, especially identification, can again make the interaction more pleasant and attractive. While in many contexts of use, decisions can be made regarding visualization using the target group, research in recent years points to the potential of user-defined design, so-called customization. Although it seems obvious here that users visualize a virtual image of themselves in such cases, there are also other approaches to using customization. An essential question in this context is whether and to what extent the identification with a virtual avatar could influence the user experience of a psychological intervention. In this work, we explore the effect of visual similarity of a virtual anthropomorphic agent on the user experience in an intervention to reduce the effect of dysfunctional beliefs. In an experiment, 22 participants were asked to create a virtual agent in two groups, similar and dissimilar to them, and then, the avatar confronted them with their dysfunctional thoughts. The results show that the similarity of the virtual agent is not only associated with statistically

---

N. Ashrafi and V. Neuhaus—contributed equally to this publication.

© The Author(s), under exclusive license to Springer Nature Switzerland AG 2024
M. Kurosu and A. Hashizume (Eds.): HCII 2024, LNCS 14686, pp. 3–21, 2024.
https://doi.org/10.1007/978-3-031-60428-7_1

significant increased identification but also with a positive influence on emotions and intrinsic motivation (more interest and enjoyment). This work contributes to the exploration of customization and identification, especially with virtual agents, and the potential implications for their visual design in the context of computer-assisted therapy tools.

Keywords: Customization · Avatars · Dysfunctional Thoughts

1 Introduction

In media studies, extensive research spanning decades has focused on the crucial role of identification and its effective utilization to influence consumers [20,33]. Whether manifested through real or fictional personalities, presented in text, image, or sound, identification within the media landscape is widely acknowledged for its transformative impact on behavior, expanding consumer social perspectives, and enriching emotional experiences [20,35,39,41].

While the influence of identification in traditional media has been extensively explored, an expanding area of interest lies in immersive media, such as video games or serious games. On these interactive platforms, consumers assume a more active role. Virtual characters serve as direct interfaces between users and the virtual world, with the immersive nature often correlating with heightened levels of identification [30]. This immersive effect extends beyond entertainment media to interactive applications in fields like medicine, especially in developing computer-assisted tools to diagnose, treat, prevent, and rehabilitate mental illnesses.

The exploration of novel therapeutic approaches is particularly relevant given the increasing global prevalence of mental health issues [50]. Computer-assisted tools present several potential advantages, such as time and cost savings, increased acceptance, accessibility, availability, and reduced barriers for patients seeking assistance. In this context, virtual avatars and agents act as natural interfaces, representing users or therapists and assuming roles such as assistants, caregivers, or interview partners [15,49,52]. Examples in cognitive behavioral therapy include the text-based chatbot Woebot studied by Fitzpatrick et al. [27] and the application Help4Mood by Burton et al. [16], featuring a 3D visualization of a virtual agent.

The use of visual representations, such as avatars or agents, in these applications introduces new challenges in terms of visual design. Media effects, notably identification, can be intentionally leveraged to enhance interaction, making it more natural, pleasant, and appealing. Recent research emphasizes the potential of user-defined design, commonly called customization [12,13,57]. While it may seem intuitive for users to visualize a virtual representation of themselves, other approaches, such as individual creation, have been explored. Avatar therapy by Leff et al. [45] is an example where patients with schizophrenia give a face to imaginary voices through a virtual anthropomorphic avatar.

A similar concept was pursued in a recent pilot study targeting mental illnesses like depression and anxiety disorders [40]. Rooted in Beck's cognitive therapy [7], patients engage in a dialogue with an avatar to challenge dysfunctional beliefs with alternative, functional thoughts [40]. Although the personal customization of avatars was initially excluded in this study, discussions of the results hinted at the potential therapeutic benefits of allowing users to modify the avatar's appearance. However, another study by Pimentel and Kalyanaraman [56], exploring the visualization of negative self-concepts, suggests that increased identification following personal customization of the avatar could be negatively influenced when exposed to negative stimuli.

Hence, a pivotal question arises concerning how the degree of identification, particularly in visualizing negative self-concepts with a virtual avatar or agent, may impact the user experience of computer-assisted therapy tools addressing dysfunctional cognitions [40]. This question serves as the focal point of this paper.

To address the research question on the impact of visual similarity on user experience in computer-assisted therapy, five hypotheses have been derived to leverage existing scientific contributions. An experiment incorporating user customization features to design virtual agents will then be conducted. The potential effects, particularly those associated with increased identification, were examined using data collection instruments measuring emotional well-being and motivation.

RQ: How does a virtual anthropomorphic agent's visual similarity or dissimilarity influence identification and user experience when interacting with a computer-assisted therapeutic tool addressing dysfunctional beliefs?
H1: The confrontation with a visually self-similar virtual agent has a higher negative impact on identification than a confrontation with a dissimilar agent.
H2: After confronting a visually self-similar virtual agent, the discrepancy between positive and negative emotional well-being is significantly higher than after interacting with a dissimilar agent.
H3: Confronting a visually self-similar virtual agent has a more significant negative impact on interest and enjoyment after customization than encountering a dissimilar agent.
H4: Following the confrontation with a visually self-similar virtual agent, the perceived value and usefulness are considered overall higher than interaction with a dissimilar agent.
H5: Confronting a visually self-similar virtual agent negatively impacts perceived pressure and tension after customization more than a dissimilar agent.

2 Related Work

2.1 On Identification

In psychology, identification encompasses both a defense mechanism and a process where individuals adopt traits of significant others, contributing to personality development [44]. It is primarily an unconscious process, although it can be partially preconscious or conscious (Laughlin, 1979; Schafer, 1973). Drawing on Freud [28], Wollheim [75], and Bettelheim [9,10] theories, the identification process involves temporarily relinquishing one's identity awareness, allowing a person to view the world from another's standpoint [20]. Erikson [26] notes its development in childhood, intensifying during adolescence with influences from peers and new authorities. It is part of healthy psychological development, fostering independence [22]. In social cognitive learning theory, Bandura [2,3] emphasizes identification's role in shaping behavior, influenced by perceived similarity and motivated by rewards. Notably, identification is not limited to humans and can extend to non-human entities [63]. The consequences of identification, determined by consciously or unconsciously chosen models, can be positive, fostering self-esteem, self-transcendence, and a sense of meaning and belonging, or negative and destructive [48].

Two additional types of identification, often applied in the media context, are similarity identification and wishful identification, shedding light on consumers' relationships with media characters [20,33,41]. Similarity identification, rooted in Bandura's insight [2], emphasizes the significance of the perceived similarity between an individual and a model in predicting the replication of traits. It is synonymous with 'perceived similarity,' acknowledging the subjectivity of perceived resemblance rather than an objectively measurable one [2]. In contrast, wishful identification involves the psychological process where an individual desires or attempts to resemble a model in appearance or behavior [32,33]. The distinction lies in whether identification is based on existing, similar traits or those one wishes to incorporate into one's identity. Both forms, however, are closely interconnected, as similarity identification often triggers the desire to emulate another person or character, especially those perceived as popular or successful, such as media stars [3,4].

2.2 Virtual Agents and Avatars

After providing a concise overview of identification and its associated theories, the focus shifts to defining another pivotal term. Distinguished from a virtual avatar, a virtual agent, also known as a conversational agent, simulates human conversations through text or oral language [66]. In a broader context, it is a user interface facilitating system interactions with end users [64]. This interaction may be based on a predefined script, like a decision tree, or guided by artificial intelligence [66]. Notable examples include voice assistants like Apple's Siri, Microsoft's Cortana, and chatbots used in customer service on online retailer websites. Virtual agents fall into two categories based on appearance-those without visual representation and embodied conversational agents [17], often portrayed in two or three dimensions. Depending on the chosen level of detail, embodied conversational agents can incorporate nonverbal elements like facial expressions and gestures, enhancing the interaction's naturalness [47].

In contrast, a virtual avatar, like an agent, acts as an interface between a user and a digital application. Particularly in immersive media like video games, the critical distinction is that a virtual avatar always graphically represents a user in a virtual space, enabling interaction through controls like a gamepad [29]. They find applications in video games, social media, and other virtual spaces, representing individuals graphically [29]. Unlike virtual agents, virtual avatars always represent one or more users, controlled by the user. In immersive applications, such as video games or serious games, most scientific contributions assume real-time control of virtual avatars, in contrast to the interaction with a virtual agent. This distinction underscores the nuanced dynamics between virtual agents and avatars, influencing user experiences within digital environments.

2.3   Identification in Immersive Media and Healthcare

Virtual avatars, particularly in immersive contexts like video games, present a unique case in exploring identification. Unlike traditional media, the active role of consumers or players fosters a monadic relationship with a media character, which Kimmt et al. [39] also called "true" identification. This process involves a convergence of player and player character, leading to the adoption of feelings, goals, and perspectives [39], which is also theorized to lead to the manifestation of a distinct self-concept during exposure [8,24,39,70]. This idea is rooted in Higgins' Self-Discrepancy Theory [31] and implies that such convergence may lead to reduced self-discrepancy, especially when aspects of the ideal self of the player are present in the avatar [8,39]. Recognizing the effects of identification in immersive media also extends from Cohen's work [20,21]. Positive outcomes include enhanced media enjoyment [30,46,70] and increased persuasiveness of messages [53,54]. Moreover, heightened identification positively correlates with intrinsic motivation, impacting user engagement across various applications like serious games or self-improvement tools [12,36,55].

Another aspect that has been given much attention in recent years is customization, which is also said to impact identification positively [12,13,70]. Turkay & Kinzer [71] suggest that this is related to Self-Determination Theory [62], of which the main components are autonomy, connectedness, presence or immersion, and intuitive control [61]. User similarity [67], personality traits [25,67], time invested [71], and narrative elements [53] also foster identification, as well as the overall user motivation to get invested [39]. Understanding these factors is essential for designing applications that utilize identification for enhanced user experience and engagement.

While extensive research exists on identification in video games, the applicability of identification effects to digital applications in other domains, particularly medicine, remains a substantial area for further exploration. Computer-assisted therapy offers advantages regarding therapist time savings and self-administration by individuals [1,76]. Despite demonstrated effectiveness in treating symptoms like depression [19,27,58], adherence issues persist, significantly beyond controlled trials [18,37]. Addressing this, intrinsic motivation from increased identification, as proposed by Birk et al. [12], could prove beneficial. However, given variations in interactive elements, such as virtual avatars and agents, it is crucial to explore user relationships with virtual agents in different scenarios, as evidenced by existing research on virtual agent perception. Prior research has explored user perceptions of virtual agents, explored by studies on Woebot [27], where users anthropomorphized the virtual agent, referring to it as a "friend" or a "funny little guy". Various studies have also delved into how the appearance of agents influences user preferences [5,6,38], acceptance in different contexts [11,51], their role-model potential [6,60], and the impact of non-verbal behavior [42,43]. In the study's chosen context of addressing dysfunctional cognitions, users confront their negative beliefs through a virtual agent [40]. Like Pimentel and Kalyanaraman's [56] approach, users visualize and distance themselves from a negative self-concept. Exploring emotional responses to varied portrayals of one's negative self, this study investigates the effectiveness of confronting oneself to mitigate negative thoughts. Incorporating customization, based on prior research, enhances identification and potentially improves the application's personalization, motivation, and overall efficacy in treating dysfunctional cognitions. The study probes into how scenarios like similarity and dissimilarity may yield positive or negative effects, considering both intrinsic motivation and general well-being.

3   Methodology

3.1   Data Collection

Identification with the Virtual Agent (PIS): The identification between users and the virtual agent was measured using van Looy et al.'s [72] scale for identification in online games. Specifically, the avatar identification subscale was employed, comprising six items each for similarity identification and embodied presence, and five for wishful identification. Group and game identification scales were excluded. The items were translated into German and slightly adjusted for contextual relevance, mainly by substituting "avatar" with "agent" while maintaining the original meaning. All items were rated on a 5-point Likert scale from 1 = "Strongly disagree" to 5 = "Strongly agree".

Emotional Well-being (PANAS): Given the potential for strong emotional reactions during the engagement with negative thoughts, they were also recorded using the German version of the Positive and Negative Affect Schedule (PANAS) [14], based on the English version by Watson, Clark, and Tellegen [74] which assesses emotional well-being with 20 items, ten describing positive affects and the other ten describing negative affects in adjectives. All items were rated on a 5-point Likert scale from 1 = "Very slightly or not at all' to 5 = "Extremely" This questionnaire was chosen because it shows moderate correlations with the negative effect of the Hopkins Symptom Checklist (HSCL), Beck Depression Inventory (BDI), and State Anxiety Scale (STAI) tests, commonly used for diagnosis in the medical context [74].

Intrinsic Motivation (IMI): To measure intrinsic motivation, particularly linked to enjoyment in identification, the Intrinsic Motivation Inventory by Ryan and Deci [62] was translated into German and applied. Using the interest/enjoyment, pressure/tension, and value/usefulness subscales, the assessment delved into the relationship between these values during customization and confrontation. Participants rated items on a 7-point Likert scale (1 = "Strongly disagree" to 7 = "Strongly agree"). This framework [62] has been previously employed in a similar context [12].

Additional Data: Alongside adapted frameworks, a supplementary questionnaire was created. Users provided general ratings for the therapeutic tool, the tested settings, the virtual agent, and the interaction. They evaluated the utility of customizing the virtual agent in a therapeutic context, expressed satisfaction with available options, and offered suggestions. Ratings were on a 7-point Likert scale, and settings were on a scale from 0 to 10.

3.2 Experiment Setup

Therapy Tool: The therapy tool used in the experiment was built based on the tool used in the original study [40]. Confrontation with personal dysfunctional cognitions was facilitated through a virtual avatar controlled in real-time there, while the newly designed tool used a script-based virtual agent. To allow customization for the two different settings, a 3D model from DAZ 3D Studio [34], was used. Customization options for the upper body of the virtual agent included variations in gender, body build, facial features, facial hair, hairstyle, and eye and skin color. General customization options were selected based on users' preferences that emerged from previous scientific contributions [24,71]. When designing customization options for the therapy tool, emphasis was placed on the virtual agent's external features rather than its personality traits, given the assumption that the agent naturally assumes a personality, particularly in confrontational situations. After preparation, the 3D model was embedded into the Unity game engine [69] and using the SALSA LipSync Suite [68], audio clips of negative thoughts, created online with text-to-speech in two variations, were played in real-time with matching animations. Non-verbal automatic behavior was previously tailored to enable the virtual agent to alternate between skeptical and angry facial expressions (Fig.1).

Experiment Procedure: The experiment, approved by the Ethics Commission of the University of Applied Sciences Hamm-Lippstadt, was conducted at the Lippstadt campus in Germany over four days. Participants were briefed verbally and in writing about the experiment's content, purpose, and procedures before providing official consent. The experiment utilized a desktop computer and tablet for data collection across seven subsequent sessions. Participants recorded personal dysfunctional beliefs, and demographic data, and filled out questionnaires on dysfunctional attitudes using the Dysfunctional Attitude Scale (DAS-18 A) [59] and self-esteem with the German version of Rosenberg's Self-Esteem Scale (RSES) [73].

After completing these questionnaires, participants engaged with the therapy tool. They customized the virtual agent and filled out questionnaires on identification, positive/negative affect, and intrinsic motivation. Following this, participants faced confrontation with the agent and, once again, filled out the

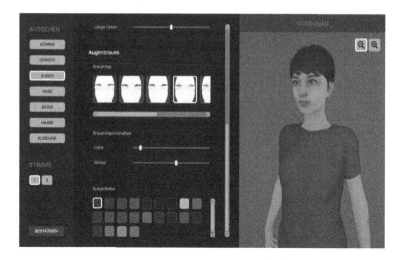

Fig. 1. Customization scene setup.

same questionnaires presented after customization. They repeated this process in both, the similarity and dissimilarity settings. In the similarity setting, participants aimed to create an agent resembling them, while in the dissimilarity setting participants aimed to customize an avatar that would not necessarily look similar to them. The order of settings alternated for each participant. The entire experiment lasted approximately 45 min.

3.3   Participants

Participants $(N = 22)$ comprised nine females, twelve males, and one non-binary person. Their age ranged from 22 to 40 years, with an average age of 27 and they were comprised of diverse educational levels. On a scale of 1 = "Not at all" to 7 = "Very good," 20 participants rated their overall technology experience with a score of four or higher. Seven of them rated their previous experience as "Very good" with an average score of about 5.7. However, only four out of the 22 participants considered their experience as good, with an average score of 2.05. Concerning mental health, five users reported a history of psychotic symptoms, three were currently on therapeutic treatment, and three had received a diagnosis of a mental disorder. Additionally, six participants exhibited conspicuous values in self-esteem, all of which also showed high values in dysfunctional attitudes. Overall, 16 individuals demonstrated elevated values for dysfunctional attitudes, with an average score of 59.2, and for self-esteem, the average score was 19.

4   Results

4.1   Identification

To confirm that the similarity and the dissimilarity settings significantly differ regarding the degree of identification, they were compared using a t-test, both after customization (PRE) and after confrontation (POST). In this section, we will provide an overarching description of our t-test analysis and the implications for our five main hypotheses.

4.2   Hypotheses

H1: The initial hypothesis, pertaining to the extent of impact of the confrontation on overall identification within the contexts of similarity and dissimilarity, was substantiated through a t-test for dependent samples. In the similarity setting, the values for comparison before (M = 2.54, SD = 0.8) and after (M = 2.26, SD = 0.82) yielded t(21) = 2.23, p = .019, and d = 0.47, signifying statistical significance with a moderate effect size. Conversely, in the dissimilarity setting with customization (PRE) (M = 1.38, SD = 0.47) and confrontation (POST) (M = 1.35, SD = 0.44), the result was t(21) = 0.37, p = .356, and d = 0.08, indicating neither significance nor a substantial effect size. A closer examination of the identification subscales unveiled a reduction in wishful identification within the similarity setting. For customization (PRE) (M = 1.8, SD = 0.82) and confrontation (POST) (M = 1.5, SD = 0.8), t(21) = 2.54, p = .01, and d = 0.54 indicated the overall strongest reduction across all subscales. Similarly, similarity identification also decreased significantly from customization (PRE) (M = 3.29, SD = 0.92) to confrontation (POST) (M = 3.05, SD = 1.09) with t(21) = 1.33, p = .034, and d = 0.41. In contrast, the overall smallest effect was observed for the embodied presence subscale in both settings. Upon direct comparison in terms of identification subscales, significant differences for each one were noted for customization (PRE) and confrontation (POST), except for wishful identification after the confrontation with the virtual agent (Fig. 2).

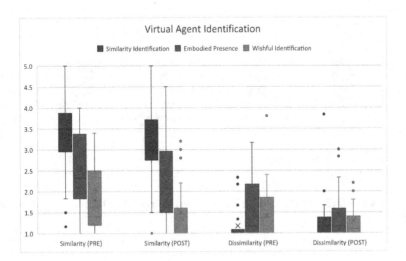

Fig. 2. Identification with Virtual Agent after Customization (PRE) and after Confrontation (POST).

H2: As anticipated, the higher discrepancy between positive and negative affect in the similarity setting after the confrontation was confirmed to be overall higher compared to the dissimilarity setting. To validate this observation, the disparities between positive (M = 29.46, SD = 7.25) and negative affect (M = 17.86, SD = 8.1) in the similarity setting (POST) were contrasted with positive (M = 26.64, SD = 6.0) and negative affect (M = 17.77, SD = 6.61) in the dissimilarity setting (POST) was calculated. The t-test examining these differences resulted in t(21) = 3.02, p = .003, and d = 0.67, indicating a statistically significant distinction (Fig. 3).

Upon closer examination, it was observed that a similar difference was found for customization (POST). The similarity setting (PRE) displayed a contrast in differences between positive (M = 29.45, SD = 6.0) and negative affect (M = 14.96, SD = 5.69) when compared to the dissimilarity setting (PRE) with positive (M = 25.41, SD = 6.48) and negative affect (M = 16.23, SD = 7.53). The t-test resulted in t(21) = 1.88, p = .037, and d = 0.4. It is noteworthy that positive affect in both settings is overall higher for the similarity setting, although only marginally significant. Another important finding is that the similarity setting exhibited a significant increase in negative affect from customization to confrontation. The comparison between customization (PRE) (M = 14.96, SD = 5.69) and after confrontation (POST) (M = 17.86, SD = 8.1) yielded t(21) = −1.82, p = .041, and d = 0.39.

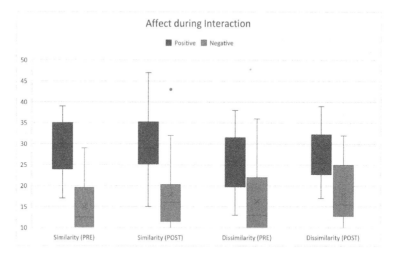

Fig. 3. Positive and Negative Affect during Customization (PRE) and Confrontation (POST).

H3: For this hypothesis, the negative impact of the confrontation on interest and enjoyment is notably more pronounced in the dissimilarity setting compared to the similarity setting, as corroborated in the following outcomes. In the similarity setting, the comparison of collected data for interest and enjoyment following customization (PRE) (M = 5.14, SD = 0.85) and confrontation (POST) (M = 4.73, SD = 1.1) yielded a t(21) = 1.91, p = .035, and d = 0.41. Conversely, in the dissimilarity setting, the comparison after customization (PRE) (M = 4.94, SD = 1.12) and confrontation (POST) (M = 4.42, SD = 1.03) resulted in t(21) = 2.28, p = .017, and d = 0.5. Therefore, statistical significance was observed in both settings in the before-after analysis, with the overall impact being higher in the case of the dissimilarity setting. Furthermore, no notable differences were observed when directly comparing the two settings before and after the confrontation.

H4: The subsequent hypothesis addresses the perceived value and usefulness of the confrontation, with the initial assumption that these factors would be significantly higher for the similarity setting (POST) (M = 4.41, SD = 1.58) compared to the dissimilarity setting (POST) (M = 4.22, SD = 1.5). However, the calculation following the confrontation yielded values of t(21) = 0.84, p = .206, and d = 0.18, indicating a lack of statistical significance. Consequently, the hypothesis is falsified. Upon closer examination of the collected data, the similarity setting exhibited a noteworthy increase when comparing customization (PRE) (M = 4.02, SD = 1.68) and confrontation (POST) (M = 4.41, SD = 1.58), resulting in t(21) = −1.95, p = .032, and d = 0.42, signifying statistical significance. In contrast, the dissimilarity setting did not yield similar results. Here as well, the direct comparison between the settings for both phases of the experiment shows no significant differences.

H5: Finally, the last hypothesis suggests that the perceived pressure and tension of each participant would increase to a greater extent in the dissimilarity setting, compared to the similarity one. This was verified using a t-test. In the similarity setting, after customization (PRE) (M = 2.54, SD = 1.35) and confrontation (POST) (M = 3.41, SD = 1.7), the values were t(21) = −2.92, p = .004, and d = 0.62. Conversely, for a dissimilar virtual agent, the comparison between customization (PRE) (M = 2.36, SD = 1.12) and confrontation (POST) (M = 3.4, SD = 1.52) resulted in t(21) = −3.6, p ¡ .001, and d = 0.77. Thus, the change is significant in both cases, but the effect is more pronounced in the dissimilarity setting, thereby verifying the hypothesis (Fig. 4).

5   Discussion

5.1   Identification, Similarity, and Dissimilarity

The results from the previous section suggest that confrontation, especially in the similarity setting, negatively affects identification. Notably, engagement with the virtual agent in a confrontation led to a general decrease in identification, potentially impacting positive effects like interest and enjoyment. However, this reduced identification could be desirable, aligning with the relevance of distancing oneself from negative beliefs.

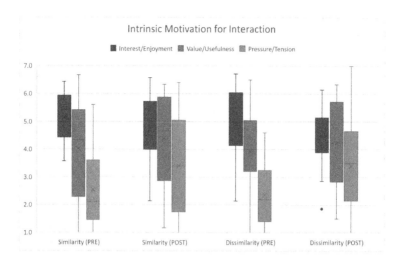

Fig. 4. Intrinsic Motivation subscale ratings for interaction with Virtual Agent for both settings.

Also, in the similarity setting, similarity identification was significantly reduced. Surprisingly, this was not the case for the dissimilarity setting, in which it showed a slight increase. Although not significant, this raises questions about users suddenly perceiving the virtual agent as similar. Given minimal differences and the possibility of reporting errors, these cases leave open questions. Unexpectedly, high presence scores challenged the assumption that virtual agents' reduced interactivity would negatively impact presence.

Overall. presence, along with similarity and wishful Identification, decreased post-confrontation, underlining the positive correlations among the subscales, as also mentioned in prior research [33, 72].

5.2   Positive and Negative Affect

Our second hypothesis suggested a greater difference between positive and negative affect would occur post-confrontation in the similarity setting compared to the dissimilarity setting. The results supported this hypothesis, showing that designing oneself might have been perceived as more satisfying than creating an arbitrary person. Although not conclusively proven in this study, it is reasonable to assume that self-design led to lower discrepancies and likely more positive feelings, as mentioned before. In the dissimilarity setting, users often deviated from their gender or chose amusing options. Thus, the dissimilar agent was likely distant from most users' self-concepts, possibly allowing more discomfort post-customization compared to the similarity setting.

Significantly, negative affect increased post-confrontation in the similarity setting, while positive affect remained unchanged on average. While an increase in negative affect when confronted with unpleasant thoughts is understandable, a similar significant increase in positive affect could have also been expected if users successfully coped with the confrontation. Despite non-significant trends in positive affect increase in the dissimilarity setting, the overall higher mean values in the similarity setting suggest that confronting a self-similar agent was perceived as more unpleasant. Consideration of these findings, however, should be relative to dissimilarity setting values, which were inherently higher.

5.3 Intrinsic Motivation

Although no significant differences in customization were observed, the dissimilarity setting's confrontation significantly decreased interest and enjoyment, aligning with the hypothesis these. A similar significant decrease was found in the similarity setting, where interest and enjoyment were higher on average. However, no significant differences emerged when comparing customization and confrontation values for similarity and dissimilarity. The subsequent hypothesis addressed the perceived value and usefulness of confronting the virtual agent, suggesting that the similarity setting post-confrontation could potentially be perceived as more valuable. However, the data contradicted this hypothesis, indicating that both settings confrontation was perceived as useful, possibly because only the core exercise of contradicting the agent was considered. Lastly, tension and pressure during interaction were considered, with anticipation of a stronger increase in the dissimilarity setting. Although pressure increased significantly for both settings, it was stronger in the dissimilarity setting, aligning with the observed increase in negative affect. It is therefore reasonable to assume that confrontation does amplify negative feelings.

5.4 Evaluation of the Therapeutic Tool

Following the implementation of the therapeutic tool, supplementary data were gathered to rate the tool, the virtual agent, and the interaction with it. The tool garnered a positive reception overall, with a noticeable inclination towards the similarity setting. Participants expressed a preference for this setting, assigning significantly higher ratings compared to the dissimilarity setting. The general rating of the interaction with the virtual agent was positive, although evaluations of visual, auditory, and non-verbal behaviors received slightly lower ratings. The incorporation of a customization feature for the virtual agent within the framework of addressing dysfunctional cognitions was well-evaluated.

5.5 Limitations

In the course of the experiment, several limitations emerged that warrant consideration for the broader application of the results. Similarly, the study encounters challenges in establishing correlations between identification and outcomes. Although moderate correlations were discerned in the similarity setting, other significant dependencies remained either unattainable or only partially demonstrated. A proposition is made for a more stringent delimitation of variables and a larger sample size to potentially reveal explicit relations.

Moreover, the study's consideration of only external attributes for identification, owing to financial and temporal constraints, resulted in limited customization options. Participant feedback indicated a desire for a broader array of options encompassing hairstyles, facial textures, voices, and even features like age and height. While the available options were generally rated as sufficient, the absence of certain options might negatively impact user satisfaction. Additionally, the study's one-week timeframe introduces a potential limitation in understanding shifts in identification levels over an extended period. Prolonged use may exert an influence on observed effects, and the procedural aspects of customization during extended use pose open questions. A suggestion was made to allow users the opportunity to modify the virtual agent over multiple sessions, considering the dynamic processes influencing self-perception. Temporary fluctuations in self-perception may occur due to factors such as mood or priming effects [23,65]. This approach aligns with the potential for shifts in identification levels over an extended timeframe, as noted in the literature [39,71].

6   Conclusion

This study explored the impact of virtual agent similarity on user identification and the user experience in a therapy tool for treating dysfunctional cognition. Customization of self-similar and dissimilar agents was followed by a confrontation phase. Results indicate higher identification with self-similar agents, especially in the similarity setting. Confrontation negatively affects identification, particularly in the similarity setting, with a significant reduction in wishful identification.

Emotional experiences vary based on agent similarity, with self-similar settings correlating with higher positive affect and dissimilar settings displaying higher negative affect. Intrinsic motivation shows fluctuations post-confrontation, with increased interest during customization but a significant decrease in both settings. Perceived value and usefulness increase post-confrontation, notably in the similarity setting. Elevated pressure and tension post-confrontation, also supported by increased negative affect, are more pronounced in the dissimilarity setting.

The study suggests potential links between identification and other factors. The visual appearance of a self-similar or dissimilar virtual agent significantly impacts emotional well-being and motivation, potentially influencing therapy success. Identification, especially when supplemented by customization, may enhance motivation for prolonged interaction. The study provides insights into customization, virtual agent identification, and their implications in therapy. Validation and further investigation into negative emotional experiences are recommended.

References

1. Andersson, G., Bergström, J., Holländare, F., Carlbring, P., Kaldo, V., Ekselius, L.: Internet-based self-help for depression: randomized controlled trial. The British J. Psych.: J. Mental Sci. **187**, 456–61 (12 2005). https://doi.org/10.1192/bjp.187. 5.456
2. Bandura, A.: Social foundations of thought and action. Englewood Cliffs, NJ **1986**(23–28) (1986)
3. Bandura, A.: Social cognitive theory of mass communication. In: Media effects, pp. 110–140. Routledge (2009)
4. Basil, M.D.: Identification as a mediator of celebrity effects. J. Broadcast. Electron. Media **40**(4), 478–495 (1996)
5. Baylor, A.L.: Promoting motivation with virtual agents and avatars: role of visual presence and appearance. Philosoph. Trans. Royal Society B: Biol. Sci. **364**(1535), 3559–3565 (2009)
6. Baylor, A.L., Kim, Y.: Pedagogical agent design: the impact of agent realism, gender, ethnicity, and instructional role. In: Lester, J.C., Vicari, R.M., Paraguaçu, F. (eds.) Intelligent Tutoring Systems, pp. 592–603. Springer Berlin Heidelberg, Berlin, Heidelberg (2004). https://doi.org/10.1007/978-3-540-30139-4_56
7. Beck, A.T.: Cognitive therapy of depression. Guilford press (1979)
8. Bessière, K., Seay, A.F., Kiesler, S.: The ideal elf: Identity exploration in world of warcraft. Cyberpsychol. Behav. **10**(4), 530–535 (2007)
9. Bettelheim, B.: Individual and mass behavior in extreme situations. Psychol. Sci. Public Interest **38**(4), 417 (1943)
10. Bettelheim, B.: The uses of enchantment: The meaning and importance of fairy tales. Vintage (2010)
11. Bickmore, T., Gruber, A.: Relational agents in clinical psychiatry. Harv. Rev. Psychiatry **18**(2), 119–130 (2010)
12. Birk, M.V., Mandryk, R.L.: Combating attrition in digital self-improvement programs using avatar customization. In: Proceedings of the 2018 CHI Conference on Human Factors in Computing Systems, pp. 1–15. CHI '18, Association for Computing Machinery, New York, NY, USA (2018). https://doi.org/10.1145/3173574. 3174234
13. Birk, M.V., Mandryk, R.L.: Improving the efficacy of cognitive training for digital mental health interventions through avatar customization: crowdsourced quasi-experimental study. J. Med. Internet Res. **21**(1), e10133 (2019)
14. Breyer, B., Bluemke, M.: Deutsche version der positive and negative affect schedule panas (gesis panel) (2016)
15. Bălan, O.: eTher – an assistive virtual agent for acrophobia therapy in virtual reality. In: Stephanidis, C., Chen, J.Y.C., Fragomeni, G. (eds.) HCII 2020. LNCS, vol. 12428, pp. 12–25. Springer, Cham (2020). https://doi.org/10.1007/978-3-030-59990-4_2
16. Burton, C., et al.: Pilot randomised controlled trial of help4mood, an embodied virtual agent-based system to support treatment of depression. J. Telemed. Telecare **22**(6), 348–355 (2016)
17. Cassell, J.: Embodied conversational agents: representation and intelligence in user interfaces. AI Mag. **22**(4), 67–67 (2001)
18. Christensen, H., Griffiths, K.M., Farrer, L., et al.: Adherence in internet interventions for anxiety and depression: systematic review. J. Med. Internet Res. **11**(2), e1194 (2009)

19. Clarke, G., et al.: Overcoming depression on the internet (odin)(2): a randomized trial of a self-help depression skills program with reminders. J. Med. Internet Res. **7**(2), e412 (2005)

20. Cohen, J.: Defining identification: a theoretical look at the identification of audiences with media characters. Mass Commun. Society **4**, 245–264 (2001). https://api.semanticscholar.org/CorpusID:1611611

21. Cohen, J.: Audience identification with media characters. Psychol. Entertain. **13**, 183–197 (01 2006)

22. Cramer, P., Cramer, P.: The defense mechanism manual. Springer (1991)

23. DeMarree, K.G., Wheeler, S.C., Petty, R.E.: Priming a new identity: self-monitoring moderates the effects of nonself primes on self-judgments and behavior. J. Pers. Soc. Psychol. **89**(5), 657 (2005)

24. Ducheneaut, N., Wen, M.H., Yee, N., Wadley, G.: Body and mind: a study of avatar personalization in three virtual worlds. In: Proceedings of the SIGCHI Conference on Human Factors in Computing Systems, pp. 1151–1160 (2009)

25. Dunn, R.A., Guadagno, R.E.: My avatar and me-gender and personality predictors of avatar-self discrepancy. Comput. Hum. Behav. **28**(1), 97–106 (2012)

26. Erikson, E.H.: Identity youth and crisis. No. 7, WW Norton & company (1968)

27. Fitzpatrick, K.K., Darcy, A., Vierhile, M.: Delivering cognitive behavior therapy to young adults with symptoms of depression and anxiety using a fully automated conversational agent (woebot): a randomized controlled trial. JMIR Mental Health **4**(2), e7785 (2017)

28. Freud, S.: Outline of psychoanalysis. The Psychoanalytic Review (1913–1957) **29**, 197 (1942)

29. Gazzard, A.: The avatar and the player: understanding the relationship beyond the screen. In: 2009 Conference in games and virtual worlds for serious applications, pp. 190–193. IEEE (2009)

30. Hefner, D., Klimmt, C., Vorderer, P.: Identification with the player character as determinant of video game enjoyment. In: Ma, L., Rauterberg, M., Nakatsu, R. (eds.) Entertainment Computing – ICEC 2007, pp. 39–48. Springer Berlin Heidelberg, Berlin, Heidelberg (2007). https://doi.org/10.1007/978-3-540-74873-1_6

31. Higgins, E.T.: Self-discrepancy: a theory relating self and affect. Psychol. Rev. **94**(3), 319 (1987)

32. Hoffner, C.: Children's wishful identification and parasocial interaction with favorite television characters. J. Broadcast. Electron. Media **40**(3), 389–402 (1996)

33. Hoffner, C., Buchanan, M.: Young adults' wishful identification with television characters: the role of perceived similarity and character attributes. Media Psychol. **7**(4), 325–351 (2005)

34. Inc., D.P.: Daz 3d studio (2022). https://www.daz3d.com

35. Jansz, J.: The emotional appeal of violent video games for adolescent males. Commun. Theory **15**(3), 219–241 (2005)

36. Kao, D., Harrell, D.F.: The effects of badges and avatar identification on play and making in educational games. In: Proceedings of the 2018 CHI Conference on Human Factors in Computing Systems, pp. 1–19 (2018)

37. Kelders, S.M., Kok, R.N., Ossebaard, H.C., Van Gemert-Pijnen, J.E.: Persuasive system design does matter: a systematic review of adherence to web-based interventions. J. Med. Internet Res. **14**(6), e152 (2012)

38. Khan, R., De Angeli, A.: The attractiveness stereotype in the evaluation of embodied conversational agents. In: Gross, T., Gulliksen, J., Kotzé, P., Oestreicher, L., Palanque, P., Prates, R.O., Winckler, M. (eds.) Human-Computer Interaction – INTERACT 2009, pp. 85–97. Springer Berlin Heidelberg, Berlin, Heidelberg (2009). https://doi.org/10.1007/978-3-642-03655-2_10

39. Klimmt, C., Hefner, D., Vorderer, P.: The video game experience as "true" identification: a theory of enjoyable alterations of players' self-perception. Commun. Theory **19**(4), 351–373 (2009)

40. Kocur, M., et al.: Computer-assisted avatar-based treatment for dysfunctional beliefs in depressive inpatients: a pilot study. Front. Psych. **12**, 608997 (2021)

41. Konijn, E.A., Nije Bijvank, M., Bushman, B.J.: I wish i were a warrior: the role of wishful identification in the effects of violent video games on aggression in adolescent boys. Dev. Psychol. **43**(4), 1038 (2007)

42. Kruzic, C., Kruzic, D., Herrera, F., Bailenson, J.: Facial expressions contribute more than body movements to conversational outcomes in avatar-mediated virtual environments. Sci. Reports **10** (11 202). https://doi.org/10.1038/s41598-020-76672-4

43. Kulms, P., Krämer, N.C., Gratch, J., Kang, S.-H.: It's in their eyes: a study on female and male virtual humans' gaze. In: Vilhjálmsson, H.H., Kopp, S., Marsella, S., Thórisson, K.R. (eds.) IVA 2011. LNCS (LNAI), vol. 6895, pp. 80–92. Springer, Heidelberg (2011). https://doi.org/10.1007/978-3-642-23974-8_9

44. Laughlin, H.: The Ego and Its Defenses. Appleton-Century-Crofts (1970). https://books.google.de/books?id=qD59AAAAMAAJ

45. Leff, J., Williams, G., Huckvale, M., Arbuthnot, M., Leff, A.P.: Avatar therapy for persecutory auditory hallucinations: what is it and how does it work? Psychosis **6**(2), 166–176 (2014)

46. Li, B.J., Lwin, M.O.: Player see, player do: testing an exergame motivation model based on the influence of the self avatar. Comput. Hum. Behav. **59**, 350–357 (2016)

47. Louwerse, M.M., Graesser, A.C., Lu, S., Mitchell, H.H.: Social cues in animated conversational agents. Appl. Cogn. Psychol.: Off. J. Society Appl. Res. Memory Cogn. **19**(6), 693–704 (2005)

48. Mael, F.A., Ashforth, B.E.: Identification in work, war, sports, and religion: Contrasting the benefits and risks. J. Theory Soc. Behav. **31**(2), 197–222 (2001)

49. Meeker, D., Cerully, J.L., Johnson, M., Iyer, N., Kurz, J., Scharf, D.M.: Simcoach evaluation: a virtual human intervention to encourage service-member help-seeking for posttraumatic stress disorder and depression. Rand Health Quart. **5**(3) (2016)

50. Melvyn, F.: World mental health report: Transforming mental health for all. World mental health report, p. 39 (2022). https://www.who.int/publications/i/item/9789240049338

51. Micoulaud-Franchi, J.A., Sagaspe, P., De Sevin, E., Bioulac, S., Sauteraud, A., Philip, P.: Acceptability of embodied conversational agent in a health care context. In: Intelligent Virtual Agents: 16th International Conference, IVA 2016, Los Angeles, CA, USA, September 20–23, 2016, Proceedings 16, pp. 416–419. Springer (2016). https://doi.org/10.1007/978-3-319-47665-0_45

52. Mitruţ, O., Moldoveanu, A., Petrescu, L., Petrescu, C., Moldoveanu, F.: A review of virtual therapists in anxiety and phobias alleviating applications. In: Chen, J.Y.C., Fragomeni, G. (eds.) HCII 2021. LNCS, vol. 12770, pp. 71–79. Springer, Cham (2021). https://doi.org/10.1007/978-3-030-77599-5_6

53. Moyer-Gusé, E., Chung, A.H., Jain, P.: Identification with characters and discussion of taboo topics after exposure to an entertainment narrative about sexual health. J. Commun. **61**(3), 387–406 (2011)

54. Moyer-Gusé, E., Nabi, R.L.: Explaining the effects of narrative in an entertainment television program: Overcoming resistance to persuasion. Hum. Commun. Res. **36**(1), 26–52 (2010)

55. Oksanen, K., Van Looy, J., De Grove, F.: Avatar identification in serious games: the role of avatar identification in the learning experience of a serious game. In: The Power of Play: Motivational Uses and Applications. In: Pre-Conference to the 63rd International Communication Association (ICA) Annual Conference (2013)

56. Pimentel, D., Kalyanaraman, S.: Customizing your demons: anxiety reduction via anthropomorphizing and destroying an "anxiety avatar." Front. Psychol. **11**, 566682 (2020)

57. Ratan, R., Rikard, R., Wanek, C., McKinley, M., Johnson, L., Sah, Y.J.: Introducing avatarification: An experimental examination of how avatars influence student motivation. In: 2016 49th Hawaii International Conference on System Sciences (HICSS), pp. 51–59. IEEE (2016)

58. Robinson, J., et al.: Can an internet-based intervention reduce suicidal ideation, depression and hopelessness among secondary school students: results from a pilot study. Early Interv. Psych. **10**(1), 28–35 (2016)

59. Rojas, R., Geissner, E., Hautzinger, M.: Das-18. dysfunctional attitude scale 18–deutsche kurzfassung (2022)

60. Rosenberg-Kima, R.B., Baylor, A.L., Plant, E.A., Doerr, C.E.: Interface agents as social models for female students: the effects of agent visual presence and appearance on female students' attitudes and beliefs. Comput. Hum. Behav. **24**(6), 2741–2756 (2008)

61. Ryan, R., Rigby, C., Przybylski, A.: The motivational pull of video games: a self-determination theory approach. Motivation Emotion **30**, 344–360 (12 2006). https://doi.org/10.1007/s11031-006-9051-8

62. Ryan, R.M., Deci, E.L.: Self-determination theory and the facilitation of intrinsic motivation, social development, and well-being. Am. Psychol. **55**(1), 68 (2000)

63. Schafer, R.: Aspects of internalization. International Universities Press, Inc (1968)

64. Sciuto, A., Saini, A., Forlizzi, J., Hong, J.I.: " hey alexa, what's up?" a mixed-methods studies of in-home conversational agent usage. In: Proceedings of the 2018 Designing Interactive Systems Conference, pp. 857–868 (2018)

65. Sedikides, C.: Changes in the valence of the self as a function of mood. Rev. Personality Social Psychol. **14**(1), 231–271 (1992)

66. Shaked, N.A.: Avatars and virtual agents-relationship interfaces for the elderly. Healthcare Technol. Lett. **4**(3), 83–87 (2017)

67. Soutter, A.R.B., Hitchens, M.: The relationship between character identification and flow state within video games. Comput. Hum. Behav. **55**, 1030–1038 (2016)

68. Studio, C.M.: Salsa lipsync suite v2 (2022). https://assetstore.unity.com/packages/tools/animation/salsa-lipsync-suite-148442

69. Technologies, U.: Unity version 2021.3.16f1 (2021). https://unity.com/de

70. Trepte, S., Reinecke, L.: Avatar creation and video game enjoyment: effects of life-satisfaction, game competitiveness, and identification with the avatar. J. Media Psychol. **22**, 171–184 (01 2010). https://doi.org/10.1027/1864-1105/a000022

71. Turkay, S., Kinzer, C.K.: The effects of avatar-based customization on player identification. In: Gamification: Concepts, Methodologies, Tools, Applications, pp. 247–272. IGI Global (2015)

72. Van Looy, J., Courtois, C., De Vocht, M.: Player identification in online games: validation of a scale for measuring identification in mmorpgs. In: Proceedings of the 3rd International Conference on Fun and Games, pp. 126–134 (2010)

73. Von Collani, G., Herzberg, P.Y.: Eine revidierte fassung der deutschsprachigen skala zum selbstwetgefühl von rosenberg. Zeitschrift für differentielle und diagnostische Psychologie (2003)

74. Watson, D., Clark, L.A., Tellegen, A.: Development and validation of brief measures of positive and negative affect: the panas scales. J. Pers. Soc. Psychol. 54(6), 1063 (1988)

75. Wollheim, R.: Identification and imagination. R. Wollheim (Ed.), Freud. A Collection of Critical Essays, Garden City/New York (Achor Press/Doubleday) 1974, pp. 172–195. (1974)

76. Wright, J.H., et al.: Computer-assisted cognitive therapy for depression: maintaining efficacy while reducing therapist time. Am. J. Psychiatry 162(6), 1158–1164 (2005)

My Energy to the Moon? Combining Human Energy Tracking with Financial Chart Analysis for Advanced Desktop Work-Life Tracking

Michael Fellmann$^{(\boxtimes)}$ ⓘ, Angelina Clara Schmidt ⓘ, Hannes Grunert ⓘ, and Baidar Bukht

Business Information Systems, University of Rostock, Rostock, Germany
{michael.fellmann,angelina.schmidt,hannes.grunert,
baidar.bukht}@uni-rostock.de

Abstract. The current working world is characterized by increased flexibility, complexity, and speed while work from home is on the rise. In this context, managing one's resources becomes even more important to stay healthy, productive and reach one's goals. One approach for this is to continuously reflect on individual work-related, mental and behavioral variables to retain a high level of human energy, productivity, and well-being during work. In this direction, we have already proposed and implemented a tool in the intersection of automatic computer-based activity tracking and continuous assessment of well-being [11]. The tool, called Desktop Work-Life Tracker (DWLT), can semi-automatically track variables such as human energy and sentiment, sleep quality as well as five user-defined variables in the evening. However, what is still missing so far are capabilities for advanced analytics to observe trends or spot patterns. In the work at hand, we first introduce the current tool. We then present two real-world datasets on human energy self-assessments and apply analysis methods known from financial chart analysis such as MA, MACD, Bollinger Bands and cross correlation. Results are promising and due to this, we report on our plans to integrate these advanced analytic capabilities into the existing DWLT.

Keywords: Self-Tracking · Desktop Logging · Human Energy · Productivity · Chart Analysis · Moving Average Convergence/Divergence · MACD

1 Introduction

These days, many employees are confronted with very high work demands [29]. High workloads, knowledge-intense products and services, as well as permanent time pressure, can make it hard to keep pace with all requirements. In addition, modern communication means can unintentionally lead to more multitasking and interruptions. All these circumstances can make it difficult to retain one's energy and drive, to stay motivated, healthy, productive, and resilient. Moreover, they can induce long-term stress, which can result in serious mental health problems such as burnout. Mental health problems are a major contributor to the overall burden of disease and are particularly concentrated in the

© The Author(s), under exclusive license to Springer Nature Switzerland AG 2024
M. Kurosu and A. Hashizume (Eds.): HCII 2024, LNCS 14686, pp. 22–40, 2024.
https://doi.org/10.1007/978-3-031-60428-7_2

working population, leading to a loss of human capital [21]. In addition, modern information and communication technology enables a higher degree of flexibility in daily work [9, 15]. On the one hand, this allows for a more seamless integration of work and life, while on the other, it challenges employees to balance their work and private life, as those boundaries increasingly tend to vanish [2, 15]. Thus, managing ones' energy and balance in life has become more challenging for individuals [2, 16].

This is a potential risk to health, as research has shown that people fail to make the best choices in their own interest [20]. It is desirable that individuals critically reflect on their own behavior in order to discover strengths as well as necessary changes. Critical reflection has already been defined by Dewey in 1933 as "the active, persistent and careful consideration of any belief or supposed form of knowledge in the light of the grounds that support it and the further conclusions to which it tends" [7] (for a comprehensive review on the notion of reflection, see [3]).

In the first place, it is information that is needed to compare different states and to target a healthier behaviour through so-called self-regulation [5]. This information can be gathered, for example, via *self-observation* [27] to systematically collect data about the own behavior e.g., on activities that serve as an energizer or activities that cause exhaustion. However, this might be time-consuming and impractical, especially in the work context. Indeed, designing and implementing IT-based tools that reduce the burden of data collection and analysis for self-reflection is a promising avenue of research [6, 10, 33]. IT can be supportive by collecting personally relevant information e.g. through desktop-based time tracking tools, mobile apps [33], or via wearable devices like smartwatches and fitness trackers. They can furthermore lead to surprising insights [28], as most humans tend to have perception biases, such as underestimating time passed. Moreover, it is even harder to identify individual patterns, as there can be complex interrelations, for example described by Abdel Hadi et al. [1] between recovery activities, work-related rumination, and motivation. Hence, tracking and analyzing one's variables of work and well-being such as human energy (cf. Sect. 2.2) is important.

However, up to now, commercial self-tracking tools, as well as those developed in the scientific field, often only provide a simple graphical display of variable values. As a result, users of self-tracking applications have to implicitly derive knowledge themselves from the (visually) presented measured values through "visual inference". However, it is well possible to identify trends, trend reversals, trend channels or extreme values with standard methods applied e.g., in financial analysis. Surprisingly, they have hardly been used so far, although they provide easy-to-interpret, action-relevant information. Therefore, the aim of this work is to test these methods and apply them to datasets of self-tracking in the context of office work. In doing so, we intend to raise the level of insights that tools such as Desktop Work-Life Tracker (DWLT) could generate.

The remainder is structured as follows. In the next section, we provide an overview of the background and related work. In Sect. 3, we present an overview of the DWLT. In Sect. 4, we introduce the datasets which we use in Sect. 5 to test various analysis methods. In Sect. 6, we discuss the results and sketch the possible integration of these methods in future versions of DWLT. In Sect. 7, we conclude our contribution.

2 Background and Related Work

In the following, we present the background, related work and position the DWLT in the intersection of time tracking, quantified self and human energy assessment. The tool has already been described in [11] with more emphasis on the requirements.

2.1 Time Tracking and the Quantified Self

To support self-observation, time tracking tools that automatically record what is done on a computer are widely used. They serve to record the working time of a user e.g., for project management. More advanced tools such as *RescueTime* (rescuetime.com) also provide additional analytics such as an estimation of productive time or tracking of work-related goals. Using these tools, it is possible to explore what are the most productive hours or how much time was lost e.g., on distracting websites. Research has confirmed that these insights are valuable, as in an empirical study, employees were surprised about various behaviors of themselves, such as their fragmentation of work [28], i.e., mixing different tasks. In other words, employees estimated various variables of their working behaviors incorrectly. Recent time tracking tools such as *Timely* (timelyapp.com) not only try to track the time spent working on a computer with various applications, files and websites, but also to automatically allocate time to projects. Given the importance of time tracking, DWLT implements an automatic tracking of computer-based activities (cf. Section 3). However, common tools have a narrow focus on work- and productivity-related measurements. They do not embrace a more holistic understanding of work-life tracking, which would include tracking a person's state in terms of well-being or health-related variables. Embracing such an understanding would also require to track physiological variables.

Tracking one's physiological variables is at the heart of the *quantified self*-movement. According to a team of authors around Gary Wolf [30], its core idea is all about "self-knowledge through numbers". That is, gaining more comprehension and understanding about oneself by measuring and interpreting some values in numbers (e.g., steps per day, heartbeats, etc.). According to Swan [39], this implies tracking any kind of biological, physical, behavioral, or environmental data about oneself. The most common tools to gather physiological data are smartwatches and other mobile devices. According to a recent study, e.g. 60% of the German population already regularly check health-related data from mobile devices [14]. However, while these devices track various parameters such as steps or heart rate, they usually lack the ability to track more experience-oriented and work-related variables, e.g. about the energetic activation or *human energy* (cf. Section 2.2) during different work tasks. Therefore, in our DWLT tool, we do not strive to duplicate the features of existing fitness trackers. Rather, we focus more on human energy and sentiment in conjunction with work variables.

2.2 Human Energy and Sentiment as a Source of Vitality

In our earlier work [25], we defined human energy as closely linked to well-being in terms of individual resource status [32]. Strain and recovery from work lead to a decrease or increase of the individual resource status over time [43], which can be characterized in terms of fatigue, (emotional) exhaustion, need for recovery, self-control capacity or vitality [37]. These states refer to different aspects of human energy [31], which in turn can be understood as high levels of subjective vitality and low levels of fatigue [13, 42]. Fritz et al. state: "Human energy is a 'fuel' that helps organizations run successfully" [13].

Quinn et al. developed an integrated model of human energy [31]. The model differentiates between two types of human energy: physical energy and *energetic activation.* Energetic activation is "the degree to which people feel energized" [31]. It is "experienced as feelings of vitality, vigor or enthusiasm" [31]. It also plays a prominent role in regard to mental well-being [35], with burnout and depression [17] being associated with a lack of energy [36].

Summarizing, energetic activation leads to intrinsic motivation, which makes people seek new challenges. Quinn et al. state that the energetic activation is the limiting factor in whether we invest our energy into an activity or not. Moreover, empirical studies suggest that long-term survival of companies is strongly associated with the employees' energy [41]. Taken together, human energy seems to be of vital importance for a more holistic work-life tracking.

Energetic activation can also be understood as the level of arousal that an individual is experiencing. In turn, arousal can be classified according to the emotional valence associated with it being positive or negative [4]. The basic idea is to classify energy according to its intensity (high or low) and sentiment (negative or positive). This distinction is also known as the *circumplex model* of Russell [34]. All in all, energy and sentiment are highly relevant variables to be tracked and managed by the individual. However, improving health behavior through digital solutions, not only for patients but also for the public, has not yet received enough attention [26].

2.3 Human Energy Tracking

In the direction of human energy assessment, Spreitzer and Grant propose an energy audit, a self-observation and intervention class to improve energy management [38]. In their article, they describe how students recorded their energy trajectories and identified behaviors that benefit or impair personal energy. The authors report positive learning experiences by students, i.e., a clearer understanding of their energy trajectories, energy depleting or promoting factors, and even strategies to improve their energy. Spreitzer and Grant furthermore describe how the increased awareness for the individual energy levels caused some students to change their behavior for improved energy management. They explicitly suggest using more semi-automated experience sampling methods in the future to automatically request energy assessments from the students.

Based on these insights, we explored the effects of continuous energy self-assessment and feedback in a prior study [23], where users received personalized feedback about their most influential factors that drive or drain their energetic activation during a workday. Results from a study with n > 100 show that there seem to be significant beneficial effects that are caused by the reflection on human energy [24]. Thus, in line with the results of Spreitzer, we can confirm empirical evidence that tracking and observing one's energy seems to be beneficial for energetic well-being, i.e., feeling higher levels of vitality instead of fatigue. Also, this study shows how different factors like micro-breaks

[22] influence an individual's energy level. Therefore, we decided to include a feature in DWLT for continuously tracking human energy and sentiment.

In summary, the DWLT is based on the insight that (i) self-observation is an important prerequisite for self-reflection, which in turn is a precondition for self-management, (ii) the integration of work-related as well as well-being and health-related variables is favorable for a more complete assessment of the work-life, and (iii) the assessment of human energy as a "high-level" variable of well-being is important. Against this background, we designed and implemented the DWLT. However, up to now, the tool presents tracking data visually and beyond a correlation analysis between the five user-defined end-of-day variables, no advanced analytics in implemented. The aim of this work is therefore to apply and test different methods known from chart analysis to generate trends, trend reversals or spot extreme values. Before we execute this analysis, we first give a brief overview of DWLT in the next section.

3 Overview of the Features of the Desktop Work-Life Tracker

In the following, we provide an overview on our *Desktop Work-Life Tracker* (DWLT) in regard to *data capturing and self-assessment features*, the *daily dashboard* (3.1) and *relation analysis* (3.2).

3.1 Data Capturing and Self-assessment Features

Since automated data capturing was identified as an important requirement in our previous work [11], we continuously collect data in the background, tracking the applications used, window titles and the timespan of usage. All data is stored locally in.*csv* files to guarantee the highest level of privacy. Regarding the self-assessments, we provide the dialogues (a)-(c) shown in Fig. 1.

For both the morning (a) and evening surveys (c), we use sliders for user input. The evening survey also shows the user-defined colors of the variables, as well as a user-defined text prompt that appears upon mouse hovering. In the more frequently appearing energy and sentiment dialogue (b) we decided to implement more visually appealing input elements. For human energy, we use our 7-point scale in the form of a battery symbol, which has been validated in an interdisciplinary research endeavor [40]. For sentiment, we use a shorter 5-point scale, which is in line with empirical research on mood tracking suggesting such a scale to be appropriate [47]. Both user input elements operate with a single click.

The evening assessment enables rating five user-adjustable variables. Our default for these variables is: perceived progress, autonomy, strength-use, social contacts and stress. While progress and stress are quite self-explanatory, autonomy, strength-use and social contacts are borrowed from the Self-Determination Theory (where they are denoted as autonomy, competence and relatedness). Finally, all the self-assessment dialogues have a text input field at the bottom for personal notes.

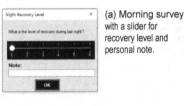

(a) Morning survey
with a slider for
recovery level and
personal note.

(c) End of day survey
with sliders for five user-defined variables and a
personal note on the day. The question of the item is
visible upon mouse hovering over the item.

(b) Energy & sentiment
with two scales for energy and mood and
personal note for describing the current situation.

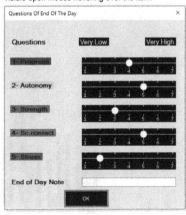

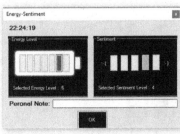

Fig. 1. Forms for Data Capturing via Self-Assessment

3.2 Current Data Analysis Features

The current implementation of the DWLT includes a Daily Dashboard with bar charts for working time and productivity. Productivity is currently approximated by a user-modifiable list of applications with productivity ratings. For example, while office applications in general are rated as "productive", games may be rated as "unproductive". Currently, we work on extending this mechanism to provide a more fine-grained estimation, considering website contents, for example. The Daily Dashboard also shows the fluctuation of energy and sentiment throughout the day via line charts as well as the values of the five user-defined variables from the evening survey and personal notes on sleep quality and for the day. The Relation Analysis Dashboard allows users to analyze their data for arbitrary time periods (cf. Fig. 2). While rich visualizations may help people with self-reflection [6], we however opted for more established visualizations known from business environments, such as bar charts or line charts as well as a matrix. At the top of the dialogue, the user can first specify the time range for the analysis using two date picker elements that allow mouse and keyboard input. Next, the user can choose to view either a line chart (cf. Fig. 4 (a)) or a matrix visualization (cf. Fig. 4 (b)) in the upper part (default is line chart).

The line chart allows to see the energy and sentiment fluctuations and optionally values of the morning assessment. The level of morning recovery as a more bodily-oriented variable fits well together with energy and sentiment. For the latter, we also include min/max values. As an alternative to the line chart, the user can activate a matrix visualization, that presents energy and sentiment states in a two-dimensional system (cf. Fig. 4 (c)). Each point can represent multiple measurements for which the date(s) and weekday(s) are indicated and personal notes are shown upon mouse hovering over

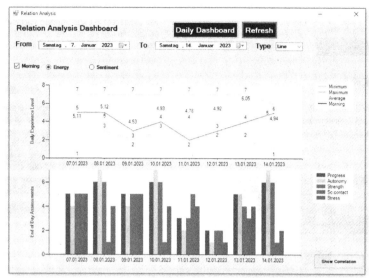

(a) Option to show a **line chart for daily fluctuation** of morning recovery, energy or sentiment incl. min/max values.

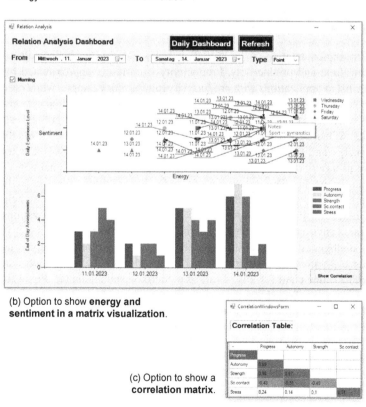

(b) Option to show **energy and sentiment in a matrix visualization**.

(c) Option to show a **correlation matrix**.

Fig. 2. Relation Analysis Dashboard with Line Charts (a), Matrix (b) and Correlation (c)

a point. In the bottom part, vertical bar charts for the values of the evening survey are displayed which represent retrospective, summative assessments of the day.

Overall, by inspecting the provided visualizations, the user can answer self-reflective questions such as "Is there a relation between my energy and sleep?", "At which times/weekdays I often feel energized and happy?", or "Are progress and strength-use correlated?". Even complex relations may be discovered in the data, such as a pattern: "High autonomy co-occurs with lower stress and higher energy on next day".

4   Datasets and Pre-processing for Human Energy Analysis

In this section, we introduce our datasets (4.1) and pre-processing steps (4.2).

4.1   Introduction to the Datasets

The first dataset *DS1* originated from a diary study on human energy carried out from June 23rd, 2020 to June 1st, 2020. The study was conducted by a group of Business Informatics students who recruited participants via social media (e.g., Xing) and word-of-mouth (convenience sampling). It consisted of three surveys (morning, noon and evening) with 18–20 items that represent factors influencing human energy. 114 people responded to the invitation and created approx. 240 data points. Due to the large number of and partially redundant items, the selection of items shown in Table 1. Was used for the cross-correlation analysis (cf. Section 5.4). The last item "Battery_energy" was measured with our single-item pictorial scale, which resembles a battery with different states from discharged to fully charged [40].

Table 1. Overview on Selected Variables of DS1

Attribute	Data Type	Description
Session	Text	Identification of the participant (token)
Created	Datetime	Timepoint when the survey was loaded
Modified	Datetime	Timepoint of last modification
Ended	Datetime	Timepoint when survey was completed
Work_with_experienced_one	Numeric	Working with an experienced colleague
Skill_utilization	Numeric	Performing tasks that match ones' skills
Vibrant_energy	Numeric	The feeling of being alive and vital
Energetic_vitality	Numeric	The feeling of being full of energy
Alert_wakefulness	Numeric	The feeling of being alert and awake
Battery_energy	Numeric	Human energy visualized as battery level

The second dataset *DS2* originated from a small human energy self-assessment used from July 2020 to April 2021 in a company as a part of their time recording software.

The company offers supervision and consulting services for individuals and families. Employees have diverse backgrounds such as pedagogues, special educators, and state-recognized educators with additional training in various fields such as systemic counselling, social therapy, trauma therapy, constellation work. The data include the session, time of recording and the energy level, again measured with our single-item scale [40] (cf. Table 2). Data was collected from 24 individuals and contains 586 data points. Employees could use the time recording software several times per day.

Table 2. Variables of DS2

Attribute	Data Type	Description
Session	Text	Identification of the participant
Timestamp	Datetime	Time of energy level recording
Battery_energy	Numeric	Human energy visualized as battery level

4.2 Data Preparation

For the implementation we used Python (v. 3.10) and the libraries: Pandas (v. 2.2.0), Numpy (v. 1.26.4), PyPlot (v. 3.7.1), Seaborn (v. 0.11.1) and SciPi (v. 1.10.1). As a first step, data was loaded from.csv-files into DataFrames, relevant columns were selected and tuples with NULL values were either dropped or filled with suitable values. Also, duplicate entries with the same timestamp were removed from the dataset. For the analysis of timeseries, the timestamp attribute was converted into a datetime format and indexed afterwards. Date and time were extracted afterwards for grouping the data later on. For preprocessing in *DS1*, missing values for the "created" attribute were filled either with the corresponding "modified" (if available) or with the "ended" attribute values. In *DS2*, the average mean of all battery levels of each day was calculated to analyze the daily behavior.

5 Results of the Analysis Methods

In this section, we discuss the different analysis methods used, Moving Average (5.1), Moving Average Crossing Divergence (5.2), Bollinger Bands (5.3) and Cross Correlation (5.4). And their significance for analyzing and predicting human energy.

5.1 Moving Average (MA)

The MA is commonly used e.g., in technical analysis in the financial domain. The reason for calculating the moving average is to smooth data by creating a constantly updated average price [12]. Analogously, the moving average allows to weaken the impact of short-term fluctuations in human energy over a specified time. Calculating the MA can be done either as simple moving average (SMAs), which uses the arithmetic average or as exponential moving averages (EMAs), which gives greater weight to more recent values. The result of calculating the SMA for the variable human energy on the Service Companies' dataset is shown in Figure 3.

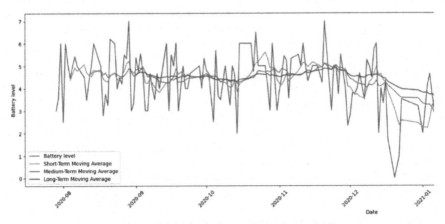

Fig. 3. Moving Average (DS2 from the Service Company)

The chart shows the battery level (blue), 7-day short-term MA (orange), 14-day medium-term MA (green), and 30-day long-term MA (red). Looking at the MA plot, we easily see that a smoothing the data leads to a much clearer picture regarding ups and downs and the overall trend. Comparing different windows, the most intuitive visualization seems to be the 14-day MA (green).

While shorter smoothing leads to many ups and downs and too closely follows the human energy, the longer smoothing shows an even clearer trend, but can be misleading. For example, at the end of the year, a clear decline in human energy took place which is shown a bit more pronounced with the 14-day MA. *Hence, we can conclude that the 14-day MA enables us to identify human energy trends in an intuitive way.*

5.2 Moving Average Crossing Divergence (MACD)

Much like MA, MACD is also very common in technical analysis. Moving Average Convergence/Divergence (MACD) is defined as a "trend-following momentum indicator that shows the relationship between two exponential moving averages (EMAs) [...]" [8]. Most commonly, it is calculated by subtracting the 26-day EMA from the 12-day EMA resulting in the MACD line. These line again is smoothed with a 9-day EMA and the result is the so-called *signal line*. Often, diagrams also include a histogram that shows the difference between MACD line and signal line [8] and hence conveys an intuitive impression for the momentum of changes. The result of calculating the MACD for the variable human energy on the Service Companies' dataset is shown in Figure 4.

The upper part of the chart shows the battery level (blue), 12-day EMA (orange), and 26-day EMA (green). In the lower part, it shows the MACD line (purple), the signal line (red) as well as a histogram view. The most interesting and useful feature of the MACD is the histogram view. Each time the MACD line crosses the signal line, it indicates an upcoming trend reversal. This is also indicated by the histogram view showing zero bars. For example, four trend reversals occurred from day 100 to 140, two upwards and two downwards (cf. Fig. 5).

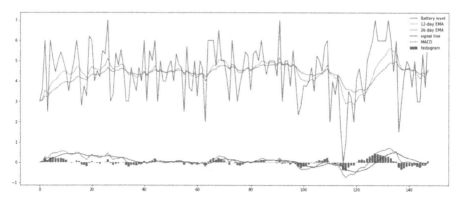

Fig. 4. MACD (DS2 from the Service Company)

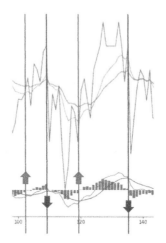

Fig. 5. Trend Reversals from Day 100 to 140 (MACD Line Crossing the Red Signal Line)

Shortly after day 100, an upward reversal occurs. This is followed are by three higher highs. Before day 110, a downward trend is indicated. Two lower lows follow. Just before day 120, an upward turn is indicated. Three very pronounced higher highs follow. *Hence, we can conclude that the MACD allows us to identify trend reversals and predict future developments of human energy.*

5.3 Bollinger Bands

A Bollinger Band is another technical analysis tool widely used in chart analysis. Bollinger Bands has been developed by technical trader John Bollinger to indicate when an asset is oversold or overbought [18]. Typically, it is visualized by a shaded "trend channel" around the underlying variable, where the upper and lower boundary are set at plus/minus two standard deviations from a 20-day simple moving average (SMA). The result of calculating the Bollinger Bands for the variable human energy using the Service Companies' dataset is shown in Figure 6.

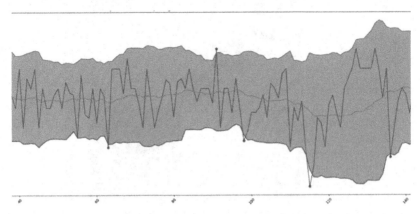

Fig. 6. Bollinger Bands (DS2 from the Service Company)

The chart shows the battery level (blue), the 20-day SMA (orange), and two additional lines (green, red) calculated by adding/subtracting the standard deviation from the 20-day SMA. Between the red and the green line, grey shading indicates that this can be regarded as the "channel" in which average fluctuations occur. The most interesting feature of the Bollinger Bands is the signal that can be generated if the underlying variable, i.e., human energy, leaves that channel. This means that some sort of extreme value has occurred. *Hence, we can conclude that Bollinger Bands allow us to signal extreme positive and negative values beyond the average fluctuation.*

5.4 Cross-Correlation

Cross-correlation is a statistical method used to measure the degree to which two variables or datasets move in relation to each other or "how closely they move in tandem" [19]. In more detail, cross-correlation measures the similarity between two variables as a function of the time lag between them. By calculating the cross-correlation, it is possible to determine a relationship between two variables and the time lag at which this relationship is most pronounced. Figure 7 shows the cross-correlation matrix for a single case (i.e., person) from DS2.

The matrix shows the linear relationship between different columns of the dataset in terms of the correlation visualized as a heatmap. The heatmap provides a color-coded representation of the correlation values, where positive correlations are shown in warm colors (e.g., red) and negative correlations in cool colors (e.g., blue). The intensity of the color indicates the strength of the correlation. Looking at the matrix, very high correlations above 0.7 can be identified between various psychological parameters of vitality (vibrant energy, energetic vitality, wakefulness) and the battery scale. This underlines the validity of the battery scale as an "umbrella" for various more detailed variables.

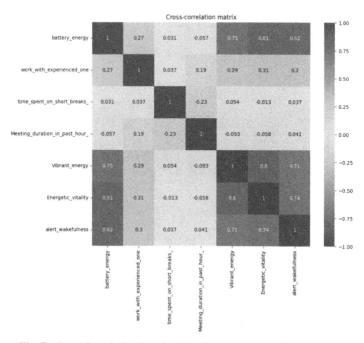

Fig. 7. Cross Correlation Matrix (DS1: Human Energy Study, Case 1)

Further, high correlations between these variables and "work with an experience one" (ca. 0.3) can be seen. This reveals that for the case (person) at hand, working with experienced and knowledgeable colleagues obviously leads to an increase in human energy. Moreover, there is a relatively strong negative correlation between meetings and breaks (−0.23), which indicates that days with many meetings breaks are neglected.

Hence, we can conclude that the cross-correlation matrix helps in understanding the relationships between different self-management variables and can reveal which factors are positively or negatively correlated with each other.

6 Discussion and Future Work

6.1 Applicability and Utility of the Analysis Methods

In general, all methods were applicable to our real-world self-assessment datasets and lead to meaningful results. The MA seems particularly useful for variables that fluctuate on a daily or weekly basis, such as human energy. A 14-day SMA provides an easy-to-read trend abstracting from these fluctuations. We furthermore could demonstrate that the MACD works well for detecting trend reversals on self-assessment data and in anticipating possible upward or downward developments of the human energy. Surprisingly, even modern self-tracking tools such as fitness trackers do not generate such signals so that transferring these analysis methods from the domain of (financial) chart analysis to self-management seems promising. Trend reversal signals may be most useful to predict changes of self-management variables that relate over weeks rather than days. Besides human energy, other variables such as sleep quality or physical activity seem to be highly relevant for MACD-based analysis. For example, an individual might receive a warning "Attention: your sleep quality starts to decrease" shortly after she or he engaged in a new project. This might initiate job crafting behaviors such as acquiring more work resources to prevent exhaustion or even burnout. *Hence, trend reversals could make the potential impact of lifestyle changes more salient to the user, even before they fully materialize.* In a similar direction, signals from the Bollinger Bands might foster self-reflection in which situations extreme values occur and possibly how to avoid them if they are perceived as negative (e.g., extreme low energy).

Regarding cross-correlation, applicability and results are somewhat inconclusive. In general, cross-correlation has shown the ability to detect interesting relations between variables, thereby abstracting from time so that variables do not have to rise or fall simultaneously. While this clearly is a merit of this analysis method, the usefulness of displaying a matrix to the user seems unclear. In the dataset we used, many correlations are somewhat trivial and do not lead to any insights. For example, the high correlation of the "battery energy" with similar variables for vitality and energy could be considered as an artifact of our dataset containing redundant variables due to the applied scales used from psychology. Even if the data contains more diverse variables, it is questionable if many interesting correlations could be identified in the matrix. In the given example of one case (person), there were only two interesting correlations with a sufficient strength (energy and working with experienced one; meeting and breaks). For other persons it looked similar. *Hence, displaying the full matrix seems less beneficial. Instead, only the strongest correlations may be selected and conveyed to the user (e.g., above ±0.2).*

One limitation of our study is that we have applied the calculations for MA, MACD and Bollinger Bands to aggregated values and not to time series of individuals. However, we expect even greater fluctuations and trends in individual time series, e.g., due to changing work demands and individual stress and recovery cycles, which cancel each other out when analyzing the data at an aggregated level.

6.2 Prospects of Integration into DWLT

Since it has been demonstrated that MA is relevant for trend analysis and MACD enables to detect trend reversals, we elaborate on prospects of integrating these analysis methods into the DWLT. In general, the presentation of a smoothed energy, sentiment or sleep quality curve is relevant in the Relation Analysis. However, since the user needs to collect some data first (e.g., for 14-day SMA), displaying the SMA should clearly be an optional element of the tool. Moreover, many people are interested in their current incoming data, as evidenced by many fitness trackers, providing both direct plots and advanced analytics on top of them. In line with this, plotting the data and optional derived values such as SMA seems to be the best option. Translated into concrete features, this could mean an additional switch to turn on/off the 14-day SMA line in Relation Analysis. Nevertheless, additional lines in the line chart could easily overwhelm the user. So, another option would be a separate window or report generation component that also plots the trend for each variable.

Regarding MACD and Bollinger Bands, these methods are clearly more focused towards experts, so they should be displayed only upon request. Still, it seems more realistic for average users to convey trend reversals or extreme values with very simple additional text/icon messages at the bottom of the Relation Analysis. An example for this would be an arrow pointing upwards and a small text "Your energy is increasing" when a trend reversal has been detected. An even more subtle way of providing this information would be via a generic icon for notifications. It could be highlighted when new information is available and the user may display it upon request.

Besides the representation form, frequency is also an important aspect to consider. Specifically regarding MACD, it should be avoided that too many trend reversal signals are displayed in phases of continuous or minor variable fluctuation. This problem could be circumvented by only sending a signal when a threshold value is exceeded, based on the difference or height of the bars (plus and minus) in the MACD histogram before and after a trend reversal signal is generated. In regard to Bollinger Bands, based on our demonstration, we observe that the frequency of extreme values (at least with the standard 20-day window) was rather low, so no adjustment seems to be required here.

In regard to cross-correlation, a reasonable application of this method still requires more research. In theory, our findings from analyzing the cross-correlation in DS1 can be transferred to the 5 end-of-day variables of DWLT. Yet, future research is still needed to determine whether enough meaningful correlations can be calculated. Finally, other analysis methods such as association rules and timed sequential patterns would also be relevant to derive more complex patterns from the data.

7 Conclusion

In today's working world, there is a need for advanced self-management support with an emphasis on human energy. Having enough energy throughout the day is a prerequisite for both productivity and well-being. To support advanced self-management via self-observation support, we introduced our Desktop Work-Life Tracker (DWLT). With the help of the tool, it is possible to track energy and sentiment via recurring small assessments, computer-based activity and productivity over the day (via automated tracking) as well as sleep quality (via self-assessment). In addition, five user-defined variables for the end-of-day questionnaire allow to track personally relevant variables such as progress, autonomy, strength-use, social contacts, and stress.

Up to now, the tool provides various components, mainly for data display and some limited forms of analysis. These include a Daily Dashboard for inspecting a single day and a Relation Analysis Dashboard for more long-term analysis. By inspecting the provided visualizations, users can already answer questions such as "Is there a relation between my energy and sleep?". Also, more complex questions such as "How does working late in the evening influence my next day energy level?" can be answered. Thereby, the user can perform "visual inference", e.g., look at the provided visualizations and draw conclusions. However, besides these possibilities, there is no advanced data analytics available (besides a simple correlation) that could notify the user about trend reversals, extreme values or more complex time-lagged correlations.

As a first step to address this shortcoming, we selected well-known analysis methods from financial chart analysis and investigated if these methods work on self-management data. For this purpose, we used real-world datasets collected in our ongoing research on human energy and IT-based self-management. In more detail, we tested Moving Average (MA), Moving Average Crossing Divergence (MACD), Bollinger Bands and Cross-Correlation. The results are that MA can well be used to display trends, MACD is useful for detecting trend reversals and anticipating increasing or decreasing energy levels while the Bollinger Bands can be used to generate signals for extreme values. In regard to Cross-Correlation, results are somewhat inconclusive and require further research. As an additional step towards enhancing the DWLT, we discussed possible strategies and features to include these advanced methods into the DWLT.

In summary, we presented our ongoing research om IT-based self-management and successfully demonstrated that methods from the financial chart analysis can be transferred to the domain of self-management. The results are promising, as the methods produce meaningful results for real-world self-assessment data with an emphasis on human energy. We hope that with our research, we contribute to the design and development of even more powerful self-management tools that will improve peoples' self-management towards a more sustainable, health and well-being aware work and life.

References

1. Hadi, S.A., Mojzisch, A., Krumm, S., Häusser, J.A.: Day-level relationships between work, physical activity, and well-being: testing the physical activity-mediated demand-control (pamDC) model. Work Stress. 36(4), 355–376 (2021). https://doi.org/10.1080/02678373.2021.2002971
2. Barber, L.K., Jenkins, J.S.: Creating technological boundaries to protect bedtime: examining work-home boundary management, psychological detachment and sleep. Stress. Health 30(3), 259–264 (2014). https://doi.org/10.1002/smi.2536
3. Baumer, E.P., Khovanskaya, V., Matthews, M., Reynolds, L., Schwanda Sosik, V., Gay, G. Reviewing reflection: on the use of reflection in interactive system design. In: Proceedings of the 2014 Conference on Designing Interactive Systems. ACM, New York, NY, USA, pp. 93–102 (2014). https://doi.org/10.1145/2598510.2598598
4. Bruch, H., Vogel, B.: Strategies for creating and sustaining organizational energy. Employ. Relat. Today 38(2), 51–61 (2011)
5. Burkert, S., Sniehotta, F.: Selbstregulation des Gesundheitsverhaltens. In: Handbuch der Gesundheitspsychologie und Medizinischen Psychologie. Hogrefe Verlag GmbH & Company KG, pp. 98–106 (2009)

6. Choe, E.K., Lee, B., Zhu, H., Riche, N.H., Baur, D.: Understanding self-reflection. How People Reflect on Personal Data Through Visual Data Exploration. In: Proceedings of the 11th EAI International Conference on Pervasive Computing Technologies for Healthcare. PervasiveHealth 2017 :23–26 May 2017, Barcelona, Spain. ICPS: ACM International Conference Proceeding Series. Association for Computing Machinery, New York, NY, USA, 173–182 (2017). https://doi.org/10.1145/3154862.3154881

7. Dewey, J.: How we think: A restatement of the relation of reflective thinking to the educative process. College S. D.C. Heath, Lexington, MA (1933)

8. Dolan, B.: MACD Indicator Explained, with Formula, Examples, and Limitations. Investopedia (Dec. 2023)

9. Eurofound.: Working conditions and sustainable work. An analysis using the job quality framework. Challenges and prospects in the EU series. Publications Office of the European Union, Dublin (2021)

10. Fallon, M., Spohrer, K., Heinzl, A.: Wearable Devices: A Physiological and Self-regulatory Intervention for Increasing Attention in the Workplace. In: Davis, F.D., Riedl, R., vom Brocke, J., Léger, P.-M., Randolph, A.B. (eds.) Information Systems and Neuroscience: NeuroIS Retreat 2018, pp. 229–238. Springer International Publishing, Cham (2019). https://doi.org/10.1007/978-3-030-01087-4_28

11. Fellmann, M., Lambusch, F., Schmidt, A.C.: Combining Computer-Based Activity Tracking with Human Energy and Sentiment Self-assessment for Continuous Work-Life Reflection. In: Kurosu, M., Hashizume, A. (eds.) Human-Computer Interaction: Thematic Area, HCI 2023, Held as Part of the 25th HCI International Conference, HCII 2023, Copenhagen, Denmark, July 23–28, 2023, Proceedings, Part II, pp. 164–181. Springer Nature Switzerland, Cham (2023). https://doi.org/10.1007/978-3-031-35599-8_11

12. Fernando, J.: Moving Average (MA): Purpose, Uses, Formula, and Examples. *Investopedia* (Mar. 2023)

13. Fritz, C., Lam, C.F., Spreitzer, G.M.: It's the Little Things That Matter: An Examination of Knowledge Workers' Energy Management. AMP **25**(3), 28–39 (2011). https://doi.org/10.5465/amp.25.3.zol28

14. 2023. Gesundheitstracker: Zwei Drittel der Smartphone-Eigner nutzen laut Umfrage Gesundheitsdaten. *Springer Medizin Verlag GmbH, Ärzte Zeitung* (Nov. 2023)

15. Green, F.: It's been a hard day's night: the concentration and intensification of work in late twentieth-century Britain. Br. J. Ind. Relat. **39**(1), 53–80 (2001). https://doi.org/10.1111/1467-8543.00189

16. Green, F., McIntosh, S.: The intensification of work in Europe. Labour Econ. **8**(2), 291–308 (2001). https://doi.org/10.1016/S0927-5371(01)00027-6

17. Grobe, T.G., Frerk, T.: BARMER Gesundheitsreport: Schriftenreihe zur Gesundheitsanalyse, vol. 24. Barmer, Berlin (2020)

18. Hayes, A.: Bollinger Bands®: What They Are, and What They Tell Investors. *Investopedia* (Sep. 2023)

19. Hayes, A.: What Is Cross-Correlation? Definition, How It's Used, and Example. *Investopedia* (Dec. 2023)

20. Hsee, C.K., Hastie, R.: Decision and experience: why don't we choose what makes us happy? Trends Cogn. Sci. **10**(1), 31–37 (2006). https://doi.org/10.1016/j.tics.2005.11.007

21. James, S.L., et al.: Global, regional, and national incidence, prevalence, and years lived with disability for 354 diseases and injuries for 195 countries and territories, 1990–2017: a systematic analysis for the global burden of disease study 2017. Lancet **392**(10159), 1789–1858 (2018). https://doi.org/10.1016/S0140-6736(18)32279-7

22. Kim, S., Park, Y., Headrick, L.: Daily micro-breaks and job performance: general work engagement as a cross-level moderator. J. Appl. Psychol. **103**(7), 772–786 (2018). https://doi.org/10.1037/apl0000308

23. Lambusch, F., Richter, H.D., Fellmann, M., Weigelt, O., Kiechle, A.K.: human energy diary studies with personalized feedback: a proof of concept with formr. In: Proceedings of the 15th International Joint Conference on Biomedical Engineering Systems and Technologies (BIOSTEC 2022), Vol. 5: HEALTHINF. SciTePress, pp.789–800. https://doi.org/10.5220/0010974100003123

24. Lambusch, F., Weigelt, O., Fellmann, M., Fischer, J., Kiechle, A.K.: Towards personalized feedback as an energizer: a randomized controlled trial. In: 2023 IEEE 25th Conference on Business Informatics (CBI). IEEE

25. Lambusch, F., Weigelt, O., Fellmann, M., Siestrup, K.: Application of a Pictorial Scale of Human Energy in Ecological Momentary Assessment Research. Presented at the (2020). https://doi.org/10.1007/978-3-030-49044-7_16

26. Li, J., Vogel, D.:. Digital health education for self-management: a systematic literature review. In: PACIS 2021 Proceedings (2021)

27. Manz, C.C., Sims, H.P.: Self-management as a substitute for leadership: a social learning theory perspective. AMR 5(3), 361–367 (1980). https://doi.org/10.5465/amr.1980.4288845

28. Pammer, V., Bratic, M.: Surprise, surprise: activity log based time analytics for time management. In: CHI '13 Extended Abstracts on Human Factors in Computing Systems. ACM, New York, NY, 211–216 (2013). https://doi.org/10.1145/2468356.2468395

29. Parent-Thirion, A., et al.: 6th European Working Conditions Survey. Overview report (2017 update). EF, 16/34. Publications Office of the European Union, Luxembourg (2017)

30. Quantified Self. 2023. *Homepage - Quantified Self* (2023). Retrieved March 6, 2023 from https://quantifiedself.com/

31. Quinn, R.W., Spreitzer, G.M., Lam, C.F.: Building a sustainable model of human energy in organizations: exploring the critical role of resources. Acad. Manag. Ann. 6(1), 337–396 (2012). https://doi.org/10.1080/19416520.2012.676762

32. Ragsdale, J.M., Beehr, T.A.: A rigorous test of a model of employees' resource recovery mechanisms during a weekend. J. Organ. Behav. 37(6), 911–932 (2016). https://doi.org/10.1002/job.2086

33. Rapp, A., Cena, F.: Self-monitoring and Technology: Challenges and Open Issues in Personal Informatics. In: Stephanidis, C., Antona, M. (eds.) Universal Access in Human-Computer Interaction. Design for All and Accessibility Practice: 8th International Conference, UAHCI 2014, Held as Part of HCI International 2014, Heraklion, Crete, Greece, June 22-27, 2014, Proceedings, Part IV, pp. 613–622. Springer International Publishing, Cham (2014). https://doi.org/10.1007/978-3-319-07509-9_58

34. Russell, J.A.: A circumplex model of affect. J. Pers. Soc. Psychol. 39(6), 1161–1178 (1980). https://doi.org/10.1037/h0077714

35. Ryan, R.M., Frederick, C.: On energy, personality, and health: subjective vitality as a dynamic reflection of well-being. J. Pers. 65(3), 529–565 (1997). https://doi.org/10.1111/j.1467-6494.1997.tb00326.x

36. Schippers, M.C., Hogenes, R.: Energy Management of people in organizations: a review and research agenda. J. Bus. Psychol. 26(2), 193–203 (2011). https://doi.org/10.1007/s10869-011-9217-6

37. Sonnentag, S., Venz, L., Casper, A.: Advances in recovery research: what have we learned? what should be done next? J. Occup. Health Psychol. 22(3), 365–380 (2017). https://doi.org/10.1037/ocp0000079

38. Spreitzer, G.M., Grant, T.: Helping students manage their energy. J. Manag. Educ. 36(2), 239–263 (2012). https://doi.org/10.1177/1052562911429431

39. Swan, M.: The quantified self: fundamental disruption in big data science and biological discovery. Big data 1(2), 85–99 (2013). https://doi.org/10.1089/big.2012.0002

40. Weigelt, O., et al.: Time to recharge batteries – development and validation of a pictorial scale of human energy. Eur. J. Work Organ. Psy. **31**(5), 1–18 (2022). https://doi.org/10.1080/135 9432X.2022.2050218

41. Welbourne, T.M.: Two numbers for growth, innovation and high performance: Working and optimal employee energy. Organ. Dyn. **43**(3), 180–188 (2014). https://doi.org/10.1016/j.org dyn.2014.08.004

42. Zacher, H., Brailsford, H.A., Parker, S.L.: Micro-breaks matter: a diary study on the effects of energy management strategies on occupational well-being. J. Vocat. Behav. **85**(3), 287–297 (2014). https://doi.org/10.1016/j.jvb.2014.08.005

43. Zijlstra, F.R.H., Cropley, M., Rydstedt, L.W.: From recovery to regulation: an attempt to reconceptualize 'recovery from work.' Stress Health J. Int. Society Invest. Stress **30**(3), 244–252 (2014). https://doi.org/10.1002/smi.2604

Overcome Psychological Alienation Through Artificial Intelligence Painting Healing Workshops

Tanhao Gao$^{(\boxtimes)}$ ⓘ, Mengshi Yang ⓘ, Jin Ning ⓘ, Yue Qiao ⓘ, and Hongtao Zhou ⓘ

College of Design and Innovation, Tongji University, Shanghai, China
tanhaogao@gmail.com

Abstract. Intense competition across various aspects of contemporary society burdens individuals with tremendous pressure, while extreme public crises like natural disasters and pandemics further heavier residents' mental problems. Artificial Intelligence (AI) painting combines technology and art, lowering the barriers to creation and offering a promising avenue for alleviating feelings of isolation, fostering self-discovery, and improving mental health. This research organized several AI painting healing workshops, engaging 136 volunteers, and randomized them into groups using computer-generated sequences. Researchers conducted a Pre-Post Descriptive Analysis and chose the Profile of the Mood States 2nd Edition (POMS 2) to measure participants' psychological states before and after their AI painting workshop experience, thereby calculating the mean (μ) and standard deviation (σ) for analysis. The results revealed a decrease in values associated with negative emotions among participants after the workshop, particularly in Confusion-Bewilderment (CB) scores (from 15.56 to 12.03) and Tension-Anxiety (TA) scores (from 14.92 to 12.48). By contrast, Scores related to positive emotions, like Vigor-Activity (VA), showed an increased trend (from 5.92 to 9.47). The Pre-Post Descriptive Analysis demonstrated the healing potential of AI painting workshops, offering an innovative interdisciplinary approach that combines technology, art therapy, and mental health strategies. As AI technology continues to intertwine with society, AI could not only enhance economic productivity but also serve as a tool for human connection, creativity, and psychological well-being.

Keywords: Artificial Intelligence Painting · Co-creative Workshops · Emotional Healing Design

1 Introduction

The development of contemporary society has propelled intense competition across various domains, including education, economics, social standing, and personal accomplishments. Those competitions are deeply entrenched within the complex dynamics of modern society (Turner et al. 2020). Such environments often put significant pressure on individuals, forcing them to distinguish themselves, achieve success, validate their values, and fulfill societal expectations. The pressure to meet societal standards

M. Kurosu and A. Hashizume (Eds.): HCII 2024, LNCS 14686, pp. 41–50, 2024.
https://doi.org/10.1007/978-3-031-60428-7_3

can become overwhelming, resulting in severe psychological and emotional stress. Concurrently, extreme public crises like natural disasters, pandemics, economic recessions, political instability, or societal upheavals disrupt daily life, stability, and overall well-being. These crises burden community members with negative psychological problems, including stress, anxiety, depression, and lethargy (Cénat et al. 2021). Worse still, individuals might refuse to seek psychological help due to societal discrimination regarding psychological issues and a sense of shame.

With the burgeoning influence of artificial intelligence (AI) and its pervasive integration into multifarious spheres of existence, the advent of AI-generated art delineates a nuanced amalgamation of technology, artistic expression, and psychological intricacies (Ragot et al. 2020). This intersection signifies a paradigmatic shift, not merely in the creative landscape, but also the cognitive and emotional dimensions of human experience. The phenomenon of AI-generated art serves as an empirical illustration of the intricate synthesis of algorithmic processes, computational prowess, and the subjective facets of artistic expression (Floridi 2021). This symbiosis transcends conventional paradigms, deconstructing barriers to artistic creation and affording individuals within communities, irrespective of their formal artistic training, the unprecedented ability to articulate and manifest their emotional experiences in innovative and culturally resonant forms (Wang and Sun 2023).

The democratization of artistic expression, facilitated by AI-generated art, bears profound implications for interpersonal dynamics and psychological phenomena. Empirical insights from (Mazzone and Elgammal 2019) illuminate the transformative impact on understanding and empathy within creative communities. Dismantling traditional hierarchies engenders an inclusive milieu that fosters collaboration and mutual comprehension among creators (Crowder et al. 2020). Moreover, the ramifications extend into mental health and well-being, offering a compelling avenue for mitigating the prevalent sense of social isolation (Yalçın et al. 2020). The democratization of creative expression through AI-generated art emerges as a potential therapeutic modality, underscoring its capacity to serve as a conduit for emotional release and connection in the digitized landscape (Lyu et al. 2022).

This phenomenon underscores the need for comprehensive investigations into the psychological implications of human interaction with AI-generated artistic endeavors, offering a fertile ground for future interdisciplinary research at the intersection of AI, psychology, and the arts (Guerreiro 2022). As we navigate this epoch of technological evolution, the profound implications of AI-generated art on human cognition, emotion, and societal dynamics necessitate rigorous scientific exploration to unravel its full potential and ramifications.

2 Aim

The goal of organizing the "Artificial Intelligence Painting Healing Workshop" is to utilize the power of technology and creative expression to assist individuals on a journey toward psychological well-being and self-discovery, thereby providing a therapeutic platform that integrates the innovative capabilities of artificial intelligence with humanity's intrinsic desire for artistic expression. Additionally, the workshop aims to validate the potential of AI painting for community emotional healing through Pre-Post descriptive analysis, laying an empirical foundation for future research on the integration of AI and therapeutic practices.

3 Methodology

3.1 Pre-post Descriptive Analysis

We chose the Profile of Mood States 2nd Edition (POMS 2) to measure the volunteers' psychological states before and after participating in the AI painting workshop. The POMS 2, published in 2012 by Multi-Health Systems (MHS), is an evolution from the original POMS (Shacham 1983). The POMS 2 assesses six distinct dimensions of mood fluctuations over a specified period. These dimensions comprise Anger-Hostility (AH), Confusion-Bewilderment (CB), Depression-Dejection (DD), Fatigue-Inertia (FI), Tension-Anxiety (TA), and Vigor-Activity (VA). Each category consists of five questions rated on a five-point scale, ranging from "not at all (scored as 0)" to "extremely (scored as 4)," resulting in a total score range of 0 to 20 for each category.

3.2 Computer Random Grouping

We publicly recruited 136 volunteers to participate in the AI painting workshop through online platforms and offline posters. Due to spatial constraints (maximum capacity of 40 people during one workshop), we utilized computer-generated random sequences to form groups. The detailed steps are as follows:

1. We Numbered the 136 volunteers based on their order of registration (From No.001 to No.136).
2. We used the Excel random number command (=RAND()*(1–0)) to generate a random number between 0 and 1 for each participant.
3. We Sorted the generated random numbers in ascending order [command: = SORT(A1:A136)], resulting in a shuffled order of participant numbers.
4. Based on the new order, we divided all participants into four groups, each consisting of 34 people. The random participant numbers are as follows (Fig. 1):

3.3 Artificial Intelligence Painting Platform

We chose an AI painting platform called "Midjourney (MJ)" and invited 136 participants with various professional backgrounds. The algorithmic painting generation logic of the MJ platform is as follows:

1. First, the participants need to enter the "/imagine: prompt" in the MJ platform and then enter a series of keywords to define the proportions, colors, materials, elements, and other characteristics of the picture. They can also add artists, games, movies, or rendering software to describe the picture style further.
2. MJ's AI algorithm generates four images at a time within 30 s.

GROUP A	126	019	099	026	125	022	010	071	129
	050	067	018	002	089	028	078	120	118
	135	012	112	083	058	116	132	087	
	102	081	128	047	044	015	074	110	
GROUP B	055	123	013	038	070	023	020	052	045
	035	006	039	124	043	092	072	049	122
	063	053	011	040	086	054	093	100	
	034	104	088	014	103	108	133	025	
GROUP C	069	094	111	075	115	085	059	046	027
	009	095	117	134	029	036	080	068	066
	098	079	056	065	091	017	003	073	
	061	064	131	127	114	077	042	082	
GROUP D	031	109	096	105	005	113	021	136	048
	084	001	106	004	016	076	097	119	032
	051	062	024	060	130	033	041	057	
	121	101	008	037	030	090	007	107	

Fig. 1. Four groups of participants were randomly disrupted by computers. Source: the author.

3. The participants can select one of them individually and execute the "U" command (U is to upscale the chosen picture and further generate richer details) or the "V" command (V is to use the selected picture based on Similar elements and create the variation of four images).
4. The picture after "U" or "V" can be further upscale or variation, and finally, they can find an image that obtained their psychological expectations.

4 Outcome

As depicted in Fig. 2, approximately 47.06% (N = 64) of participants in the AI painting healing workshop were male, and about 38.24% (N = 52) were female. Regarding age distribution, the majority were in the 21–30 age group, accounting for approximately 52.94% (N = 72).

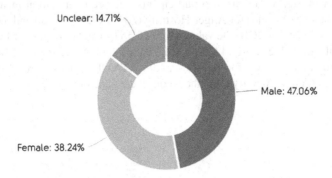

Fig. 2. Gender distribution of 136 participants. Source: the author.

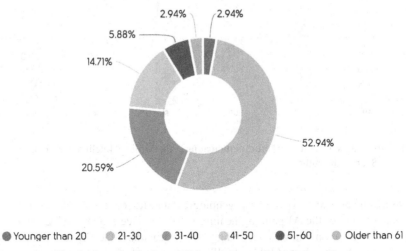

Fig. 3. Age distribution of 136 participants. Source: the author.

We collected all participants' psychological state data before they attended the AI healing workshop and calculated their mean values (μ) using the following formula:

$$\mu = \frac{1}{N} \sum_{i=1}^{N} x_i$$

The deviation of samples from the sample mean is used to measure the dispersion of an array. The formula for calculating the standard deviation (σ) is:

$$\sigma = \sqrt{\frac{1}{N}\sum_{i=1}^{N}(x_i - \mu)^2}$$

As shown in Fig. 3, For the 136 participants, the pre-intervention mean (μ) and standard deviation (σ) values for Anger-Hostility (AH) were 15.09 (μ) and 3.07 (σ), for Confusion-Bewilderment (CB) the values were 15.56 (μ) and 3.33 (σ), for Depression-Dejection (DD) the values were 14.92 (μ) and 2.95 (σ), for Fatigue-Inertia (FI) the values were 15.53 (μ) and 2.71 (σ), for Tension-Anxiety (TA) the values were 14.92 (μ) and 2.86 (σ), and for Vigor-Activity (VA) the values were 5.92 (μ) and 3.09 (σ).

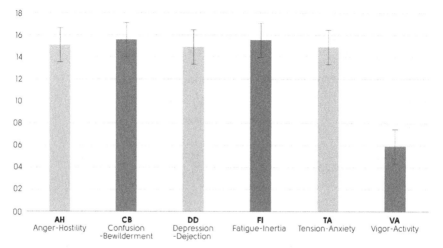

Fig. 4. Participants' mental state before participating in the Artificial Intelligence painting healing workshop. Source: the author.

We conducted a post-experience psychological state test on the participants following their engagement in the AI painting healing workshop (see Fig. 4). Values associated with negative emotions showed declining trends, particularly the CB value (from 15.56 to 12.03) and TA value (from 14.92 to 12.48). Conversely, the VA value related to positive emotions demonstrated an upward trend (from 5.92 to 9.47). The AI painting experience shows promising healing potential through pre-post descriptive analysis (Figs. 5, 6, 7 and 8).

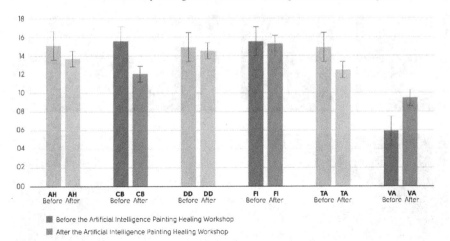

Fig. 5. Comparison of participants' mental state before and after participating in the workshop. Source: the author.

Fig. 6. Images generated by participants in AI painting healing workshops. Source: the author.

Fig. 7. The image generation process by one of the participants, "Arya," in the AI workshop. Source: the author.

Fig. 8. Color tendencies of images generated by participants in AI workshops. Source: the author.

5 Conclusion

The AI painting healing workshop represents an innovative interdisciplinary approach, integrating emerging technology, art therapy, and mental health strategies. Although further research is essential to understand the long-term impacts of such interventions, AI-based painting offers a promising path to address the widespread psychological dissonance caused by intense social competition and extreme public crises. AI technology can serve not only to enhance economic productivity but also as a tool for human connection, creativity, and mental well-being. Future research can expand these workshops, incorporating insights and advancements from AI and mental health studies to foster a more empathetic, interconnected, and emotionally resilient society.

References

Cénat, J.M., et al.: Prevalence of symptoms of depression, anxiety, insomnia, posttraumatic stress disorder, and psychological distress among populations affected by the COVID-19 pandemic: a systematic review and meta-analysis. Psychiatry Res. **295**, 113599 (2021)

Crowder, J.A., Carbone, J., Friess, S. (eds.): Artificial Psychology: Psychological Modeling and Testing of AI Systems. Springer, Cham (2020). https://doi.org/10.1007/978-3-030-17081-3

Floridi, L.: Artificial intelligence, deepfakes and a future of ectypes. In: Ethics, Governance, and Policies in Artificial Intelligence, pp. 307–312 (2021)

Guerreiro, R.I.C.: Using artificial intelligence to create paintings: How type of artist impacts WTP through emotional intelligence and perceived quality [PhD Thesis] (2022). https://repositorio.ucp.pt/handle/10400.14/38837

Lyu, Y., Wang, X., Lin, R., Wu, J.: Communication in human–AI co-creation: perceptual analysis of paintings generated by text-to-image system. Appl. Sci. **12**(22), 11312 (2022)

Mazzone, M., Elgammal, A.: Art, creativity, and the potential of artificial intelligence. Arts **8**(1), 26 (2019)

Ragot, M., Martin, N., Cojean, S.: Ai-generated vs. Human artworks. A perception bias towards artificial intelligence? In: Extended Abstracts of the 2020 CHI Conference on Human Factors in Computing Systems, pp. 1–10 (2020)

Shacham, S.: A shortened version of the profile of mood states. J. Pers. Assess. **47**(3), 305–306 (1983). https://doi.org/10.1207/s15327752jpa4703_14

Turner, A.I., et al.: Psychological stress reactivity and future health and disease outcomes: a systematic review of prospective evidence. Psychoneuroendocrinology **114**, 104599 (2020)

Wang, Y., Sun, Y.: The relevance of emotional AI-generated painting to the painting subject and main colors. In: Mori, H., Asahi, Y., Coman, A., Vasilache, S., Rauterberg, M. (eds.) HCI International 2023 – Late Breaking Papers, vol. 14056, pp. 390–399. Springer, Cham (2023). https://doi.org/10.1007/978-3-031-48044-7_28

Yalçın, Ö.N., Abukhodair, N., DiPaola, S.: Empathic ai painter: a computational creativity system with embodied conversational interaction. In: NeurIPS 2019 Competition and Demonstration Track, pp. 131–141 (2020). https://proceedings.mlr.press/v123/yalcin20a.html

Quantification and Analysis of Stress Levels While Walking Up and Down a Step in Real Space and VR Space Using Electrocardiogram

Masanao Koeda[1](✉), Yoshio Tsukuda[2], Katsuhiko Onishi[3], and Hiroshi Noborio[3]

[1] Okayama Prefectural University, Okayama, Japan
koeda@ss.oka-pu.ac.jp
[2] Embedded Wings Co., Ltd., Osaka, Japan
[3] Osaka Electro-Communication University, Osaka, Japan

Abstract. The purpose of this study is to quantify the fear during walking in VR space. We conduct an experiment where subjects walk up and down steps in real and VR spaces. A path with steps of 10cm high was placed in the real and VR spaces. Subjects wore an HMD and walked along the path. The coordinate systems of the real and VR spaces were calibrated in advance, and the real and virtual steps were placed at the same position. It is considered that fear relates to the stress level. We used ECG (Electrocardiogram) to measure the degree of stress during the experiment and Poincare plot and LF/HF for analyzing the feeling of fear. The results indicate that it is possible to give stress to subjects when they walk through a space with steps in a VR space.

Keywords: VR Exposure Therapy · Post-fall Syndrome · Stress · ECG · Poincare plot

1 Introduction

In recent years, falling accidents have become more frequent in Japan due to the increase of elderly people. One in three elderly people falls at least once a year [1]. When an elderly person falls, they may suffer from a disease called post-fall syndrome. Post-fall syndrome is a psychiatric disorder in which patients have fear of walking. As a treatment for this, exposure therapy is effective [2]. Exposure therapy is an effective treatment for this syndrome [2], and it has been reported that virtual reality (VR)-based exposure therapy is also effective as reality-based therapy [3].

Tsujishita et al. [4] conducted an experiment that showed an actual falling down scene in a VR to elderly people with a fear of falling. They measured the sense of fear from the heart rate. The results suggested that the subjects felt fear when they saw a falling down scene, and the effect of exposure therapy on reducing the fear of falling was also confirmed.

In this study, we evaluate the change in the stress state when walking in a VR space in which the subjects feel fear of walking by analyzing electrocardiographic measurements.

© The Author(s), under exclusive license to Springer Nature Switzerland AG 2024
M. Kurosu and A. Hashizume (Eds.): HCII 2024, LNCS 14686, pp. 51–62, 2024.
https://doi.org/10.1007/978-3-031-60428-7_4

2   VR Space with a Step to Make Walking Fearful

To give subjects a fearful feeling, we placed a step (10 cm in height, 60 cm in length, and 60 cm in width) in the VR space. The walking range in the VR space was approximately 2.5 m × 3 m (Fig. 1). The experiments were conducted in real and virtual spaces, switching alternately with and without steps (Fig. 2). For example, we assume that subjects feel danger when there is no step in the real space but there is a step in the virtual space.

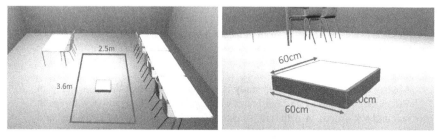

Fig. 1. VR space with a step and the size of the step

Fig. 2. Real space (left) and virtual space (right) with a step

A motion tracker was attached to each ankle of the subject, and a 3D lower limb model in the VR space were synchronized with the leg movements in the real space (Fig. 3). The subject was asked to walk in the VR space in several situation, and the ECG was measured.

In this study, HTC VIVE Pro Eye was used as the HMD. VIVE Trackers were used as the motion tracker. BITalino (r)evolution (hereafter, BITalino) was used to measure ECG. OpenSignals (r)evolution was used for data recording. Unity 2019 3.5f1 (64bit) was used to develop the VR system.

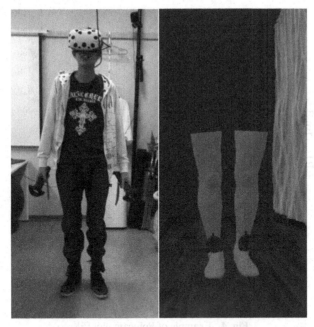

Fig. 3. Motion tracker attached to each ankle (left) and 3D lower limb model

3   Analysis of ECG for Estimation of Stress State

The Poincare plot (hereafter, PP) and LF/HF are used to analyze the ECG. PP plots the nth and n + 1st R-R Interval (hereafter, RRI) on the horizontal and vertical axes, respectively. Normally, the distribution is elliptical, with the major axis along a 45-degree line passing the origin (Fig. 4).

In general, the heart rate falls in the resting state. Therefore, the center of gravity of the ellipse moves to the upper right. Conversely, in a state of stress or tension, the heart rate increases. Therefore, the center of gravity of the ellipse moves to the lower left.

L and T in Fig. 4 are the standard deviations in the major axis (L) / minor axis (T) of the ellipse including 90% of the plotted points (called the confidence ellipse). Normally, L/T is larger in the resting state and smaller in the stress/strain state. LF/HF is the ratio of the power ratio in the low-frequency and high-frequency regions of the RRI.

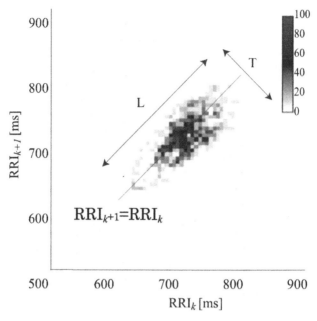

Fig. 4. Example of Poincare plot [5]

4 Experiment

The subjects were 10 male students in their 20 s. The subjects sat on chairs placed at the initial position, wore HMDs, and attached electrodes to their chests for electrocardiographic measurements. A step was placed approximately 1.5 m away from the initial position. The subject walks to the front of the step, steps up to the step, walks over the step, steps down, and then walks about 1.5 m more and finishes (Fig. 5).

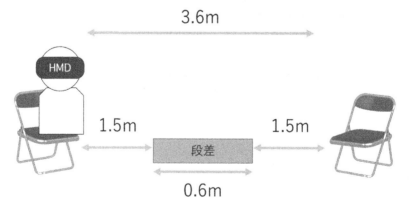

Fig. 5. Experimental environment

Experiments are conducted according to the order shown in Table 1, and consists of 11 phases.

Table 1. The order of the experiments

Phase	Contents	Time (min)
1	Rest in a chair before the experiment	2
2	Watch videos in a chair with HMD	2
	Interval	1
3	Walk in VR space: Outward, without a step in real and virtual space	2
	Interval	1
4	Walk in VR space: Return, without a step in real and virtual space	2
	Interval	1
5	Walk in VR space: Outward, with a step in real and virtual space	2
	Interval	1
6	Walk in VR space: Return, with a step in real and virtual space	2
	Interval	1
7	Walk in VR space: Outward, without a step in real space, with a step in virtual space	2
	Interval	1
8	Walk in VR space: Return, without a step in real space, with a step in virtual space	2
	Interval	1
9	Walk in VR space: Outward, with a step in real space, without a step in virtual space	2
	Interval	1
10	Walk in VR space: Return, with a step in real space, without a step in virtual space	2
11	Rest in a chair after the experiment	2

4.1 Rest in a Chair Before the Experiment (Phase 1)

The subject rests in a chair for 2 min wearing the HMD. A dark landscape (Fig. 6) is displayed on the HMD. ECG is measured during this period.

4.2   Watch Videos in a Chair with HMD (Phase 2)

After Phase 1, without interval, the subject watches a video image of walking up and down the steps in VR space (Fig. 7) for 2 min. ECG is measured while the subject only watches the video without moving the body.

Fig. 6. The video image displayed on the HMD in Phase 1

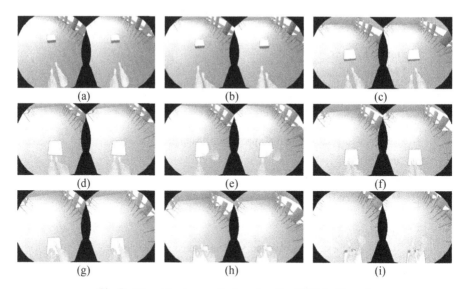

Fig. 7. The video image displayed on the HMD in Phase 2

4.3   Walk in VR Space (Phase 3 – 10)

The subject stands up and walks in the real and virtual spaces with and without steps in the order shown in Table 1 (Fig. 8). ECG is measured during walking.

Before the start of walking, we asked the first subject to "Walk straight". The subject walked checking for obstacles with his feet on the ground. Therefore, we asked the second subject to " Walk straight, and if there is a step, lift up your foot and walk up the step". However, the subject walked without looking at his feet. Therefore, we asked the fourth subject and the following subjects to "Walk straight, look at your feet, and if there is a step, lift up your foot and walk up the step".

4.4 Rest in a Chair After the Experiment (Phase 11)

The subject rests in a chair for 2 min wearing the HMD. A dark landscape (Fig. 6) is displayed on the HMD. ECG is measured during this period.

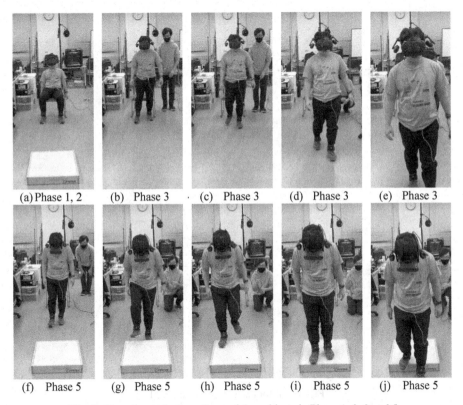

(a) Phase 1, 2   (b)   Phase 3   ·   (c)   Phase 3   (d)   Phase 3   (e)   Phase 3

(f)   Phase 5   (g)   Phase 5   (h)   Phase 5   (i)   Phase 5   (j)   Phase 5

Fig. 8. Experimental view of one of the subjects in Phase 1, 2, 3 and 5

5 Experimental Results

Due to space limitations, the data for all subjects cannot be included. As an example, we show the PP with confidence ellipse (Fig. 9), variance ratios and center of gravity of confidence ellipses, LF/HF and HF (Fig. 10) of a subject. In the walking experiment in the VR space, only the ECGs during walking were analyzed.

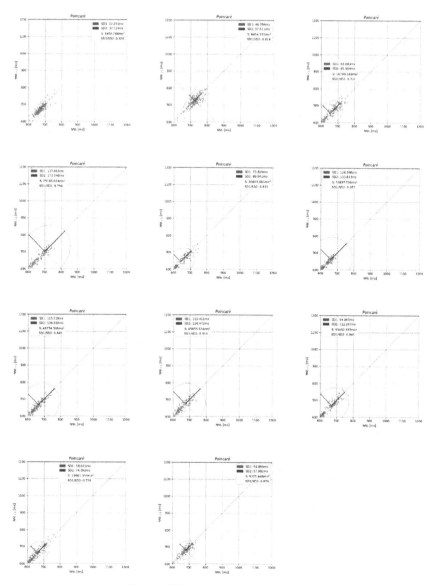

Fig. 9. PP for each phase of subject 1

Figures 11, 12 and 13 show boxplots of the normalized variance ratio of the confidence ellipse, the normalized center of gravity of the confidence ellipse, and LF/HF in each phase for all subjects. In these figures, the orange line indicates the median value, and the green triangle indicates the mean value.

Table 2 shows the results of the t-tests for significant differences between the various phases.

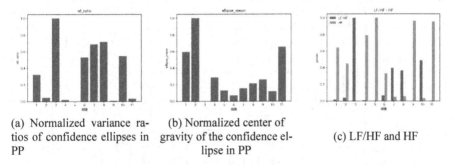

(a) Normalized variance ratios of confidence ellipses in PP

(b) Normalized center of gravity of the confidence ellipse in PP

(c) LF/HF and HF

Fig. 10. Analysis results for PP of subject 1

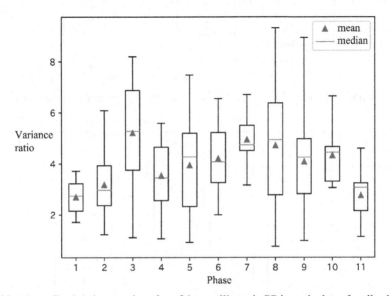

Fig. 11. Normalized variance ratios of confidence ellipses in PP in each phase for all subjects

The experimental results indicated that the subjects were more stressed during the walking experiment (Phase 3–10) than when they were at rest (Phase 1) or watching the walking video (Phase 2). This suggests that the subjects may feel fear when walking. The outward walking (Phase 3, 5, 7, and 9) tended to be more stressful than the return walking (Phase 4, 6, 8, and 10), but there were no significant differences between the two.

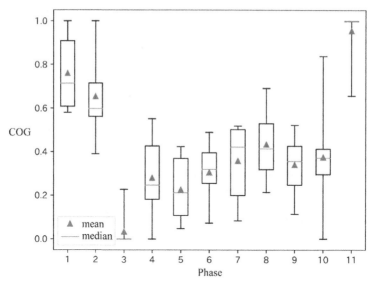

Fig. 12. Normalized center of gravity of the confidence ellipse in PP in each phase for all subjects

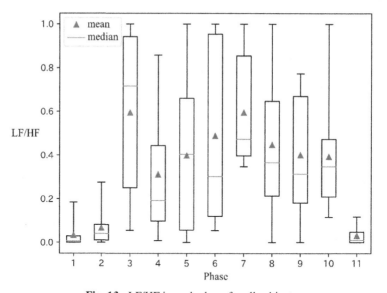

Fig. 13. LF/HF in each phase for all subjects

Table 2. Significant differences between phases calculated by T-test (* is 5% significant)

Compared Phases	Variance ratios of confidence ellipses in PP	Center of gravity of the confidence ellipse in PP	LF/HF
Phase 1 - Phase 2	0.27390	0.1380066	0.30371
Phase 3 - Phase 4	0.05024*	0.0075461*	0.11423
Phase 5 - Phase 6	0.52944	0.0149794*	0.58112
Phase 7 - Phase 8	0.66429	0.3483707	0.19814
Phase 9 - Phase 10	0.96816	0.4790195	0.95526
Phase 1 - Phase 3	0.00045*	0.0000002*	0.00113*
Phase 1 - Phase 4	0.03758*	0.0003561*	0.02688*
Phase 1 - Phase 5	0.02865*	0.0159423*	0.00929*
Phase 1 - Phase 6	0.00406*	0.0000232*	0.01242*
Phase 1 - Phase 7	0.00006*	0.3648217	0.00009*
Phase 1 - Phase 8	0.01884*	0.0006338*	0.00482*
Phase 1 - Phase 9	0.03501*	0.0002127*	0.00444*
Phase 1 - Phase 10	0.00116*	0.0045362*	0.00299*
Phase 1 - Phase 11	0.51220	0.0904004	0.96195*
Phase 2 - Phase 3	0.02808*	0.0000009*	0.00232*
Phase 2 - Phase 4	0.40749	0.0021307*	0.03910*
Phase 2 - Phase 5	0.18311	0.0157353*	0.01854*
Phase 2 - Phase 6	0.10993	0.0022322*	0.01581*
Phase 2 - Phase 7	0.00861*	0.3592728	0.00004*
Phase 2 - Phase 8	0.07306	0.0348665*	0.00718*
Phase 2 - Phase 9	0.19187	0.0041963*	0.00907*
Phase 2 - Phase 10	0.03533*	0.0432202*	0.00605*
Phase 3 - Phase 5	0.16723	0.01509*	0.46303
Phase 3 - Phase 6	0.08732	0.68871	0.19000
Phase 3 - Phase 7	0.00227*	0.33893	0.04673*
Phase 3 - Phase 8	0.06669	0.07348	0.28024
Phase 3 - Phase 9	0.24133	0.39913	0.44442
Phase 3 - Phase 10	0.04617*	0.23637	0.45061

6   Conclusion

In this study, we measured the stress state when walking in a VR space with a 10-cm-high step. The step was carefully placed to avoid the difference between the real and virtual space. The stress state was estimated from the Poincare plot and LF/HF calculated from ECG data. The results showed that the system could quantitatively estimate the stress state and fear during walking in the VR space. This is the first step toward the realization of a VR exposure therapy system for treating post-fall syndrome.

As a future issue, it is necessary to conduct experiments with a large number of subjects over a long period of time and to analyze the results from enough data. Also, it is required to separately analyze the physical stress caused by walking and the visual stress caused by the HMD.

References

1. Otaka, Y.: Fall prevention in older people: present and future perspectives. Jpn. J. Fall Prevent. **1**(3), 11–20 (2015)
2. Huppert, J.D., Roth, D.A.: Treating obsessive-compulsive disorder with exposure and response prevention. Behav. Analyst Today **4**, 66–70 (2003)
3. Emmelkamp, P.M.G., et al.: Virtual reality treatment versus exposure in vivo: a comparative evaluation in acrophobia. Behav. Res. Ther. **40**(5), 509–516 (2002)
4. Tsujishita, M., Noborio, H., Masutani, Y., Koeda, M., Onishi, K.: The efficacy of virtual reality exposure therapy for fear of falling (FOF) in the elderly. In: Kurosu, M. (ed.) Human-Computer Interaction. Human Values and Quality of Life: Thematic Area, HCI 2020, Held as Part of the 22nd International Conference, HCII 2020, Copenhagen, Denmark, July 19–24, 2020, Proceedings, Part III, pp. 178–187. Springer International Publishing, Cham (2020). https://doi.org/10.1007/978-3-030-49065-2_13
5. Matsumoto, Y., Mori, N., Mitajiri, R., Jiang, Z.: Study of mental stress evaluation based on analysis of heart rate variability. Life Support **22**(3), 105–111 (2010)

Mapping Epilepsy Monitoring Challenges for Enhanced Patient Experience

Mafalda Morgado[1]([✉]), Hande Ayanoğlu[1,2] [iD], and Rodrigo Hernández Ramírez[2,3] [iD]

[1] IADE, Faculdade de Design, Tecnologia e Comunicação, Universidade Europeia,
Av. D. Carlos I, 4, 1200-649 Lisbon, Portugal
mafalda.morgado@tecnico.ulisboa.pt,
hande.ayanoglu@universidadeeuropeia.pt
[2] UNIDCOM/IADE, Unidade de Investigação em Design e Comunicação, Av. D. Carlos I, 4,
1200-649 Lisbon, Portugal
rodrigo.hernandez@sydney.edu.au
[3] Sydney School of Architecture, Design and Planning, University of Sydney,
Wilkinson Building G04, Camperdown, NSW 2006, Australia

Abstract. Epilepsy is one of the most common neurological diseases, affecting people of all ages. A considerable number of patients with epilepsy (PWE) are resistant to drug therapy and require constant monitoring. In the scope of developing a wearable for constant epilepsy monitoring, this study addresses four aspects, at a theoretical level, providing a brief overview of: the condition; particular biosignals in epilepsy monitoring; use of textile electrodes; and the importance of a user-centric approach. The paper highlights the importance of a holistic, iterative, user-centric design approach, prioritizing the needs and experiences of PWE, caregivers and medical professionals. Ultimately, it seeks to contribute to developing synergies between the human and technological dimensions of the problem, to develop solutions that are effective and seamlessly integrate into the patient's daily life, improving adherence to the technology, and, overall, enhancing patient care and their well-being.

Keywords: Epilepsy · Constant Monitoring · User Experience. · Biosignals · Wearable

1 Introduction

Recent technological advancements have created new opportunities for wearable development and commercially available digital solutions in the medical field [1–4]. Studies indicate that patients with epilepsy are becoming more curious about wearable technologies [5–8]. Textile-based wearable solutions [9–11] offer new opportunities from a User Experience (UX) standpoint, due to their flexibility, elasticity, comfort, and ease of integration with sensing technologies.

The research project presented here concerns the development of a textile-based epilepsy monitoring device to improve the well-being and, potentially, the Quality of

M. Kurosu and A. Hashizume (Eds.): HCII 2024, LNCS 14686, pp. 63–77, 2024.
https://doi.org/10.1007/978-3-031-60428-7_5

Life (QoL) of Patients with Epilepsy (PWE) by combining textiles and electronics in a user-centric development process.

Continuous collection of specific physiological signals allows to detect and (potentially) predict epileptic seizures—which in turn allows for timely interventions. Moreover, early detection and prediction contribute to an increased sense of security and autonomy for PWE, particularly for those who have not yet achieved seizure freedom. Finally, the data collected through constant monitoring can contribute to a more comprehensive diagnosis and, subsequently, a more accurate treatment of the condition, supporting greater patient care.

Developing a device capable of accomplishing those tasks while enabling a positive long-term user experience requires a human-centred approach. Firstly, due to the multitude of challenges that PWE face, including perceived and enacted stigma as well as anxiety, fear, and lack of autonomy. Secondly, because such a device should be comfortable, non-obstructive, discreet, and adaptable. Finally, because user experience greatly influences acceptance and adherence to the device and its monitoring protocol.

Besides seeking to positively and meaningfully impacting the everyday well-being of PWE, at psychological and physical levels, we also aim to contribute to the continuous advancements in health and well-being design.

Consequently, the main goal of this paper is providing a theoretical contextualization of wearable monitoring devices. The paper is organized in four sections: (i) Epilepsy: Characterizing symptoms, available treatments, and the overall impact of the condition; (ii) Biosignal Modalities: Investigating their roles in seizure occurrence, focusing on their integration into epilepsy monitoring; (iii) Conductive Fabrics Overview, related to their application in the developed work; (iv) User Experience and wearable monitoring devices: Examining user experience, particularly within healthcare contexts, as it relates to the developed work. Current practices in epilepsy monitoring, both in clinical environments and at-home, are discussed, including autonomous health and epilepsy monitoring through wearables.

2   Understanding Epilepsy

Epilepsy is a chronic neurological disorder that affects over 70 million individuals globally, irrespectively of their sex, age, ethnicities, and socio-economic backgrounds [12–15] although these variables may affect the incidence and prevalence of the condition amongst certain groups. Research indicates a marginally higher prevalence and incidence in males compared to females—possibly correlated to higher risk factors normally found in the male population [13]. Incidence and prevalence are also higher in the elderly age-group, attributed primarily to an increased incidence of cardiovascular and neurodegenerative conditions, although focal seizures are most common in children and adults [12]. Socio-economic factors also affect epilepsy rates, as lower to middle-income countries, as well as lower socio-economic segments within high-income countries, report higher prevalence and incidence rates. This trend may be influenced by several factors, including population demographics, environmental risk factors, lower quality healthcare management, reduced access to health care system, hygiene and sanitation factors, infections, and trauma-related incidents [12, 15, 16]. In fact, the reduction of mortality rates among people suffering from idiopathic epilepsy is correlated with enhancements in health care quality, access, and treatment [12]. Furthermore, epilepsy incidence and prevalence might be underestimated in certain areas where cultural and social stigma lead to the concealment of symptoms and conditions, resulting in undiagnosed or unreported cases [16].

Diagnosing epilepsy requires an extensive evaluation of the patient. This evaluation includes several factors, including medical history, age at onset, present health, seizure characterization, and tests such as magnetic resonance imaging (MRI), electrocardiogram (ECG) and electroencephalogram (EEG) [17].

Epilepsy can be classified according to its origin. Idiopathic epilepsy is that in which no clearly identified causing factor has been identified and a genetic predisposition is assumed; symptomatic, attributed to a specific brain injury; and cryptogenic, in which the condition is assumed to be symptomatic but requires further exploration to identify the underlying factor causing it [16]. The role of genetics in epilepsy varies widely, ranging from the primary cause (commonly related to generalized epilepsy) to the underlying predisposing to develop epilepsy following a brain injury [15]. Although genetic and environmental factors are known to contribute to the heterogeneity of epilepsy distribution, nearly half of epilepsy cases have no known cause [12].

The neurological condition is characterized by recurrent, unprovoked epileptic seizures [12, 14, 15]. Unprovoked seizures occur without any precipitating factors, contrasting with acute symptomatic, or provoked, seizures, which occur as a symptom of an acute central nervous system insult, thus not integrating an epilepsy diagnosis [12]. Recurrent, unprovoked seizures are related to abnormal, transient, synchronous excitatory and inhibitory activities within neuronal network, which leads to abnormal electrical discharges and the consequent disruption of the affected neuronal network and, potentially, others [15, 17, 18]. Seizures are associated with irregular cortical activity and can be characterized as focal or generalized, depending on whether the epileptogenic networks are distributed in one or both brain hemispheres, respectively [12, 15, 19]. Moreover, seizures are classified as motor or non-motor according to physically exhibited symptoms [18].

According to Epilepsy Foundation Eastern Pennsylvania and the Centers for Disease Control and Prevention, both generalized and focal onset seizures can exhibit motor and non-motor symptoms; generalized seizures may further develop according to motor manifestations such as tonic or atonic (respectively, muscle stiffness or relaxation) and myoclonic or clonic (respectively, event or period of muscle jerking). In terms of patient consciousness, absence seizures are characterized by a period of consciousness impairment while presenting with minimal or no motor symptoms [19]. Convulsions is a term often used to describe the physical manifestations of generalized onset motor seizures; however, this term is not officially recognised in the International League Against Epilepsy seizure classification [18].

2.1 Comorbidities

The simultaneous presence of multiple health conditions in the same individual is termed comorbidity. PWE experience a higher rate of comorbidities, potentially up to eight times greater than the general population, and these comorbidities affect the treatment outcomes and QoL of patients. Comorbidities observed in PWE include cognitive impairments, psychiatric and psychological comorbidities, such as depression, anxiety, and autism spectrum disorders, and somatic comorbidities, such as diabetes, arthritis, and digestive, cardiovascular, and respiratory issues [15, 17, 20, 21]. Notably, PWE report a higher prevalence of psychiatric disorders, particularly mood and anxiety disorders, and a higher suicide rate, ten times greater than in the general population [22]. The causative relationship between epilepsy and some comorbidities is considered bidirectional, since comorbidities may be the precipitating factors or the results of epilepsy and its treatment [15, 17]. This is particularly evident in psychiatric conditions like depression or anxiety, where these disorders can be a consequence and a risk factor for developing epilepsy [20, 21, 23], in some cases affecting the patient's response to treatment [22], which may be indicative of a neurological mechanism shared by epilepsy and these psychiatric comorbidities [17].

Comorbidities are a leading factor for premature death among PWE [15]. Epilepsy patients face a higher mortality risk than the general population [20], and approximately one-third of premature deaths can be linked to epilepsy, such as *status epilepticus* and Sudden Unexpected Death in Epilepsy (SUDEP), or indirectly from the occurrence of, for instance, drowning or suicide [12, 15, 17]. SUDEP is an unexpected death that occurs without evidence of other traumatic, toxicologic, anatomic or *status epilepticus*-related causes, and while evidence suggests that it follows an epileptic seizure, the exact causes of SUDEP remains unclear. The nature and persistence of seizures are related to risk factors for SUDEP; nocturnal seizures, in particular, are strongly correlated with SUDEP, and supervision remains the most effective preventive strategy [12, 15].

2.2 Treatment

Comorbid conditions impact the efficacy of epilepsy treatments [17]. Pharmaceutical treatment is the main approach, usually through the administration of antiseizure and Antiepileptic Drugs (AED). However, about one-third of patients are pharmacoresistant, rendering the approach ineffective [14, 15, 17]. The cause of pharmacoresistance is likely multifactorial, and a personalized treatment that accounts for individual factors such as potential underlying causes, medical and familial history, drug efficacy, and comorbid conditions, might be necessary [14].

When pharmaceutical approaches fail, alternative strategies can be employed, including surgery, electrical neurostimulation, reducing brain inflammation through brain cooling, immunosuppressants and mTOR pathway inhibitors, and dietary modifications such as the ketogenic diet [14, 15]. Surgical interventions, particularly in focal epilepsy, involve removing or disconnecting the epileptogenic area of the brain. While cost-effective and successful in seizure control, surgery is suitable for only a limited number of pharmacoresistant patients, and its effectiveness largely depends on the comprehensive evaluation and identification of the epileptogenic zone. Neurostimulation is a palliative approach that involves regular or responsive electrical stimulation of specific brain regions or nerves, like the vagus nerve, to mitigate seizure generation and propagation [15, 17].

Moreover, the use of antiseizure medications is not without side effects, which are primarily neuropsychiatric [15] but may also cause cardiovascular, gastrointestinal, cognitive, dermatological, and visual issues [17]. The impact of these medications on a patient's physical and emotional well-being varies depending on their effectiveness and the severity of their side effects [20]. Notably, there is a strong correlation between the number of administered AEDs, perceived stigma, and difficulties in emotional regulation [22]. Around 90% of patients report some degree of AED treatment side effects, and these can be debilitating and significantly diminish the QoL of PWE [20]. Factors such as the severity of the condition, polytherapy, and mental health conditions such as depression or anxiety have been linked to the increased frequency and severity of reported side effects [24].

2.3 Impact

The QoL of epilepsy patients is multidimensional and extends past the interrelated QoL health-related factors such as the severity of epilepsy, disability, seizure management, and the perception of medication effects [24], encompassing also their physical, mental, and social well-being [25]. Epilepsy patients' QoL encompasses several aspects of the social dimension, encompassing quality of their social life, level of external support, autonomy, and independence; the psychological dimension, pertaining to the impact of social stigma, isolation, self-esteem, and coping capabilities; the cognitive dimension, involving cognitive capabilities such as memory, communication, and attention; the influence of psychiatric comorbidities; and the patient's education and employment [26]. When compared to the general population, PWE tend to report lower QoL, and while this may be attributed to various factors, the most common include depressions, anxiety, and perceived social stigma [27]. In fact, diagnosis of anxiety or depression are twice as prevalent among PWE, affecting up to one in three PWE [17]. Furthermore, those with pharmacoresistant epilepsy tend to exhibit a higher frequency of depressive symptoms. These psychological aspects not only affect the person's mood but also their perception of the medication's side effects, and therefore influencing their adherence to treatment and condition severity [24]. A causal relationship has been established between depression and increased drug treatment side-effects, accidents, injuries, and mortality [22].

Epilepsy, its symptoms, and treatment result in a range of neurobiological, neurocognitive, psychosocial, social, and physical burdens that significantly impact the well-being and QoL of PWE [12, 15, 28, 29]. PWE, particularly those who have not yet achieved seizure freedom, usually face significant challenges in their relationships, education, and employment, primarily due to social stigma, seizure-related concerns, and functional disabilities [30].

In general, PWE suffer from a higher frequency of cognitive issues, including difficulties with memory and concentration. This decline in cognitive abilities is particularly linked to tonic-clonic seizures. Psychosocial issues encompass depression, anxiety, and sexual, social, and communication difficulties. Physical limitations are related to a higher level of physical inactivity, attributed to the fear of experiencing seizures [28]. Epilepsy significantly impacts the brain regions responsible for social cognition on both focal and generalized onsets [25]. Impairments in social skills, often stemming from fear or stigmatization, as well as higher rates of psychiatric conditions and neurocognitive issues, such as attention deficits, memory problems, and communication difficulties, are interconnected factors contributing to social deficits in PWE. These deficits in social well-being have repercussions on external support, family constitution, employment prospects, and social engagement, ultimately leading to a reduced QoL and coping abilities [25]. Therefore, effective epilepsy management should involve more than seizure control and the minimization of side effects in order to include social and psychological interventions [31].

The burden of epilepsy extends beyond the condition itself, with social stigma as a significant contributor to this burden by introducing additional challenges and distress for patients [29], such as social exclusion and difficulties in education or employment [20]. Its impact and perception play a substantial role in emotional dysregulation and depressive symptoms experienced by PWE [22]. Stigma can be categorized as 'felt' or 'enacted', respectively, referring to the fear or shame of facing social stigma and the actual instances of discriminatory attitudes [20]. In developed countries, felt stigma tends to weigh more than enacted stigma, indicating that the belief in discrimination prevails in patients despite improvements in public attitudes [29]. In developing countries, conversely, enacted stigma is of greater priority and concern [20]. Even in view of a favorable prognosis, PWE and their families tend to express negative feelings and concerns regarding social discrimination and stigma [31], underscoring the impact and weight of patients' fears of facing discrimination.

It is crucial to approach epilepsy care in a personalized and comprehensive manner [14, 24].

3   The Role of Biosignals

While seizure documentation is instrumental for the diagnosis and characterization of the condition, accurate self-reporting and logging seizure occurrences can be challenging for PWE, particularly those involving loss of awareness, consciousness, or occurring during sleep [32]. Continuous seizure monitoring and detection devices can aid and enhance the accuracy of seizure reporting and documenting, promoting more timely and more effective interventions [15, 33], as well as assessing the risk and contributing to the prevention of SUDEP by tracking the progression of related risk factors [15, 34]. Additionally, such technologies also reduce the burden of the condition for PWE [33]. Wearable multimodal devices integrating various sensors, particularly in a wristband form, are a highly desirable, non-invasive, and non-stigmatizing alternative to EEG-related techniques for continuous outpatient monitoring, as they monitor the autonomic nervous system and detect seizures with minimal disruption to patient's lives [32, 33, 35]. Despite their contribution to diagnosis and monitoring, however, their performance is inconsistent across different types of seizures [32], making them particularly unreliable when it comes to accurately detecting non-convulsive seizures [15].

Factors related to accelerometry, body temperature, skin conductance, and hemodynamics are commonly measured in epilepsy monitoring [33, 35] as they facilitate the detection of physiological changes associated with autonomic nervous system disturbances during seizure episodes, which include the pre-ictal phase (early symptoms and aura), the ictal phase (active period), and the post-ictal phase (recovery period). Accelerometry monitoring enables detection of patterns and changes in velocity, position, and movement through the measurement of acceleration, which is particularly relevant for motor seizure detection. Seizure occurrence also frequently induces fluctuations in body temperature, typically an increase, thus being a contributing factor to seizure detection [36].

ANS dysfunction caused by seizure occurrence impacts heart rate variability and fluctuations in the intervals between heartbeats; additionally, the excessive release of catecholamines, neurotransmitters that act as anticonvulsants, as a response to seizure occurrence affects vascular modulation, impacting the constriction and dilation of blood vessels. The application of a photoplethysmogram (PPG) optical sensor, which detects blood flow volumetric changes through the reflection of emitted light waves, reflecting the variations occurring in the cardiovascular system, facilitates the detection of consistent variation patterns in hemodynamics, with seizure detection performance comparable to ECG methods [32, 35]. However, PPG monitoring is highly sensitive to movement, which reduces the quality of a significant portion of the data; thus, it requires limited movement in the signal acquisition area as well as further data processing to remove artifacts [35]. While fingertip placement is standard for PPG signal acquisition in clinical settings, experimental studies also support the use of palmar placements, particularly the thenar eminence of the palm, as it is less susceptible to disruptions caused by hand and finger movements. Moreover, palmar placements facilitate the integration of multiple sensors in a single area, which is useful in multimodal monitoring device applications [37].

The ANS activation during epileptic seizures can also be reflected in detectable transient changes in Electrodermal Activity (EDA), the sympathetic response of eccrine sweat glands; the physiological response during seizure occurrence results in sweat gland activity changes, subsequently impacting skin conductance (galvanic skin response, GSR). Thus, EDA signal acquisition and monitoring can be instrumental in seizure detection. In clinical settings, EDA is typically monitored through the measurement of GSR, commonly through the application of two disposable Ag/AgCl gel electrodes, in placements with higher electrodermal responses, such as the face, palms, or soles. The effectiveness of this measurement varies across different types of seizures, particularly according to laterality and awareness: EDA sensors placed on one specific side may not detect lateral focus seizures on the opposite side, and a retained awareness state during seizures seemingly does not elicit a response [34]. Additionally, hand-based EDA signal acquisition also varies among the different fingers [38, 39]. Nevertheless, wrist-based acquisitions have been identified as a practical and effective placement for outpatient EDA monitoring [34]. While EDA entropy may be a promising predictive feature by potentially capturing the ANS changes occurring at the pre-ictal stage [33], the current knowledge on pre-ictal electrodermal responses remains limited and contradictory [34]. Therefore, further research into pre-ictal EDA changes and factors at play is crucial.

In the context of daily life seizure prediction, challenges include low sampling rates, sensor placement, and artifacts from poor fitting or movement [33]. However, as the overall physiological response to seizures typically follows a common pattern, understanding the evolution of these patterns and the interplay between different physiological responses could enhance the accuracy of multimodal seizure monitoring devices [34]. Moreover, while palm-based EDA acquisition offers greater signal quality, it is essential to consider the trade-offs between wrist-based acquisition quality and the advantages of continuous, daily monitoring outside the clinical setting [40].

4 Conductive Fabrics in EDA Acquisition

Due to the versatility of skin conductance as a biosignal that allows for Sympathetic Nervous System monitoring, it has integrated health monitoring as an indicator of different dimensions, such as emotional or neurological. While Ag/AgCl gel electrodes are the standard application in clinical settings, they are not appropriate for extended use due to possible skin reactions caused by the adhesive, are not a sustainable option as a single-use item [39], and their gradual dehydration decreases their effectiveness [41]. The application of dry electrodes presents a sustainable alternative as well as being unobtrusive and easily integrated into everyday items. While commercially available wearables rely predominantly on rigid EDA monitoring electrodes, these can become uncomfortable over time [39], textile-based wearables offer a flexible, user-friendly alternative for long-term monitoring with positive performance [42].

Textile electrodes may be integrated through embroidering plated yarn in specific patterns, through the application of the conductive fabric [39], through knitting and weaving, or direct application through coating methods such as plating or printing [41]. The application of different integration methods impacts the elasticity of the product; for instance, direct integration of conductive yarn can be suboptimal in terms of fabric flexibility, and weaving can create rigid sections to provide more structure to the product; conversely, application, coating, and knitting can help retain stretchiness and elasticity [43, 44]. Compared against standard Ag/AgCl gel electrodes, copper-based conductive fabric and densely embroidered silver-based conductive yarn perform best. While larger and denser contact areas can outperform standard wet electrodes due to reduced surface resistance [39], this aspect is also affected by deformations and reactions to environmental factors [43].

Ensuring direct contact between the skin and the electrode is crucial; otherwise, it results in data acquisition disruption, which is particularly challenging in dynamic contexts as movement also introduces artifacts in data collection. Loss of contact and movement may be mitigated through the application of textile electrodes on elastic substrates, relying on the provided tension to maintain signal quality [41]. Additionally, woven cotton substrates perform better than nylon or polyester substrates, possibly due to breathability and moisture absorption, resulting in improved interfacing stability [38].

Textile-based wearable solutions must take into account aspects such as breathability, weight, abrasion, resistance to abrasion, chemicals, and washing cycles, among others [42, 43]; optimizations may be performed to improve the durability of the electrodes, such as protective polymer coating of the conductive fabric, and the quality of the acquisition, such as adjusting the configuration and distance between the electrodes (Anusha et al., 2018).

5   User Experience in Wearable Monitoring Devices

The potential for mobile and wearable technologies lies in significantly enhancing the management of chronic conditions, by fostering greater physical activity and self-efficacy among patients [46]. These technologies, when designed with a user-centered approach, can provide tailored feedback and real-time monitoring, which are pivotal in motivating individuals to engage in healthier behaviors. However, the adoption and effectiveness of these tools are not without challenges. Issues such as device wearability, data accuracy, and the personalization of feedback are crucial for ensuring patient engagement and the successful integration of these technologies into daily life [47].

Moreover, the impact of wearables and mobile applications extends beyond physical health improvements, influencing psychological aspects such as patient confidence and self-management capabilities [48]. Research underscores the importance of designing these technologies to support the psychological needs of chronic disease patients, enhancing their belief in their ability to manage their conditions effectively. Nevertheless, the diversity in user experience highlights the necessity for a broad spectrum of solutions. Not all interventions require wearable devices; alternative unobtrusive sensing technologies and non-wearable solutions play a significant role in chronic disease management, offering versatility in addressing the unique needs and preferences of individuals [49]. While wearables offer promising avenues for health monitoring and management, a multifaceted approach that includes both wearable and non-wearable solutions is essential for catering to the complex and varied needs of chronic disease patients.

During the design process of medical devices and given that these artefacts are used by both patients and medical professionals, it is imperative to consider not just User Experience (UX), ergonomic principles, and usability, but also the different user groups of said medical devices (such as patients, medical professionals, and caregivers) and the context in which these will be employed. As medical devices directly impact comfort, expended effort, operational efficiency, diagnostics and treatment efficacy, and subsequent errors affecting the patients' health, the design process should ensure ease of use, safety and risk reduction, efficiency, maintenance and repair simplification, and the subsequent quality of patient care. This is facilitated through the application of quantitative and qualitative UX research methods, providing, respectively, objective conclusions of statistical nature and subjective insights into emotional dimensions; these include observations, questionnaires, interviews, and focus groups, among others [50]. The application of holistic and pragmatic approaches such as the User-Centered Design methodology allows us to ensure solutions are user-centric and engaging through iterative development that focuses on validating requirements and design choices with end-users, and engagement and usability directly impact functionality and mistake occurrence [51].

The shift towards wearable devices as they emerge in the healthcare context has facilitated collecting large amounts of continuously acquired data in the patients' everyday context and created new opportunities for applying it towards the enhancement of patient care and, particularly in epilepsy management, the improvement of patient safety and treatment decisions through continuous monitoring, detecting, reporting, and documenting seizure occurrences outside clinical contexts, considering particularly that PWE awareness and consciousness may be impaired during these incidents [52, 53]. Ensuring users' expectations and perceptions related to factors such as software, hardware, value, and design are incorporated and met in the design and development process can impact their adherence to the devices and their intention to continue using them [54]. Wearable devices with clinical and healthcare applications, particularly seizure detection, continuously monitor PPG, EDA, temperature, accelerometers, gyroscopes, and GPS, among other measurements, to enable reports and alerts to caregivers and medical professionals, facilitating timely interventions.

Despite the continuous progress and improvement of this technology, data acquisition outside the clinical setting still presents many challenges in terms of data reliability [55]. According to Brinkmann et al. [56], there are currently several form factors specifically designed for wearable devices with epilepsy monitoring and seizure detection applications. These include smartwatches, which are preferred for their comfort and ease of use; smart rings, which have limitations related to battery capacity, real-time data linkage capabilities, and compromised PPG data due to movement; arm bands, which are generally less comfortable and accepted and have data quality issues due to movement of unsecured devices; and adhesive sensor patches, which are versatile but not suitable for extended monitoring over several weeks. Wearable devices such as the Empatica E4 [57], the SPEAC system of Brain Sentinel [58], Nightwatch [59], and Epi-care [60] are examples of currently available solutions in epilepsy management and seizure detection.

Despite a general acceptance of epilepsy management wearables by PWE [53], and the improvement of these technologies, human factors are neglected during wearable development, consequently leading to short life cycles and limited user acceptance [61]. Seizure detection devices, particularly their aesthetic characteristics, strongly impact the self-image of the patient, their outlook on the condition, and their routine experiences; their visual appearance and visibility may cause the devices to become a reminder of the condition, leading to heightened feelings of being different or being observed, ultimately deterring them from adhering to the technology [7]. Thus, the long-term adherence to medical wearable devices can be enhanced through aligning its aesthetics with the experiences and preferences of epilepsy patients [56], as well as those of other user groups, such as caregivers and medical professionals [52, 53]. This required synergy between technology and human factors can be created through the incorporation of requirements of different ergonomic natures: physical, including comfort, safety, and durability; cognitive, including usability and reliability; and emotional, including engagement and aesthetics [61].

Considering the visual appearance and visibility of epilepsy management solutions, a discreet, non-stigmatizing, non-intrusive design is largely preferred, where the wearable device incorporates the daily lives of PWE [7, 52], such as by easily integrating everyday items such as smartphones, wristbands, smartwatches, jewelry, or clothing [53, 62]. The attraction of unwanted attention through heightened visibility can lead to both felt and enacted discrimination; thus, it is crucial to ensure the device is familiar-looking, can be easily hidden, is not large or bulky, and is fashionable and comfortable [52]. Concerning their weight and placement, wearable devices worn closer to the center of the body mass, such as the waist area, are generally better tolerated; conversely, users report a heightened sensitivity to discomfort on wearables worn on their extremities, being particularly sensitive to excessive weight and insecure attachments. Thus, wearable devices should be produced using flexible materials that evenly distribute pressure and weight and ensure a comfortable and secure attachment. The prevention of long-term discomfort or orthopedic issues caused by the alteration of users' posture must also be taken into account [63]. In terms of functionality, PWE report a preference for customizable alert and feedback; waterproof devices [52]; longer battery lives [53] to avoid challenges in charging opportunities and compliance, as such devices are meant to be worn continuously through day and night [56]; and real-time detection efficacy and the collection and documentation of physiological and psychological data [53].

While the design process of wearables often involves trade-offs between user expectations for aesthetics and comfort and functional priorities from a medical and technological standpoint [64], these insights highlight the importance of a user-centric approach in the design of wearable epilepsy monitoring devices in which usability, engagement, and meeting user expectations are key to enhancing the patient and user experience [50, 51, 54, 65].

6 Conclusion

In the scope of developing a textile-based solution for long-term, continuous epilepsy monitoring and seizure detection, in this article we explored four critical areas that contribute to the understanding of textile-based biosignal monitoring for epilepsy patients from a user-centric perspective.

The burden of the condition affects PWE beyond seizure occurrence, as its symptomology, comorbidities, and treatment deeply impact the QoL of patients. Accurate seizure detection and documentation greatly contribute to epilepsy management, enabled by prolonged, continuous monitoring of patients; the application of biosignal monitoring wearable devices facilitates epilepsy monitoring in their daily lives, enhancing patient care not only through the collected data but also by facilitating timely interventions and improving patient safety. Given the context of use of such devices, these solutions have a significant impact on the patient's routine, daily experiences, self-image, outlook on the condition, emphasizing the need for discreet, non-stigmatizing, comfortable devices that seamlessly integrate into the daily lives of PWE. The integration of textile-based solutions offers a sustainable and user-friendly alternative, creating new opportunities for improving the patient experience of continuous monitoring devices by promoting their integration into other daily objects and improving comfort in the context of continuous, long-term use. A focus on usability, comfort, and alignment with user expectations is crucial during the development of epilepsy monitoring technologies, as neglecting the experience of PWE directly impacts their adherence to the technology and willingness to continuously use the medical device.

Moving forward, there is a clear need for aligning technology with human factors in the development of wearable epilepsy monitoring devices. This can be done through a holistic, iterative, user-centric approach that prioritizes the preferences, needs, requirements, and monitoring experience of PWE, as well as those of their caregivers and medical professionals, without neglecting the functional performance requirements to ensure the efficacy and quality of data acquisition.

Acknowledgments. The study was supported by UNIDCOM under a grant from the Fundação para a Ciência e Tecnologia (FCT) No. UIDB/00711/2020 attributed to UNIDCOM – Unidade de Investigação em Design e Comunicação, Lisbon, Portugal.

Disclosure of Interests. The authors have no competing interests to declare that are relevant to the content of this article.

References

1. Lu, L., et al.: Wearable health devices in health care: narrative systematic review. JMIR Mhealth Uhealth **8**, e18907 (2020). https://doi.org/10.2196/18907
2. Motti, V.G.: Wearable Health. Opportunities and Challenges. In: PervasiveHealth 2019: Proceedings of the 13th EAI International Conference on Pervasive Computing Technologies for Healthcare, pp. 356–359 (2019). https://doi.org/10.1145/3329189.3329226
3. Kim, J., Campbell, A.S., De Ávila, B.E., Wang, J.: Wearable biosensors for healthcare monitoring. Nat. Biotechnol. **37**, 389–406 (2019). https://doi.org/10.1038/s41587-019-0045-y
4. Rodgers, M.M., Pai, V., Conroy, R.: Recent advances in wearable sensors for health monitoring. IEEE Sens. J. **15**, 3119–3126 (2015). https://doi.org/10.1109/jsen.2014.2357257
5. Simblett, S., et al.: Patient perspectives on the acceptability of mHealth technology for remote measurement and management of epilepsy: a qualitative analysis. Epilepsy Behav. **97**, 123–129 (2019). https://doi.org/10.1016/j.yebeh.2019.05.035
6. Beck, M., Simonÿ, C., Zibrandtsen, I.C., Kjær, T.W.: Readiness among people with epilepsy to carry body-worn monitor devices in everyday life: a qualitative study. Epilepsy Behav. **112**, 107390 (2020). https://doi.org/10.1016/j.yebeh.2020.107390
7. Olsen, L.S., Nielsen, J., Simonÿ, C., Kjær, T.W., Beck, M.: Wearables in real life: A qualitative study of experiences of people with epilepsy who use home seizure monitoring devices. Epilepsy Behav. **125**, 108398 (2021). https://doi.org/10.1016/j.yebeh.2021.108398
8. Simblett, S., et al.: Patients' experience of wearing multimodal sensor devices intended to detect epileptic seizures: a qualitative analysis. Epilepsy Behav. **102**, 106717 (2020). https://doi.org/10.1016/j.yebeh.2019.106717
9. Choudhry, N.A., Arnold, L., Rasheed, A., Khan, I.A., Wang, L.: Textronics—a review of textile-based wearable electronics. Adv. Eng. Mater. **23**(12), 21200469 (2021). https://doi.org/10.1002/adem.202100469
10. Coccia, A., et al.: Design and validation of an e-textile-based wearable system for remote health monitoring. ACTA IMEKO **10**(2), 220 (2021). https://doi.org/10.21014/acta_imeko.v10i2.912
11. Baskan, A.D., Göncü-Berk, G.: User experience of wearable technologies: a comparative analysis of textile-based and accessory-based wearable products. Appl. Sci. **12**, 11154 (2022). https://doi.org/10.3390/app122111154
12. Beghi, E.: The epidemiology of epilepsy. Neuroepidemiology **54**, 185–191 (2019). https://doi.org/10.1159/000503831
13. Fiest, K.M., et al.: Prevalence and incidence of epilepsy. Neurology **88**, 296–303 (2017). https://doi.org/10.1212/wnl.0000000000003509
14. Löscher, W., Potschka, H., Sisodiya, S.M., Vezzani, A.: Drug resistance in epilepsy: clinical impact, potential mechanisms, and new innovative treatment options. Pharmacol. Rev. **72**, 606–638 (2020). https://doi.org/10.1124/pr.120.019539
15. Thijs, R.D., Surges, R., O'Brien, T.J., Sander, J.W.: Epilepsy in adults. The Lancet. **393**, 689–701 (2019). https://doi.org/10.1016/s0140-6736(18)32596-0

16. Banerjee, P.N., Filippi, D., Hauser, W.A.: The descriptive epidemiology of epilepsy—a review. Epilepsy Res. **85**, 31–45 (2009). https://doi.org/10.1016/j.eplepsyres.2009.03.003

17. Moshé, S.L., Perucca, E., Ryvlin, P., Tomson, T.: Epilepsy: new advances. The Lancet. **385**, 884–898 (2015). https://doi.org/10.1016/s0140-6736(14)60456-6

18. Fisher, R.S., et al.: Operational classification of seizure types by the international league against epilepsy: position paper of the ILAE commission for classification and terminology. Epilepsia **58**, 522–530 (2017). https://doi.org/10.1111/epi.13670

19. Blumenfeld, H.: Consciousness and epilepsy: why are patients with absence seizures absent? In: Progress in Brain Research, pp. 271–603 (2005)

20. Kerr, M.P.: The impact of epilepsy on patients' lives. Acta Neurol. Scand. **126**, 1–9 (2012). https://doi.org/10.1111/ane.12014

21. Shlobin, N.A., Sander, J.W.: Learning from the comorbidities of epilepsy. Curr. Opin. Neurol. **35**, 175–180 (2021). https://doi.org/10.1097/wco.0000000000001010

22. Tombini, M., et al.: Depressive symptoms and difficulties in emotion regulation in adult patients with epilepsy: association with quality of life and stigma. Epilepsy Behav. **107**, 107073 (2020). https://doi.org/10.1016/j.yebeh.2020.107073

23. Löscher, W., Stafstrom, C.E.: Epilepsy and its neurobehavioral comorbidities: insights gained from animal models. Epilepsia **64**, 54–91 (2022). https://doi.org/10.1111/epi.17433

24. Sajobi, T.T., et al.: Quality of Life in Epilepsy: same questions, but different meaning to different people. Epilepsia **62**, 2094–2102 (2021). https://doi.org/10.1111/epi.17012

25. Yogarajah, M., Mula, M.: Social cognition, psychiatric comorbidities, and quality of life in adults with epilepsy. Epilepsy Behav. **100**, 106321 (2019). https://doi.org/10.1016/j.yebeh.2019.05.017

26. Szemere, E., Jokeit, H.: Quality of life is social – towards an improvement of social abilities in patients with epilepsy. Seizure. **26**, 12–21 (2015). https://doi.org/10.1016/j.seizure.2014.12.008

27. Ridsdale, L., et al.: Characteristics associated with quality of life among people with drug-resistant epilepsy. J. Neurol. **264**(6), 1174–1184 (2017). https://doi.org/10.1007/s00415-017-8512-1

28. Henning, O., Landmark, C.J., Henning, D., Nakken, K.O., Lossius, M.I.: Challenges in epilepsy—The perspective of Norwegian epilepsy patients. Acta Neurol. Scand. **140**, 40–47 (2019). https://doi.org/10.1111/ane.13098

29. Jacoby, A.: Stigma, epilepsy, and quality of life. Epilepsy Behav. **3**, 10–20 (2002). https://doi.org/10.1016/s1525-5050(02)00545-0

30. Asadi-Pooya, A.A., Homayoun, M., Keshavarz, S.: Education, marriage, and employment in people with epilepsy: the barriers that patients perceive. Int. J. Epilepsy **6**, 50–53 (2020). https://doi.org/10.1055/s-0040-1715767

31. Cianchetti, C., et al.: The perceived burden of epilepsy: Impact on the quality of life of children and adolescents and their families. Seizure. **24**, 93–101 (2015). https://doi.org/10.1016/j.seizure.2014.09.003

32. Safavi, S.M., et al.: Analysis of cardiovascular changes caused by epileptic seizures in human photoplethysmogram signal. arXiv (Cornell University). (2019) https://doi.org/10.48550/arXiv.1912.05083

33. Vieluf, S., et al.: Autonomic nervous system changes detected with peripheral sensors in the setting of epileptic seizures. Sci. Rep. **10**(1), 11560 (2020). https://doi.org/10.1038/s41598-020-68434-z

34. Ortega, M.C., Bruno, E., Richardson, M.P.: Electrodermal activity response during seizures: a systematic review and meta-analysis. Epilepsy Behav. **134**, 108864 (2022). https://doi.org/10.1016/j.yebeh.2022.108864

35. Atrache, R.E., et al.: Photoplethysmography: a measure for the function of the autonomic nervous system in focal impaired awareness seizures. Epilepsia **61**, 1617–1626 (2020). https://doi.org/10.1111/epi.16621

36. Sohn, H.S., Kim, S.K., Lee, S.-Y.: Inflammatory markers associated with seizures. Epileptic Disord. **18**, 51–57 (2016). https://doi.org/10.1684/epd.2016.0794

37. Silva, H., Sousa, J., Gambôa, H.: Study and evaluation of palmar blood volume pulse for heart rate monitoring in a multimodal framework. (2012). https://doi.org/10.5220/0003884900350040

38. Haddad, P.A., Servati, A., Soltanian, S., Ko, F., Servati, P.: Breathable dry Silver/Silver chloride electronic textile electrodes for electrodermal activity monitoring. Biosensors **8**, 79 (2018). https://doi.org/10.3390/bios8030079

39. Janka, M., Kujala, J., Helminen, T.M., Kylliäinen, A., Virkki, J.: Development, fabrication and evaluation of textile electrodes for EDA measurements. (2022). https://doi.org/10.1109/segah54908.2022.9978571

40. Van Der Mee, D.J., Gevonden, M., Westerink, J.H.D.M., De Geus, E.J.C.: Validity of electrodermal activity-based measures of sympathetic nervous system activity from a wrist-worn device. Int. J. Psychophysiol. **168**, 52–64 (2021). https://doi.org/10.1016/j.ijpsycho.2021.08.003

41. Nigusse, A.B.B., Malengier, B., Mengistie, D.A., Tseghai, G.B., Van Langenhove, L.: Development of washable silver printed textile electrodes for Long-Term ECG monitoring. Sensors. **20**, 6233 (2020). https://doi.org/10.3390/s20216233

42. Das, P.S., Kim, J.W., Park, J.Y.: Fashionable wrist band using highly conductive fabric for electrocardiogram signal monitoring. J. Ind. Text. **49**, 243–261 (2018). https://doi.org/10.1177/1528083718779427

43. Tseghai, G.B., Malengier, B., Fante, K.A., Nigusse, A.B.B., Van Langenhove, L.: Integration of conductive materials with textile structures, an overview. Sensors. **20**, 6910 (2020). https://doi.org/10.3390/s20236910

44. Ismar, E., Bahadir, S.K., Kalaoglu, F., Koncar, V.: Futuristic clothes: electronic textiles and wearable technologies. Global Challenges **4**(7), 1900092 (2020). https://doi.org/10.1002/gch2.201900092

45. Anusha, A.S., Preejith, S.P., Akl, T.J., Joseph, J., Sivaprakasam, M.: Dry electrode optimization for wrist-based electrodermal activity monitoring. In: IEEE International Symposium on Medical Measurements and Applications (MeMeA) (2018).https://doi.org/10.1109/memea.2018.8438595

46. Mattison, G., et al.: The influence of wearables on health care outcomes in chronic disease: systematic review. J. Med. Internet Res. **24**, e36690 (2022). https://doi.org/10.2196/36690

47. Hadady, L., Klivényi, P., Fabó, D., Beniczky, S.: Real-world user experience with seizure detection wearable devices in the home environment. Epilepsia. 64, (2022). https://doi.org/10.1111/epi.17189

48. Wulfovich, S., Fiordelli, M., Rivas, H., Concepcion, W., Wac, K.: "I must try harder": design implications for mobile apps and wearables contributing to self-efficacy of patients with chronic conditions. Front. Psychol. **10**, 478889 (2019). https://doi.org/10.3389/fpsyg.2019.02388

49. Guo, Y., et al.: A review of wearable and unobtrusive sensing technologies for chronic disease management. Comput. Biol. Med. **129**, 104163 (2021). https://doi.org/10.1016/j.compbiomed.2020.104163

50. Vl, O., Bitkina, H.K., Kim, J.P.: Usability and user experience of medical devices: an overview of the current state, analysis methodologies, and future challenges. Int. J. Indus. Ergon. **76**, 102932 (2020). https://doi.org/10.1016/j.ergon.2020.102932

51. Mival, O., Benyon, D.: User experience (UX) design for medical personnel and patients. In: Fricker, S.A., Thümmler, C., Gavras, A. (eds.) Requirements Engineering for Digital Health, pp. 117–131. Springer, Cham (2015). https://doi.org/10.1007/978-3-319-09798-5_6

52. Bruno, E., Viana, P.F., Sperling, M.R., Richardson, M.P.: Seizure detection at home: do devices on the market match the needs of people living with epilepsy and their caregivers? Epilepsia 61(S1), 16521 (2020). https://doi.org/10.1111/epi.16521

53. Sivathamboo, S., et al.: Preferences and user experiences of wearable devices in epilepsy. Neurology. 99, e1380–e1392 (2022). https://doi.org/10.1212/wnl.0000000000200794

54. Park, E.: User acceptance of smart wearable devices: an expectation-confirmation model approach. Telematics Inform. 47, 101318 (2020). https://doi.org/10.1016/j.tele.2019.101318

55. Rukasha, T., Woolley, S., Kyriacou, T., Collins, T.: Evaluation of wearable electronics for epilepsy: a systematic review. Electronics 9, 968 (2020). https://doi.org/10.3390/electronics9060968

56. Brinkmann, B.H., et al.: Seizure diaries and forecasting with wearables: epilepsy monitoring outside the clinic. Front. Neurol. 12, 690404 (2021). https://doi.org/10.3389/fneur.2021.690404

57. Empatica: E4 wristband | Real-time physiological signals | Wearable PPG, EDA, Temperature, Motion sensors. https://www.empatica.com/en-gb/research/e4/. Accessed 16 Feb 2024

58. Szabó, C.Á., et al.: Electromyography-based seizure detector: preliminary results comparing a generalized tonic–clonic seizure detection algorithm to video-EEG recordings. Epilepsia 56(9), 1432–1437 (2015). https://doi.org/10.1111/epi.13083

59. NightWatch Epilepsy Seizure Detection: NightWatch|Epilepsy seizure detection during sleep. https://nightwatchepilepsy.com/. Accessed 16 Feb 2024

60. Epi-Care mobile — Epilepsy alarms for children and adults with seizures. https://danishcare.co.uk/epicare-mobile. Accessed 16 Feb 2024

61. Francés-Morcillo, L., Morer-Camo, P., Rodríguez-Ferradas, M.I., Cazón, A.: Wearable design requirements identification and evaluation. Sensors. 20, 2599 (2020). https://doi.org/10.3390/s20092599

62. Bruno, E., et al.: Wearable technology in epilepsy: the views of patients, caregivers, and healthcare professionals. Epilepsy Behav. 85, 141–149 (2018). https://doi.org/10.1016/j.yebeh.2018.05.044

63. Park, H., Pei, J., Shi, M., Xu, Q., Fan, J.: Designing wearable computing devices for improved comfort and user acceptance. Ergonomics 62, 1474–1484 (2019). https://doi.org/10.1080/00140139.2019.1657184

64. Motti, V.G., Caine, K.: Human factors considerations in the design of wearable devices. Proc. Human Factors Ergon. Soc. Ann. Meet. 58, 1820–1824 (2014). https://doi.org/10.1177/1541931214581381

65. Wolf, J.A., Niederhauser, V., Marshburn, D., LaVela, S.L.: Defining patient experience. Patient Exp. J. 1(1), 7–19 (2014). https://doi.org/10.35680/2372-0247.1004

Exploring the Mediating Role of Smartphones Between Meaning in Life and Well-Being

Rageshwari Munderia[1]($\boxtimes$) and Rajbala Singh[2]

[1] Department of Psychology, Sunandan Divatia School of Sciences NMIMS, Mumbai, India
rageshwari.munderia@nmims.edu
[2] Department of Humanities and Social Sciences, The LNM Institute of Information Technology, Jaipur, India
rajbala@lnmiit.ac.in

Abstract. Meaning in life (MIL) is a deeply ingrained and enduring part of human existence that extends well beyond happiness or success and encompasses the desire for fulfillment and contentment. MIL can stem from many sources, from social connections to pursuing passions and contributions to society. In the modern age of technology, smartphones provide instant access to various opportunities such as communication, search for knowledge, entertainment, security, etc. Individuals may find themselves adrift in search of meaning in life and the sphere of digital life, which may impact their well-being (WB). Thus, in this context, this study examines the mediating effect of perceived positive smartphone usage (PPSU) on the relationship between MIL and WB. The present study comprised 509 adults ranged from 19 to 40 years from India's capital and national capital region. All participants were requested to complete the assessments on meaning in life, positive smartphone usage, and well-being. The study's data was analyzed using Haye's PROCESS macro model, which indicated that PPSU significantly mediated the relationship between MIL and WB. The findings underscore the importance of promoting positive smartphone usage to improve well-being, especially among individuals on a quest for meaning in their lives. Future research may investigate intervention strategies to promote the positive usage of smartphones for a greater perception of MIL and well-being in different populations and contexts.

Keywords: Smartphone Usage · Meaning in Life · Subjective Well-Being · Purpose · Search for Meaning

1 Introduction

1.1 Perceived Positive Smartphone Usage (PPSU)

The interaction between humans and information and communication technology (ICT) has become increasingly intimate over the years. According to the

M. Kurosu and A. Hashizume (Eds.): HCII 2024, LNCS 14686, pp. 78–86, 2024.
https://doi.org/10.1007/978-3-031-60428-7_6

Statista report (2023), worldwide smartphone mobile network subscriptions have reached almost 6.4 billion in 2022 and are forecast to exceed 7.7 billion by 2028. ICT is an umbrella term encompassing various technological devices such as mobile phones, radios, televisions, smartphones, laptops, etc. According to [34], in addition to making phone calls, individuals also use smartphones for other purposes, such as appointment calendars, calculators, maps, and gaming devices, among other things. The advancement of this portable technology has wholly transformed almost every traditional activity performed on a typical desktop or laptop, thereby diluting the temporal and locative constraints [20].

According to [14], smartphones are 'cognitive attractors' since they offer short-moment satisfaction at a low cost and with high stimulus salience. Smartphone technology enables the acquisition of information from various sources and assists in storing and managing information, similar to human memory. Smartphones can be viewed as an 'instantiation of the extended mind', representing a form of cognitive efficiency [3, p.13].

According to [25], the mobile phone "has become such an important aspect of a user's daily life that it has moved from being a mere 'technological object' to a key' social object' (p.111)". The virtual environment facilitated by smartphones has become a 'default habitat' of individuals across all age groups [13]. Unlike mobile phones, smartphones are more than interpersonal connectivity devices because they serve various functions ranging from simple connectivity to entertainment and the portrayal of self on social media or similar platforms without locative and temporal constraints [23]. They have enabled individuals to access the internet and other applications from anywhere and anytime for diverse purposes, which was possible via desktop or laptop only at a specific location and at a specified time.

According to [5], smartphone use motives can be classified into two types: communicative and non-communicative. Communicative usage broadly includes interacting with people through voice calls and messages. In contrast, non-communicative usage refers to seeking knowledge for careers, jobs, leisure, and information. According to [19], digitally mediated communications via smartphones have reshaped society in the form of a 'little box.' A few decades back, communities were closely connected more locally (door-to-door). In contrast, in the present time, it is moving towards 'networked individualism,' where individuals are connected virtually. Therefore, smartphones offer an environment for fulfilling hierarchical needs that span from basic to more advanced cognitive needs without locative and temporal constraints.

Different theoretical perspectives of ICT usage provide a broader lens to understand the different motivations behind ICT usage. These theoretical perspectives have been studied mainly in the area of internet and social media usage. However, there needs to be more studies investigating the implications of these studies in the area of smartphone usage. According to the uses and gratification theory of media effect research [21], media usage caters to a range of individual needs, including entertainment, socialization, and relaxation. According to [26], internet usage is associated with three gratification motives:

1. Content gratification: It involves information and entertainment
2. Process gratification: It encompasses the overall experience derived from media usage, including the internet and smartphones
3. Social gratification: The satisfaction derived from virtual interaction and engagement with social networking sites.

Smartphones also contribute significantly to gratifying content, process, and social needs, in accordance with the uses and gratification theory.

1.2   Meaning in Life (MIL)

According to Frankl [11], meaning in life (MIL) is the primary motivation of humans. MIL is a "process of discovery within the world that is intrinsically meaningful" [7, p.4]. Steger [27] defined MIL as a network of connections, comprehension and analysis of these connections that help them plan and achieve their goals. He identified two components of MIL: cognitive component and motivational component. The cognitive component helps individuals understand and consolidate their daily life experiences, and the motivational component enables them to define the goals of their lives. Thus, MIL cultivates a deeper understanding of oneself by utilizing one's daily life experiences to help cultivate an in-depth understanding of oneself. Numerous studies have explored the connection between meaning in life and well-being. Doğan et al. [9] found that the presence and the search for meaning in life significantly predicted subjective well-being. Santos et al. [22] also reported similar findings. Suar et al. [30] discovered that satisfaction with personal relationships and emotional stability significantly predicted subjective well-being among Indians. Steger [27] emphasized the importance of meaning in life, noting its positive correlation with happiness, life satisfaction, autonomy, positive relationships, competence, and conscientiousness. While recent studies have explored the link between smartphone addiction and meaning in life [10,18,24,35], only a handful of studies have investigated the positive aspects of smartphone use about meaning in life. For instance, Singh and Munderia [24] reported that individuals seeking meaning in life use smartphones to establish social capital by providing mental reassurance, easy access to information, emotional expression, and an enhanced social image.

1.3   Well-Being (WB)

According to [15], well-being is an umbrella term that includes psychological and physical health. Subjective well-being encompasses an individual's cognitive and emotional life assessments [8, p.63]. These assessments involve emotional reactions to events and cognitive judgments regarding satisfaction and fulfillment. Integrating smartphones into individuals' daily lives has acquired a significant role, and thus, it has also impacted their well-being. Past research conducted in the area of technology use and well-being has reported mixed findings. [6] examined how smartphone use influences subjective well-being and social capital. Chan found that voice and online communication through mobile phones were linked with positive affect, an indicator of subjective well-being. However, the non-communicative features of mobile phones, such as information search, adversely impacted feelings of positive affect. Moreover, leisure activities on smartphones were positively associated with adverse effects. [2], in a longitudinal study, found that using smartphones to communicate was positively related to subjective well-being.

1.4 Present Study

Finding MIL is the constant and fundamental drive that embarks to satisfy psychological and emotional needs [11]. MIL refers to "the sense made of, and significance felt regarding, the nature of one's being and existence" [28, p.81]. MIL is instrumental for optimal human development and well-being [29]. Social relationships play a crucial role in finding MIL. The social surroundings are not merely an overt feature of an individual's world. They also have a salient impact on an individual's covert behavior. Being part of a meaningful social group makes an individual feel unique, distinctive, efficient, and successful. It helps individuals find purpose in life, alleviates their efficacy, and provides a platform to evaluate their values system and self-worth. These effects buffer during adversities and when one's well-being is in danger [12]. In the contemporary context, smartphones provide a unified platform to fulfill a spectrum of needs, ranging from social to cognitive. Smartphones serve as a platform for social engagement and self-presentation in the virtual world that helps people weave their social relationships and tinker with their identities on various social media platforms. Existing literature has shown a positive association between smartphone addiction and MIL [10,24,35]. We must recognize that the non-negligible aspect of smartphones is their positive usage. The relationship between MIL, positive smartphone usage, and well-being, however, is understudied. In this context, this study explores the mediating role of perceived positive smartphone usage between MIL and psychological well-being. Thus, the present study investigates the mediating role of perceived positive smartphones between MIL and well-being.

2 Method

2.1 Participants

The study employs a convenience sampling technique, and the present study's sample was collected from the capital and national capital region of India. The inclusion criteria for the sample selection were primarily based on smartphone usage, accessibility, readiness to participate, and parsimoniousness. The sample consisted of 509 adults ($n = 313$) who were male and ($n = 196$) female participants. The ages of the participants ranged from 19 years to 40 years, with a mean age of 23.9 years (SD = 6.30). Most participants ($n = 300$) were pursuing their graduation, while ($n = 209$) were working professionals.

2.2 Measures

Meaning in Life. The Meaning in Life Questionnaire (MLQ), designed by Stegar et al. [28], was utilized to assess Meaning in Life (MIL). This scale includes ten items, rated on a seven-point Likert scale. Within the MLQ, nine items are phrased positively, while one item is framed negatively and scored in reverse. The scale gauges two dimensions: the presence of meaning and the pursuit of meaning. The reliability of the presence of meaning dimension is indicated by Cronbach's α of 0.80, and for the search for meaning dimension, it is Cronbach's α of 0.90. The factor's overall reliability, with a Cronbach's α of 0.76, was determined to be satisfactory.

Positive Smartphone Usage. The authors devised a scale for gauging perceived positive smartphone usage, undertaking a literature review and formal interviews with 15 participants (average age: 23 years) to delineate the comprehensive dimensions of positive smartphone usage. Six dimensions surfaced from this exploration: connectivity, security, utility, expression of emotions, entertainment, and knowledge. Initially, 33 items were crafted to represent these dimensions. Additionally, six items were borrowed from [20] media and technology usage and attitude scale, substituting 'technology' with 'smartphone'. All items underwent critical evaluation with the input of two other department professors. A preliminary administration of the scale, utilizing a seven-point Likert scale with 15 participants (average age $= 25$), aimed to assess item comprehension and clarity.

Feedback from this phase guided the authors in refining the scale by eliminating or merging conceptually similar items to enhance precision and meaningfulness. Ultimately, 19 items were chosen to measure perceived smartphone usage. An exploratory factor analysis was carried out, revealing five dimensions: emotional expression via smartphone (Cronbach's $\alpha = .79$), hedonistic motivation (Cronbach's $\alpha = 0.59$), security (Cronbach's $\alpha = 0.65$), utility (Cronbach's $\alpha = 0.76$), image enhancer, and knowledge (Cronbach's $\alpha = 0.70$). The overall reliability, with Cronbach's $\alpha = .744$, was deemed satisfactory for further study.

Wellbeing. Diener et al.'s [8] satisfaction with life scale was utilized to measure subjective well being. This scale consists of five items gauging overall cognitive evaluations of life satisfaction. All items were phrased positively, offering seven-point Likert scale options from strongly disagree to strongly agree. This scale holds significance across diverse psychosocial domains, including personality, cognition, cross-cultural investigations, temperament, life satisfaction, and self-esteem, as highlighted by [31]. The reliability of the scale, with a Cronbach's α of 0.79, was determined to be satisfactory (Fig. 1).

3 Results

The data is analyzed using Haye's PROCESS macro model in Statistical Package for Social Sciences (SPSS, version 21.0). The results revealed a significant

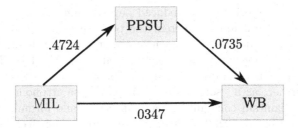

Fig. 1. Mediation model of indirect relationship between meaning in life (MIL) and well-being (WB) through perceived positive smartphone usage (PPSU).

positive relationship between positive smartphone usage and meaning in life, as indicated by a coefficient of .4724($p = .00$). Additionally, the impact of positive smartphone usage on wellbeing was investigated, yielding a coefficient of .0735($p = .00$). Furthermore, the direct effect of positive smartphone usage on wellbeing was $b = -.1601, p < 0.001$). The study also examined the indirect effects, revealing an indirect effect of .0347 (BootSE = .0135, BootLLCI = .0111, BootULCI = .0640) of positive smartphone usage on meaning in life. Further, the results suggest that (i) MIL and PPSU significantly predicted WB, and (ii) PPSU significantly mediated the relationship between MIL and WB.

4   Discussion

The mediation analysis results demonstrated that perceived positive smartphone usage mediates the relationship between meaning in life and subjective well-being. The study utilizes Stafford et al.'s [26] uses and gratification theory of media effect to explain the results. Like media usage, the three most critical gratifying factors associated with smartphone usage are content, process, and social gratification. Smartphones tend to gratify both social and cognitive needs. Individuals seeking meaning in their lives perceive smartphones as a valuable tool for exploring and retrieving information through various applications that give them a sense of security, help them enhance their knowledge, and maintain contact with significant others. As a result, they may develop a positive outlook on the world and people, gain control over daily life situations, and plan and develop effective life strategies, leading to a better perception of subjective well-being. Since smartphones facilitate access to information, individuals can enrich their knowledge through them. It leads to the holistic development of human potential, encouraging freedom from biases, compulsions, hostility, self-doubt, and lack of understanding [36]. Together, these factors may contribute to a higher level of life satisfaction.

According to [14], smartphones are like "cognitive attractors" as they provide instant access to information, making it easier to achieve momentary satisfaction and heightened stimulus salience in the short term. Consequently, these aspects may contribute to individuals experiencing increased life satisfaction, enhanced positive emotions, and reduced negative emotions. Abbasi et al. [1] illustrated a structural model wherein the positive impact of children's emotional engagement, enjoyment, and sensory interactions with smartphones was evident in their relationship with subjective well-being. Similarly, Nie et al. [17] revealed a positive association between smartphone usage, life satisfaction, and happiness. Further, as a "social tool" [25, p.111], smartphones have enabled individuals to maintain constant social connections and formulate and consolidate social relationships that, in turn, have helped them feel secure. Similar results were also reported by [6]. He investigated the relationship among smartphone users (voice, email, SMS, Facebook, and WhatsApp), perceived relationship quality, and subjective well-being. Results of the study demonstrated that mobile voice communication was positively related to friendship satisfaction and social support.

According to Walther's 'hyper-personal communication theory' [33], computer-mediated communication (CMC) is primarily characterized by diminished visual, auditory, and contextual cues. Moreover, CMC interactants are less troubled about how others would view them, and as a result, their communication becomes hyper-personal, i.e., more intimate in nature. Similarly, according to [32] self-disclosure hypothesis, the internet provides a landscape to individuals for sharing one's thoughts and feelings with their friends, which has a positive association with well-being. Brunell [4] also reported that self-disclosure is one of the critical aspects of initiating and maintaining social relationships and is defined as the process of revealing one's personal and intimate information to others. According to [16], mobile phone social networking sites (MSNPs) enable individuals to engage and maintain a constant exchange of social information and self-presentation and call this process "technology-based social comparison" (TSC).

The results confirm that MIL significantly influences PPSU and WB. Individuals with MIL use smartphones to build social networks. It also helps them perceive more significant well-being levels in their lives. The study yielded important findings with certain limitations. The sample for this study was primarily selected from urban and suburban areas of India, potentially limiting the generalizability of the results. Future research could consider broader geographical sampling to enhance the external validity of the findings. Additionally, incorporating longitudinal data would be beneficial in validating the enduring significance of the current study's results.

The research findings have important implications. Positive utilization of smartphones is associated with a heightened perception of overall well-being in their lives. The study pinpointed noteworthy sources of content and social gratification that could contribute to meaning in life and greater well-being. A comprehensive awareness program can be designed to educate children, adolescents, young adults, parents, and educators about these gratifying factors and their potential implications. These findings highlight the potential of designing specialized visual and interactive human interfaces that facilitate goal achievement, promote positive content consumption, and promote journaling.

Developing awareness of smartphones' positive aspects and tailoring interfaces to meet these aims can help users achieve elevated levels of MIL and well-being.

References

1. Abbasi, A.Z., Shamim, A., Ting, D.H., Hlavacs, H., Rehman, U.: Playful-consumption experiences and subjective well-being: children's smartphone usage. Entertain. Comput. **36**, 100390 (2021)
2. Bae, S.M.: The relationship between smartphone use for communication, social capital, and subjective well-being in Korean adolescents: Verification using multiple latent growth modeling. Child Youth Serv. Rev. **96**, 93–99 (2019)
3. Barr, N., Pennycook, G., Stolz, J.A., Fugelsang, J.A.: The brain in your pocket: evidence that smartphones are used to supplant thinking. Comput. Hum. Behav. **48**, 473–480 (2015)
4. Brunell, A.B.: Self-disclosure. Encyclopedia of Social Psychology, pp. 811–812 (2007)
5. Chan, M.: Social identity gratifications of social network sites and their impact on collective action participation. Asian J. Soc. Psychol. **17**(3), 229–235 (2014)
6. Chan, M.: Mobile-mediated multimodal communications, relationship quality and subjective well-being: an analysis of smartphone use from a life course perspective. Comput. Hum. Behav. **87**, 254–262 (2018)
7. Debats, D.L.H.M.: Meaning in Life: Psychometric, Clinical And Phenomenological Aspects. Groningen, s.n. (1996)
8. Diener, E., Lucas, R.E., Oishi, S., Suh, E.M.: Looking up and down: weighting good and bad information in life satisfaction judgments. Pers. Soc. Psychol. Bull. **28**(4), 437–445 (2002)
9. Doğan, T., Sapmaz, F., Tel, F.D., Sapmaz, S., Temizel, S.: Meaning in life and subjective well-being among Turkish university students. Procedia. Soc. Behav. Sci. **55**(5), 612–617 (2012)
10. Dursun, P., Bedir, S.A.L.A., Ahmet, Ü.Z.E.R.: The internet and smartphone addictions in a sample of university students: the role of search for meaning in life. Anatolian Clinic J. Med. Sci. **26**(3), 249–258 (2021)
11. Frankl, V.E.: Man's Search for Meaning: An Introduction to Logotherapy. Beacon Press, Massachusetts (1992)
12. Haslam, S.A., Jetten, J., Postmes, T., Haslam, C.: Social identity, health and well-being: an emerging agenda for applied psychology. Appl. Psychol.: An Int. Rev. **58**(1), 1–23 (2009)
13. Hernández-Ramírez, R.: Technologies of the self: How are digital tools affecting human ontologies? In: Fifth Conference on Computation, Communication, Aesthetics and X (xCoAx). Lisbon, Portugal (2017)
14. Lahlou, S.: Human activity modeling for systems design: a trans-disciplinary and empirical approach. In: Harris, D. (ed.) Engineering Psychology and Cognitive Ergonomics, pp. 512–521. Springer, Berlin Heidelberg, Berlin, Heidelberg (2007)
15. Nair, A.R., Ravindranath, S., Thomas, J.: Can social skills predict wellbeing?: an exploration. Eur. Acad. Res. **1**(5), 712–720 (2013)
16. Nesi, J., Prinstein, M.J.: Using social media for social comparison and feedback-seeking: gender and popularity moderate associations with depressive symptoms. J. Abnorm. Child Psychol. **43**(8), 1427–1438 (2015)

17. Nie, P., Ma, W., Sousa-Poza, A.: The relationship between smartphone use and subjective well-being in rural China. Electron. Commer. Res. **21**, 983–1009 (2021)
18. Qiu, C., Liu, Q., Yu, C., Li, Z., Nie, Y.: The influence of meaning in life on children and adolescents' problematic smartphone use: a three-wave multiple mediation model. Addict. Behav. **126**, 107199 (2022)
19. Rainie, L., Wellman, B.: Networked: The New Social Operating System. The MIT Press (Apr 2012)
20. Rosen, L., Whaling, K., Carrier, L., Cheever, N., Rokkum, J.: The media and technology usage and attitudes scale: an empirical investigation. Comput. Hum. Behav. **29**(6), 2501–2511 (2013)
21. Ruggiero, T.: Uses and gratification theory in the 21st century. Mass Commun. Society **3**(1), 3–37 (2000)
22. Santos, M.C.J., Magramo, C., Jr., Oguan, F., Jr., Paat, J.J., Barnachea, E.A.: Meaning in life and subjective well-being: is a satisfying life meaningful? Res. World **3**(4), 32–40 (2012)
23. Schrock, A.R.: The emergence of mobile social network platforms on the mobile internet. In: Rosen, L.D., Cheever, N.A., Carrier, L.M. (eds.) The Wiley Handbook of Psychology, Technology, and Society, pp. 321–338. Wiley, 1 edn. (Apr 2015)
24. Singh, R., Munderia, R.: Relationship between four needs of meaning and smartphone usage. In: Meaning in Life International Conference 2022-Cultivating, Promoting, and Enhancing Meaning in Life Across Cultures and Life Span (MIL 2022), pp. 112–125. Atlantis Press (December 2022)
25. Srivastava, L.: Mobile phones and the evolution of social behaviour. Behav. Inform. Technol. **24**(2), 111–129 (2005)
26. Stafford, T.F., Stafford, M.R., Schkade, L.L.: Determining uses and gratifications for the Internet. Decis. Sci. **35**(2), 259–288 (2004)
27. Steger, M.F.: Meaning and well-being. In: Diener, E., Oishi, S., Tay, L., Zhu, Z. (eds.) Handbook of Well-Being. DEF Publishers, Salt Lake City, UT (2018)
28. Steger, M.F., Frazier, P., Oishi, S., Kaler, M.: The meaning in life questionnaire: Assessing the presence of and search for meaning in life. J. Couns. Psychol. **53**, 80–93 (2006)
29. Steger, M.F., Kashdan, T.B., Oishi, S.: Being good by doing good: Daily eudaimonic activity and well-being. J. Res. Pers. **42**(1), 22–42 (2008)
30. Suar, D., Jha, A.K., Das, S.S., Alat, P.: The structure and predictors of subjective well-being among millennials in India. Cogent Psychol. **6**(1), 1584083 (2019)
31. Suh, E.M., Oishi, S.: Culture and subjective well-being: Introduction to the special issue. J. Happiness Stud. **5**(3), 219–222 (2004)
32. Valkenburg, P.M., Peter, J.: Social consequences of the Internet for adolescents: a decade of research. Curr. Dir. Psychol. Sci. **18**(1), 1–5 (2009)
33. Walther, J.B.: Computer-mediated communication: Impersonal, interpersonal, and hyperpersonal interaction. Commun. Res. **23**(1), 3–43 (1996)
34. Wilmer, H.H., Sherman, L.E., Chein, J.M.: Smartphones and cognition: A review of research exploring the links between mobile technology habits and cognitive functioning. Front. Psycholo. **8** (2017)
35. Zhao, H., et al.: The reciprocal relationships between meaning in life and smartphone addiction among Chinese college students: Evidence from a three-wave cross-lagged panel model. Front. Public Health **11** (2023)
36. Živko, M.: Psychological aspects of cyberspace (2011). http://darhiv.ffzg.unizg.hr/id/eprint/8206/1/1-11%20Zivko%2C%20Psychological%20Aspects%20of%20Cyberspace.pdf

Next-Gen Stress Monitoring: Social Robot and AI Integration

Bhavana Nachenahalli Bhuthegowda⬡, Akshara Pande⬡, and Deepti Mishra(✉)⬡

Educational Technology Laboratory, Intelligent Systems and Analytics Group, Norwegian
University of Science and Technology, Teknologivegen 22, 2815 Gjøvik, Norway
{bhavana.n.bhuthegowda,akshara.pande,deepti.mishra}@ntnu.no

Abstract. In recent years, there has been a surge in the popularity of social robots
in various fields, including healthcare, which has affected people's health over
time. In today's fast-paced world, many people experience stress and other emotional conditions that can affect their well-being. Social robots are increasingly
being developed to provide emotional support and companionship to individuals
in need. Early identification of stress is essential in order to address and deal with
it. Artificial intelligence can play an important role in the detection of stress using
facial expressions. The objective of this study is to detect emotions such as stress
and no stress using the facial expressions of the persons. To achieve this goal, we
examine the hybrid performance of three AI libraries- VGGFace, DLib, and Deep-
Face. Furthermore, a humanoid robot, Nao, is integrated with AI libraries, which
helps in capturing people's facial images. The stress and non-stress situations are
simulated by playing a game and watching an entertaining video, respectively and
labelled accordingly. These images are then processed by algorithms individually, with detected emotions labeled as stress and non-stress. The findings of this
study report 93.589% accuracy in classifying emotions. In the future, the robot's
suggestions will also be incorporated to promote relaxation and stress reduction.

Keywords: Artificial Intelligence · Social robots · Facial image analysis ·
Emotion recognition · Stress detection

1 Introduction

Stress has become a growing concern in our modern world, affecting individuals in various ways. Stress occurs when an individual is overwhelmed by adverse environmental
factors or stressors [1]. It can significantly impact productivity, causing a decline in output and efficiency. Psychological stress is the primary focus of our study, as it is one of
the most common types of stress experienced by individuals. Lazarus et al. [2] discussed
various effects of stress on performance, including verbal performance and perceptual-
motor performance. Similarly, Cohen et al. [3] illustrated stress association with disease
and depression. Furthermore, Seiler et al. [4] demonstrated the impact of stress on the
immune system, which may lead to diseases such as cardiovascular, diabetes and cancer.

Early identification of stress is beneficial for effectively treating it. Alberdi et al.
[5] conducted a review of multimodal measurements for the early detection of stress in

© The Author(s), under exclusive license to Springer Nature Switzerland AG 2024
M. Kurosu and A. Hashizume (Eds.): HCII 2024, LNCS 14686, pp. 87–98, 2024.
https://doi.org/10.1007/978-3-031-60428-7_7

office environments, and they identified three main modalities: psychological, physiological and behavioural. Psychological [6] responses are related with increase in negative emotions such as depression. On the other hand, physiological responses are associated with variations in factors such as blood pressure [5], hormones [7], and heart rate [8]. Behavioural reactions [5] are connected to changes in facial expression, including eye gaze and blink rate.

Artificial Intelligence (AI) plays a crucial role in the identification of stress. Several algorithms in the area of AI, such as machine learning and deep learning, are helpful in stress detection. Ahuja et al. [9] evaluated the mental stress of students before an examination using machine learning classification algorithms. Li et al. [10] utilized deep neural networks for identifying stress and classifying emotions. Zhang et al. [11] considered a fused dataset of ECG, voice and facial expression and used a deep learning algorithm to detect mental stress. Bobade et al. [12] demonstrated the use of a multimodal dataset, including modalities such as ACC, ECG, EMG, body temperature, and respiration, for identifying stress with the help of both machine learning and deep learning methods.

There are many ways to handle stress, including exercises [13], meditation [14] and listening to music [15]. It can be challenging for an individual to identify stress and take appropriate action to cope with it on their own. However, having a companion around for support can be beneficial in handling stress more effectively. A support companion can provide emotional comfort and practical suggestions. Social robots can play a companion role in social settings, and there are studies [16, 17] that demonstrate that they are helpful in coping with stress. In the present study, social robot Nao is utilized, to capture facial expression of a person.

Nao, a humanoid robot developed by SoftBank Robotics [18], can perceive its environment through a camera and sensors. Nao has a module called ALFaceCharactristics [19], which is able to identify five emotional states of a person – happy, surprise, neutral, angry and sad. However, Filippini et al. [20] suggested that this module is not sufficient for more features and effective computing. Therefore, in the present study, the aim is to employ AI libraries with the social robot Nao to identify stress and non-stress facial expressions effectively. Previous reports [21, 22] suggested that negative emotional facial expressions can accurately predict stress, these facial expressions include anger, sadness and fear. On the other hand, other reports [23, 24] suggested positive emotions such as happiness and surprise, are considered as non-stress indicators. Based on these facts, in the present study, stress is measured through negative emotional facial expressions - such as anger, sadness, and fear and non-stress emotional facial expressions are measured through happiness, and surprise.

The objective of the study is to evaluate the hybrid performance of AI libraries, including VGGFace, dlib, and DeepFace, in identifying emotions as a means of classifying stress levels. To achieve this goal, the Nao robot is incorporated to capture facial images of individuals in both stressful and non-stressful situations. These situations are simulated through engaging activities such as playing a game such as sudoku game and watching entertaining video clips. Previous studies showed that playing sudoku can induce stress [25] while watching entertaining video clips can help in providing relaxation [26]. Subsequently, these captured images are individually processed by the selected AI libraries. The robot responses after stress detection are not included in this paper, but we will incorporate them and test the overall system in the future. The paper is organized as follows: Sect. 2 includes the methodology. Results and discussions are illustrated in Sect. 3. Conclusion and future work are discussed in Sect. 4.

2   Methodology

The experiment pipeline is shown in the Fig. 1. The experiment is setup as described in the following section. The images captured during the experiment are transferred to the local computer for processing and analysis, wherein labelling is verified and used as data for facial analysis via DeepFace, VGGFace and dlib techniques. Thus, obtained emotions are then classified into stress and no-stress categories and the details are explained in the later subsections.

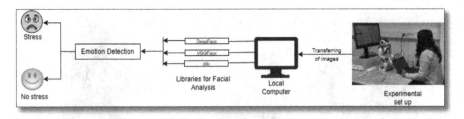

Fig. 1. The overall pipeline for detecting stress and no-stress using Nao and AI libraries.

2.1   Experiment Setup

Participants. The study involved four female adult volunteer participants in the age group of 25 to 55. They were selected to represent a diverse range of ages to enhance the generalizability of the findings.

Robot. A humanoid robot named Nao was used as the primary data capture tool. It was placed in front of a monitor, facing the user, and positioned in a crouched position to maintain a consistent image capture perspective. The robot had an inbuilt camera capable of capturing facial images.

Stimuli. Two distinct scenarios were created for this experiment to evoke varying emotional responses:

Non-stress Scenario. Participants were exposed to a 4-min entertaining video carefully chosen because of its universal appeal and its ability to elicit positive emotions [26].

Stress Scenario. Participants played an online Sudoku game, which was selected for its potential to induce stress and concentration. This idea was based on the similar approach used by Chen et al. [25] wherein sudoku games was used to evaluate the stress level of students during their gameplay.

Image Capture Interval. The Nao robot was programmed to capture facial images at regular intervals of 10 s during both scenarios. This resulted in a total of 18 images for each scenario per participant, leading to 36 images in total for each participant.

Image Labeling. Images were labelled in real-time according to the scenario they were captured in (non-stress or stress) to ensure accurate classification of emotions.

2.2 Experiment Execution

Non-stress Scenario. Participants were seated comfortably in front of the Nao robot (Fig. 2). A 4-min entertaining video was played on the monitor. During the video, the robot captured facial images at 10-s intervals. Participants were encouraged to watch the video without any specific emotional instruction.

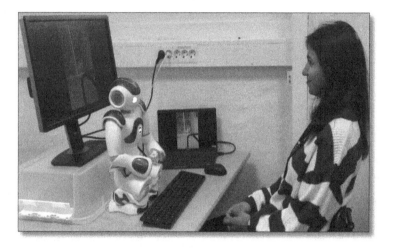

Fig. 2. Participant watching an entertaining video clip (non-stress scenario)

Stress Scenario. Participants were seated in front of the Nao robot (Fig. 3). They were asked to play an online Sudoku game on the monitor. Facial images were captured at 10-s intervals during the game. Participants were informed that they were being monitored but were not provided any specific instructions about their emotional expressions.

Capture and Transfer of Images to the Local Computer. To capture and transfer images from the Nao robot to a local computer, a Python 2.7 program is used. The program is designed to be compatible with Nao. It utilizes several libraries like qi, paramiko, and naoqi. The process involves a series of steps that make it easy to capture and transfer images.

Firstly, the program initiates the qi framework to establish communication and interaction with the robot through its IP address. The ALPhotoCapture [27] proxy is then used to access the robot's image capture functionality. This allows the program to take and store images in specified locations or directories on the robot's system. To transfer these images to the local machine, the program uses Paramiko [28], a Python library for SSH communication. This library enables the program to establish a secure connection between the local computer and the image path stored on the Nao robot. With this connection, the image files from the robot's system can be downloaded to the local machine for further processing or analysis. This approach makes image processing and analysis on the local system more efficient.

Algorithm Execution. Once captured images were transferred to a local system, the labeling for each image was done appropriately. Three emotion recognition libraries, namely keras_vggface [29], dlib [30], and deepface [31], were imported and executed on the labeled images with Python3. These algorithms are designed to detect facial expressions and recognize basic emotions.

VGGFace model is imported from keras_vggface libraray [29]. Resnet50 architecture [32] was used as the backbone of VGGFace model. Dlib [33] is a famous C + + toolkit for face detection. A facial landmark predictor 'shape_predictor_68_face_landmarks.dat' was employed to detect the landmarks in the images. A pre-trained emotion recognition model 'emotion_model.hdf5' [34] was loaded. The 'emotion_model.hdf5' file contains a Convolution Neural Network (CNN) model designed specifically for recognizing emotions in facial images. DeepFace module was imported from deepface library to perform emotion analysis on images.

Fig. 3. Participant playing a Sudoku game (stress scenario)

2.3 Dominant Emotion Detection

The criteria for determining primary emotion in the given situation, also called as dominance, were as follows:

Consensus Dominance. If more than two algorithms predicted the same emotion or emotions belonging to the same category (stress or non-stress), the dominant emotion was classified based on this consensus.

Contradictory Dominance. In cases where any of the two algorithms predicted emotions from different categories, the dominant emotion was classified as contradictory.

2.4 Accuracy of Emotion Detection

We imported accuracy score from the sklearn library to predict the accuracy of the predicted output. The module accuracy score takes two inputs: the actual label and the algorithm predicted output.

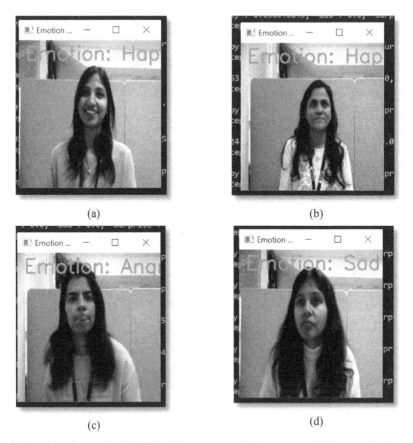

Fig. 4. Emotions detected by VGGFace (a) non-stressed (b) non-stressed (c) stressed (d) stressed

3   Results and Discussion

The detection of emotions on data collected from four participants in both stress and non-stress scenarios is done using three libraries - VGGFace, dlib and DeepFace. A few examples of some scenarios are demonstrated in Figs. 4, 5 and 6. Previous research has frequently employed watching videos as a method of data collection for facial expression analysis [35–37]. Chen et al. [25] utilized sudoku games to evaluate the stress level of students during their gameplay. We used the same approach to create scenarios where an entertaining video induced non-stressful conditions and playing Sudoku induced stress. The images were captured by Nao robot, and then they were processed by AI algorithms. Figure 4 illustrates the images processed by using VGGFace in both non-stress and stress scenarios. Similarly, in Fig. 5, the output of images processed by dlib has been shown. In the Fig. 6, the results of DeepFace are presented.

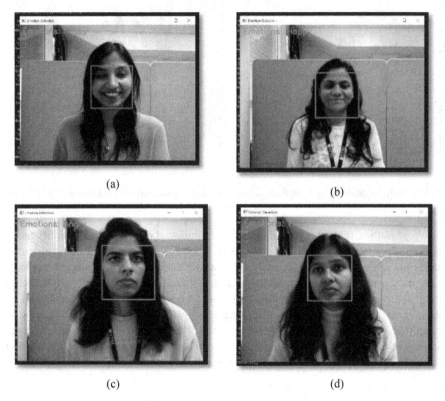

Fig. 5. Emotions detected by dlib (a) non-stressed (b) non-stressed (c) stressed (d) stressed.

The analysis involved determining the dominant emotion based on the outputs of the three algorithms and predicting their accuracy (shown in Fig. 7). The accuracy of the dominant emotion classification, derived from the outputs of three emotion recognition libraries (VGGFace, dlib and DeepFace), was assessed with the actual labels denoting stress and non-stress categories assigned to the images.

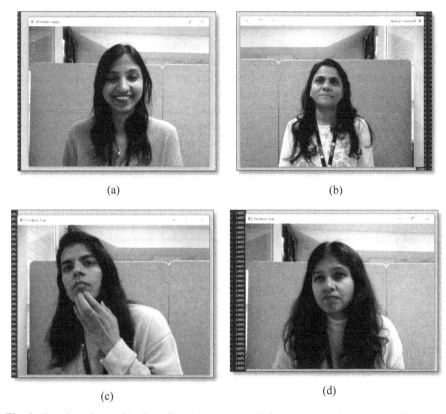

(a)   (b)

(c)   (d)

Fig. 6. Emotions detected by DeepFace (a) non-stressed (b) non-stressed (c) stressed (d) stressed

In past studies, these three AI libraries were employed individually to identify facial emotions. Jaquetti et al. [38] fine-tuned VGGFace for emotion analysis using facial images and achieved an accuracy of 92.1%. Canedo et al. [39] utilized dlib library with CK + database and 68 facial landmarks to detect faces. In our study, we followed a similar approach and utilized the dlib library and 68 facial landmarks for face detection. Patil et al. [40] illustrated that the DeepFace framework is effective for facial emotion recognition. Previous studies [41, 42] demonstrated that the hybrid model increases the accuracy of emotion detection. Our analysis revealed that the accuracy of the method in classifying the dominant emotions as stress or non-stress categories was 93.589% (Fig. 8).

	A	B	C	D	E	F	G
1	Image Detail	VGGFace	DeepFace	dlib	Dominant Emotion	Classification of Image	
2	naooct_ar_happy10.jpg	Sad	sad	Neutral	sad	stress	
3	naooct_ar_happy15.jpg	Happy	sad	Sad	sad	stress	
4	naooct_ar_stress15.jpg	Angry	sad	Sad	sad	stress	
5	naooct_ar_stress17.jpg	Happy	sad	Sad	sad	stress	
6	naooct_dm_stress0.jpg	Happy	sad	Sad	sad	stress	
7	naooct_dm_stress17.jpg	Happy	sad	Sad	sad	stress	
8	naooct_dm_stress4.jpg	Happy	sad	Sad	sad	stress	
9	naooct_nb_stress1.jpg	Happy	sad	Sad	sad	stress	
10	naooct_nb_stress10.jpg	Happy	fear	Fear	fear	stress	
11	naooct_ap_happy0.jpg	Happy	happy	Happy	happy	no_stress	
12	naooct_ap_happy1.jpg	Happy	happy	Happy	happy	no_stress	
13	naooct_ap_happy10.jpg	Surprise	happy	Happy	happy	no_stress	
14	naooct_ap_happy11.jpg	Happy	happy	Happy	happy	no_stress	
15	naooct_ap_happy12.jpg	Happy	happy	Happy	happy	no_stress	
16	naooct_ap_happy13.jpg	Happy	happy	Neutral	happy	no_stress	
17	naooct_ap_happy14.jpg	Happy	happy	Happy	happy	no_stress	
18	naooct_ap_happy15.jpg	Happy	happy	Happy	happy	no_stress	
19	naooct_ap_happy16.jpg	Happy	happy	Happy	happy	no_stress	
20	naooct_ap_happy17.jpg	Happy	happy	Happy	happy	no_stress	
21	naooct_ap_happy2.jpg	Happy	happy	Happy	happy	no_stress	

Fig. 7. Screenshot of classification of emotions as stress and no stress based on dominant emotion category

```
import pandas as pd
from sklearn.metrics import accuracy_score

df = pd.read_csv('sk_emo.csv',sep=';') #contains actual and predicted emotions as stress and no-stress

actual = df['actual']
predicted = df['predicted']

accuracy = accuracy_score(actual, predicted)

print(f'Accuracy: {accuracy}')

Accuracy: 0.9358974358974359
```

Fig. 8. Screenshot of calculating accuracy using sklearn library.

4   Conclusion and Future Work

Stress identification is important in almost every field, including home and work. AI inclusion with social robots can be beneficial for dealing with stress. In the present study, we considered the hybrid output from VGGFace, dlib and DeepFace. By combining the performance of the selected AI algorithms in stress detection through emotional analysis, we gain valuable insights into identifying stress while allowing for early intervention strategies and real-time monitoring. This study leads to a deeper understanding of the potential of AI-driven humanoid robots in addressing stress and underscores the significance of early stress detection for well-being and health including their applications in mental health services, education and schools, workplace and corporate environments, home assistance as well in public spaces. The proposed system used in this study accurately identifies stress with 93.589% accuracy. However, we have not yet integrated robot suggestions after identifying stress based on a person's emotions. We plan to incorporate this in the future.

In this study, the experiment was conducted in laboratory settings using a small sample of four volunteers. However, in the future, we plan to conduct it in natural settings with a larger sample size that includes more participants. Additionally, we will focus on multimodal data like sensor data (heart rate, electrodermal activity etc.) from wearable device, not just facial images, 'to capture a person's emotional state more effectively. Alongside this, we will collect qualitative data, such as interviews and questionnaires, to understand participants' perceptions of stress and evaluate the effectiveness of robot-assisted stress management.

References

1. Schuler, R.S.: Definition and conceptualization of stress in organizations. Organ. Behav. Hum. Perform. **25**(2), 184–215 (1980)
2. Lazarus, R.S., Deese, J., Osler, S.F.: The effects of psychological stress upon performance. Psychol. Bull. **49**(4), 293–317 (1952)
3. Cohen, S., Janicki-Deverts, D., Miller, G.E.: Psychological stress and disease. JAMA **298**(14), 1685–1687 (2007)
4. Seiler, A., Fagundes, C.P., Christian, L.M.: The impact of everyday stressors on the immune system and health. In: Choukèr, A. (ed.) Stress Challenges and Immunity in Space: From Mechanisms to Monitoring and Preventive Strategies, pp. 71–92. Springer International Publishing, Cham (2020)
5. Alberdi, A., Aztiria, A., Basarab, A.: Towards an automatic early stress recognition system for office environments based on multimodal measurements: a review. J. Biomed. Inform. **59**, 49–75 (2016)
6. Brown, T.A., Chorpita, B.F., Barlow, D.H.: Structural relationships among dimensions of the DSM-IV anxiety and mood disorders and dimensions of negative affect, positive affect, and autonomic arousal. J. Abnorm. Psychol. **107**(2), 179 (1998)
7. Ranabir, S., Reetu, K.: Stress and hormones. Indian J. Endocrinol. Metab. **15**(1), 18–22 (2011)
8. Oh, J., Lee, H., Park, H.: Effects on heart rate variability of stress level responses to the properties of indoor environmental colors: a preliminary study. Int. J. Environ. Res. Public Health **18**(17), 9136 (2021). https://doi.org/10.3390/ijerph18179136
9. Ahuja, R., Banga, A.: Mental stress detection in university students using machine learning algorithms. Procedia Comput. Sci. **152**, 349–353 (2019)
10. Li, R., Liu, Z.: Stress detection using deep neural networks. BMC Med. Inform. Decis. Mak. **20**(11), 285 (2020)
11. Zhang, J., et al.: Real-time mental stress detection using multimodality expressions with a deep learning framework. Front. Neurosci. **16**, 947168 (2022)
12. Bobade, P., Vani, M.: Stress detection with machine learning and deep learning using multi-modal physiological data. In: 2020 Second International Conference on Inventive Research in Computing Applications (ICIRCA). IEEE (2020)
13. Jackson, E.M.: STRESS RELIEF: the role of exercise in stress management. ACSM's Health Fitness J. **17**(3), 14–19 (2013)
14. Edwards, M.K., Loprinzi, P.D.: Experimental effects of brief, single bouts of walking and meditation on mood profile in young adults. Health Promot. Perspect. **8**(3), 171–178 (2018)
15. Thoma, M.V., et al.: The effect of music on the human stress response. PLoS ONE **8**(8), e70156 (2013)
16. Dang, T.-H.-H., Tapus, A.: Coping with stress using social robots as emotion-oriented tool: potential factors discovered from stress game experiment. In: Herrmann, G., Pearson, M.J., Lenz, A., Bremner, P., Spiers, A., Leonards, U. (eds.) Social Robotics. LNCS (LNAI), vol. 8239, pp. 160–169. Springer, Cham (2013). https://doi.org/10.1007/978-3-319-02675-6_16

17. Yorita, A., et al.: A robot assisted stress management framework: Using conversation to measure occupational stress. In: 2018 IEEE International Conference on Systems, Man, and Cybernetics (SMC). IEEE (2018)
18. NAO webpage. https://www.aldebaran.com/en/nao. Accessed 28 Nov 2023
19. Nao Module ALFaceCharacteristics. http://doc.aldebaran.com/2-1/naoqi/peopleperception/alfacecharacteristics.html. Accessed 28 Nov 2023
20. Filippini, C., Perpetuini, D., Cardone, D., Merla, A.: Improving human–robot interaction by enhancing NAO robot awareness of human facial expression. Sensors **21**(19), 6438 (2021). https://doi.org/10.3390/s21196438
21. Das, S., Yamada, K.: Evaluating instantaneous psychological stress from emotional composition of a facial expression. J. Adv. Comput. Intell. Intell. Inform. **17**(4), 480–492 (2013)
22. Zhang, J., et al.: Detecting negative emotional stress based on facial expression in real time. In: 2019 IEEE 4th International Conference on Signal and Image Processing (ICSIP). IEEE (2019)
23. Stanković, M., Nešić, M.: Functional brain asymmetry for emotions: psychological stress-induced reversed hemispheric asymmetry in emotional face perception. Exp. Brain Res. **238**(11), 2641–2651 (2020)
24. Zhang, B., et al.: Classroom monitoring system based on facial expression recognition. In: 2021 20th International Symposium on Distributed Computing and Applications for Business Engineering and Science (DCABES). IEEE (2021)
25. Chen, Q., Lee, B.G.: Deep learning models for stress analysis in university students: a sudoku-based study. Sensors **23**(13), 6099 (2023). https://doi.org/10.3390/s23136099
26. Bartsch, A.: Emotional gratification in entertainment experience. Why viewers of movies and television series find it rewarding to experience emotions. Media Psychol. **15**(3), 267–302 (2012). https://doi.org/10.1080/15213269.2012.693811
27. ALPhotoCapture Webpage. http://doc.aldebaran.com/2-1/naoqi/vision/alphotocapture.html. Accessed 28 Nov 2023
28. Paramiko library. https://www.paramiko.org/. Accessed 28 Nov 2023
29. VGGFace. https://github.com/rcmalli/keras-vggface. Accessed 28 Nov 2023
30. King, D.E.: DLIB-ML: a machine learning toolkit. J. Mach. Learn. Res. **10**, 1755–1758 (2009)
31. Serengil, S.I., Ozpinar, A.: Lightface: a hybrid deep face recognition framework. In: 2020 Innovations in Intelligent Systems and Applications Conference (ASYU). IEEE (2020)
32. He, K., et al.: Deep residual learning for image recognition. In: Proceedings of the IEEE Conference on Computer Vision and Pattern Recognition (2016)
33. Dlib. http://dlib.net/. Accessed 28 Nov 2023
34. Github. https://github.com/petercunha/Emotion/blob/master/models/emotion_model.hdf5. Accessed 28 Nov 2023
35. Dharanesh, M., et al.: Video based facial emotion recognition system using deep learning. In: 2023 Second International Conference on Electronics and Renewable Systems (ICEARS) (2023)
36. Turabzadeh, S., et al.: Facial expression emotion detection for real-time embedded systems. Technologies **6**(1), 17 (2018)
37. Zhang, J., et al.: Trusted emotion recognition based on multiple signals captured from video. Expert Syst. Appl. **233**, 120948 (2023)
38. Jaquetti, P.F., Pilla, V., Borba, G.B., Gamba, H.R.: VGG FACE fine-tuning for classification of facial expression images of emotion. In: Bastos-Filho, T.F., de Oliveira Caldeira, E.M., Frizera-Neto, A. (eds.) XXVII Brazilian Congress on Biomedical Engineering. IP, vol. 83, pp. 1539–1546. Springer, Cham (2022). https://doi.org/10.1007/978-3-030-70601-2_226
39. Canedo, D., Neves, A.J.R.: Facial expression recognition using computer vision: a systematic review. Appl. Sci. **9**(21), 4678 (2019). https://doi.org/10.3390/app9214678

40. Patil, V.K., et al.: Theory, Practical Concepts, Strategies and Methods for Emotion Recognition. In: Advanced Sensing in Image Processing and IoT, pp. 81–108. CRC Press (2022)
41. Kim, J.-C., et al.: Hybrid Approach for Facial Expression Recognition Using Convolutional Neural Networks and SVM. Appl. Sci. **12**(11), 5493 (2022)
42. Mishra, R.K., et al.: Deep hybrid learning for facial expression binary classifications and predictions. Image Vis. Comput. **128**, 104573 (2022)

Open Issues in Persuasive Technologies: Six HCI Challenges for the Design of Behavior Change Systems

Amon Rapp[1]([⊠]) [iD] and Arianna Boldi[2] [iD]

[1] Computer Science Department, University of Turin, Torino, Italy
amon.rapp@unito.it
[2] Department of Psychology, University of Turin, Torino, Italy

Abstract. Persuasive technologies are increasing in popularity due to the widespread availability of devices that are able to automatically collect and process behavioral data. However, most of these technologies merely focus on the behavior to be changed, overlooking both the user's subjective experience of the behavior change process and the wider life context in which it is situated. In this paper, we identify six challenges that the HCI community should address in the near future to account for the complexity of the lived experience of behavior change, also proposing several technological opportunities for moving the field of persuasive technology forward. First, technology should focus on the subjective meanings that people ascribe to the behavior. Second, technology should support reflection rather than the rational analysis of data. Third, technology should promote the person's agency instead of relying on external motivators. Fourth technology should address the living body, which is essential in driving the change of many behaviors (e.g., in dieting and exercising). Fifth, designers should consider the person's life context, which refers to routines, social relations, and everyday matters that point to the complexity of "life". Sixth, designers should account for the person's life time, as behavior change intertwines with the entire past of the individual and projects into their distant future(s).

Keywords: Behavior change · Persuasive technologies · Self-tracking · Personal Informatics · Wearable technologies · Activity trackers

1 Introduction

Persuasive technologies, or behavior change systems, are devices and software applications designed to modify users' behavior or habits [12, 23]. Over recent years, these technologies have become popular among the general population, because of the spreading of wearable devices that automatically collect behavioral data with the aim of encouraging people, for example, to do more physical activity [54]. Concurrently, the Human-Computer Interaction (HCI) community has shown a growing interest in designing technologies that promote healthier or more sustainable behaviors (e.g., [15, 39]). However, despite the popularity of commercial persuasive devices and the increasing academic

© The Author(s), under exclusive license to Springer Nature Switzerland AG 2024
M. Kurosu and A. Hashizume (Eds.): HCII 2024, LNCS 14686, pp. 99–116, 2024.
https://doi.org/10.1007/978-3-031-60428-7_8

research on technology for behavior change, there is a rising wave of concern within the HCI community about these systems' actual capabilities of yielding enduring changes in behavior and maintaining the user engagement over time [6, 15].

A significant flaw is that these technologies often exclusively focus on the behavior that they aim to modify. They offer a variety of tools for analyzing the behavior as an "objective phenomenon" (e.g., graphs and statistics), and for influencing it "from the outside" (e.g., by using incentives like points). In this way, however, they tend to overshadow the lived and idiosyncratic experience of the behavior change process, which is primarily subjective, meaning-laden, and driven "from the inside" [61]: in fact, changing behavior is closely linked to subjective meanings, such as personal values and motivations, and influenced by broader "life" factors, like preexisting social relationships and everyday routines, which play a fundamental role in the dynamics of change [52, 60]. Therefore, despite the current approach on persuasive technology has brought successes, for example, by supporting people in modifying their behavior in the short term (e.g., [22, 24, 47]), several open issues still need to be addressed by HCI researchers and practitioners.

In this article, drawing from a decade of our empirical research on self-tracking devices and behavior change systems (e.g., [54, 56, 58, 59, 62]), we identify six pivotal challenges for persuasive technology, as well as emerging opportunities for its development arising from the evolving technology landscape.

First, technology should focus on meaning rather than on the target behavior to be modified. In fact, when a person attempts to modify their own behavior, often their main concern is not the behavior itself. For instance, dieting may relate to the desire to please others, the fear of becoming ill, or the need of being in control. The subjective meanings that people ascribe to the behavior are thus a fundamental part of the behavior change process. Second, technology should support reflection rather than the rational analysis of data. To change their behavior, people often need to reflect on it and rework what they think about themselves, making sense of the behavior change process itself. Encouraging people to examine behavioral data is often not sufficient to trigger and sustain reflection, as many users may not find such data meaningful. Third, technology should promote the person's agency rather than driving the behavior from the outside. Designs that rely on external motivators treat individuals as executors of pre-defined behavioral programs and can hardly sustain the change once these motivators are removed. Fourth, technology should address the living body, rather than the "physiological body" only. Most persuasive devices use body data automatically collected by sensors (e.g., the heartbeat) to provide feedback and tailor the intervention: however, these are rarely able to capture the lived experience of the body (e.g., how the body is felt by the person), which is essential in driving the change of many behaviors, such as dieting and exercising. Fifth, designers should consider the person's life context for designing the intervention. While current persuasive technologies focus on the varying conditions of the user's physical context (e.g., location, hour), changing behavior is embedded in routines, social relations, and everyday matters that point to the complexity of "life". Sixth, designers should account for the person's life time when settling the behavioral program. While current technologies rely on the "objective time" that regulates the timeliness of the intervention, the management of relapses, and the duration of the program, behavior change intertwines with the subjective time of the person's life, which embraces their entire past and projects into their distant future(s).

These challenges highlight the complexity of the behavior change process pointing to a series of "existential" and "life" matters that play a fundamental role in the modification of the person's behavior. Such matters are certainly difficult to be addressed by current technology, and this may explain why effective solutions have not yet been found. However, this difficulty could not be a reason to ignore essential aspects of behavior change: otherwise, it would mean to consciously build "suboptimal" technologies, which, in certain cases, might not even work at all. By pointing out six important challenges that persuasive technologies should address in future research, in the following, we aim to offer a theoretical contribution built on evidence about how people really experience the change of behavior in their everyday life, encouraging researchers and practitioners to experiment novel solutions and approaches that can really account for the complexity of the process of change.

2 Background

Persuasive technologies commonly rely on strategies that either focus on conscious processing and rational analysis to yield change in behavior (e.g., [21, 70]), or exploit subconscious mechanisms to influence people's choices through nudging techniques (e.g., [6, 49]).

The conscious approach is fueled by the increasing availability of behavioral data that are collected by self-tracking instruments, like wearable activity trackers and tracking apps. These instruments are based on the assumptions that individuals are not aware of their own behaviors and habits and need to increase their self-knowledge to effectively start the process of change [61]. Cognitive theories like the Social Cognitive Theory [2] and the Transtheoretical Model of behavior change [50], which often backdrop technologies belonging to the conscious approach, precisely highlight the role of conscious, rational processing in affecting people's intentions of enacting a change [49]. By contrast, the mindless approach mainly embraces Applied Behavior Analysis [8] and behavioral economics [73], either acting upon the environment to reinforce the emissions of a certain behavior (e.g., [76]), or shaping the choice architecture to alter people's decisions in a predictable way. For instance, mindless persuasive technologies may leverage people's biases (i.e., systematic deviations from rational judgment) and heuristics (i.e., mental shortcuts) to modify their behavioral choices (e.g., [19, 34]).

As we highlighted in our previous work [52, 60], however, HCI designs that rely on both these approaches share, on a deeper theoretical level, what we have called the "behavioral model of change": this model conceptualizes behavior as an objective, discrete and isolated phenomenon, which can be manipulated from the outside through circumscribed interventions that exclusively target the behavior that needs to be modified. More precisely, in this model behavior change is seen as i) externalistic, since the internal experience of change (e.g., the psychological states connected with it) is overlooked in favor of its observable and measurable manifestations; ii) monistic, since change appears to have a univocal sense, while personal meanings and motivations, which people may ascribe to a certain behavior, are completely ignored by technology; iii) mechanistic, as change appears to occur as an automatic reaction, once certain "tools" are provided, be they behavioral or environmental; iv) fragmented, because it is viewed as an isolated event, whereby a change can be induced in independent, specific target behaviors, leaving the wider life of the individual substantially untouched; v) episodic, namely, change is framed as a discrete event, as it were a transition from one substantially steady state to another, or through a normative sequence of predefined phases [60].

This model is dominant in the current persuasive technology landscape. Persuasive self-tracking systems, for instance, which at first glance seems to give value to the interiority of the individual encouraging "self"-reflection and "self"-knowledge, mostly understand the person's "self" as a database, that is, a conglomerate of quantified data [72] meant as objective traces of the user's behavior [61]: here, behavior change may occur through self-monitoring and feedback loop mechanisms [68], as if it were a thermostat tending to homeostasis.

Despite its dominance, however, the behavioral model may cloud the lived experience of change, which is fundamentally subjective and meaning-laden, whereby the meaning that people ascribe to the behavior and the process of change often pertain to important existential concerns, like the need to have control on life, the fear of suffering or dying, and the desire to be recognized by others [52]. We have then suggested to shift the focus from the target behavior to be modified to the wider life context in which the behavior change attempts are embedded, proposing an "existential model of behavior change" as an alternative take on persuasive technology design. This model gives value to the internal meanings that individuals develop throughout their lives and accounts for the existential matters that are intertwined with their behavior change endeavors, putting in foreground the "life" in which they are situated [52].

This perspective resonates with alternative approaches that have been previously explored within HCI. For instance, work on health coaching and counseling has noticed the importance of meaning in the behavior change process [69]. For example, Rutjes et al. [69] investigated the health coaches' perspective on behavior change, who report that often there is a more profound problem underlying a stated behavior change goal and that it is needed to capture contextual information and the lived experience of the client for a successful intervention. Likewise, Bhattacharya et al. [3] interviewed providers with diverse experiences in smoking cessation counseling, finding that they consider essential understanding the care and social context in which the intervention occurs.

3 Six HCI Challenges for the Design of Persuasive Technologies

In this section, we will outline six pivotal challenges for persuasive technology design, to account for the complexity of the behavior change process. In so doing, we also identify several promising lines of research that may help the HCI community explore novel technological opportunities for influencing people's behavior. We base our considerations on relevant literature and, more importantly, on the theoretical reflections and the empirical research that we conducted on behavior change and self-tracking technologies over the last ten years. In fact, we have explored how people with no experience with self-tracking attempt to integrate activity trackers in their daily routines [53, 54] and react to novel forms of visualization of personal data [56]; how amateur and elite athletes use wearables to tune their trainings and improve their sports performance [58, 59]; how self-tracking design may account for the fundamental subjectivity that characterizes our experience of the world and ourselves [61]; how people face and live important changes in their lives, including behavioral changes [60, 64]; how self-tracking technologies affect individuals' perceptions and awareness of their body [4]; and how people use technology when they attempt to modify their habits and behaviors [52].

3.1 Focusing on Meaning

A first fundamental challenge for persuasive technologies relates to the subjective meanings that people ascribe to the behavior that they want to modify and to the process of change itself. In fact, changing behavior is not an endeavor that is merely important per se: rather, it is endowed with meanings that point to personal and existential matters, which often drive the process of change.

These meanings are fundamentally subjective and idiosyncratic, because they are constructed by the person in the course of their life [61], thus varying from individual to individual, influenced by how they intertwine with their intimate life. It follows that the same behavior may have diverse meanings for different individuals: for example, people report that modifying a specific behavior, like doing more physical activity, may be connected with the need to gain control over their body, the worry of being harmed, the willingness to become a better person or be pleased by others, or the desire for experiencing pleasure [52]. Likewise, different behaviors may point to the very same meaning: for instance, dieting, exercising, and regularizing the daily routines may all be linked to the need of being in control by a certain individual.

The meanings that people construct play an essential role in behavior change, as the willingness to achieve the change, the sense of having succeeded or failed, and, more in general, how the change is managed may be deeply affected by them [52]. This happens not only for people attempting to modify their own behavior, but also for those who undergo important changes in their life, like relocating, starting a new relationship, or facing a loss [60].

However, current persuasive technologies hardly address the subjective and idiosyncratic nature of these meanings. Technology support for sense-making is scarce, because often persuasive systems feed the behavior back merely in a quantified form, which nonetheless does not account for our "natural" way of understanding the behavior and ourselves [61]: for instance, an important life matter like taking care of one's health may be reduced to the number of steps taken in a month. This may cause the scarce integration of the "meanings" prompted by the technology into the user's previous knowledge [52], the early abandonment of the device, and also the failure of the behavioral intervention [32]. Moreover, a variety of side-effects may follow from the usage of technologies that do not account for the meanings that people attribute to behavior change: as technology is not able to drive the sense-making process around the behavior and its modification, people may start developing undesired and unexpected meanings: for instance, excessively quantifying their understanding of the behavior may produce harmful effects, like reducing the pleasure of eating when attempting to reduce the food intakes [52]. This is confirmed by research examining the features of popular self-tracking tools [7] and exploring tracking practices in chronic illness management [43], which highlighted that tracking devices may limit meaning-making or are simply not helpful in guiding people's own sense-making processes.

Sense-making is a narrative process based on language, entailing the active reworking of previous linguistic meanings. Considering and possibly modifying the meanings associated with the target behavior in a way that is positive for the process of change is essential for a successful intervention: for instance, if smoking is understood by the person as a form of "protection" during stressful times, or eating is seen as a comfort during challenging life situations, changing the meanings associated with the target behaviors is paramount to make the person aware that its modification is important.

Effectively managing language may be an extremely difficult endeavor for current persuasive technologies. In this sense, conversational agents could support people's sense-making by simulating, for example, active listening [36]. However, these agents suffer from serious limitations in tackling conversational topics that fall outside the narrow domain of expertise of the agent [55]. Being behavior change intertwined with personal and existential matters that may go beyond the domain to which pertains the target behavior, it is difficult to support sense-making around the individual's relevant issues with traditional chatbots.

Nevertheless, recent advances in Large Language Models (LLMs) and Generative AI may open new opportunities for helping people construct new meanings around their behavior. Pre-trained LLMs (e.g., ChatGPT) can engage in fluent, multi-turn conversations out-of-the-box and, especially when their outputs are improved by prepending prompts - textual instructions and examples of their desired interactions - to LLM inputs, they may produce conversational outcomes that are close to human-like interactions [78]. These models could then be used to stimulate conversations around the behavior to be changed, connecting it with the "life issues" that the person thinks are relevant, and sustain the formation of alternative, more "positive" meanings. Certainly, much research should be still conducted on this line, as LLMs do not have any proper access to "meaning", possibly being extremely harmful by providing inappropriate or hallucinated responses or those without sufficient empathy [9]: in fact, even with prompt engineering, it can be hard to control what an LLM may say to an individual, and in domains like health and wellness it may give dangerous advice to users, especially if they tackle existential matters that are paramount to them. Despite significant development is yet required, this technology appears to be extremely promising, and there is an increasing urgency for future research focused on designing open-ended conversations that facilitate meaning-making. This mirrors the approach used in clinical practices addressed to modify the client's behavior, where human therapists guide the process of change.

3.2 Supporting Reflection

The second challenge points to the need to go beyond the rational examination of behavior and the data that should represent it. Technologies that track behavior with the aim of encouraging its modification, like activity trackers, mostly display the collected information through stats and graphs. These may further offer analytical tools to detect correlations among different kinds of data or forecast the future "fluctuations" of behavior [67].

However, an emerging stream of HCI research has highlighted the limits of such visualizations and instruments, which may lack meaning for the user [32, 54]. In fact, people with no experience in data analysis often find the visualizations and features offered by these tools hard to understand, requiring a high cognitive load and long time to discover thought-provoking insights on their behavior [54]. During a diary study, we found that this kind of users perceive such visualizations too abstract and removed from what they expect, not allowing them to recognize themselves in the information displayed [54]. As a consequence, these people show lack of engagement with the given visualizations, eventually reducing their initial curiosity and interest in the technology, which prevents them from continuing reflecting on the data and themselves.

This lack of help for reflection in current technology is relevant, since (self-)reflection appears fundamental in processes of change. People commonly reflect on their own changes and link them to parallel modifications of their inner states, like personality, values, beliefs, and emotions [60]. These reflections tell us that changes, whether positive or negative, need to be "mentally tamed" to make people feel having a quota of control over them. Moreover, HCI research has noticed that reflection may be a catalyst for behavior change [30, 35]. After all, change primarily happens in the "self," and only subsequently may affect behavior. In fact, major and enduring changes often derive from a substantial shift of the perspective that we have on ourselves [61]: if we may say that the sense of our stability is granted by the fact that we reflect on and constantly tell ourselves the same stories about "our self" [71], (behavior) change may occur as we begin reflecting differently on it and creating different stories about it [61].

What may be needed, therefore, to move further the landscape of persuasive design is a technology support that is able to elicit fruitful reflection. HCI researchers have seldom explored how to design systems that allow for an easier, more efficient and engaging analytical reflection on behavioral data [45]. For example, they studied how to improve the readability of displayed data [11] and experimented on alternative ways of recounting and visualizing information about behavior, for example through stories [25], metaphorical depictions [56], or tangible interactions [29].

However, novel opportunities for encouraging reflection in people attempting to change their own behavior may come from designs leveraging ambiguous - rather than clear – data representations, in order to stimulate open-ended, multiple, and unexpected interpretations of data, beyond utility and rationality [14]. On this line, there are systems that display ambiguous visualizations of biosignals, like heart rate, as social cues for interpersonal relationships, showing the role of ambiguity in triggering conversations that can encourage reflection [26, 66]. Beyond these examples, Gaver et al. [14] identified different kinds of ambiguity, which could be fruitfully exploited in persuasive designs: ambiguity of information focuses on creating or reflecting uncertainties about information, making the system seem mysterious, but more importantly compelling people to join in the work of making sense of it and the information it conveys; ambiguity of context refers to blocking the interpretation of a system in terms of an established discourse, thus spurring people to approach it with an open mind and questioning the assumptions they have about it; ambiguity of relationship creates the condition for a deeply personal projection of imagination and values onto a design, allowing systems to become psychological mirrors for people trying new identities or questioning their values and activities. Gaver et al. [14] also provides a variety of ambiguity strategies that could be usefully explored in persuasive designs, making behavior change technologies more open to interpretation, instead of prescriptive and addressed to provide a unique and "correct" perspective about the behavior to be changed.

3.3 Promoting the Person's Agency

The third challenge points to the way people manage their own changes. When we interviewed people undergoing relevant changes in their lives, we discovered that those individuals who have a strong internal locus of control, namely, they perceive themselves as the main drivers of changes even when they happen as fortuitous events, tend to embrace them favorably and actively [60]. By contrast, those who ascribe the agency of their changes to external entities like society or fate, have the tendency to frame them negatively and to become passive in their face: the perception of not being in control may provoke states of anxiety and worry. However, these individuals still attempt to reduce their feeling of helplessness, by "taming" the change mentally or emotionally, for example, by reframing the emotions triggered by it [60]. We may say, therefore, that a sense of agency is fundamental in the management of relevant changes because it may allow people to take over the reins of them. However, when people attempt to modify their own behavior through technology but do not have sufficient competence to drive the process, they may experience a loss of agency and become dependent on the device [52].

Persuasive technologies could then benefit from designs aimed at bringing the agency of change back to the user. This would empower them, making them feel the protagonist of the intervention. Working on food habits, Gao [13] noticed that designs should offer opportunities for people to actively express their own understandings of what is healthy. Purpura et al. [51] emphasized that, in the context of dieting and exercising, persuasive technologies might enforce sublimated social goals, reinforcing taken-for-granted conceptions of what it means to be healthy or fit; then, they proposed that users should set their own goals. In light of this, future research should experiment with designs that support users in achieving their goals, on the basis of their values and conceptions of what is good or bad for them, in order to avoid the sensation of being dominated by the technology, which may negatively impact on the management of change. In fact, the problem of domination in persuasive design has been also emphasized by potential users: when we asked students to imagine the future of behavior change technologies through the creation of a series of design fictions, namely, fictional prototypes inserted into a long distant future shaped by the fictional design, they mostly proposed dystopian scenarios, signaling an attitude of mistrust and suspect toward these systems [62]. More precisely, their design fictions pointed out that in persuasive designs it is not immediately clear who is promoting a certain behavior and why, stressing that a variety of actors could exploit this technology for their own ends, like private companies, governments, and even society and family [62].

In fact, it is undoubtable that persuasive technologies inscribe in themselves instances of power that state what is right and what is not and define why and how we should or should not behave in a certain way. Moreover, practitioners and researchers might forget or underestimate that their work can be driven by external agencies, conveying social values and visions of the world as if they were unquestionable and unchangeable. Lupton [41], for example, claimed that health behavior change technologies promote healthism, an ideology that values those individuals that take self-responsibility about their own health, who, nonetheless, are the socio-economically privileged, being able to make health a priority in their lives, since they have the educational and economic resources to do so.

In this context, it becomes crucial to further explore research questions related to the responsibility of persuasive design, which implies decisions on who has the right, the willingness, or the duty of driving the change, and whether the shift of agency from humans to technology on these matters is acceptable under any circumstances. Moreover, as behavior change designs become more pervasive, it becomes essential considering ethical issues more seriously, asking whether this technology is strengthening, weakening, or subverting certain values and weltanschauungs, as well as how we can rebalance the power asymmetries that persuasive technology may establish.

3.4 Addressing the Living Body

The fourth challenge relates to the need to consider the living body more than the physiological body, which is automatically detected by sensors of many persuasive devices. It has been noticed that activity trackers encompass a reductionist, abstract, and fragmented view of the body, which is scattered across a variety of data [4, 75], potentially causing disembodiment and dissatisfaction [42]. In a large mixed-methods study involving 321 first-time wearable activity tracker users, we precisely explored the impact of these technologies on people's body perceptions and representations [5]. We discovered that several individuals improved their body awareness, as well as the knowledge of their own body, following the usage of an activity tracker, without, however, significantly altering their body representations. Nevertheless, we noticed that the tracker offered a "narrow" image of people's own body, often misaligned with their self-perception. This discrepancy led to a psychological detachment from the collected data, which were then considered almost irrelevant [5].

Similar findings can be found among athletes using wearable devices for tuning their training and increasing their performance. These technologies are rarely effective in modifying athletes' lifestyle and behavior because they fail to elucidate the rationale behind the "lifestyle recommendations" they provide, or how these suggestions can benefit the athlete's sports performance. Furthermore, they fall short in linking the collected "lifestyle data", like the food intakes and sleep pattern, with their core functionalities, like the heartbeat monitoring feature [58]. Consequently, amateur athletes are not able to identify useful relations between lifestyle data and sports performance data and are not encouraged to change their behavior. By contrast, elite athletes are not concerned with the monitoring of "lifestyle" parameters, because they already follow a strict discipline, tuned on the basis of their coaches' suggestions and on their own deep understanding of their own bodies [58]: they use the tracker as a supplementary tool, a commodity that can ease their trainings but that does not impact their overall lifestyle.

Nonetheless, these devices can make the athletes more aware of internal body processes that they are not able to identify by themselves, like the heart rate. Moreover, they can support the athletes in learning how to "read" their body signals, in order to detect such hidden processes (e.g., those body signals that indicate that they are in certain heart zones) and, in this way, positively impact on their sports performance [58]. However, the benefits involving an increased body awareness are not exempt from side-effects, especially if we consider amateur athletes, who completely rely on the device to understand their own body processes. While elite athletes are able to distinguish when it is appropriate to rely on the tracked data or rather it is best to trust their own sensations, for amateur athletes, reliance on a tracker may undermine their confidence in personal sensations, leading to an excessive dependence on the device. This shift may eventually reduce awareness of bodily cues, potentially impairing sports performance [58]. Similarly, Lupton [40] highlights that technology can extend the capacities of the body, but can also convey a totally quantified, objective, and "aseptic" body knowledge where data substitute meaningful body experiences, and where the repository of body knowledge shifts from the internality of the subject to the externality of the device.

Therefore, for persuasive technologies it becomes important to start framing the person's body not merely as a physiological assemblage of data, but as a "living body", that is the body experienced from a first-person point of view [58]. In fact, by exclusively providing quantitative information, persuasive tracking devices may turn the lived experience of the body into a merely intellectual activity, where the body is regulated from the outside through continuous rational choices (e.g., looking at the current heart rate displayed by the device, and then deciding to increase the physical activity). The living body, instead, calls for the exploration of novel interaction modalities that support its internal regulative mechanisms, which are subjective and visceral [58].

Here, Augmented Reality (AR) and wearable simulations may help persuasive technologies evoke and experiment with novel, alternative or distorted body experiences [16]. Take, for instance, "Force Jacket": this device integrates an array of pneumatically-actuated airbags and force sensors that provide feel effects to make the person experience an entirely new perceptual experience, which reverberates to the wearer's whole body. An example of its application includes simulating heartbeat effects to control people's sense of fatigue when running [10]. Likewise, "TreeSense" is a tactile experience of being a tree, where wearables trigger novel tactile sensations that are not naturally possible: it stimulates a variety of perceptual variations allowing the individual to experience what it feels like to be a tree from a seedling to its full-size form, to its final destiny [37].

Technologies of this kind may enable people to live different health conditions, simulating how the body could be transformed following different lifestyles, eventually making them reflect on the modification of behavior. Persuasive technologies research, therefore, could explore how to make wearables more transparent, integrating them into the person's sensorial apparatus in order to provide them with novel full-body experiences and perceptions [65]. For instance, a health activity tracker paired with AR glasses could modify the individual's perception of food: in the case of someone with hypercholesterolemia, it could visually mark "harmful" foods in red; conversely, for someone adhering to a low-fat diet, it could use different shades to indicate foods with different fat content [65].

3.5 Considering the Person's Life Context

The fifth challenge relates to the context in which behavior change occurs. Commonly, this context is conceived as "local" to the behavior to be changed: for example, a persuasive application aimed at modifying the users' food habits only considers their eating behavior, overlooking its connections with other behaviors and the wider life context in which it is situated. However, both people undergoing relevant changes in their lives and those undertaking behavioral changes report that such changes reverberate throughout the different aspects of their life, also being linked to more complex, overarching processes, which tie together different life domains [62]. In this sense, changing behavior is not a local event, but a process inserted into a nexus of life circumstances that may directly affect the change itself [52].

For example, favorable life circumstances, like starting a new relationship, might open opportunities for doing more physical activity, since the new partner may motivate the person to exercise together; by contrast, unfavorable ones, like starting a new job, may reduce the person's efforts in exercising, since this activity may not fit in her everyday routines anymore. In other words, behavior change is only one aspect that people have to manage in their life among others and intertwines with many other conditions that make up their everydayness [52]. Persuasive technology, instead, often only targets the behavior to be modified, leaving unconsidered the other behaviors and the wider life context in which it is embedded: this may reduce its effectiveness, and even produce a variety of unexpected and unmanaged side effects, since the modification of the behavior may negatively impact on other aspects of the person's life (e.g., dieting may worsen the overall mood of the user or undermine her social life).

Of course, the "life context" in which behavior change is situated is extremely difficult to capture and consequently to act upon. This kind of context is subjective and made up of a variety of life circumstances, representing all those everyday conjunctures that the individual considers to be linked to the process of change: these do not necessarily refer to its immediate "surroundings" (e.g., the physical place where the behavior change happens), but entail the routines, practices, and relationships that are perceived as connected with the behavior to be changed [52]. Even the current advances in ubicomp technologies, allowing researchers to collect "objective data" about the behavior that were unmanageable until recent times [48], cannot capture the subjective nature of the wider context of life.

To this aim, the "help" provided by the person appears fundamental. However, as self-reporting is allegedly considered a burdensome task for the user (e.g., [54]), technology should provide ways to support them in this activity. In this sense, novel opportunities for persuasive design may be found in the world of games [63]. "Gameful" approaches could encourage users to report their own data and meanings about the circumstances that they consider relevant for the behavioral intervention within the enjoyable frame of the game. For example, a full-fledged "behavior change game" that puts great emphasis on the "fun factor" to make the gameplay engaging could foster self-reporting by making it appear as a task of the game. Moreover, by connecting the users' real-life behaviors with the gameplay, it could possibly change the meanings that they ascribe to the behavior, making them feel that behavior change is a game itself: for instance, walking more than usual could have an impact on their in-game performance, linking their daily steps to their endeavors in the game and providing supplementary meaning to the process of change [77].

3.6 Accounting for the Person's Life Time

The last challenge points to the temporality of behavior change, which is commonly circumscribed to the time of the behavioral intervention by current technologies (e.g., from when the individual shows the intention to change to the end of the behavioral program, possibly considering (close) subsequent follow-ups). However, in the people's experience, the temporality of behavior change is by no means so narrow, rather unfolding over long periods of time or even embracing their entire life course. In fact, we noticed that albeit changing behavior may result from a specific event that can trigger the person's willingness to undertake the change, most often the process cannot be limited to precise temporal boundaries: for many individuals, behavior change has roots in their distant past and is projected toward their distant future(s) [52]. In other words, it points to a long and complex "life time", which is the time that is experienced by the person in their everyday life, aligning with the subjective time of the phenomenology [64].

The flowing of this life time may transform the person's life circumstances and personality, as well as the meanings that are ascribed to the behavior, consequently affecting how behavior change is managed by them. Moreover, life time itself may be endowed with meanings potentially pointing to existential concerns, which may further impact the behavior change process: for instance, a person may apply the meanings that pervaded their past, when they perceived food as an emotional support, to the present time, negatively impacting their present attempts to lose weight.

Similarly, we found that the time of the important changes that people face in their life, like changes in relationships and work, deeply influence how they perceive, make sense of, and manage the change themselves [64]. For example, extremely slow changes risk going unnoticed, thus limiting the individual's possibilities to act upon the change, whereas fast changes may be experienced as anxious and worrisome; moreover, when the directionality of change is conceived as a progress, people may see more opportunities to steer the change, whereas when the direction of change is perceived as an involution, it may be lived as a fate that can only be accepted [64].

In this sense, the narrow time tackled by persuasive technologies may become problematic: by relying on the "clock time", which is objective, linear, exact and measurable [64], behavior change technologies mostly consider only the timeliness of the intervention [33], the management of relapses [1], or the duration of the person's adherence to the behavioral program [31], whereby the pasts and the futures addressed are only those that are close to the site of the intervention [28, 67]. In doing so, however, they do not acknowledge how people live the subjective time of the behavior change process.

Opportunities for moving forward persuasive technology design, therefore, may be found in all those alternative perspectives on time that have been explored by the HCI community, but are still not sufficiently applied to behavior change: those approaches that attempt to shape time by design, like the slow technology movement [20], which proposes slowness as encouragement for reflection [46]; those that focus on time as an existential concern [64], tying it to fundamental existential issues, like the desire for longevity and immortality, or the need to be remembered in the future [57], like

HCI work on aging [38], legacy [18], and death [44]. All these perspectives might be of inspiration for future research on persuasive designs. Anja, Memonile, Seaweed, and Woody, for example, are 4 artifacts supporting temporal experiences that challenge dominant conceptions of time, being designed to embed the Wabi-Sabi philosophy: this philosophy acknowledges that nothing lasts, nothing is finished, and nothing is perfect, encouraging people to experience the impermanence of time, while contrasting assumptions of timeless endurance entailed by traditional industrial design [74].

In this line, opportunities for research may lie in Virtual Reality (VR) technologies intervening on the subjective perception of behavior change time: for instance, by providing the user with simulations of how changes may evolve at different paces, such technologies may make visible how very small changes could produce bigger impacts in a distant future [64]. VR paired with Generative AI technology could further make the person experience alternate futures, encouraging them to change the meanings that they connect to the present behavior. For instance, an individual that is thinking that exercising is not worthy of their time could be prompted with virtual scenarios generated by the AI, in which their alternate selves live different possible futures, highlighting the consequences of persisting or not in their attempts to change.

4 Conclusion

In this paper, we outlined six relevant HCI challenges that persuasive technologies need to tackle in the near future to account for the complexity of behavior change dynamics, going beyond the more simplistic "behavioral model", which considers the target behavior to be modified as an objective, isolated, and fragmented phenomenon. More precisely, we pointed out that the HCI community should focus on *meaning* rather than on the target behavior to be modified; should support *reflection* rather than the rational analysis of data; should promote the person's *agency* rather than driving the behavior from the outside; should address the *living body*, rather than the physiological body; should consider the person's *life context* for designing the intervention, rather than the physical context; and should account for the person's *life time* when settling the behavioral program, rather than the objective time of the technology.

These challenges are meant to be considered together with the "existential model of behavior change" [52], which we have defined after more than a decade of research on behavior change and on how people experience and live persuasive and tracking technologies. The model, which is extensively recounted in a TOCHI article entitled *"Exploring the Lived Experience of Behavior Change Technologies: Towards an Existential Model of Behavior Change for HCI"* [52], is thought of as an alternative to the dominant behavioral model of change: it gives value to the subjective meanings that people develop throughout their lives and ascribe to the process of change, and accounts for the existential matters that are intertwined with behavior change attempts, thus shifting the focus from the behavior to be modified to the life (time and context) in which it is situated.

We hope that both the challenges and the model will pave the way for novel lines of research, enabling researchers to explore alternative paths for effectively supporting people in modifying their own behavior. Ideally, these research directions should originate from an understanding of people's subjective experience and perception of change, rather than relying solely on external prescriptive design suggestions.

References

1. Agapie, E., Avrahami, D., Marlow, J.: Staying the course: system-driven lapse management for supporting behavior change. In: Proceedings of the 2016 CHI Conference on Human Factors in Computing Systems (CHI 2016), pp. 1072–1083. ACM, New York, NY (2016)
2. Bandura, A.: Social Foundations of Thought and Action: A Social Cognitive Theory. Prentice-Hall Inc., Englewood Cliffs (1986)
3. Bhattacharya, A., Vilardaga, R., Kientz, J.A., Munson, S.A.: Lessons from practice: designing tools to facilitate individualized support for quitting smoking. In: Proceedings of the 2017 CHI Conference on Human Factors in Computing Systems (CHI 2017), pp. 3057–3070. ACM, New York, NY (2017)
4. Boldi, A., Rapp, A.: Quantifying the body: body image, body awareness and self-tracking technologies. In: Wac, K., Wulfovich, S. (eds.) Quantifying Quality of Life. HI, pp. 189–207. Springer, Cham (2022). https://doi.org/10.1007/978-3-030-94212-0_9
5. Boldi, A., et al.: Exploring the impact of commercial wearable activity trackers on body awareness and body representations: a mixed-methods study on self-tracking. Comput. Hum. Behav. **151**, 108036 (2024)
6. Caraban, A., Karapanos, E., Gonçalves, D., Campos, P.: 23 Ways to nudge: a review of technology-mediated nudging in human–computer interaction. In: Proceedings of the 2019 CHI Conference on Human Factors in Computing Systems (CHI 2019), pp. 1–15. ACM, New York, NY (2019)
7. Cho, J., Xu, T., Zimmermann-Niefield, A., Voida, S.: Reflection in theory and reflection in practice: An exploration of the gaps in reflection support among personal informatics apps. In: Proceedings of the 2022 CHI Conference on Human Factors in Computing Systems (CHI 2022), pp. 1–23. ACM, New York, NY (2022)
8. Cooper, J.O., Heron, T.E., Heward, W. L.: Applied Behavior Analysis. Pearson/Merrill-Prentice Hall Upper Saddle River, NJ (2007)
9. De Choudhury, M., Pendse, S.R., Kumar, N.: Benefits and Harms of Large Language Models in Digital Mental Health. arXiv preprint arXiv:2311.14693 (2023)
10. Delazio, A., Nakagaki, K., Klatzky, R.L., Hudson, S.E., Fain Lehman, J., Sample, A.P.: Force jacket: pneumatically-actuated jacket for embodied haptic experiences. In: Proceedings of the 2018 CHI Conference on Human Factors in Computing Systems (CHI 2018), pp. 1–12. ACM, New York, NY, USA (2018)
11. Epstein, D., Cordeiro, F., Bales, E., Fogarty, J., Munson, S.: Taming data complexity in lifelogs: exploring visual cuts of personal informatics data. In: Proceedings of the Conference on Designing interactive Systems (DIS 2014), pp. 667–676. ACM, New York, NY (2014)
12. Fogg, B.J.: A behavior model for persuasive design. In: Proceedings of the 4th International Conference on Persuasive Technology (Persuasive 2009), pp. 1–7. ACM, New York, NY (2009)
13. Gao, F., Costanza, E., Schraefel, M.C.: "Honey=sugar" means unhealthy: investigating how people apply knowledge to rate food's healthiness. In: Proceedings of the 2012 ACM Conference on Ubiquitous Computing (UbiComp 2012), pp. 71–80. ACM, New York, NY (2012)
14. Gaver, W.W., Beaver, J., Benford, S.: Ambiguity as a resource for design. In: CHI 2003: Proceedings of the SIGCHI Conference on Human Factors in Computing Systems, pp. 233–240. ACM Inc., Ft. Lauderdale, Florida (2003)

15. Gentile, V., Mylonopoulou, V.: Exploiting social comparison using pervasive displays and mobile notifications for reducing energy consumption. In: Proceedings of the 6th ACM International Symposium on Pervasive Displays (PerDis 2017), pp. 1–2. ACM, New York, NY (2017)

16. Gibb, A., Cook, S., Nyateka, N., Bust, P., Jones, W., Finneran, A.: Wearable simulations for ill-health conditions in construction. Proc. Inst. Civil Eng. Civil Eng. **168**(6), 51–56 (2015). https://doi.org/10.1680/cien.14.00055

17. Gulotta, R., Kelliher, A., Forlizzi, J.: Digital systems and the experience of legacy. In: Proceedings of the 2017 Conference on Designing Interactive Systems (DIS 2017), pp. 663–674. ACM, New York, NY, USA (2017)

18. Gulotta, R., Odom, W., Faste, H., Forlizzi, J.: Legacy in the age of the internet: reflections on how interactive systems shape how we are remembered. In: Proceedings of the 2014 conference on Designing interactive systems (DIS 2014), pp. 975–984. ACM, New York, NY, USA (2014)

19. Gunaratne, J., Nov, O.: Informing and improving retirement saving performance using behavioral economics theory-driven user interfaces. In: Proceedings of the 33rd Annual ACM Conference on Human Factors in Computing Systems (CHI 2015), pp. 917–920. ACM, New York, NY (2015)

20. Hallnäs, L., Redström, J.: Slow technology – designing for reflection. Pers. Ubiquit. Comput. **5**(3), 201–212 (2001)

21. Halttu, K., Oinas-Kukkonen, H.: Persuading to reflect: Role of reflection and insight in persuasive systems design for physical health. Human-Comput. Interact. **32**(5–6), 381–412 (2017)

22. Hamari, J., Koivisto, J., Pakkanen, T.: Do persuasive technologies persuade? - A review of empirical studies. In: Spagnolli, A., Chittaro, L., Gamberini, L. (eds.) Persuasive Technology. LNCS, vol. 8462, pp. 118–136. Springer, Cham (2014). https://doi.org/10.1007/978-3-319-07127-5_11

23. Hekler, E.B., Klasnja, P., Froehlich, J.E., Buman, M.P.: Mind the theoretical gap: interpreting, using, and developing behavioral theory in HCI research. In: Proceedings of the SIGCHI Conference on Human Factors in Computing Systems (CHI 2013), pp. 3307–3316. ACM, New York, NY (2013)

24. Hermsen, S., Frost, J., Renes, R.J., Kerkhof, P.: Using feedback through digital technology to disrupt and change habitual behavior: a critical review of current literature. Comput. Hum. Behav. **57**, 61–74 (2016)

25. Hilviu, D., Rapp, A.: Narrating the quantified self. In: Adjunct Proceedings of the 2015 ACM International Joint Conference on Pervasive and Ubiquitous Computing and Proceedings of the 2015 ACM International Symposium on Wearable Computers (UbiComp/ISWC 2015 Adjunct), pp. 1051–1056. ACM, New York (2015)

26. Howell, N., Devendorf, L., Vega Gálvez, T.A., Tian, R., Ryokai, K.: Tensions of data-driven reflection: A case study of real-time emotional biosensing. In: CHI 2018. Proceedings of the SIGCHI Conference on Human Factors in Computing Systems, vol. 2018-April, pp. 1–13. ACM Inc., New York, NY (2018)

27. Jones, J., Ackerman, M.S.: Co-constructing family memory: understanding the intergenerational practices of passing on family stories. In: Proceedings of the 2018 CHI Conference on Human Factors in Computing Systems (CHI 2018), pp. 1–13. ACM, New York, NY, USA (2018)

28. Kersten-van Dijk, E.T., Westerink, J.H.D.M., Beute, F., IJsselsteijn, W.A.: Personal informatics, self-insight, and behavior change: a critical review of current literature. Human–Comput. Interact. **32**(5–6), 268–296 (2017)

29. Khot, R.A.: Exploring material representations of physical activity. In: Proceedings of the 2014 Companion Publication on Designing Interactive Systems (DIS Companion 2014), pp. 177–180. ACM, New York, NY (2014)

30. Konrad, A., Isaacs, E., Whittaker, S.: Technology-mediated memory: Is technology altering our memories and interfering with well-being? ACM Trans. Comput. Human Interact. **23**(4), 29 (2016)

31. Kovacs, G., Wu, Z., Bernstein, M.S.: Not now, ask later: users weaken their behavior change regimen over time, but expect to re-strengthen it imminently. In: Proceedings of the 2021 CHI Conference on Human Factors in Computing Systems (CHI 2021), pp. 1–14. ACM, New York, NY (2021)

32. Lazar, A., Koehler, C., Tanenbaum, J., Nguyen, D.H.: Why we use and abandon smart devices. In: Proceedings of the UbiComp 2011 Conference on Ubiquitous Computing. ACM, New York, NY (2015)

33. Lee, J., Walker, E., Burleson, W., Kay, M., Buman, M., Hekler, E.B.: Self-experimentation for behavior change: design and formative evaluation of two approaches. In: Proceedings of the 2017 CHI Conference on Human Factors in Computing Systems (CHI 2017), pp. 6837–6849. ACM, New York, NY (2017)

34. Lee, M.K., Kiesler, S., Forlizzi, J.: Mining behavioral economics to design persuasive technology for healthy choices. In: Proceedings of the SIGCHI Conference on Human Factors in Computing Systems (CHI'11), pp. 325–334. Association for Computing Machinery, New York, NY (2011)

35. Lee, M.K., Kim, J., Forlizzi, J., Kiesler, S.: Personalization revisited: a reflective approach helps people better personalize health services and motivates them to increase physical activity. In: Proceedings of the 2015 ACM International Joint Conference on Pervasive and Ubiquitous Computing (UbiComp 2015), pp. 743–754. ACM, New York, NY (2015)

36. Lim, C.Y., et al.: Facilitating self-reflection about values and self-care among individuals with chronic conditions. In: Proceedings of the 2019 CHI Conference on Human Factors in Computing Systems (CHI 2019), pp. 1–12. ACM, New York, NY (2019)

37. Liu, X., Qian, Y.: If you were a tree. http://www.media.mit.edu/posts/tree-treesense/MitMediaLab. Accessed 01 Nov 2018

38. Loup, J., Subasi, Ö., Fitzpatrick, G.: Aging, HCI, & personal perceptions of time. In: Proceedings of the 2017 CHI Conference Extended Abstracts on Human Factors in Computing Systems (CHI EA 2017), pp. 1853–1860. ACM, New York, NY, USA (2017)

39. Luo, Y., Lee, B., Wohn, D.Y., Rebar, A.L., Conroy, D.E., Choe, E.K.: Time for break: understanding information workers' sedentary behavior through a break prompting system. In: Proceedings of the 2018 CHI Conference on Human Factors in Computing Systems (CHI 2018), pp. 1–14. ACM, New York, NY (2018)

40. Lupton, D.: M-health and health promotion: the digital cyborg and surveillance society. Soc. Theory Health **10**, 229–244 (2012)

41. Lupton, D.: Quantifying the body: monitoring and measuring health in the age of mHealth technologies. Crit. Public Health **23**, 393–403 (2013)

42. Lupton, D.: You are your data: self-tracking practices and concepts of data. In: Selke, S. (ed.) Lifelogging, pp. 61–79. Springer VS, Wiesbaden (2016)

43. Mamykina, L., Mynatt, E.D., Kaufman, D.R.: Investigating health management practices of individuals with diabetes. In: Proceedings of the SIGCHI Conference on Human Factors in Computing Systems (CHI 2006), pp. 927–936. ACM, NY (2006)

44. Moncur, W., Bikker, J., Kasket, E., Troyer, J.: From death to final disposition: roles of technology in the post-mortem interval. In: Proceedings of the SIGCHI Conference on Human Factors in Computing Systems (CHI 2012), pp. 531–540. ACM, New York, NY, USA (2012)

45. Nafus, D., et al.: As simple as possible but no simpler: creating flexibility in personal informatics. In: Proceedings of the 2016 CHI Conference Extended Abstracts on Human Factors in Computing Systems (CHI EA 2016), pp. 1445–1452. ACM, New York, NY (2016)

46. Odom, W., Banks, R., Durrant, A., Kirk, D., Pierce, J.: Slow technology: critical reflection and future directions. In: Proceedings of the Designing Interactive Systems Conference (DIS 2012), pp. 816–817. ACM, New York, NY, USA (2012)

47. Orji, R., Moffatt, K.: Persuasive technology for health and wellness: state-of-the-art and emerging trends. Health Inform. J. **24**(1), 66–91 (2018)

48. Perera, C., Zaslavsky, A., Christen, P., Georgakopoulos, D.: Context aware computing for the internet of things: a survey. IEEE Commun. Surv. Tutor. **16**(1), 414–454 (2014)

49. Pinder, C., Vermeulen, J., Cowan, B.R., Beale, R.: Digital behaviour change interventions to break and form habits. ACM Trans. Comput.-Human Interact. **25**(3), 1–66 (2018). https://doi.org/10.1145/3196830

50. Prochaska, J.O., Velicer, W.F.: The transtheoretical model of health behavior change. Am. J. Health Promot. **12**(1), 38–48 (1997)

51. Purpura, S., Schwanda, V., Williams, K., Stubler, W., Sengers, P.: Fit4life: the design of a persuasive technology promoting healthy behavior and ideal weight. In: Proceedings of the SIGCHI Conference on Human Factors in Computing Systems (CHI 2011), pp. 423–432. ACM, New York, NY, USA (2011)

52. Rapp, A., Boldi, A.: Exploring the lived experience of behavior change technologies: towards an existential model of behavior change for HCI. ACM Trans. Comput. Human Interact. **30**(6), 1–50 (2023). https://doi.org/10.1145/3603497

53. Rapp, A., Cena, F.: Affordances for self-tracking wearable devices. In: Proceedings of International Symposium on Wearable Computers, ISWC 2015, pp. 141–142. ACM, New York (2015)

54. Rapp, A., Cena, F.: Personal informatics for everyday life: how users without prior self-tracking experience engage with personal data. Int. J. Human-Comput. Stud. **94**, 1–17 (2016). https://doi.org/10.1016/j.ijhcs.2016.05.006

55. Rapp, A., Curti, L., Boldi, A.: The human side of human-chatbot interaction: a systematic literature review of ten years of research on text-based chatbots. Int. J. Human-Comput. Stud. **151**, 102630 (2021)

56. Rapp, A., Marcengo, A., Buriano, L., Ruffo, G., Lai, M., Cena, F.: Designing a personal informatics system for users without experience in self-tracking: a case study. Behav. Inf. Technol. **37**(4), 335–366 (2018)

57. Rapp, A., Odom, W., Pschetz, L., Petrelli, D.: Introduction to the special issue on time and HCI. Human-Comput. Interact. **37**(1), 1–14 (2022)

58. Rapp, A., Tirabeni, L.: Personal informatics for sport: meaning, body, and social relations in amateur and elite athletes. ACM Trans. Comput. Human Interact. **25**(3), 1–30 (2018). https://doi.org/10.1145/3196829

59. Rapp, A., Tirabeni, L.: Self-tracking while doing sport: comfort, motivation, attention and lifestyle of athletes using personal informatics tools. Int. J. Hum Comput Stud. **140**, 102434 (2020)

60. Rapp, A., Tirassa, M., Tirabeni, L.: Rethinking technologies for behavior change: a view from the inside of human change. ACM Trans. Comput. Human Interact. **26**(4), 1–30 (2019). https://doi.org/10.1145/3318142

61. Rapp, A., Tirassa, M.: Know thyself: a theory of the self for personal informatics. Human-Comput. Interact. **32**(5–6), 335–380 (2017)

62. Rapp, A.: Design fictions for behaviour change: Exploring the long-term impacts of technology through the creation of fictional future prototypes. Behav. Inf. Technol. **38**(3), 244–272 (2019)

63. Rapp, A.: Gamification for self-tracking: from world of warcraft to the design of personal informatics systems. In: Proceedings of the 2018 CHI Conference on Human Factors in Computing Systems (CHI 2018), 15p. ACM, New York, NY, USA, Paper 80 (2018)

64. Rapp, A.: How do people experience the temporality of everyday life changes? Towards the exploration of existential time in HCI. Int. J. Human Comput. Stud. **167**(102899), 1–14 (2022)

65. Rapp, A.: Wearable technologies as extensions: a postphenomenological framework and its design implications. Human-Comput. Interact. **38**(2), 79–117 (2023)

66. Ren, X., Yu, B., Lu, Y., Brombacher, A.: Exploring cooperative fitness tracking to encourage physical activity among office workers. Proc. ACM Human-Comput. Interact. **2**(CSCW), 1–20 (2018). https://doi.org/10.1145/3274415

67. Rho, S., et al.: FutureSelf: what happens when we forecast self-trackers' future health statuses? In: Proceedings of the 2017 Conference on Designing Interactive Systems (DIS 2017), pp. 637–648. ACM, New York, NY (2017)

68. Ruckenstein, M., Pantzar, M.: Beyond the quantified self: thematic exploration of a dataistic paradigm. New Media Soc. **19**, 401–418 (2017)

69. Rutjes, H., Willemsen, M.C., IJsselsteijn, W.A.: Beyond behavior: the coach's perspective on technology in health coaching. In: Proceedings of the 2019 CHI Conference on Human Factors in Computing Systems (CHI 2019), pp. 1–14. ACM, New York, NY (2019)

70. Saksono, H., Castaneda-Sceppa, C., Hoffman, J., Seif El-Nasr, M., Morris, V., Parker, A.G.: Social reflections on fitness tracking data: a study with families in Low-SES neighborhoods. In: Proceedings of the 2019 CHI Conference on Human Factors in Computing Systems (CHI 2019), pp. 1–14. ACM, New York, NY (2019)

71. Schechtman, M.: Stories, lives and basic survival: a refinement and defense of the narrative view. R. Inst. Philos. Suppl. **60**, 155–178 (2007)

72. Schüll, N.D.: Data for life: wearable technology and the design of self-care. BioSocieties **11**, 317–333 (2016)

73. Thaler, R.H., Sunstein, C.R.: Nudge: Improving Decisions About Health, Wealth. And Happiness. Yale University Press, New Haven (2008)

74. Tsaknaki, V., Fernaeus, Y.: Expanding on Wabi-Sabi as a design resource in HCI. In: Proceedings of the 2016 CHI Conference on Human Factors in Computing Systems (CHI 2016), pp. 5970–5983. ACM, New York, NY, USA (2016)

75. van Dijk, E.T., Westerink, J.H.D.M., Beute, F., Ijsselsteijn, W.A.: In sync: the effect of physiology feedback on the match between heart rate and self-reported stress. BioMed Res. Int. **2015**, 1–9 (2015). https://doi.org/10.1155/2015/134606

76. Villamarín-Salomón, R.M., Brustoloni, J.C.: Using reinforcement to strengthen users' secure behaviors. In: Proceedings of the SIGCHI Conference on Human Factors in Computing Systems (CHI 2010), pp. 363–372. ACM, New York, NY (2010)

77. Villata, S., Rapp, A., Cena, F.: Towards an adaptive behavior change game based on user-tailored and context-aware interventions. In: Proceedings of the International Workshop on Behavior Change and Persuasive Recommender Systems at the 17th ACM RecSys 2023. CEUR Workshop Proceedings, vol. 3544 (2023)

78. Zamfirescu-Pereira, J.D., Wong, R.Y., Hartmann, B., Yang, Q.: Why Johnny Can't prompt: how non-AI experts try (and Fail) to design LLM prompts. In: Proceedings of the 2023 CHI Conference on Human Factors in Computing Systems (CHI 2023), Article 437, pp. 1–21. ACM, New York, NY (2023)

iCare: Findings from the Design and Initial Evaluation of a Mental Health App Prototype for Working-Class Women in India

Jaisheen Kour Reen$^{(\boxtimes)}$ ⓘ, Aniefiok Friday ⓘ, Gerry Chan ⓘ, and Rita Orji ⓘ

Faculty of Computer Science, Dalhousie University, Halifax, NS, Canada
js346515@dal.ca

Abstract. Researchers have long recognized women's prevalence of stress, anxiety, and depression. The role of a professional or a housewife can significantly negatively impact stress and anxiety, so a better understanding of gender as a social predictor of workplace health is required. In this paper, we designed a mental health app prototype iCare which was evaluated by 40 women to determine the perceived effectiveness of mobile health apps in helping working-class Indian women to manage stress. Based on our qualitative study, we found that the Aesthetics, Anonymity, Customization, Personalization, Usefulness of Feedback Provided by the App, App User Interface, and Effectiveness of the App for Stress and Anxiety Management, are critical needs of this target audience from an app of this type. We believe that India and many countries in Africa share numerous similarities, particularly in the experiences of working-class women. Thus, the findings from this research can be effectively applied to an African context as well.

Keywords: Persuasive Strategies · Personalization · Mental Health · Working-Class Indian Women · Well-Being

1 Introduction

Mental health is an essential aspect of overall well-being. The World Health Organization (WHO) defines health as more than just physical well-being; it also encompasses mental well-being [1]. The high frequency of psychological stress, anxiety, and depression in women has been widely acknowledged worldwide [2]. In 2011, the American Psychological Association (APA) advised that stress is becoming a public health crisis [3]. The National Institute of Mental Health director has described technological approaches to mental health care as "likely…crucial," implying interest in research and innovation in this area by both government and practitioners [4]. Although the mental health care system has traditionally prioritized the treatment of mental disorders over prevention, it is now widely acknowledged that mental wellness is more than just the absence of mental illness [5]. For example, stress and anxiety are viewed as challenges to mental health conditions [6], and stress is a growing problem, and each person requires a different

M. Kurosu and A. Hashizume (Eds.): HCII 2024, LNCS 14686, pp. 117–132, 2024.
https://doi.org/10.1007/978-3-031-60428-7_9

approach to deal with it because they are different. Research suggests that women are substantially more prone than men to stress and anxiety problems during their lives [7]. Particularly in a developing country like India, where discussing topics such as mental health is still considered taboo [8], people who are going through mental distress ignore sharing it with their family members or life partners to avoid becoming the cause of their stress, cause panic [9], and to avoid being stereotyped.

Some people are uncomfortable sharing their thoughts with another individual, making it more challenging to reach the root cause of stress. According to Karampela, Ouhbi, and Isomursu [10], there appear to be differences in the acceptability of sharing information with doctors versus having it linked into a more broadly accessible electronic medical record for persons with depression and anxiety. Understanding how these difficulties impact modern user perceptions is an important research goal because digital health relies on patients' and the general public's willingness to use technologies like applications (apps). Mobile health (mHealth) interventions can enable patients to become active participants in their healthcare plan while remaining in a secure environment. Despite all these efforts, there are very few studies focusing on mHealth interventions for stress management, particularly for women. Most notably, while most existing apps cater to people in Western countries, our research finds little or no apps targeting women from developing countries, especially working-class women. Our study aims to fill this gap by focusing on marginalized groups such as working-class (people who are part of the workforce) Indian women using a user-centric design approach [11].

In this research, our goal is to investigate how mobile apps can be designed to help working-class Indian women manage their mental health by looking into their mental health challenges, causes, techniques they use to manage their stress, and their needs for apps that can help them manage their mental health. In this study, we asked the participants to evaluate a prototype (iCare) of a mental health app. iCare was used to test the interaction, navigation, and effectiveness of the features and simulate the user experience before the development of a fully functional app.

iCare was designed based on the insights drawing on the work of Reen and Orji [12]. iCare uses persuasive technology, which is intended to "change attitudes or behaviors or both (without using coercion or deception)" [13], and Persuasive Strategies to "motivate users and help them to achieve their goals better" [14]. We used eight Persuasive Strategies in our design. The Persuasive Strategies were adopted from the Persuasive System Design (PSD) model [15], as this model could be used to analyze the potential persuasiveness of the system [16]. The Persuasive Strategies used in our design are Customization, Feedback, Self-monitoring, Rehearsal, Praise, Tunneling, Reminder, and Social Facilitation.

2   Related Works

2.1   mHealth and HCI

mHealth apps can minimize appointment wait times, eliminate the need to meet with a clinician in person, reduce the strain on mental health practitioners, be more cost-effective for practices, and encourage self-care techniques [17, 18]. A growing number of these apps are geared toward assisting people who are dealing with mental health concerns such as stress, anxiety, depression, Post-Traumatic Stress Disorder (PTSD), and Obsessive-Compulsive Disorder (OCD), but are not limited to these mental health concerns [17]. Furthermore, mHealth apps can encourage people to be more honest about their mental health symptoms [19]. This demonstrates the app's efficacy, as it is critical for a patient to be open about their mental health to receive the best medical care. Also, the capacity of technology-enabled interventions' to scale and lower entrance obstacles such as cost and stigma can help alleviate some of the burdens of mental illness [14]. For example, in one study, Moberg, Niles, and Beermann [14] conducted a randomized control trial with an intervention and control group. Results showed that popular, commercially available guided self-help tools can help people manage stress, anxiety, and depression symptoms while also increasing self-efficacy.

Furthermore, Wang, Varma, and Prosperi [20] systematically reviewed 17 full-text articles describing mental health apps and reported that mobile apps for mental health can monitor or improve symptoms of a variety of mental disorders, including anxiety, stress, alcoholism, sleep difficulties, depression, suicidal behavior, and PTSD. Hwang [21] conducted a randomized control experiment with 56 nurses in which the effectiveness of a mental healthcare app built for workers to self-manage stress and use mental healthcare programs such as meditation, music, and yoga through the app was evaluated. According to the findings, stress management software significantly enhanced mental health. In a different study, Coelhoso et al. [5] conducted a randomized controlled trial with 490 females to evaluate the effectiveness of an app developed to promote stress management and well-being among working women. Both groups showed a significant improvement in overall happiness over time. Still, only the intervention group experienced a substantial rise in work-related satisfaction as well as a significant reduction in work-related and general stress.

2.2 Designing for Women from Low-Resource Communities

There is observed evidence suggesting that women suffer much more from mental health issues than men, this observation holds even when factors such as perceived work circumstances and traditional gender roles are taken into account [22]. For example, in one interview study, Reen, and Orji [12] interviewed 31 working-class Indian women to better understand how they deal with mental health issues and what they felt about the design of mental health apps. Results revealed that participants used the following strategies to deal with their mental health issues: *"doing something to distract themselves from their current negative mood, using relaxation exercises and methods to relieve symptoms, trying to be alone"* [12].

Even though a significant amount of research has been done to understand users' impressions of mental health app design, the above-mentioned gender difference has not been considered broadly and more importantly among women in developing countries where significant gender differences exist. This study primarily focuses on understanding the strategies used by Indian women participants (who have experienced/experiencing mental health issues) to deal with mental health issues in their lives, their perspectives, and opinions about popular mental health apps, and how these strategies and ideas could be leveraged in the design of a mental health app, all of which have received little attention in previous studies.

2.3 Gaps in the Literature

One of the gaps observed in existing works is the low use of Digital Recovery Support Services (D-RSS) and gender-based mHealth in addressing stress among working-class women. At the time of our study, research on D-RSS and mHealth, in general, did not focus on the needs of working-class women in developing economies [23]. Also, we found limited information on the broad adoption of both mobile and web tools in managing stress amongst working-class women in our target audience. Contrasting this with findings from Curtis et al. [23] where community or social support groups were identified to play a vital role in helping patients recover. Women in developing economies like India are faced with possible stigma in discussing mental health conditions or seeking support from family and friends [12].

Another gap we observed in the existing literature includes the limitation of stress apps in addressing working women in different phases and marital statuses. Working-class women comprise different categories which can include but are not limited to single mothers, widows, divorcees, and married women to name a few. We found limited information on how stress is managed by these subgroups of working-class women. A study by Sawyer et al. [24] shows mobile intervention can be helpful for mothers dealing with pressure from childbirth and postnatal depression. However, there was not sufficient data to indicate what stressors can lead to stress in mothers who may still be actively engaged at work as is common in developing economies.

Given previous research findings, the mobile intervention was considered a good choice for our current work despite its identified limitations. Similar to the results by Fischer et al. [13] investigated the impact of using a sensor and a mobile tablet to monitor user stress and sleep patterns to help users better manage stress, we believe our work will enable users to perform self-management by using a mood tracker along with other features like meditation music, and a diary or voice memo to manage their mental health.

This study fills a gap in the literature by pointing out that socio-cultural contexts are not considered when designing mHealth interventions. It also suggests that these socio-cultural contexts be considered and addressed systematically by defining a design process for involving users in mHealth interventions. Our work attempts to advance knowledge about designing for cultural groups considering this.

3   iCare Design and Features

The app prototype features are designed mostly from the findings of a research study conducted by Reen and Orji [12] which involved 31 working-class Indian women. The prototype was designed using proto.io [25]. Participants in their research mentioned that the key requirements in a mental health app are features such as being able to relax and practice meditation in their own free time, learn task management, and opportunities to express their feelings in the form of writing or voice notes and dedicate time for their hobbies or activities.

(a). The home screen displays all the features in the app.

(b). Mood Tracker helps the user to track their mood.

Fig. 1. Example screenshots of the iCare prototype.

This section describes the different prototype features of iCare. Table 1 shows all the features, their purpose, and the Persuasive Strategies implemented, while Fig. 1 shows the Home Screen and Mood Tracker features of the iCare prototype.

Table 1. iCare features, purpose, and persuasive strategies.

Features	Purpose	Persuasive Strategies
Welcome page	Provides users with a place where they are greeted by their chosen name	N/A
Profile page	It represents the user, containing their details	Customization
Home screen	Contains the entire menu of the prototype (Fig. 1a)	Feedback, Tunneling
Hobby corner	Helps the user to add their hobbies and set and create timers to perform them	Self-monitoring, Praise, and Customization
Meditation music, and breathe	Helps the users to relax their minds and control their breathing	Tunneling, Customization
Mood tracker	Helps the user to monitor their mood (Fig. 1b)	Self-monitoring

(*continued*)

Table 1. (*continued*)

Features	Purpose	Persuasive Strategies
Diary, voice memo, and gratitude corner	Helps the user to be expressive	Self-monitoring
Self-awareness	Creates awareness among the user regarding important topics of life	Tunneling
To do, reminder	Helps the users in task and time management	Reminders
Social community	Helps the user to be a part of the community	Social facilitation
Settings	Gives the option to set up a fingerprint and change the theme	Customization

4 Method

Upon receiving clearance from our institutional ethics review board, we advertised the study on social media, including LinkedIn, Facebook, and WhatsApp. The study is divided into three steps: (1) a pre-study questionnaire (to check eligibility criteria and individuals' awareness of mHealth apps), (2) the usability of the prototype before the interview, and (3) one-on-one interviews (to collect feedback about the prototype). To analyze the interview data, we performed a thematic analysis [26]. This section discusses the procedures we followed to collect and analyze our data. The following sections discussed these steps in more detail.

4.1 Selection Criteria

We conducted the study with 40 working-class Indian women who were experiencing or have experienced mental health issues such as stress, anxiety or depression, or mood swings based on self-diagnosis. Participants must be working-class Indian women living in India, know basic English, and be at least 18 years of age. Participants must also be individuals who are experiencing or have experienced mental health issues such as stress or anxiety or low mood or negative feelings or thoughts or worry or fear or panic attack, or depression based on self-diagnosis, and must own a mobile phone to run the prototype on a browser. Table 2 summarizes the demographic information of the participants.

Table 2. Participants' characteristics ($N = 40$).

Characteristics	Percentage
Mental health apps used	Did not use (72.5%), Use (27.5%)
Age	18–24 (40%), 25–34 (45%), 35–44 (15%)
Marital Status	Single (62.5%), married (32.5%), divorced (2.5%), widowed (2.5)
Education	Bachelor's degree (50%), master's degree (50%)

4.2 Study Procedure

Our pre-study questionnaire had a total of six questions, constituting demographics and awareness about mHealth apps. This filtered participants who matched our inclusion criteria and understood their attention regarding mHealth apps. After selecting participants who met the inclusion criteria, we invited them to use iCare for at least five minutes. Participants were also provided with a video explaining how to use the prototype. After using the prototype (Fig. 1), the participants were invited for one-on-one interviews lasting 30 min. The one-on-one format further allowed each participant to share their thoughts about the design and offer recommendations to improve the app and their views on the prototype. All interviews were conducted over Microsoft Teams [27], which was approved by the research ethics board of our university. The interview questions also focused on the support features like the ability to customize the user interface and we asked questions related to all the features in the prototype and whether they would want to have it modified, their reasoning behind any changes, and how they will use it.

4.3 Data Collection and Analysis

Interviews were voice recorded and transcribed using Microsoft Teams. Then, we conducted a thematic analysis to analyze the collected data. A thematic analysis was chosen because it allows us to evaluate a large data set systematically, revealing patterns in the text while considering the context of what participants said, allowing us to interpret the data. Mainly, all the responses were fed into NVivo 12 Pro[1], a qualitative and mixed-methods research software tool used to analyze the unstructured text, audio, video, and picture data, such as interviews, focus groups, and surveys [28]. We used NVivo because it is a popular tool used in Human-Computer Interaction research to conduct qualitative analysis [29]. Data were assigned to different sections following the thematic codes generated. We used an inductive approach (extracting meaning and identifying themes from data with no preconceived ideas [30]) to generate the codes.

A thematic analysis was undertaken as suggested by Braun and Clarke [31] following a six-step process: (1) understanding the data, (2) creating initial codes, (3) looking for themes, (4) defining themes, (5) iteratively reviewing themes, and (6) reporting the findings. The thematic analysis of our user responses indicated that participants had an overall perception of these features as being effective in managing stress.

---

[1] NVivo 12 Pro: https://lumivero.com/products/nvivo/.

5   Results

After exploring all the features proposed in the prototype, participants shared their opinions on what they liked or disliked and offered a variety of design suggestions for improving the app. Our thematic analysis identified nine core themes: (1) The Importance of Aesthetics, (2) The Benefits of Being Anonymous, (3) The Power of Customization, (4) The Power of Personalization, (5) The Effectiveness of the App for Stress and Anxiety Management, (6) The Usefulness of Feedback Provided by the App, (7) User Interface of the Prototype, (8) Finding a Safe Space, and (9) Suggestions for Improving the Design of the App. The sample comments are presented with minor spelling and grammatical corrections.

5.1   Theme 1: The Importance of Aesthetics

Aesthetics is defined as "the study of the mind and emotions concerning the sense of beauty" of a thing [32]. In the context of User Interface, aesthetics can be defined as a fundamental design principle that makes a design appealing [33]. Aesthetics comprises elements like balance, color, movement, pattern, scale, shape, and visual weight in terms of the visible world. The notion of beauty does not only apply to artworks but is seen to play an important role even in persuasive apps.

We attempted to achieve aesthetics in our prototype using color, font types, images, and whitespaces (white areas surrounding a page's content and valuable features. White space's primary purpose is to create breathing room for your design by minimizing the quantity of text and functional items people view at once [34]). Our study shows that participants highlighted aesthetics as essential to the stress and anxiety management app. In particular, users commented on the Breathe, Mood Tracker, Hobby Corner, and Setting features had content relating to aesthetics. For example, one participant mentioned that providing them with the option to change the app theme in the setting feature can change their mood, when they said "*I think these are all **great features in settings**. Maybe one day, I can pick another color and just **change the background theme** and **it can lift my mood**"* [P1].

Furthermore, many participants were impressed by the change of color in the Breathe feature and attempted it even though it was a prototype. For example, one participant thought that "*Breathe is one of the best features of this app. **I am personally looking forward to using this feature**"* [P3], while a different participant said "*I liked the Breathe feature. I was even doing it even though it is a prototype. It is awe-inspiring and **I like the color change**"* [P4]. Some participants also mentioned that they liked the interface of the app when one participant said "*I **liked the confetti falling** from the message in the hobby corner…"* [P10].

5.2   Theme 2: The Benefits of Being Anonymous

Anonymity is defined as "the state or quality of being anonymous" [35]. Previous studies on anonymity have shown that it affects users' reporting on mental health conditions. For example, Fear, Seddon, Jones, Greenberg and Wessely [36] researched the effect of anonymity in reporting mental health among veterans. Their work shows that anonymity in a psychological questionnaire has implications for mental health screening. They found an increase in the prevalence of PTSD and stigmatizing beliefs when using an anonymous questionnaire compared to an identifiable questionnaire. In the iCare app, participants would be able to use an anonymous username to post in the social community and communicate with fellow users.

For example, participants mentioned that they would feel safe sharing their feelings with others without the fear of judgment and knowing that people are also in the same situation when one participant said: *"I think this is great. **We feel we can talk whatever, as our identities are anonymous"** [P11], while another participant said "It **will be anonymous, and we can share without the fear of judgment"** [P22]. However, participants mentioned that apart from being anonymous, they should be able to report any danger when one participant explained that "It is **good to talk and be anonymous** in the social community. I should be able to report to any user** I do not feel I am safe talking to"* [P24].

5.3 Theme 3: The Power of Customization

Customization allows users to specify their preferences, and the app produces tailored services based on the set preferences [37]. Orji, Tondello, and Nacke [38] conducted a large-scale study with 543 people to examine how various user types reacted to 10 persuasive strategies shown in persuading game-based health systems. According to their research results, for those with stronger socializer and disruptor tendencies, customization would encourage behaviors as it gives users a sense of control, choice, and personal touch.

Participants' feedback indicated that customization is important for stress management apps targeted at working-class Indian women in our interview. Comments relating to the need for customization mechanisms in the app attributes were raised across multiple features including Diary, Meditation music, Mood tracker, and the app's color scheme. Comments indicated that users perceived the customization feature positively. For example, participants wanted to change colors when one said: *"Blue is like a neutral color. You can also have a feature where users can choose their screen colors"* [P1]. Furthermore, participants considered the option to create their playlist in the meditation music feature as a symbol of their touch to the app when one participant said *"Meditation music is good and allows the user to add their very own music"* [P12], where as another participant said *"I think music is very subjective. I would like to have my playlist"* [P5].

5.4 Theme 4: The Power of Personalization

Personalization does not require users' inputs to provide personalized services [37]. Orji, Nacke, and Marco [39] conducted large-scale studies to examine the persuasiveness of 10 Persuasive Strategies. They found that most people like personalized systems, people were more inclined to use the default features provided by personalization [40] and some people place a high value on personalization because of its ability to boost the utility, relevance, credibility, and user confidence and trust in the system [38].

In our project, we received suggestions from participants to provide features that allow them to provide data that can help the app personalize the contents and feedback it provides to them. Feedback from participants shows that personalization is essential to target users. For example, many participants wanted the app to change its appearance according to their moods when they said the following:

*"Giving people the liberty to enter **how they are feeling today**, so **according to that, they can have their avatars**. So, I think I like the idea of it"* [P13].

*"That change avatar option makes us feel good, **we can change according to our moods**"* [P27].

*"It would be great if the **theme of the app changes according to the mood entered**"* [P32].

In contrast, one participant wished to receive positive affirmation based on their app activity when they said: *"I will feel good if **I get positive notifications based on my activity in the app**"* [P16].

5.5 Theme 5: The Effectiveness of the App for Stress and Anxiety Management

Effectiveness is the degree to which something successfully produces the desired result. Alqahtani, Winn, and Orji [41] explored persuasive approaches in mental health apps, and they found that motivation types significantly influence the perceived persuasiveness of different features. This theme shows that participants perceived that this app would help them achieve the desired behavior of managing their stress and anxiety. In our design, we adopted features that made the user feel more in control of their mental health state. For example, the Gratitude feature will enable users to focus their thoughts on people, and having a to-do list will be a useful reminder to keep their tasks on track when one participant said: *"**To-do list is beneficial to me** I usually forget things"* [P4].

Moreover, participants considered having a gratitude corner will affect their mood when one participant said *"Gratitude corner is a wonderful feature, when we show gratitude, **we feel good**, and it is the **most important thing at the end of the day**"* [P28], while a different participant said *"It will help us to **enlighten our mood whenever we are sad**"* [P34].

5.6 Theme 6: The Usefulness of Feedback Provided by the App

Previous research has shown the need for health literacy and providing patients with information regarding their current health status [16, 42, 43]. Researchers such as Stormacq et al. [44] and Wittink and Oosterhaven [45] stated that individuals with limited literacy have higher rates of illness and more hospitalizations and recommended that efforts should be made to enable patients with limited reading abilities to access health information in a way they can interpret and relate to the given information.

In our design, we provided features such as the Hobby Corner and Mood Tracker to give users an overview of their hobbies and mental and emotional state over a period. Participants' responses show that users were glad to see how these features will provide feedback. For example, one participant mentioned that they would be excited to see how their mood was throughout the month and how they could reflect on it when they said *"the Mood Tracker is impressive. I would be excited to see how many days I was happy and sad or calm or tired"* [P2]. Many participants also appreciated having a hobby corner as they believed that it would be a reminder for them to dedicate time to self-love. This is exemplified when one participant said *"I forget to spend time on my hobbies. So, if I have a hobby corner, I can at least see that I am spending a week working on my hobby"* [P17].

5.7 Theme 7: User Interface of the Prototype

Shirazi et al. [46] investigated the User Interface pattern in mobile apps using the 400 most downloaded free apps from the Android store. They found that the complexity of mobile interface differs between app categories (Tools, Communication, Entertainment, Efficiency, Social Networks, and so on). Comments from the prototype review demonstrated that the design was well-received by the target audience and that having an organized screen makes the users feel good and in control of their app. For example, participants clearly understood the prototype when they said *"Every option is so clear by even reading the name, you can understand and directly start with the app"* [P15], while another participant said *"The Home screen is simple and properly organized; it made me feel calm"* [P22].

Further, a participant mentioned how the functionality of this app would replace various apps on her phone when she said *"I would say I was very impressed by the number of elements...you just bring everything together in one home screen, and I can delete all unnecessary apps...makes me feel better"* [P27].

5.8 Theme 8: Finding a Safe Space

Pernice-Duca [47] highlighted the positive role of family support in recovering patients with mental health issues. The researcher found that interactions of family members through regular contact are essential dimensions of a support network related to recovery. Likewise, Avasthi [48] noted that the family is a crucial resource for patients with mental health problems in India because of: (1) the Indian tradition of interdependence and concern for a family member in adversities and (2) the lack of trained mental health professionals required for the large population. Indian psychiatry care integrates family support into patient care. In the present study, the comments collected during the optional interview session suggest that participants felt these features provided them with a space where no one would judge them. For example, one participant mentioned that this will be their safe space when they said *"This is a good way of providing people with a safe space or corner where they can have some positivity in their day-to-day life"* [P17]. On the other hand, one participant believed that no one would judge them if they boasted about their lives in the gratitude corner when they said *"No one will judge you that you are feeling proud"* [P20].

5.9 Theme 9: Suggestions for Improving the Design of the App

One of the main goals of our study is to design a persuasive user-centric app. In the User-Centered Design approach, it is essential to involve users in the design process and include the vital suggestions they made. This ensures that the user's needs are taken into consideration to personalize the features and the design of the app. For example, participants mentioned the following areas for improving the iCare app:

"*For meditation music, **put a background of music***" [P2].

"*For **breathing, you can add a timer**, the user should stop and have a break of 5 min*" [P7].

"*Option of **guided breathing**, I will use it as **many people are not aware of the correct technique***" [P11].

6 Discussion

The goal of this research was to better understand the viewpoints, preferences, opinions, and requirements of working-class Indian women regarding iCare explicitly designed for them to manage their stress and anxiety. Given the well-documented challenges of engaging individuals in mental health promotion, especially among our target audience, insights from this study are critical for designing and developing apps for providing effective mental health intervention. A careful examination is especially important for apps that claim to improve mental health.

We found that allowing users to tailor the app to their specific requirements and preferences is an excellent method to increase user satisfaction and engagement, minimizing the low morale currently associated with mental health apps. Participants with mental health concerns typically want assistance from someone who will not judge or stereotype them. As a result, including an anonymous social community in the app will match the participants' method of dealing with their challenges in real life. Because of the stigma associated with mental health difficulties, few participants stated that contacting and talking to an anonymous person who has no way of knowing them would be preferable to finding and talking to someone who knows about them.

Furthermore, we found that participants wanted to keep their lives organized, so having a to-do list feature, a mood tracker feature, and a hobby corner feature will make them feel in control and on the correct path to self-discipline and love. They also viewed certain features like the gratitude corner and social community as a safe space, where they will freely express themselves. Also, giving participants options like a diary or voice memo to express themselves will make them feel that they are not restricted to just one feature.

6.1 Design Recommendations

Based on the results of this study, we found many different features that can be used to design mHealth apps for underserved populations and their requirements for mental health apps. Below, we offer a list of design recommendations for mental health apps that are likely to increase their persuasiveness, usefulness, and ability to assist in managing mental health issues.

- **Recommendation 1: Include a mechanism for users to anonymize themselves.** Mental health app designers should consider adding an option where users can hide their identities when using mental health apps. As can be seen from our participants' comments (e.g., "*I think this is great. We feel we can talk whatever, as our identities* *are anonymous*" [P11]), they believe having this option can give them the confidence to express themselves to others without the fear of having their identity revealed.

- **Recommendation 2: Integrate features for users to engage in social interactions**. Adding a social community feature in mental health apps can be empowering for the users. This can allow them to communicate with people who are in the same situation as they are. The idea of having a social community was taken positively by our participants (e.g., "*It is good to talk and be anonymous in the social community. I should be able to report to any user I do not feel I am safe talking to*" [P24]). Designers can also provide users with the option to report any unwanted activity.

- **Recommendation 3: Offer ways for users to express gratitude and feel more positive emotions.** Being able to practice gratitude daily can make a better impact on the lives of users looking for positivity. Designers should provide users with such a feature so that they can rehearse gratitude and share in the social community with others at their own will. Our participants were impressed by the idea of expressing gratitude and they believed that it would make them feel good (e.g., "*Gratitude corner is a wonderful feature, when we show gratitude, we feel good, and it is the most important thing at the end of the day*" [P28]).

- **Recommendation 4: Help users to strategically plan and organize their activities.** Designers should add features like a to-do list or reminders to help users to keep their tasks organized. One of the sources of stress and anxiety can be the inability to get organized and running behind on tasks [49]. Our participants mentioned that being able to strike off tasks from a to-do list will make them happy.

- **Recommendation 5: Add a journaling feature so users can write about their feelings and thoughts related to stressful events.** Designers should add features like diary or voice memos so that it helps users to engage in journaling habits and be expressive. Being able to vent out their emotions in written or spoken form can help them manage their stress and anxiety. Our participants mentioned that having a diary feature will help to vent their emotions and relax.

6.2   Limitations and Directions for Future Research

One limitation is that right now, the data surrounding the use of the prototype is very limited to immediate perceptions and reflections on its potential benefits. Another limitation is that our findings are based on the design and one-time use of the prototype, and thus, we expect the possibility of different results when a study is conducted in the wild. Also, our prototype is focused on working-class Indian women, so the findings may not generalize to other user groups in economies with high per capita income.

This research is part of a larger project to develop and evaluate the efficacy of a mHealth app for improving mental health. Based on the rich data collected through the one-on-one interviews' evaluation of the app prototype, we are planning to develop a stress and anxiety management app that incorporates our findings from all the themes and suggestions and conduct a long-term evaluation with our target audience (working-class Indian women). The next step is to conduct a quantitative evaluation and collect more insight into how the app can be improved.

7   Conclusions

In closing, we sought to better understand how mobile apps can be designed to help working-class Indian women manage their mental health. The findings of this study shed light on Indian women's attitudes, views, and preferences for mental health mobile apps and how such apps should be developed. According to our findings, we identified the following nine themes: (1) The Importance of Aesthetics, (2) The Benefits of Being Anonymous, (3) The Power of Customization, (4) The Power of Personalization, (5 The Effectiveness of the App for Stress and Anxiety Management, (6) The Usefulness of Feedback Provided by the App, (7) User Interface of the Prototype, (8) Finding a Safe Space, and (9) Suggestions from the Participants. Understanding end users' needs and concerns about mental health apps can aid designers and developers in designing mental health apps that are usable, valuable, acceptable, and effective in the future for improving mental health and emotional well-being. Once again, most existing apps cater to people in wealthy countries, however, our research fills that gap by focusing on marginalized communities, such as Indian working-class women.

References

1. Harrison, J.E., Weber, S., Jakob, R., Chute, C.G.: ICD-11: an international classification of diseases for the twenty-first century. BMC Med. Inform. Decis. Mak. **21** (2021). https://doi.org/10.1186/S12911-021-01534-6
2. Kilkkinen, A., et al.: Prevalence of psychological distress, anxiety and depression in rural communities in Australia. Aust. J. Rural Health. **15**, 114–119 (2007). https://doi.org/10.1111/J.1440-1584.2007.00863.X
3. Adams, P., et al.: Towards personal stress informatics: comparing minimally invasive techniques for measuring daily stress in the wild. In: Proceedings of the PERVASIVEHEALTH 2014 8th International Conference on Pervasive Computing Technologies for Healthcare, pp. 72–79 (2014). https://doi.org/10.4108/icst.pervasivehealth.2014.254959
4. Gordon, J.A., Borja, S.E.: The COVID-19 pandemic: setting the mental health research agenda. Biol. Psychiatry **88**, 130 (2020). https://doi.org/10.1016/J.BIOPSYCH.2020.05.012
5. Coelhoso, C.C., et al.: A new mental health mobile app for well-being and stress reduction in working women: randomized controlled trial. J. Med. Internet Res. **21**, e14269 (2019). https://doi.org/10.2196/14269
6. Academic stress, parental pressure, anxiety and mental health among Indian high school students|QUT ePrints
7. McLean, C.P., Asnaani, A., Litz, B.T., Hofmann, S.G.: Gender differences in anxiety disorders: prevalence, course of illness, comorbidity and burden of illness. J. Psychiatr. Res. **45**, 1027–1035 (2011). https://doi.org/10.1016/J.JPSYCHIRES.2011.03.006
8. For How Long Will Mental Illness Remain A Taboo in India?|Youth Ki Awaaz
9. Pendse, S.R., et al.: Mental health in the global south: challenges and opportunities in HCI for development. In: COMPASS 2019 – Proceedings of 2019 Conference on Computing and Sustainable Societies, pp. 22–36 (2019). https://doi.org/10.1145/3314344.3332483
10. Karampela, M., Ouhbi, S., Isomursu, M.: Exploring users' willingness to share their health and personal data under the prism of the new GDPR: implications in healthcare. In: Proceedings of Annual International Conference of the IEEE Engineering in Medicine and Biology Society (EMBS), pp. 6509–6512 (2019). https://doi.org/10.1109/EMBC.2019.8856550
11. What is User Centered Design?|Interaction Design Foundation (IxDF)

12. Reen, J.K., Orji, R.: Improving mental health among working-class Indian women: insight from an interview study. In: Conference on Human Factors in Computing Systems - Proceedings (2022). https://doi.org/10.1145/3491101.3519781
13. Fischer, N., et al.: Exploring the effects of technology-enabled mindfulness and meditation on stress management. Iproceedings 3, e23 (2017). https://doi.org/10.2196/iproc.8463
14. Moberg, C., Niles, A., Beermann, D.: Guided self-help works: randomized waitlist controlled trial of Pacifica, a mobile app integrating cognitive behavioral therapy and mindfulness for stress, anxiety, and depression. J. Med. Internet Res. 21, 1–17 (2019). https://doi.org/10.2196/12556
15. Oinas-Kukkonen, H., Harjumaa, M.: Persuasive systems design: key issues, process model, and system features. Commun. Assoc. Inf. Syst. 24, 28 (2009)
16. Musiat, P., Hoffmann, L., Schmidt, U.: Personalised computerised feedback in E-mental health. J. Mental Health 21, 346–354 (2012). https://doi.org/10.3109/09638237.2011.648347
17. Rathbone, A.L., Prescott, J.: The use of mobile apps and SMS messaging as physical and mental health interventions: systematic review. J. Med. Internet Res. 19, 1–13 (2017). https://doi.org/10.2196/jmir.7740
18. Spurgeon, J.A., Wright, J.H.: Computer-assisted cognitive-behavioral therapy. Curr. Psychiatry Rep. 12, 547–552 (2010). https://doi.org/10.1007/S11920-010-0152-4/TABLES/2
19. Kauer, S.D., et al.: Self-monitoring using mobile phones in the early stages of adolescent depression: randomized controlled trial. J. Med. Internet Res. 14(3), e67 (2012). https://www.jmir.org/2012/3/e67, https://doi.org/10.2196/JMIR.1858
20. Wang, K., Varma, D.S., Prosperi, M.: A systematic review of the effectiveness of mobile apps for monitoring and management of mental health symptoms or disorders. J. Psychiatr. Res. 107, 73–78 (2018). https://doi.org/10.1016/j.jpsychires.2018.10.006
21. Jo, H.H.: Evaluation of the Effectiveness of Mobile App-Based Stress-Management Program: A Randomized Controlled Trial (2019)
22. Linos, A., Kirch, W.: Promoting Health for Working Women. Springer, New York (2008). https://doi.org/10.1007/978-0-387-73038-7
23. Curtis, B., et al.: Characterizing participation and perceived engagement benefits in an integrated digital behavioral health recovery community for women: a cross-sectional survey. JMIR Ment. Heal. 6, e13352 (2019). https://doi.org/10.2196/13352
24. Sawyer, A., et al.: The effectiveness of an app-based nurse-moderated program for new mothers with depression and parenting problems (EMUMS Plus): pragmatic randomized controlled trial. J. Med. Internet Res. 21, e13689 (2019). https://doi.org/10.2196/13689
25. Proto.io - Prototyping for all
26. Terry, G., Hayfield, N., Clarke, V., Braun, V.: Thematic analysis. SAGE Handbook of Qualitative Research in Psychology, pp. 17–36 (2017). https://doi.org/10.4135/9781526405555.N2
27. Video Conferencing, Meetings, Calling|Microsoft Teams
28. Best Qualitative Data Analysis Software for Researchers|NVivo
29. Gauthier, R.P., et al.: Agency and amplification: a comparison of manual and computational thematic analyses by public health researchers. Proc. ACM Human-Computer Interact. 7, 22 (2023). https://doi.org/10.1145/3567552
30. How to Do Thematic Analysis|Step-by-Step Guide & Examples
31. Braun, V., Clarke, V.: Using thematic analysis in psychology. Qual. Res. Psychol. 3, 77–101 (2006). https://doi.org/10.1191/1478088706qp063oa
32. Aesthetics Definition & Meaning|Dictionary.com
33. What is Aesthetics?|Interaction Design Foundation (IxDF)
34. What's White Space Design? 5 Real Examples|Adobe XD Ideas
35. Anonymity Definition & Meaning|Dictionary.com

36. Fear, N.T., Seddon, R., Jones, N., Greenberg, N., Wessely, S.: Does anonymity increase the reporting of mental health symptoms? BMC Public Health **12**, 1–7 (2012). https://doi.org/10.1186/1471-2458-12-797/TABLES/3
37. Zo, H.: Personalization vs. Customization: which is more effective in e-services? p. 32 (2003)
38. Orji, R., Tondello, G.F., Nacke, L.E.: Personalizing persuasive strategies in gameful systems to gamification user types. In: Conference on Human Factors in Computing Systems - Proceedings (2018). https://doi.org/10.1145/3173574.3174009
39. Orji, R., Nacke, L.E., Di Marco, C.: Towards personality-driven persuasive health games and gamified systems, pp. 1015–1027 (2017). https://doi.org/10.1145/3025453.3025577
40. Orji, R., et al.: Modeling the efficacy of persuasive strategies for different gamer types in serious games for health. User Model. User-Adap. Inter. **24**, 453–498 (2014). https://doi.org/10.1007/s11257-014-9149-8
41. Alqahtani, F., Winn, A., Orji, R.: Co-designing a mobile app to improve mental health and well-being: focus group study. JMIR Form. Res. **5**(2), e18172 (2021). https://www.formative.jmir.org/2021/2/e18172, https://doi.org/10.2196/18172
42. Weiss, B.D.: Health literacy: an important issue for communicating health information to patients. Zhonghua Yi Xue Za Zhi (Taipei) **64**, 603–608 (2001)
43. Mild Traumatic Brain Injury: Symptom Validity Assessment and Malingering - Google Books
44. Stormacq, C., Wosinski, J., Boillat, E., Van Den Broucke, S.: Effects of health literacy interventions on health-related outcomes in socioeconomically disadvantaged adults living in the community: a systematic review. JBI Evid. Synth. **18**, 1389–1469 (2020). https://doi.org/10.11124/JBISRIR-D-18-00023
45. Wittink, H., Oosterhaven, J.: Patient education and health literacy. Musculoskelet. Sci. Pract. **38**, 120–127 (2018). https://doi.org/10.1016/J.MSKSP.2018.06.004
46. Shirazi, A.S., Henze, N., Schmidt, A., Goldberg, R., Schmidt, B., Schmauder, H.: Insights into layout patterns of mobile user interfaces by an automatic analysis of Android apps. In: EICS 2013 – Proceedings of ACM SIGCHI Symposium on Engineering Interactive Computing Systems, pp. 275–284 (2013). https://doi.org/10.1145/2480296.2480308
47. Pernice-Duca, F.: Family network support and mental health recovery. J. Marital Fam. Ther. **36**, 13–27 (2010). https://doi.org/10.1111/J.1752-0606.2009.00182.X
48. Avasthi, A.: Preserve and strengthen family to promote mental health. Indian J. Psychiatry. **52**, 113 (2010). https://doi.org/10.4103/0019-5545.64582
49. Albrecht's Four Types of Stress - From MindTools.com

Connecting Patients and Clinicians: Shedding Light on Functionalities for Mental Health Apps in Depression Care

Philipp Reindl-Spanner[1]([✉]), Barbara Prommegger[1], Tedi Ikonomi[1], Jochen Gensichen[2], and Helmut Krcmar[1]

[1] TUM School of Computation, Information and Technology, Technical University of Munich, Garching, Germany
philipp.spanner@tum.de
[2] Institute of General Practice and Family Medicine, University Hospital of the Ludwig-Maximilians-University, Munich, Germany

Abstract. This paper evaluates the functionalities of mental health apps by developing and testing a smartphone application focusing on depression. This article follows a design science research approach, reviewing existing literature and app functionalities to identify essential functionalities for mental health care apps. The application integrates the PHQ-9 questionnaire and supports passive data collection for activity levels. The app provides real-time feedback and monitoring to patients and data access to their treating clinician. We evaluated usability and functionality with potential end users and healthcare professionals. The results show high usability scores and highlight the importance of features such as in-app access to emergency services, self-monitoring tools, and progress tracking. Our findings indicate a strong preference for functionalities that support active engagement and immediate access to support in crises.

Keywords: depression monitoring · mobile app · mHealth · smartphone data · PHQ-9 · design science · patient monitoring · requirement engineering

1 Introduction

Mental health care, specifically for depression, is crucial for individuals as it directly affects their overall well-being and quality of life [1]. Without proper care, depression can escalate and lead to more severe consequences such as suicide [2]. Mental health care, including therapy, medication, and self-care practices, can help individuals manage their symptoms and improve their mental and emotional health. By addressing depression early and effectively, individuals can return to fulfilling and productive lives, ultimately benefiting themselves and their families and communities [3].

Mental health clinicians use validated screening tools like the Patient Health Questionnaire (PHQ) [4] to monitor patients' progress during depression treatment. Usually, patients complete the questionnaires according to their recollections of past experiences

M. Kurosu and A. Hashizume (Eds.): HCII 2024, LNCS 14686, pp. 133–148, 2024.
https://doi.org/10.1007/978-3-031-60428-7_10

during the face-to-face sessions with their therapist. However, despite the validity of these tools, retrospective recollection can cause patients to frame or forget important information [5]. Moreover, as conventionally done, filling out questionnaires through pen and paper can be labor-intensive and intrusive for patients [6].

The widespread adoption of smartphones and smart devices has the potential to revolutionize the treatment of depression [7]. By adopting eHealth and mHealth solutions, patients can quickly access their medical records and receive remote care and monitoring through telemedicine apps and other digital health tools. In addition, it can improve patient outcomes by allowing more frequent and convenient check-ins, enabling early detection and intervention of potential health problems, and reducing the need for in-person visits [8]. As technology continues to evolve and integrate with healthcare, it has the potential to improve the patient experience and facilitate better health outcomes.

Currently, it is possible to accompany the therapy of depression by using mobile applications. Still, there are hardly any or no applications that provide the questionnaire data collected from the patients directly to the clinicians in the process. Therefore, this article investigates the functionalities of a mental health monitoring application to improve the connection between patients and clinicians in mental health care, especially depression care, by adopting smartphone usage and mental health apps. Due to the great importance of increasing the acceptance of mental health apps among potential users from the patient group, in this article, we concentrate primarily on the functionalities from the perspective of potential end users. For this reason, we aim to answer the following research question with the present article:

RQ: What are important functionalities of a mental health app for depression care?

Therefore, to answer the research question, we proceed as follows: First, we review existing literature and app store applications to identify functionalities for a mental health app. Then, based on these functionalities, we implemented an application combining and extending the identified functionalities by making the data directly available to the treating clinician. Finally, we evaluate the application in two ways. First, we evaluate the application's usability to ensure a good base for functionality evaluation, and second, we evaluate the implemented functionalities with potential users to rank them according to their importance.

2   Theoretical Background

This section offers an overview of the theoretical underpinnings that informed the development of the present paper.

2.1   Patient Clinician Interaction

The chronic care model (CCM) [9] is a theoretical framework developed to guide the provision of high-quality care to individuals with chronic conditions, such as diabetes, heart disease, and depression. The CCM emphasizes the need for a proactive, patient-centered approach to care delivered through a coordinated, integrated healthcare system. While the model comprises different vital elements, it emphasizes that patients should be actively involved in their treatment to improve its outcome. Mental health patients pose a particular challenge regarding active monitoring because they tend towards non-adherence and lack collaboration [10]. Moreover, active monitoring may exacerbate stress levels in already vulnerable patients, leading them to discontinue tracking [11]. Despite the challenges, methods like mental health questionnaires for active data collection remain relevant [12]. This paper connects to this theory and explores a technology-enabled approach to actively engage depression patients in their treatment while highlighting patient/physician interaction. A suitable path from a data perspective is integrating patient-generated health data (PGHD) into the treatment workflow.

PGHD refers to health-related information created, recorded, or gathered by individuals outside traditional healthcare settings [13]. PGHD can include a wide variety of data, such as information about symptoms, physical activity, mood, sleep patterns, and diet and measurements of physiological parameters like blood pressure, heart rate, and blood glucose levels [14]. PGHD is often collected using various digital devices, such as smartphones, wearables, and sensors, and can be transmitted to healthcare providers for analysis and use in clinical decision-making. By enabling patients to collect and share their health data with their healthcare providers, PGHD has the potential to facilitate more personalized and precise healthcare. This way, PGHD enables treatment that is tailored to an individual's unique health needs and, at the same time, involves patients actively in their treatment [15, 16].

2.2 Mental Health Applications

In recent years, mental health applications have become increasingly popular to support and improve mental health [17]. These apps offer a range of features, including mood tracking, meditation and mindfulness exercises, cognitive behavioral therapy techniques, and access to mental health professionals. They can potentially increase access to mental health care, particularly for underserved populations, by providing low-cost or free resources that may be accessed from the comfort and privacy of one's own home [18]. However, the quality and effectiveness of mental health apps can vary widely, and their use should be considered complementary, rather than a replacement, to traditional mental health care. It is crucial that mental health apps are evidence-based (especially when recommended by a clinician) and that their effectiveness is evaluated to ensure they provide safe and practical support to individuals struggling with mental health concerns [19].

Incorporating the above-described PGHD in patient-clinician interactions can enhance consultations by better understanding the evolving disease and treatment outcomes [20]. For instance, mental health questionnaires can collect these patients' reported outcomes through mental health applications. However, directly communicating the collected data from the patient to the clinician (i.e., through an application) is still not very common [21].

3 Research Methodology

To answer our research question, we decided to use a design science research approach [22]. We divided the procedure into three different cycles [23]. This structure supports our implementation in representing the individual steps in a targeted way and implementing an application on a well-founded basis to perform the intended evaluation.

For the Rigor Cycle, we chose a two-fold approach. First, to create a basis for developing the application, we conducted a selective literature review on depression screening in the context of smartphones to get further insights into how scientific studies suggest collecting mental health questionnaire data from patients and additional functionalities for the artifact. For this purpose, we searched the journals listed in the Association for Information Systems (AIS) Special Interest Group (SIG) of "IT in Healthcare" [24] and the sub-journals of the Journal of Medical Internet Research (JMIR), like JMIR mental health. Overall, we identified 11 articles that suit our demands.

In addition to this literature review, we identified applications from the App Store and investigated their functionalities for mental health care applications. Due to the large number of apps in the App Store that meet our expectations, we constrain our review to apps with more than twenty user ratings and scores better than four stars. We believe that these limitations allow us to disregard lower-quality apps. Moreover, our analysis excludes applications designed as educational or therapeutic tools. With these limitations, we identified 17 applications that met our requirements.

Following identifying functionalities for mental health monitoring apps through the Rigor Cycle, we created a prototype iOS app during this project's Design Cycle. This step aimed to create the first version of a possible app, which we could use to evaluate the functionalities from the Rigor Cycle with potential users.

Finally, for this paper's Relevance Cycle, we chose a two-stage approach to evaluate the functionalities we identified through the implemented prototype. Therefore, we first evaluated the iOS application with healthcare professionals and potential users for its usability. We included this step to ensure the app provided good usability before using it for the functionality evaluation. Lastly, we tested the application with potential users to determine the importance of the functionalities for mental health apps and used the

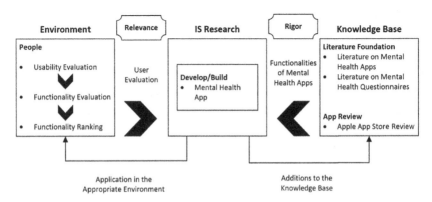

Fig. 1. Conceptual framework of the research approach. Based on Hevner [23]

app to create a ranking for the identified functionalities. Figure 1 shows a conceptual schematic representation of the employed research methodology.

4 Functionalities

In the first step of the Rigor Cycle, we looked at functionalities for mental health monitoring apps from the literature in the IS field, as described above. We were able to identify 11 relevant articles that met our requirements. Although both patients and healthcare professionals can use our prototype, we are concentrating exclusively on functionalities for patients in this step. We could derive five functionalities relevant to implementing the planned app from these articles. First, the app should offer depression screening via a questionnaire [25–31]. Based on the questionnaire, the app should provide users with feedback on their entries as part of self-monitoring, thereby promoting and supporting patient self-monitoring [32]. The app should offer patients mood monitoring, which can predict depressive moods [28, 30, 33]. Some of the included articles describe that patients can be discharged using passively collected data via sensors or smartwatches, for example, and that further valuable data can be included in the monitoring [29, 31, 33]. Table 1 shows the functionalities we identified within the included literature.

Table 1. Functionalities from literature review.

Functionality	Description
Questionnaire Screening	Enables completion of mental health assessment questionnaires [25–31]
Feedback on questionnaire results	Analyzes and provides insights on questionnaire responses [32]
Implements self-monitoring	Tracking of symptoms and behaviors over time [28, 30, 33]
Mood Monitoring	Logging and tracking of emotional states [28, 30, 33]
Supports passive data collection	Automatic data gathering, like sleep and activity patterns [29, 31, 33]

In the second step of this Rigor Cycle, we reviewed mental health apps from the Apple App Store to complement the functionalities identified in the scientific literature. We observed three main App Store categories to where these apps belong: Health and Fitness, Lifestyle, and Medical, of which Health and Fitness were the most popular. Through this step, we identified nine further functionalities for our application.

We divide these functionalities into five categories for a better overview. The categories contain at least one functionality and can also contain functionalities identified in the literature research. The first category, "Track Progress," describes functionalities that track the user's progress. This includes tracking the patient's progress (e.g., Display of Trends), viewing previous results, and feedback based on the questionnaire (e.g., Evaluation of Questionnaires). The second category, "Track Consistency," describes functionalities that track how regularly the user completed the screening of either mood or depression in the past. This category also includes the functionality to overview the results and history of past questionnaires and mood entries. The third category describes screening for depression. This refers to the functionalities that allow the app to provide clues for a diagnosis of depression based on the questionnaires used. The next category includes all functionalities that give the patient/user access to the contact details of the attending physician in the app or the case of a suicidal result, the number of the suicide prevention hotline. The last category contains functionalities that allow the app to collect further health data about the user. Table 2 provides an overview of the categories of functionalities included in the applications. Table 3 shows the identified functionalities with a brief description.

Table 2. Functionality Categories and App Store Applications

App	Track Progress	Track Consistency	Depression Screening	Contact Data	Health Data Collection
Moodnotes	X	X			
Moodflow	X	X			X
Depression Test	X		X		
InnerHour	X	X	X		
Depressed			X	X	
Vos	X	X			X
Emoods	X	X	X	X	X
Moodistory	X	X			
Youper	X	X	X		X
Woebot	X			X	
Daylio Journal	X	X			
Mind Doc	X	X	X	X	X
Inquiry Health	X		X	X	
Selfapy	X	X		X	
Hello Better	X	X			
CBT Thought Diary	X	X			

Table 3. Functionalities from App Store Review

Functionality	Description
Monitoring patient's progress	Progress tracking through charted questionnaire scores
Tracking Questionnaire Consistency	Tracking questionnaire completion by marking calendar days
In-app access to the clinician's contact information	Clinicians' contact information is visible to the patient
In-app access to emergency services	The patient can use the app to contact the suicide prevention hotline
Review previous results	The patient can see the questionnaire scores achieved in the past
Depression Screening	Tools to diagnose depression such as the use of the PHQ-9 questionnaire
Tracking Activity Data	Collecting activity data from the health app to present it on a timeline
Questionnaire result overview and history	The app provides an overview of the results of past questionnaires
Patient's insights in the clinician component	The clinician can monitor patients' progress through questionnaire scores and activity data

5 Design Cycle

Subsequently, we applied the knowledge we gathered during the Rigor Cycle. Within the Design Cycle, we implemented a prototypical application. Our application combines and implements the functionalities we identified in the Rigor Cycle. Therefore, we added basic functionalities to feed the collected data directly to the clinicians. In this section of the paper, we showcase the features of the designed artifact.

5.1 Common Functionalities

The app uses the same views for both components with minor differences to implement standard functionalities. Further, both share the same color scheme that changes depending on the appearance of the device's display. The essential functionalities available to both user categories are the app settings, patient insights, and authentication and registration. The last one is responsible for securing a user's private data and providing a safe link for data transfers between clinicians and their patients.

5.2 Patient View

After the user login, the home screen displays a calendar with a completion ring for every day the user completed the questionnaire. Within the application, the PHQ-9 questionnaire is the only active task for the patient. The questionnaire is designed in a nine-item form and is available in German and English, with the answer possibilities transformed to a 5-point Likert scale. After completing the questionnaire, the app presents the user with their score and a short explanation of the score. If the patient receives an alarming score, they are prompted to contact their clinician, friend, and the suicide prevention hotline [25, 32, 34].

The Insights view features two charts: one for the questionnaire results and one for the activity data. The questionnaire chart is updated in real-time for the patient and their clinician after completing it. Additionally, we synchronize all patient activity data gathered by HealthKit from the day preceding the patient's final app interaction to the current date. The data is visualized in a chart. The y-axis on the questionnaire chart indicates the scores of the patients, whereas the y-axis on the activity chart shows the step count. The y-axis's maximum value corresponds to the highest data point gathered in the chosen period, while the x-axis represents the duration over which the data was collected.

In Fig. 2, the first three screenshots present the questionnaire screen, the insights feature, and the screen the user receives after completing the questionnaire with an alarming score.

5.3 Clinician View

The main page of the clinician component is the Patient Overview. This page displays a list of all the patients currently in treatment by the clinician in the form of small cards showing the patient's full name. The clinician can tap on a patient to view their insights through charts. The name of the respective patient is displayed at the top of the Insights tab. After selecting a patient, the app provides the same insights for the clinician as for the patient. The collected data/screenings are always accessible for later examination, as real-time data assessment is not always feasible for clinicians [30]. In addition to presenting the collected data to the patients, clinicians can see the patient's progress over time [30].

In Fig. 2, the last screenshot represents the clinicians' patient overview. The charts/insights screen is the same for patients and clinicians and can be seen in screenshot two.

6 Evaluation

We opted for a two-stage approach to evaluate our application and the identified functionalities. In the first step, we check the application's usability, and in the second step, we check the functionalities identified during the Rigor Cycle.

For the first step, we evaluated the developed artifact using the System Usability Scale (SUS) questionnaire [35] to assess the usability of the implemented artifact. We decided to use the SUS questionnaire for its reliability and robustness in measuring subjective usability. Additionally, we added open questions to the questionnaire to explore further aspects of such applications. We chose to evaluate the artifact with potential users for the patient side of the applications and healthcare professionals.

Fig. 2. Patient-Clinician Application Screenshots

For the evaluation, we first introduced the participants to the app and asked them to complete several typical tasks, including registering, logging in, and accepting terms and conditions. We then showed them the app's core functionalities, such as the charts, completing a questionnaire, and the ability to contact care providers, and introduced them to its charting function. In addition, we presented the clinical side of the application to healthcare professionals. These tasks aimed to determine if the app met the usability goals. After completing the tasks, we asked the participants to complete the questionnaire.

We went conducted the evaluation of the functionalities in a modified form. We presented the application to the participants and gave them a list of all identified functionalities. The participants could then rate these functionalities on a 7-point Likert scale according to their importance for the application.

6.1 Usability Evaluation

For the usability evaluation, we recruited 30 participants with potential interest in such an application. The recruited group consists of potential end users and healthcare professionals. For the end user group, we recruited 26 participants. The participants ranged from 21 to 35 years old, with different backgrounds, most of whom were students. Additionally, four healthcare professionals with expertise in mental health research participated in this evaluation process. Their backgrounds are psychotherapists in training, general practitioners, and medical researchers.

Table 4 describes the results of the SUS survey. The application scored well above average. SUS scores of 82.6 and 86.25 are generally considered a good rating for the usability of an application. These high usability values for the app enabled us to ensure that the implemented functionalities are well integrated and, therefore, suitable for testing the functionalities.

6.2 Functionality Evaluation

For the final step in this design science project, we evaluated the functionalities implemented in the app. For this purpose, we recruited 36 participants from the group of potential end users with an age range from 18 to 62 years old, averaging around 36.8 years old. The group is predominantly male, with 24 male participants compared to 10 females. Additionally, two people either did not respond or did not identify as either male or female. Fifteen participants answered that they suffered from depression, and 21 answered that they did not. This diversity in both age and mental health status provides a broad perspective on preferences and needs concerning the functionalities of mental health apps, particularly in the context of depression treatment.

The evaluation results provide insightful data on the preferences and perceived importance of various features in the implemented app. The highest-rated feature, with an average score of 6.25, is in-app access to emergency services. This highlights the critical need for immediate support in crises. This is closely followed by the implementation of self-monitoring (6.19) and patient progress monitoring (6.05), with scores above 6, showing a strong preference for features allowing users to track their mental health status and progress. Feedback on questionnaire results (6.03) and the ability to view previous results (5.84) were also rated as very important, suggesting that the users appreciate insights into their collected data. At the lower end of the scale, the tracking of activity data (4.75) and passive data collection (4.48) were considered the least important, although still important on the absolute scale. The results' standard deviations range from 1.16 to 1.87. This data highlights the importance of active user engagement and direct access to support in mental health apps but also recognizes the value of comprehensive monitoring and feedback mechanisms. Table 5 provides a complete overview of the ranking.

Table 4. SUS Results

Participant	No. Participants	Mean	Min	Max
End-Users	26	82.8	50	95
Professionals	4	86.25	75	92.5

Table 5. Results of Functionality Evaluation

Ranking	Functionality	Avg Score	Std Dev
1	In-app access to emergency services	6.25	1.47
2	Implements self-monitoring	6.19	1.22
3	Monitoring patient's progress	6.05	1.16

(*continued*)

Table 5. (*continued*)

Ranking	Functionality	Avg Score	Std Dev
4	Feedback on questionnaire results	6.03	1.30
5	Review previous results	5.84	1.35
6	Questionnaire result overview and history	5.66	1.55
7	In-app access to the clinician's contact information	5.61	1.57
8	Depression Screening	5.44	1.46
9	Tracking Questionnaire Consistency	5.33	1.25
10	Mood Monitoring	5.31	1.56
11	Questionnaire Screening	5.26	1.52
12	Patient's insights in the clinician component	4.89	1.78
13	Tracking Activity Data	4.75	1.77
14	Supports passive data collection	4.48	1.87

7 Discussion

This article aims to analyze functionalities for mental health apps that facilitate data communication. The following section discusses the opportunities for improvement and the potential of introducing such apps in depression treatment.

Based on the CCM, involving patients in their treatment is essential [9]. Mental health apps give patients access to mental health support and monitoring, some of which they would not have had without these apps [36]. With the implemented artifact, we implement functionalities described in scientific literature and used in established apps. The implemented app allows clinicians to access their patients' data whenever they want and always have the most up-to-date data. This accessibility and richness of data enable clinicians to track the effectiveness of treatment over a more extended period, anticipate mood fluctuations in the short term, and identify the early onset of deteriorating symptoms [37]. The usability evaluation results clearly show that healthcare professionals are willing to use such an application in the future. However, the functionality that the healthcare professional has direct access to the data in the doctor component is rated less important by patients compared to other functionalities. Therefore, it is essential to address the potential concerns of end-users and ensure that the application can be easily integrated into the existing treatment processes. This leads to the fact that the app does not represent an additional burden for the patients which can lead to less adherence [10] and increase patients' stress levels [11]. We think that such applications will be used primarily for patients who have overcome the worst phase of their depression and for whom the application can be used to monitor the progress of the subsequent therapy.

Our functionalities evaluation shows that, overall, quick access to help when it is needed is essential to potential users. Access to the suicide emergency number directly from the app highlights the critical importance of having immediate access to help in the event of a crisis. In comparison, the participants rated the access to the contact details of the treating doctor as not reasonably as necessary. We assume that this rating is related to the fact that the participants rated the urgency differently. In the event of an acute suicidal crisis, immediate action must be taken to prevent suicide using the emergency number; for example, the attending physician is more likely to be called in for help in non-life-threatening crises. Given the critical role of crisis support features, it is crucial for applications to enhance their implementation to ensure optimal assistance for patients facing urgent crises. Thus, it appears logical to adopt further strategies as outlined in Martinengo, Van Galen [38], enabling the timely and optimal support of at-risk patients.

Surprisingly, the functionalities for passive data collection and activity tracking were rated the lowest in our app. We can attribute this rating to the different characteristics of these functionalities. First, we think that some of the users might not know or do not make the direct connection between these functionalities and depression or mental health in general. The participants might not be fully aware of how activity data and passive data collection can benefit their mental health and undervalue these features [12]. Due to the implemented and presented functionalities, the participants might perceive features like mood tracking or depression screening as more relevant to their immediate needs. Education on how passive data collection and activity tracking can contribute to a holistic understanding of their health might increase their perceived value. We also think users might prefer more active engagement with the app. Activity data tracking and passive data collection are often background processes that do not require direct user interaction. Users may find active features, like completing questionnaires or receiving direct feedback, more engaging and immediately rewarding. This preference might stem from the users feeling that manually entered data is more accurate or relevant to their condition.

8 Contribution

8.1 Theoretical Contribution

With the present article, we contribute to several research areas. First, our paper can contribute to understanding how user-centered design principles apply specifically to mental health applications. User-centered design principles are fundamental in our context of mental health and depression in particular. Depression is a highly individual illness, which means that user-centered design can help to ensure that the functionalities implemented can be helpful in diagnosis and therapy. Functionalities such as the inclusion of the suicide emergency number or the contact to the attending physician for crises, which were rated very highly in our evaluation, can often be overlooked in technology-centered approaches.

Furthermore, our paper contributes to a broader understanding of PGHD (through self-report questionnaires or passive data collection). Our results show that although data is actively collected, for example, through questionnaires, it is still rated as necessary by the users concerned without much effort in everyday life through smart sensors, smartwatches, or smartphones. This primarily supports theories that support a mix of actively and passively collected PGHD as the most sensible option. This combination of data collected in everyday life can ultimately provide the treating physician with further essential clues in diagnosing and treating the disease.

8.2 Practical Contribution

In addition to our contribution to theory, we also make a practical contribution with our article. First of all, the evaluation of the functionalities can be used by developers to implement Mental Health applications. The ranking can be used to equip the apps with the needed functionalities. This eliminates less popular or less required functionalities, increasing acceptance among potential users. In addition, this allows the focus to be placed on more essential functionalities, thus preventing users from being overwhelmed by too many functionalities. As a result, such apps can be designed to be more user-friendly.

Another practical contribution of our article is the evaluation of the functionalities. The results show a low assessment of the importance of passive data collection and activity data. As described in the discussion, this can be attributed to the fact that respondents potentially do not see much benefit in these data types or believe that a more significant effort is involved in collecting this data. Other studies [12] have shown that facilitators for the use of PGHD in general, including these types of data, are influenced by user characteristics. These include, for example, the perceived usefulness and relevance of these types of data. This article, therefore, demonstrates the need to educate potential users on the relevance and usefulness of passively collected PGHD.

9 Limitations

Like other studies, some constraints apply to our research. In this paper, we tested an application, and despite our efforts to remain impartial, confirmation bias could have influenced our results. Specifically, through being present during user testing and evaluation, we may unintentionally have influenced participants' perceptions of the usability and usefulness of the application. Respondents might provide socially desirable answers or might not have a complete understanding of their behaviors and preferences. This could lead to inaccuracies in the data about the importance and effectiveness of different app functionalities.

A further potential limitation of our app evaluation is the small sample size. With only 36 respondents in the functionality evaluation, the sample size is relatively small, which may limit the generalizability of the findings. In addition, the sample appears biased towards a younger, predominantly male population. This lack of diversity in terms of age and gender may not accurately reflect the needs and preferences of the wider population, especially considering that mental health problems and the usability of mental health apps can vary significantly across age groups and between genders. With a larger sample size, we could have gathered more diverse perspectives and identified additional issues or opportunities for improvement that were not captured by our current sample.

With our study setup, we primarily focus on the functionalities of mental health apps for depression care. This excludes the consideration of the broader context in which these apps are used. Additionally, the user's acceptance of technology, the severity of their conditions, and treatment methods may influence their perception and relevance of the evaluated functionalities.

10 Future Research

Future research could focus on investigating clinical workflows to incorporate mental health applications. This research could entail examining existing clinical workflows to identify gaps in mental health monitoring, particularly concerning patient adherence and patient-clinician collaboration. Furthermore, it may involve evaluating the feasibility of incorporating mental health monitoring applications like the implemented prototype into existing clinical workflows. This research could also explore the effectiveness of these monitoring tools in improving patient outcomes and identify barriers to their adoption and strategies for overcoming them. Ultimately, the findings from this research could inform the development of more effective clinical workflows that incorporate mental health applications to enhance mental health care delivery.

A future addition to the present study could be a more comprehensive study on the functionalities of mental health apps. It would be conceivable to create a more comprehensive list of functionalities based on this study and to test them quantitatively with a larger sample. This could result in a more meaningful list of functionalities for all demographic groups. This more comprehensive quantitatively validated list could then be used to implement a new prototype to be evaluated in a longitudinal study. This could help understand whether certain features become more or less important to users as their mental health journey progresses.

11 Conclusion

In this paper, we address the question of which functionalities of a doctor-patient interface are most important to potential users. For this purpose, we developed a prototype for a mental health app for depression care, which we evaluated for its functionalities and their importance after a usability evaluation. Both evaluations confirm such applications' importance and their functions' value. The implemented app shows high usability, and by evaluating the implemented functionalities, we identified a strong preference for quickly accessible crisis support and self-monitoring options. Our paper contributes to a broader understanding of information systems within the field of mHealth apps for mental health care and depression care.

Acknowledgments. The POKAL-Study-Group (PrädiktOren und Klinische Ergebnisse bei depressiven ErkrAnkungen in der hausärztLichen Versorgung (POKAL, DFG-GRK 2621)) consists of the following principle investigators: Tobias Dreischulte, Peter Falkai, Jochen Gensichen, PeterHenningsen, Markus Bühner, Caroline Jung-Sievers, Helmut Krcmar, Barbara Prommegger, Karoline Lukaschek, Gabriele Pitschel-Walz and Antonius Schneider. The following doctoral students are as well members of the POKAL-Study-Group: Jochen Vukas, Puya Younesi, Feyza Gökce, Victoria von Schrottenberg, Petra Schönweger, Hannah Schillock, Jonas Raub, Philipp Reindl-Spanner, Lisa Hattenkofer, Lukas Kaupe, Carolin Haas, Julia Eder, Vita Brisnik, Constantin Brand and Katharina Biersack.

References

1. World Health Organization Depression (2021). https://www.who.int/news-room/fact-sheets/detail/depression. Cited 7 Oct 2023
2. World Health Organization, Preventing suicide: A global imperative: World Health Organization (2014)
3. World Health Organization Mental health: strengthening our response (2022). https://www.who.int/news-room/fact-sheets/detail/mental-health-strengthening-our-response. 16 Feb 2023
4. Kroenke, K., Spitzer, R.L.: The PHQ-9: a new depression diagnostic and severity measure. In: SLACK Incorporated Thorofare, NJ, pp. 509–515 (2002)
5. Sandstrom, G.M., et al.: Opportunities for smartphones in clinical care: the future of mobile mood monitoring. J. Clin. Psychiatry 77(2), 13476 (2016)
6. Depp, C.A., et al.: A pilot study of mood ratings captured by mobile phone versus paper-and-pencil mood charts in bipolar disorder. J. Dual Diagn. 8(4), 326–332 (2012)
7. Perna, G., et al.: The revolution of personalized psychiatry: will technology make it happen sooner? Psychol. Med. 48(5), 705–713 (2018)
8. Reindl-Spanner, P., et al.: Insights on Patient-Generated Health Data in Healthcare: A Literature Review (2022)
9. Wagner, E.H., Austin, B.T., Von Korff, M.: Organizing care for patients with chronic illness. Milbank Q. 74, 511–544 (1996)
10. Chakrabarti, S.: What's in a name? Compliance, adherence and concordance in chronic psychiatric disorders. World J. Psychiatry 4(2), 30–36 (2014)
11. Wu, D.T., et al.: Clinician perspectives and design implications in using patient-generated health data to improve mental health practices: mixed methods study. JMIR Formative Res. 4(8), e18123 (2020)
12. Nittas, V., et al.: Electronic patient-generated health data to facilitate disease prevention and health promotion: scoping review. J. Med. Internet Res. 21(10), e13320 (2019)
13. Shapiro, M., et al.: Patient-generated health data. In: RTI International, April 2012
14. Turner, K., et al.: Sharing patient-generated data with healthcare providers: findings from a 2019 national survey. J. Am. Med. Inform. Assoc. 28(2), 371–376 (2021)
15. Burgermaster, M., et al.: A new approach to integrating patient-generated data with expert knowledge for personalized goal setting: a pilot study. Int. J. Med. Informatics 139, 104158 (2020)
16. Hartmann, R., et al.: Utilization of patient-generated data collected through mobile devices: Insights from a survey on attitudes toward mobile self-monitoring and self-management apps for depression. JMIR Mental Health 6(4), e11671 (2019)
17. Baumel, A., et al.: Objective user engagement with mental health apps: systematic search and panel-based usage analysis. J. Med. Internet Res. 21(9), e14567 (2019)
18. Krishna, S., Boren, S.A., Balas, E.A.: Healthcare via cell phones: a systematic review. Telemed. e-Health 15(3), 231–240 (2009)
19. Torous, J.B., et al.: To use or not? Evaluating ASPECTS of smartphone apps and mobile technology for clinical care in psychiatry. J. Clin. Psychiatry 77(6), 6729 (2016)
20. Austin, L., et al.: Providing 'the bigger picture': benefits and feasibility of integrating remote monitoring from smartphones into the electronic health record: findings from the Remote Monitoring of Rheumatoid Arthritis (REMORA) study. Rheumatology 59(2), 367–378 (2020)
21. Zhu, H., et al.: Sharing patient-generated data in clinical practices: an interview study. In: AMIA Annual Symposium Proceedings. American Medical Informatics Association (2016)
22. Bichler, M.: Design science in information systems research. Wirtschaftsinformatik 48(2), 133–135 (2006). https://doi.org/10.1007/s11576-006-0028-8

23. Hevner, A.R.: A three cycle view of design science research. Scand. J. Inf. Syst. **19**(2), 4 (2007)
24. AIS. Senior Scholars' Basket of Journals, Association for Information Systems SIG: "IT in Healthcare" (2023). https://aisnet.org/page/SeniorScholarBasket. Cited 15 Feb 2023
25. BinDhim, N.F., et al.: Depression screening via a smartphone app: cross-country user characteristics and feasibility. J. Am. Med. Inform. Assoc. **22**(1), 29–34 (2014)
26. Torous, J., et al.: Utilizing a personal smartphone custom app to assess the patient health questionnaire-9 (PHQ-9) depressive symptoms in patients with major depressive disorder. JMIR Mental Health **2**(1), e3889 (2015)
27. Price, M., et al.: Usability evaluation of a mobile monitoring system to assess symptoms after a traumatic injury: a mixed-methods study. JMIR Mental Health **3**(1), e5023 (2016)
28. Kim, J., et al.: Depression screening using daily mental-health ratings from a smartphone application for breast cancer patients. J. Med. Internet Res. **18**(8), e5598 (2016)
29. Faherty, L.J., et al.: Movement patterns in women at risk for perinatal depression: use of a mood-monitoring mobile application in pregnancy. J. Am. Med. Inform. Assoc. **24**(4), 746–753 (2017)
30. Hetrick, S.E., et al.: Youth codesign of a mobile phone app to facilitate self-monitoring and management of mood symptoms in young people with major depression, suicidal ideation, and self-harm. JMIR Mental Health **5**(1), e9041 (2018)
31. Goltermann, J., et al.: Smartphone-based self-reports of depressive symptoms using the remote monitoring application in psychiatry (ReMAP): interformat validation study. JMIR Mental Health **8**(1), e24333 (2021)
32. Patoz, M.-C., et al.: Patient and physician perspectives of a smartphone application for depression: a qualitative study. BMC Psychiatry **21**(1), 1–12 (2021)
33. Cao, J., et al.: Tracking and predicting depressive symptoms of adolescents using smartphone-based self-reports, parental evaluations, and passive phone sensor data: development and usability study. JMIR Mental Health **7**(1), e14045 (2020)
34. Qu, C., et al.: Functionality of top-rated mobile apps for depression: systematic search and evaluation. JMIR Mental Health **7**(1), e15321 (2020)
35. Brooke, J.: SUS - a quick and dirty usability scale. Usability Eval. Ind. **189**(194), 4–7 (1996)
36. Borghouts, J., et al.: Barriers to and facilitators of user engagement with digital mental health interventions: systematic review. J. Med. Internet Res. **23**(3), e24387 (2021)
37. Nuij, C., et al.: Smartphone-based safety planning and self-monitoring for suicidal patients: rationale and study protocol of the CASPAR (Continuous Assessment for Suicide Prevention And Research) study. Internet Interv. **13**, 16–23 (2018)
38. Martinengo, L., et al.: Suicide prevention and depression apps' suicide risk assessment and management: a systematic assessment of adherence to clinical guidelines. BMC Med. **17**(1), 1–12 (2019)

A Study on the Effects of Experiencing a Falling Situation in Virtual Reality on EEG and Heart Rate Variability in the Elderly

Morihiro Tsujishita[1]($\boxtimes$), Hiroshi Noborio[2], Katsuhiko Onishi[2], and Masanao Koeda[3]

[1] Nara Gakuen University, Nara, Nara, Japan
tuzisita@nara-su.ac.jp
[2] Osaka Electro-Communication University, Shijonawate, Osaka, Japan
[3] Okayama Prefectural University, Soja, Okayama, Japan

Abstract. With the rapid aging of the Japanese population, the number of elderly people who fall over is increasing. Falls, including femoral neck fractures, constitute a significant cause of injuries in the elderly, leading to the primary need for nursing care. Hence, fall prevention and rehabilitation are expected to become increasingly important in the future, requiring active introduction of new technologies. The fear of falling can be a genuine concern often associated with the apprehension of the actual act of falling. This fear encompasses anxiety of experiencing a subsequent fall, even in the absence of resulting fractures or other injuries. This study aimed to comprehend the mechanism of fear of falling and contribute to the development of rehabilitation for this syndrome by assessing the effects of experiencing a fall on the EEG and HRV in elderly subjects through a virtual reality (VR) experience.

Keywords: VR Falling Experience · EEG · HRV

1 Introduction

As of the end of February 2021, 6.66 million people required long-term care, an increase of approximately 1 million people over eight years since 2013, and this upward trend is expected to continue [1]. Falls and fractures are the fourth leading cause of people requiring long-term care, following stroke, dementia, and age-related debilitation.

Falls not only necessitate nursing care but also limit daily life activities due to fear of falling, leading to confinement, depression, and an increased risk of further falls and development of dementia [2]. Considering fear of falling as a form of anxiety disorder, a behavioral therapy called exposure therapy can be used. This treatment gradually exposes individuals to specific fearful stimuli, such as people or confined spaces, reducing fear reactions and promoting habituation [3].

Recent studies on virtual reality (VR) exposure therapy, using VR technology for exposure to fearful stimuli, was reported to be effective in treating specific phobias such as fear of heights and airplanes, panic disorder, and anxiety disorders such as post-traumatic stress disorder (PTSD) [4].

M. Kurosu and A. Hashizume (Eds.): HCII 2024, LNCS 14686, pp. 149–159, 2024.
https://doi.org/10.1007/978-3-031-60428-7_11

However, no study has yet attempted VR exposure therapy for fear of falling in the elderly. Conventional fall prevention systems for the elderly focus of exercises and gymnastics to improve general muscle strength and balance. Although the fear of falling is considered important, specific approaches to addressing this fear have not been introduced. However, rehabilitation medicine employing VR technology, called virtual rehabilitation, has been active overseas. Studies have explored the effects of VR technology and treadmill training in preventing falls, but their objective was improving physical abilities rather than addressing the fear of falling [5].

Therefore, utilizing VR exposure therapy to reproduce a falling experience, and alleviating fear of falling through biofeedback (BF) could prevent confinement and inactivity in elderly people who have experienced a fall. Hence, VR exposure therapy could aid in fall prevention, thus helping to reduce the number of people requiring long-term care.

The study aims to elucidate the mechanism of the onset of fear of falling and contribute to the rehabilitation development for this syndrome by studying the effects of the VR experience of falling on EEG and heart rate variability (HRV) in the elderly and verifying the effectiveness of breathing techniques.

2 Methods

2.1 VR Fall Experience System

VR fall experience system was developed using Unreal Engine ver. 5 and Meta Quest2 as the HMD. The virtual space created resembles a typical Japanese house with a garden and a Japanese-style room with a table, cushions, and tatami mats laid out. The initial screen contains a button to start the fall experience and pressing it with the Meta Quest2 controller initiates the experience. Instructions are played from a speaker in the HMD, guiding the examinee forward to the edge of the Japanese-style room. When the examinee proceeds from the end of the Japanese-style room to the mark on the corridor, the examinee automatically steps off the ledge and falls into the garden below. After the fall, the experience ends with the individual lying in a prone position in the yard (Fig. 1). Following the complete experience, a video replay of the fall scene is automatically played (Fig. 2).

The time required for a single experience is approximately one minute from the initial screen to the reproduced video. This system can induce fear of falling by reproducing not only the experience of falling but also the scene of falling. Additionally, it can be used for experiments and also as a tool for fall prevention, as the HMD speaker also provides guidance to warn the individual against falls.

2.2 EEG Measurement

The EEG headset (iSyncWave®: iMediSync, Inc., Seoul, South Korea) had a built-in design positioned and based on the international 10–20 system (Fp1, Fp2, F7, F3, Fz, F4, F8, T3, C3, Cz, C4, T4, T5, P3, Pz, P4, T6, O1 and O2). Dry electrodes were used to derive brain potentials (Fig. 3). EEG was recorded at a sampling rate of 500 Hz

Fig. 1. VR fall experience system (opening screen)

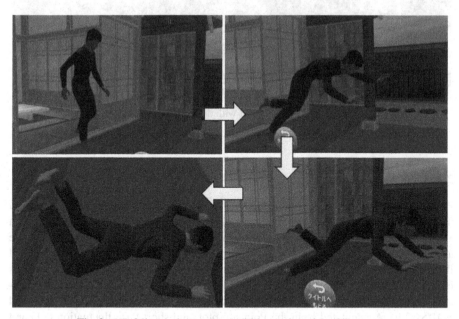

Fig. 2. VR fall experience system (Video replay of the fall scene)

and filtered through a band-pass of 0.53–120 Hz. The electrodes impedance was kept under 500 kΩ. Artifact removal was conducted using independent component analysis (ICA) individually for each channel. At the sensor level, the relative power of eight frequency bands (delta [1–3.99 Hz], theta [4–7.99 Hz], alpha1 [8–9.99 Hz], alpha2

[10–11.99 Hz], beta1 [12–14.99 Hz], beta2 [15–19.99 Hz], beta3 [20–29.99 Hz], and gamma [30–44.99 Hz]) was calculated using the iSyncBrain® software, v.2.1, 2018 (iMediSync, Inc., Seoul, South Korea). Owing to the considerable variability in EEG data among examinees, standardization was performed using EEG data from normal subjects adjusted for gender and age. All the processing and analysis were handled automatically by iSyncBrain® software.

Fig. 3. The EEG headset with dry electrodes in place.

2.3 HRV Measurement

HRV was measured using a photoelectric volumetric pulse wave sensor in the EEG headset. The volume pulse wave can be evaluated autonomously using the maximum amplitude value of each feature point from the waveform components within one cycle and the variation of pulse wavelength. Poincaré plots of heartbeat intervals and detrended fluctuation analysis (DFA) fractal properties were used to analyze HRV. The analysis utilized the iSyncHeart software (iMediSync, Inc., Seoul, South Korea), which automatically processed the pulse wave data acquired from the EEG headset. SD1, SD2, and SD1/SD2 were calculated from the Poincaré plot, and short-term fluctuation (α1) and long-term fluctuation (α2) were calculated from the DFA.

2.4 Experiment Procedures

After briefing the subjects on experimental procedures and obtaining their written consent, they were fitted with EEG headsets. Initially, the subjects were asked to gaze at a mark on the wall in front of them with open eyes for 90 s while they remained at rest. The measurements were then taken for 90 min while wearing the HMD and undergoing the VR fall experience (Fig. 4). After the fall experience, measurements were again taken in a resting state with open eyes for 90 s. This study was approved and conducted by the Research Ethics Review Committee of Nara Gakuen University.

Fig. 4. Scene of subject wearing EEG headset and HMD

3 Experimental Results

3.1 Subjects

Out of 12 recruited subjects, only four healthy elderly subjects who agreed to participate and were able to take measurements while wearing the HMD were selected for the experiment (Table 1).

Table 1. Subject Characteristics

Subject	Age	Sex	experience of falling
A	75	M	no
B	69	F	no
C	78	M	no
D	75	M	no

3.2 EEG Analysis

The EEG was divided into relative power at eight frequency bands, standardized with normal EEG data, and displayed as a topography for each of the four subjects (Figs. 5,

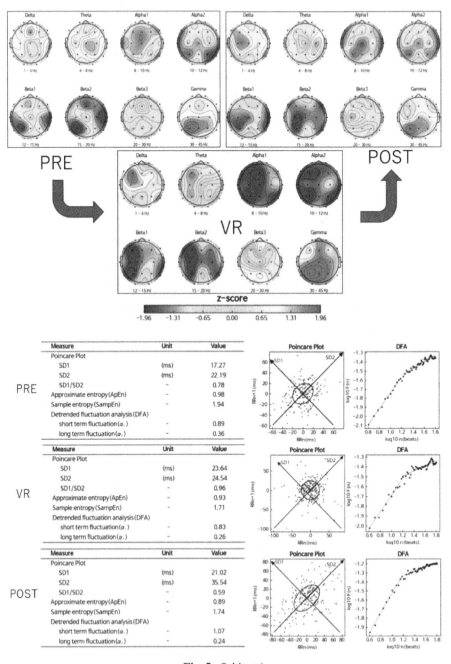

Fig. 5. Subject A

6, 7 and 8). The four subjects, being elderly, had high delta and theta wave power. Subjects A and B experienced a decrease in total head power for α1 and α2 during the VR experience compared to the resting state. β1 and β2 exhibited reduced power during

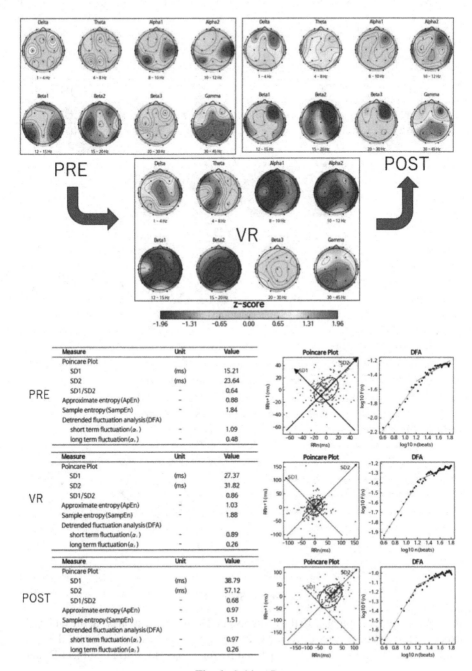

Fig. 6. Subject B:

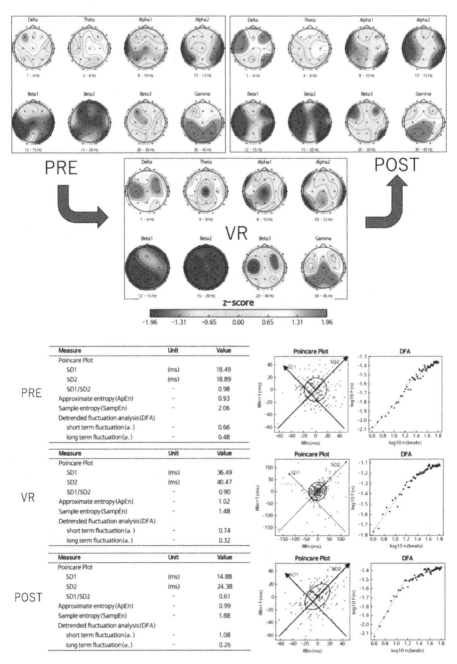

Fig. 7. Subject C:

the VR experience compared to the resting state. During the rest phase at the end of the experience, the patients had recovered to their pre-experience state. However, there was no downward trend in α1 and α2 or β1 and β2 for Subjects C and D. Subject D had a

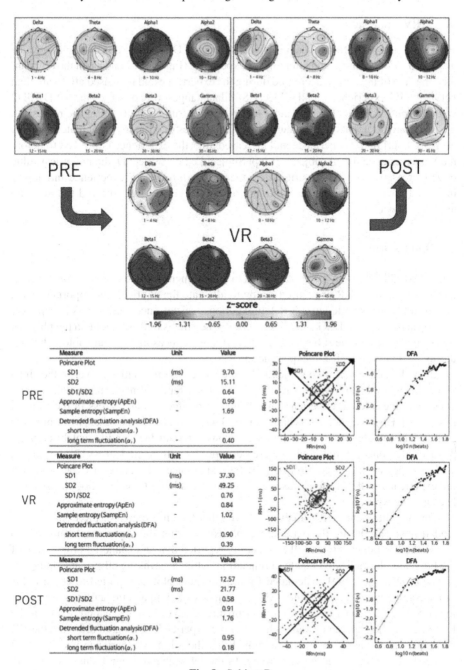

Fig. 8. Subject D:

marked decrease in β3 and Gamma during the VR experience and recovered after the VR experience. Subject C showed no characteristic changes throughout the VR experience.

3.3 HRV Analysis

HRV analysis was performed using Poincaré plots and DFA, with subject-specific results displayed before, during, and after the VR experience (Figs. 5, 6, 7 and 8). In the Poincaré plot, the area of the ellipse decreased during the experience and increased afterward than before the VR experience for all subjects. Similar changes were observed in the SD1/SD2 values calculated using the Poincaré plot, except for Subject D. In DFA, the regression plot diagram did not show the change well. The values of $\alpha1$ and $\alpha2$ calculated by DFA decreased during the experience and increased after the experience compared to before the VR experience for all subjects except Subject D. For Subject D, the numerical value of $\alpha1$ increased during the experience compared to before the VR experience and further increased after the experience, while the numerical value of $\alpha2$ showed the opposite tendency to decrease.

4   Discussion

Since post-fall phobia in the elderly leads to confinement and the need for nursing care, the development of VR exposure therapy to alleviate the phobia is an important issue. In this study, we developed a VR fall experience system necessary for VR exposure therapy and measured EEG and HRV to clarify the effects of this system on the physical and mental health of the subjects. EEG and HRV were measured in four subjects before, during, and after the VR fall experience.

In the EEG analysis, two subjects showed a decrease in relative power in the alpha wave frequency band. Alpha wave power has been reported to decrease with mental stress, and the VR fall experience was found to produce mental stress in the form of anxiety [6]. However, since no change in EEG was observed in the other two subjects, it could not be said that this was a common and constant trend due to individual differences. β-waves are generally reported to increase in power with mental stress [7], but in this study the power decreased after the VR fall experience. Therefore, it is possible that the experience in this system was not a mental stress but a transient shock experience because the exposure was brief.

On the other hand, HRV analysis showed that the ellipse area of the Poincaré plot tended to shrink during the experience and expand after the experience compared to before the VR fall experience. It is generally reported that an expanding ellipse area of the Poincaré plot indicates a state of relaxation, while a shrinking ellipse area indicates a state of stress [8]. SD1, calculated from a Poincaré plot, is reported to be an index of parasympathetic activity, while SD2 is an index of sympathetic activity. Therefore, lower SD1/SD2 values indicate more sympathetic nerve activity, which tended to be lower during the experience and higher after the experience compared to before the VR fall experience. Therefore, it was assumed that the VR fall experience had an effect of increasing sympathetic nerve activity. In the DFA analysis, we focused on $\alpha1$, an index of fractal characteristics at short durations of about 10 s, because the VR fall experience is a short duration experience. Except for subject C, $\alpha1$ values decreased during the experience and increased after the experience compared to before the VR fall experience. It has been reported that $\alpha1$ decreases at night and increases during the day, and the increase in this value is thought to be associated with activation of sympathetic nervous activity [9]. Therefore, the decrease in α1 during the experience was inconsistent with the results of the Poincaré plot. The reason for this discrepancy could be that the HRV measurement time was as short as 90 s, which was thought to support the results of the Poincaré plot.

Finally, since the number of subjects in this study was only four and could not be statistically verified, we would like to consider increasing the number of subjects in the future. In addition, the results of the EEG and HRV measurements showed that it is possible to understand the effects of the VR fall experience on the body and mind. However, it is necessary to investigate the measurement methods of EEG and HRV to improve the accuracy of the effect evaluation.

5 Conclusion

In this study, we investigated the effects of the developed VR fall experience system on the subjects' EEG and HRV. The results showed that the EEG tended to show a decrease in alpha and beta wave power during the VR experience, indicating that the subjects were under mental stress, while the HRV showed sympathetic activity in the Poincaré plot during the VR experience, but the DFA showed a decrease in sympathetic activity. The results were not consistent. Future work should include increasing the number of subjects and investigating measurement methods.

References

1. Ministry of Health, Labour and Welfare: Long-Term Care Insurance Business Status Report, 1 February 2024. https://www.mhlw.go.jp/topics/0103/tp0329-1.html
2. Kawahara, K., Utsunomiya, H., Hashizume, H.: T relationship between fear of falling, body composition, and fall risk. J. Japan Mibyo Syst. Assoc. 21(2), 148–151 (2015)
3. Roberts, R.J.: Passenger fear of flying: behavioural treatment with extensive in-vivo exposure and group support. Aviat. Space Environ. Med. 60(4), 342–348 (1989)
4. Banos, R.M., Botella, C., Perpina, C., et al.: Virtual reality treatment of flying phobia. IEEE Trans. Inf. Technol. Biomed. 6(3), 206–212 (2002)
5. Anat, M., et al.: Addition of a non-immersive virtual reality component to treadmill training to reduce fall risk in older adults (V-TIME): a randomized controlled trial. LANCET 388, 1170–1182 (2016)
6. Chang, P.F., Arendt-Nielsen, L., Chen, A.C.: Dynamic changes and spatial correlation of EEG activities during cold pressor test in man. Brain Res. Bull. 57(5), 667–675 (2002)
7. Wen, T.Y., Aris, S.M.: Electroencephalogram (EEG) stress analysis on alpha/beta ratio and theta/beta ratio. Indones. J. Electr. Eng. Comput. Sci 17(1), 175–182 (2020)
8. Rahman, S., Habel, M., Contrada, R.J.: Poincaré plot indices as measures of sympathetic cardiac regulation: responses to psychological stress and associations with pre-ejection period. Int. J. Psychophysiol. 133, 79–90 (2018)
9. Norihiro, H.: Detrended fluctuation analysis (DFA) of heart rate fluctuations and its clinical use of heart rate variability in elderly communication-dwelling people and in patients with transplanted human hearts. J. Tokyo Women's Med. Univ. 77(2), 47–61 (2007)

HCI in Healthcare

Developing Prosthetic Hand: Innovation in Hand Movement for Paralyzed Individuals

Md. Tariquzzaman Azad[1], Md. Farhad Hossain[1] (iD), Safin Rahman[1],
Mohammad Shidujaman[2] (iD), and Mengru Xue[1(✉)] (iD)

[1] Ningbo Innovation Center, Zhejiang University, Ningbo, China
{22251396,22151447,22251411,mengruxue}@zju.edu.cn
[2] RIoT Research Centre, Department of Computer Science and Engineering,
Independent University, Dhaka, Bangladesh
Shidujaman@iub.edu.bd

Abstract. The impaired mobility and limited freedom of individuals paralyzed due to spinal cord injuries or neurological illnesses present significant challenges. An innovative solution is urgently needed to provide adjustable and affordable hand prostheses. The integration of 3D printing technology has the potential to revolutionize prosthetic production with rapid prototyping, personalization, and low-cost manufacturing. Previous studies and projects have presented prototypes with limited hand movements, highlighting the need for fully functional and personalized hand prostheses. By addressing current limitations and leveraging advancements in 3D printing, this research highlights the potential of prosthetic hands to perform tasks such as removing shoes, opening lids, and zipping clothing, thus significantly improving the lives of paralyzed individuals.

Keywords: Biomechanics · Gesture · Prosthetic Hand model · Paralyzed · Wearable Hand · Spiral cord

1 Introduction

The impaired mobility and restricted freedom faced by individuals paralyzed due to spinal cord injuries or neurological illnesses pose significant challenges to their daily lives. The lack of customization, rigidity, and high cost of traditional prosthetic solutions prevent paralyzed people from recovering their usual hand movements [1, 4]. The considerable customization needs of current prosthetic devices provide issues that drive up costs and lengthen wait times. These problems are further exacerbated by financial difficulties and restricted access to specialized healthcare facilities, making these therapies costlier and less widely available [3]. Despite the considerable potential of 3D printing technology to revolutionize prosthetic manufacture by enabling rapid prototyping, customization, and cost-effective production [2, 4, 7], its integration into the prosthetic environment remains largely unexplored. This lack of exploration represents a critical gap in leveraging the trans-formative capabilities of 3D printing for enhancing

M. Kurosu and A. Hashizume (Eds.): HCII 2024, LNCS 14686, pp. 163–176, 2024.
https://doi.org/10.1007/978-3-031-60428-7_12

the development of prosthetic solutions. Iterative design upgrades ensure a personalized and adaptive fit for each users. The flexibility provided by 3D printing allows for the customizing of prosthetic devices to the specific needs and preferences of users, overcoming the constraints of one-size-fits-all solutions. Furthermore, the possibility of low-cost manufacturing might democratize access to modern prosthetic technology, making them more inexpensive and accessible to a larger population.

A novel technology that overcomes these limits and delivers adaptable and cheap hand prosthesis is urgently needed to solve this issue and improve the quality of life for paralyzed persons. Current prosthetic options, on the other hand, frequently need substantial customization, resulting in greater prices and longer wait times. Exploring and utilizing 3D printing's full potential in the prosthetic environment is critical for improving the industry and overcoming present limits in conventional prosthetic choices. Prophecies of prosthetic hands have been shown in a few studies and initiatives, however they are usually limited in what they can do, such grip items [8–13]. The lack of a broad range of hand movements and capabilities is another drawback of many conventional prosthetics.

In order to provide paralyzed people with completely functioning and customized hand prosthetics, this project aims to investigate the viability and efficacy of using 3D printing technologies. The extensive capabilities of prosthetic hands offered by 3D printing technology through a series of experiments. These studies seek to overcome present constraints in prosthetic devices by using advances in 3D printing. The emphasis is on showcasing the adaptability of these prosthetic hands, demonstrating their ability to execute a variety of everyday chores such as taking off shoes, opening lids, and zipping garments. These trials aim to present a paradigm shift in the field of prosthetics by addressing current constraints and leveraging the unique attributes of 3D printing, providing a glimpse into a future where individuals with paralysis can regain a broader range of functional hand movements, thereby improving their overall independence and quality of life.

Furthermore, this research aims to address imbalance by investigating and proposing novel solutions that cater specifically to the unique needs and challenges faced by individuals who are paralyzed, thereby enhancing their quality of life and functional independence. The approach used in the study is multidimensional, including biomechanical investigations, 3D printing technologies, and quantitative assessments. The process of fitting the 3D-printed prosthetic hands for individuals with paralysis proved to be straightforward, emphasizing simplicity in design and ease of use. The resulting 3D-printed hands demonstrated exceptional comfort, characterized by a lightweight structure, ergonomic considerations, and a seamless adaptation to the unique characteristics of the remaining limb. In contrast, real-world hand data was meticulously collected using sophisticated imaging techniques, ensuring the capture of the nuanced intricacies inherent in genuine finger motions. This advanced imaging approach facilitates a thorough understanding of natural finger movements, allowing for a precise and detailed comparison between real hand and 3D-printed prosthetic hand finger angles. Real-hand data is obtained through advanced imaging techniques, capturing the intricacies of natural finger movements.

Developing a set of experiments to test the capabilities of 3D-printed prosthetic hands in performing various daily tasks and engaging in routine activities. Evaluating how well the prosthetic hand can carry out a wide range of tasks beyond simple pinching, such complex hand movements needed for daily activities.

2 Related Work

Rehabilitation following a stroke presents significant hurdles for patients, sometimes necessitating access to specialized treatment in private clinics or hospitals [24, 25]. The procedure is complex, comprising supervised exercises aimed at reactivating neurons and restoring motor function [28, 29]. The issue resides not only in the physical components of rehabilitation, but also in the availability of proper facilities and the efficacy of therapies [28].

Stroke survivors frequently face a difficult path, balancing the need for individualized, comprehensive rehabilitation that extends beyond traditional hospital settings. Because of the multifaceted nature of post-stroke recovery, it is critical to investigate novel ways to rehabilitation that may address both the logistical and psychological components of this complex process. Fuzzy logic is used by the underlying software of the glove, which is controlled by an image processing technique and replicates motions that are recorded by a camera [15]. Exploration of ontology in the field of rehabilitation technology is a significant step forward, particularly in terms of enhancing grip type recognition skills in portable robotic gloves. The research goes into the subtle application of ontology for item type difference, giving a comprehensive way to categories and comprehend various items in a user's environment. The project intends to improve the precision of fingertip geometry modelling, which is crucial in assuring accurate and context-aware grip type recognition, by using ontological concepts.

Several studies intend to establish a strong framework that not only recognize the physical properties of objects but also comprehends their functional value in the context of motor control and rehabilitation through a synthesis of data from many sources [21, 27, 30]. These studies innovative approach signifies a departure from conventional methods, showcasing the potential to revolutionize how portable robotic gloves perceive and interact with objects, ultimately contributing to more effective and personalized rehabilitation. As a challenging but important job, estimating a hand's three-dimensional (3D) location from a single RGB snapshot is here tackled by training on a large data-set of RGB hand photographs combined with precise 3D hand key-point annotations [16]. The reliance on a large data-set is intended to increase the accuracy of the model's predictions for the location of hand key-points, which will enhance the effectiveness of the suggested method.

The ability to visually explore a virtual area with collision detection and the ability to interact with virtual items through tactile or aural feedback are other benefits of integrating a virtual 3D representation [17]. The immersive environment reacts to human activity in a dynamic way, making the rehabilitation process more interesting and successful. Nevertheless, difficulties result from the fingers' limited vision because of the camera's wrist angle. The restriction significantly reduces the accuracy and efficiency of the image processing method by making it more difficult to accurately record hand and finger motions.

Movement control recovery and nerve reactivation are challenging issues, and the combination of image processing, fuzzy logic, ontology, and virtual 3D representation shows how to approach them from several angles [26]. Although finger visibility presents certain problems, the innovations suggested in the research open the door to a more inclusive and engaging rehabilitation process, which might revolutionize the field of stroke recovery. Furthermore, the study is extremely valuable in furthering the debate on technology-assisted healthcare, particularly in the domain of rehabilitation. The foundations presented that provides a solid platform for future research and technical improvements. Its ramifications go beyond the specific application of stroke rehabilitation, giving a road map °C for using modern technology in a broader range of healthcare scenarios. The restriction significantly diminishes the accuracy and efficiency of the image processing method by making it more challenging to accurately record hand and finger motions [22, 23].

Analyzing the cost-effectiveness of 3D printing technology in comparison to traditional prosthetic solutions and its potential to increase accessibility for a broader population. Investigating the durability and longevity of 3D-printed prosthetic hands under various conditions to ensure their practical viability over time. The investigation of the feasibility and usefulness of 3D printing in making personalized, fully functional prosthetic hands are a key step towards a future in which technology improves accessibility and patient outcomes in paralysis rehabilitation. Although finger visibility presents certain problems, the innovations suggested in this study open the door to a more inclusive and engaging rehabilitation process, which might revolutionize the field of stroke recovery. In addition to advancing the conversation around technology-assisted healthcare, especially in the area of rehabilitation, this study lays the groundwork for future advancements and improvements in the pursuit of better patient outcomes.

3   Design Overview

This design overview focuses on the development of a prosthetic hand that harnesses the possibilities of technology to enhance the daily lives of paralyzed individuals. By incorporating advanced technology and addressing specific functional requirements, this prosthetic hand design aims to empower paralyzed individuals with greater independence and improved quality of life.

The rest of the section explains how the combination of removing shoes, opening lids, and zipping clothing capabilities in a single device represents a significant step forward in prosthetic hand technology, paving the way for a more inclusive and accessible future.

3.1 Zipping Clothes

This is particularly advantageous for individuals with hand losses, as it enables the recognition of grasping gestures even in the absence of a functional hand. The other methodically on the intact hand itself to capture data. Therefore, for the successful implementation of zipper clothing using a prosthetic hand, it is crucial to consider utilizing EMG-based data capturing methods, as they offer the potential to recognize and replicate the grasping gestures of amputees with hand losses (Fig. 1).

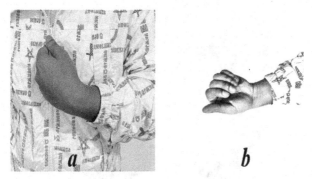

Fig. 1. Utilizing an artificial hand for the purpose of manipulating zipper and quantifying the angle of zipper opening, figure (a) shows the opening of the zipper, and figure (b) shows the angle of the hand.

3.2 Opening Lids

As previously stated, it is essential to focus on human hand motion-capturing devices while exploring the use of prosthetic hands, can be considered for an artificial hand (Fig. 2). In the realm of research, the 3D-printed prosthetic hand is engineered to encompass an actuation mechanism that facilitates the generation of the requisite force and movement for opening lids. This mechanism can comprise flexible joints or linkages that enable controlled motion of the fingers or gripping mechanism.

The control system employed in a 3D-printed prosthetic hand may vary depending on the distinct design and intended functionality [9]. It may encompass mechanical constituents, such as cables or tendons, strategically routed through the hand structure to transmit force from the user's residual limb to the fingers. These cables or tendons are connected to the interface of the user's residual limb and are controlled by muscle movements or electrical signals. The design of the 3D-printed prosthetic hand is meticulously devised to ensure a secure grip on the lid. To augment grip strength and prevent slippage during the lid-opening action, the fingers or gripping mechanism may feature flexible and textured surfaces.

The control system, driven by muscle movements or electrical signals, initiates the gripping mechanism to firmly grasp the lid [20]. The design of the 3D printed prosthetic hand may incorporate mechanical advantage mechanisms, such as leverage or gear systems, to amplify the force exerted by the user's residual limb during lid opening [10, 13]. This augmentation enables easier and more effective lid opening. The utilization of 3D printing technology allows for the customization of the prosthetic hand to accommodate the user's residual limb and specific lid-opening requirements [11].

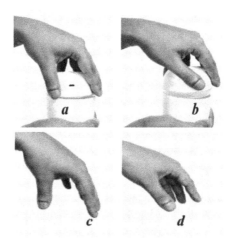

Fig. 2. Figure (a) displays the initial position for opening lids, and Figure (b) shows the completed position for opening lids using an artificial hand. Figure (c) depicts the angle of the opening lid's reflection in figure (a), where figure (d) depicts the finishing angle which is the reflection in figure (b).

Factors such as size, shape, and grip strength can be tailored based on the individual's unique needs and preferences [5]. This customization ensures a comfortable and functional fit for the user, enhancing overall usability and the user experience.

3.3   Take of Shoes

As previously noted, it is crucial to focus on human hand motion-capturing tools while exploring the implementation of prosthetic hands, can be considered as a choice for an artificial hand (Fig. 3). In the realm of research, the utilization of 3D-printing technology in the development of prosthetic hands has emerged as a noteworthy area of investigation. These 3D-printed prosthetic hands exhibit versatility by incorporating either individually articulated fingers or a simplified gripping mechanism, contingent upon the specific requirements of the user and the intricacy of the shoe removal task at hand [2]. In the process of removing a shoe, the user initiates the control system, thereby activating the gripping mechanism integrated within the prosthetic hand. Through the utilization of either the articulated fingers or the gripping mechanism, a secure grasp is established on

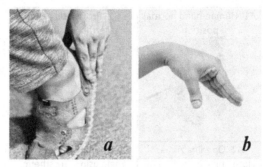

Fig. 3. Figure (a) displays the take-off shoes and figure (b) illustrates the angle of the hand while using an artificial hand for the purpose of taking off shoes and measuring the angle of taking off shoes.

the shoe, enabling the user to apply a pulling motion that facilitates the removal of the shoe from their foot.

This research aims to explore and optimize the design and functionality of 3D-printed prosthetic hands, specifically focusing on their efficacy in assisting individuals with shoe removal tasks.

4 Design Observation

In this study, we employed 3D printing technology to fabricate a prosthetic hand, aiming to investigate and compare its functionality with that of a natural human hand (Fig. 4).

Various tasks commonly associated with daily activities, such as opening lids, zipping clothing, and adjusting shoe angles, were meticulously measured using both the human hand and the prosthetic hand. The obtained results elucidate discernible differences between the capabilities of the human hand and the prosthetic counterpart, providing valuable insights into the comparative effectiveness of the prosthetic device in performing essential daily tasks. The findings of this study reveal notable distinctions between the functionality of the human hand and a prosthetic hand. This comparative analysis aims to facilitate the assessment of accuracy during real-life implementations, providing insights into the operational efficacy of both natural and prosthetic hands (Table 1).

The objective is to enable users to ascertain the level of precision achievable in various tasks, thereby enhancing their understanding of the practical capabilities of both human and prosthetic hands. This research contributes valuable information that can guide users in gauging the accuracy required for specific real-world activities, aiding them in making informed decisions about the adoption and utilization of prosthetic hands.

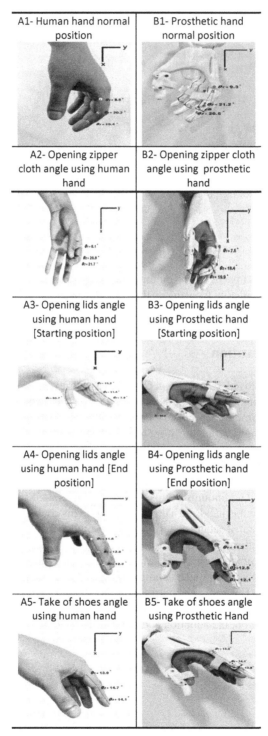

Fig. 4. The figure illustrates the angular differences between the human hand and the prosthetic hand.

Table 1. The table presents a comparative analysis of the angular differences at various key points between the human hand and prosthetic hand, elucidating the degrees of distinction.

X/Y	θ_1	θ_2	θ_3	θ_0
A1	8.5	20.2	19.4	-
B1	9.3	21.2	20.5	-
A2	8.1	20.9	21.7	-
B2	7.5	18.4	19.9	-
A3	15.2	11.4	7.9	65.7
B3	14.9	10.8	7.1	60.6
A4	11.6	12.8	12.3	-
B4	11.2	12.5	12.1	-
A5	13.9	14.7	14.1	-
B5	13.2	14.1	13.8	-

5 Design Implementation

In this research-oriented design implementation, the creation of a 3D-printed prosthetic hand is detailed, showcasing a fusion of mechanical design and electronics. The project involves a comprehensive list of materials and components, including 3D-printed parts, electronics such as Arduino boards, servo motors, flex sensors, and other miscellaneous items like rubber belts and glue. The design process begins with considering individual user factors, such as the level of amputation and desired functionalities. Using a CAD program, the mechanical features are meticulously designed based on the user's unique requirements, considering factors like hand size and shape.

The 3D model is then translated into printable layers using slicing software. The electrical aspect involves an interactive project using Arduino, servo motors, and flex sensors. The Arduino board acts as a micro-controller platform, controlling the precise movement of servo motors, which are strategically connected to the prosthetic hand's fingers. Flex sensors are utilized to measure the degree of finger bending, enhancing the prosthetic hand's responsiveness. The electrical components are interconnected using jumper wires, ensuring organized and seamless connectivity. The calibrated Arduino interprets flex sensor readings, orchestrating the servo motors to produce natural hand movements.

The integration of technology enables the prosthetic hand to work in tandem with an enabled hand, showcasing coordinated movements for various tasks like zipping clothes, removing shoes, and opening lids. The synchronization of both hands maximizes productivity and accuracy in task performance, highlighting the importance of harmonious coordination in improving overall prosthetic device functioning and user experience (Fig. 5).

The research also emphasizes the user-friendly experience facilitated by integrating flex sensors into a glove, allowing intuitive hand commands for disabling and enabling prosthetic hand movements during specific tasks. The detailed design and development

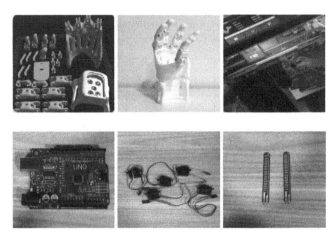

Fig. 5. The diagram illustrates the constituent elements essential for constructing a prosthetic hand, delineating the key components involved in the assembly process.

process extend to specific functionalities such as zipping clothes and taking off shoes. Flex sensors strategically embedded in a glove capture nuanced hand gestures, translating them into digital commands for the prosthetic hand (Fig. 6).

Fig. 6. The visual representation illustrates the experimental results obtained through the execution of the proposed implementation, demonstrating its efficacy in commanding the prosthetic hand.

The research emphasizes the meticulous crafting of the 3D-printed prosthetic hand to replicate the anatomical structure and functionality of a natural hand. The integration of flex sensors and smart control systems aims to enhance responsiveness and adaptability, providing individuals with limb differences a versatile tool for everyday chores. The study concludes by illustrating how the prosthetic hand, when equipped with technology, becomes more responsive and user-friendly, contributing to the empowerment of individuals with limb differences in their daily lives.

6 Discussion

In the realm of prosthetic hand design, it is imperative to closely examine and understand the differences in functional angles between prosthetic hands and their human counterparts [1, 6]. Activities such as zipping clothes, opening lids, and managing shoes entail specific joint movements and angles that are seamlessly executed by the human hand. These mundane yet crucial activities underscore the significance of precise and realistic angle replication in prosthetic hand development.

One of the primary challenges lies in the inherent dissimilarity between the intricate biomechanics of the human hand and the mechanical functionalities of prosthetic counterparts [14, 18, 19]. The human hand exhibits a remarkable degree of adaptability and dexterity, seamlessly adjusting joint angles and movements to navigate various daily tasks [31, 32]. Prosthetic hands, on the other hand, face limitations in replicating this nuanced range of motion.

For zipping clothes, the human hand effortlessly adjusts the angles of the fingers and thumb to manipulate the zipper. Prosthetic hands often struggle to emulate this intricate motion, leading to difficulties in performing what might be considered a routine task for an able-bodied individual. Addressing this discrepancy requires a deep dive into the biomechanics of zipper manipulation, pinpointing the specific joint angles involved, and incorporating this knowledge into the design and programming of prosthetic devices.

Similarly, the opening of lids and shoes involves a combination of gripping, twisting, and pulling motions that demand a precise orchestration of joint movements. Human hands instinctively adapt to the varying shapes and sizes of lids or shoes, adjusting finger and thumb angles accordingly. In contrast, prosthetic hands may lack the finesse required to perform these tasks seamlessly, underscoring the need for a more sophisticated understanding and integration of functional angles in prosthetic design.

To bridge this gap, research efforts should focus on multidisciplinary collaboration between biomechanics experts, engineers, and prosthetic users. Advanced sensors and machine learning algorithms can be employed to analyze and mimic the natural joint angles employed by the human hand during these activities. Furthermore, user feedback and real-world testing are critical components of refining prosthetic designs, ensuring that the functional angles are not only accurate but also intuitive for users.

In conclusion, understanding and addressing the discrepancy in functional angles between prosthetic hands and human hands for activities like zipping clothes, opening lids, and managing shoes is pivotal for enhancing the overall functionality and user experience of prosthetic devices. This research discussion emphasizes the importance of a comprehensive approach that integrates biomechanical insights, advanced technologies, and user feedback to create prosthetic hands that closely mirror the adaptive capabilities of the human hand in daily activities.

7 Future Work and Conclusion

In the forthcoming phase of our research, we intend to conduct an empirical study involving the implementation of a prosthetic hand on actual patients. The primary objective of this investigation is to assess and validate the accuracy of the design proposed in our prior studies. This practical application will afford us valuable insights into the real-world functionality and performance of the prosthetic hand, thereby enhancing the translational impact of our research findings. Through rigorous experimentation and observation, we aim to refine and optimize the prosthetic hand's capabilities, ensuring its efficacy and suitability for real-life usage. The outcomes of this study will contribute substantively to the advancement of prosthetic technology, providing valuable data for future developments in the field.

The study on the disparity in angle requirements between prosthetic hands and human hands during everyday tasks such as zipping clothes, opening lids, and handling shoes underscores the critical importance of optimizing prosthetic designs for enhanced functionality and user experience. Recognizing and addressing the differences in biomechanics between prosthetic and human hands is imperative for achieving optimal performance and usability.

The findings highlight the need for a nuanced approach in prosthetic hand development, taking into account the varied angles and movements essential for common activities of daily living. By understanding the specific demands posed by tasks like zipping clothes, opening lids, and handling shoes, designers and engineers can tailor prosthetic devices to closely mimic the natural range of motion exhibited by human hands.

Moreover, this research serves as a foundation for advancing prosthetic technology, promoting the creation of devices that not only restore physical capabilities but also facilitate a seamless integration into users' daily lives. The insights gained from this study can guide future innovations in prosthetic design, fostering the development of devices that contribute to a more inclusive and functional experience for individuals with limb differences.

Ultimately, by addressing the angle discrepancies between prosthetic hands and human hands in specific tasks, we can pave the way for more effective and user-friendly prosthetic solutions, enhancing the overall quality of life for those who rely on these devices. This research encourages ongoing collaboration between researchers, clinicians, and prosthetic users to refine and optimize prosthetic designs, ensuring a closer alignment with the natural movements and capabilities of the human hand.

References

1. Günay, S.Y., Quivira, F., Erdoğmuş, D.: Muscle synergy-based grasp classification for robotic hand prosthetics. In: Proceedings of the 10th International Conference on Pervasive Technologies Related to Assistive Environments, pp. 335–338 (2017)
2. Hrabia, C.E., Wolf, K., Wilhelm, M.: Whole hand modeling using 8 wearable sensors: biomechanics for hand pose prediction. In: Proceedings of the 4th Augmented Human International Conference, pp. 21–28 (2013)
3. Truong, H., Nguyen, P., Nguyen, A., Bui, N., Vu, T.: Capacitive sensing 3D-printed wristband for enriched hand gesture recognition. In: Proceedings of the 2017 Workshop on Wearable Systems and Applications, pp. 11–15 (2017)
4. Yoo, H.J., Lee, S., Kim, J., Park, C., Lee, B.: Development of 3D-printed myoelectric hand orthosis for patients with spinal cord injury. J. Neuroeng. Rehabil. **16**(1), 1–14 (2019)

5. Kawashimo, J., Yamanoi, Y., Kato, R.: Development of easily wearable assistive device with elastic exoskeleton for paralyzed hand. In: 2017 26th IEEE International Symposium on Robot and Human Interactive Communication (RO-MAN), pp. 1159–1164 (2017)

6. Liu, Y., Zhang, S., Gowda, M.: NeuroPose: 3D hand pose tracking using EMG wearables. In: Proceedings of the Web Conference 2021, pp. 1471–1482 (2021)

7. Kadhim, A.N., Abdulsattar, M., Abdulghani, A.: Lowcost design of 3D printed wearable prosthetic hand. Am. J. Eng. Res. **7**(10), 110–117 (2018)

8. Lim, C., Kim, J., Kim, M.J.: Thumble: one-handed 3D object manipulation using a thimble-shaped wearable device in virtual reality. In: Adjunct Proceedings of the 35th Annual ACM Symposium on User Interface Software and Technology, pp. 1–3 (2022)

9. Cuellar, J.S., Smit, G., Zadpoor, A.A., Breedveld, P.T.: Guidelines for the design of non-assembly mechanisms: the case of 3D-printed prosthetic hands. Proc. Inst. Mech. Eng. Part H: J. Eng. Med. **232**(9), 962–971 (2018)

10. Bai, H., Lee, G., Billinghurst, M.: Using 3D hand gestures and touch input for wearable AR interaction. In: CHI 2014 Extended Abstracts on Human Factors in Computing Systems, pp. 1321–1326 (2014)

11. Cuellar, J.S., Smit, G., Breedveld, P., Zadpoor, A.A., Plettenburg, D.: Functional evaluation of a non-assembly 3D-printed hand prosthesis. Proc. Inst. Mech. Eng. Part H: J. Eng. Med. **233**(11), 1122–1131 (2019)

12. Pérez Fernández, C., del Mar Espinosa, M., Domínguez, M.: Use of 3D printing in the manufacture of prosthetic hands. Técnica Industrial: Revista Cuatrimestral de Ingeniería, Industria e Innovación (334) (2023)

13. Shatilov, K.A., Chatzopoulos, D., Hang, A.W.T., Hui, P.: Using deep learning and mobile offloading to control a 3D-printed prosthetic hand. Proc. ACM Interact. Mob. Wearable Ubiquit. Technol. **3**(3), 1–19 (2019)

14. Selvan, M.P., Raj, R., Sai, R.G., Jancy, S., Mary, V.A.: Prosthetic hand using EMG. J. Phys. Conf. Ser. **1770**(1), 012018 (2021). IOP Publishing. Closest-Point Problems (Computational Geometry). Ph.D. Dissertation. Stanford University, Palo Alto, CA. UMI Order Number: AAT 8506171

15. Bărbulescu, M., Musat, A., Popescu, D.: 3D printed robotic glove useful for recovery of people affected by stroke (2015)

16. Wu, Z., Hoang, D., Hoang, D., Xie, Y., Chen, L., Lin, Y.Y.: 3D-aware multi-modal guided hand generative network for 3D hand pose synthesis, p. 9, Seattle, WA, USA. ACM (2020)

17. Götzelmann, T.: A 3D printable hand exoskeleton for the haptic exploration of virtual 3D scenes. Nuremberg Institute of Technology, Island of Rhodes, Greece. ACM (2017)

18. Su, H., Kim, T.-H., Moeinnia, H., Kim, W.S.: A 3D printed wearable electromyography wristband. Simon Fraser University, Surrey, BC, Canada (2023)

19. Wu, E., Yuan, Y., Yeo, H.-S., Quigley, A., Koike, H., Kitani, K.M.: Back-Hand-Pose: 3D hand pose estimation for a wrist-worn camera via dorsum deformation network, USA (2020)

20. Roy, D.P., Chowdhury, Md.Z.A., Afrose, F., Hoque, Md.E.: Design and development of a cost-effective prosthetic hand for upper limb amputees. Military Institute of Science and Technology (MIST) (2021)

21. Burns, M., et al.: Design and implementation of an instrumented data glove that measures kinematics and dynamics of human hand (2021)

22. Giovannetti, G., Buscaglione, S., Noccaro, A., Formica, D.: Design and validation of 3D printed hand interfaces for wrist stiffness assessment (2023)

23. Domínguez, R.E., Iraheta, A.S.O., Gamero V, M.A.: Design of a hand rehabilitation exoskeleton prototype for patients affected by osteoarthritis. In: 8th International Conference on Control and Robotics Engineering, Tecnológica Centroamericana (UNITEC) (2023)

24. Mohamaddan, S., Khamis, H., Awang, S.A., Zakaria, N.A.C., Hanafusa, A.: Development and control of hand exoskeleton system using intended movement. In: IEEE Eurasia Conference on Biomedical Engineering, Healthcare and Sustainability (2021)

25. Andrei, B.C., Mircea, C., Paul, S.: Gesture interaction with 3D printed hybrid compression and inertial tracking device based on plastic embedded antenna for virtual reality integration. IEEE, Romania (2022)

26. Cai, J., Cai, J.: Human-computer interaction-based robotic design and development and control system testing—prototyping and implementation testing study of a robotic. In: IEEE Asia-Pacific Conference (2022)

27. Añazco, E.V., et al.: Human-like object grasping and relocation for an anthropomorphic robotic hand with natural hand pose priors in deep reinforcement learning. ACM, Moscow (2019)

28. Miskon, A., Djonhari, A.K.S., Azhar, S.M.H., Thanakodi, S.A/L., Tawil, S.N.M.: Identification of raw EEG signal for prosthetic hand application. ACM (2019)

29. Boruah, A., Kakoty, N.M., Ali, T.: Reasoning on objects' geometric shapes for prosthetic hand grasping. ACM ISBN 978-1-4503-6650-2/19/07, Chennai, India (2019)

30. Dragos, C., Neluş-Constantin, B., Chirita, A., Ciobanu, C.: Robotic arm control via hand movements. IEEE Transilvania University, Braşov, Romania (2022)

31. Desai, R., Kelly, K., Lewis, K., Sreenivasan, V., Austin, W.: The eagle hand: innovations in 3D printing prosthetic hands. IEEE, Rutgers University-New Brunswick (2021)

32. Dragusanu, M., Achilli, G.M., Valigi, M.C., Prattichizzo, D., Malvezzi, M., Salvietti, G.: The wavejoints: a novel methodology to design soft-rigid grippers made by monolithic 3D printed fingers with adjustable joint stiffness. IEEE (2022)

Study of the Effectiveness of Gamification Design Applied to Chinese Medicine Learning App

Rongrong Fu[iD] and Yongyan Guo[(⊠)]

College of Art Design and Media, East China University of Science and Technology,
Shanghai, China
g-gale@163.com

Abstract. Gamification has become an increasingly important topic and has been researched in many fields. Chinese medicine culture is a treasure of Chinese traditional culture, but the existing Chinese medicine learning mobile apps mostly adopt the traditional way of science learning, and it is difficult to have innovative research and discovery. Gamification design can apply gamification elements to non-game scenarios to optimize the user experience and help to solve the actual problems. Based on this, the article conducted a study on the usability, effectiveness and emotional experience of gamification design applied to Chinese medicine learning mobile apps, and found that gamified Chinese medicine learning apps have multiple positive effects on promoting users' knowledge of Chinese medicine, and the results are of positive significance for optimising this kind of apps, and providing a more suitable way to learn and disseminate the Chinese medicine culture.

Keywords: Gamification Design · Chinese medicine Learning · Mobile Apps · Usability Measurement · Emotional Experience Measurement

1 Introduction

Chinese medicine, Chinese traditional medicine, is an important part of Chinese traditional culture. Under the new socio-economic and technological development situation, adhering to the concept of dissemination and promotion of Traditional Chinese Medicine Culture (TCMC), people are trying to realise the innovative development of the dissemination of TCMC. The study of its effective learning mode will be more conducive to enhancing the learning and dissemination of TCMC and promoting the value and connotation of TCMC.

The research shows that the main tasks of learning Traditional Chinese Medicine (TCM) knowledge include the understanding of herbs and prescriptions and the mastery of TCM diagnosis and treatment thinking, but the existing applications supporting the learning of TCM knowledge mostly adopt the traditional way of graphic learning and literature popularization, which is easy to catalyze negative emotions such as dullness and tedium, and reduce the efficiency of learning; another situation is that in most young groups, the impression of TCM is boring and redundant, and the traditional

M. Kurosu and A. Hashizume (Eds.): HCII 2024, LNCS 14686, pp. 177–193, 2024.
https://doi.org/10.1007/978-3-031-60428-7_13

popularization of science is difficult to stimulate the interest of such groups in exploring the culture of TCM [1] and learning motivation.

In the web 3.0 era, mobile intelligent terminals have become the main way for people to obtain information. The 52nd "Statistical Report on the Development of the Internet in China" shows that the number of Chinese cell phone netizens has reached 1.076 billion [2]. Meanwhile, mobile learning methods are increasingly receiving widespread attention for their fun, mobile, and fragmented learning experiences [3]. However, we found that the current mobile apps for learning TCM have problems such as information overload, redundant knowledge, and boring learning mechanism, which are difficult to meet the user's requirements for an interesting experience of learning TCM as well as for learning efficiency.

In this context, it is expected that gamification design theory will be integrated into TCM learning mobile apps to infiltrate culture and knowledge by means of gamification and in a fun and educational way, but there are fewer research papers on the effectiveness of the application of gamification theory in TCM learning apps. Therefore, in this paper, we take the knowledge of Chinese herbal medicine as an example, and combine it with "AIYI" (a kind of TCM learning application designed based on gamification theory) to study whether the application of gamification design theory to TCM learning application can help to improve the effectiveness of users' knowledge of Chinese herbal medicine; and whether applications incorporating gamification elements can help optimize the user learning experience, enhance the usability of TCM learning applications, positively affect the emotional experience of the users, and promote the users' continuous learning.

2   Related Work

2.1   Mobile Learning

Mobile learning usually refers to a learning mode in which learners access learning resources through mobile terminal devices and learn anytime, anywhere, and learners in mobile learning have greater autonomy in learning [4]. They are free to adjust the time of learning activities without the limitation of time and place in order to acquire knowledge when needed [5]. Mobile learning is characterized by convenience, flexibility, personalization, and good interactivity [6]. This is of great significance for learning TCM knowledge. Traditional passive receptive learning of TCM knowledge is very likely to make the user become tedious and tired, while the mobile learning approach can break down the huge and redundant learning system of TCM knowledge into a continuous learning process that can be terminated and continued at any time [7], coupled with the fact that the Internet information technology can provide a wealth of learning resources and learning methods, which creates an expandable learning space for TCM knowledge learners. Whether they are learners of Chinese medicine, Chinese medicine enthusiasts, or curiosity seekers, they can acquire the corresponding knowledge of TCM anytime and anywhere according to their own needs.

2.2   Research on Mobile Apps for Chinese Medicine Learning

Through the investigation of TCM learning apps in the Apple App Store, such as "Zhiyuan Chinese Medicine", "Chinese Medicine Wisdom", "Essence of Chinese

Medicine", etc., it is found that these apps are mainly categorized into knowledge lectures, bookstores, question banks, and knowledge encyclopedias according to the learning modules. Knowledge lectures provide users with videos explaining the theoretical knowledge of TCM; bookstores provide users with readable classics of TCM; and Chinese medicine question banks provide examination questions ranging from basic theories to those covering the thinking and skills of various disciplines of TCM. The knowledge encyclopedia includes a wide range of content from the theory to the practice of TCM.

In general, this kind of application is a comprehensive learning software, summarizing and integrating a huge amount of knowledge of TCM. We took herbs and prescriptions as the entry point for research and found that this kind of application uniformly adopts the traditional way of presenting knowledge: herbs and prescriptions are categorized according to their medicinal properties and efficacy, and are presented to the user in the form of visualized text and pictures, so that the user learns through step-by-step clicking on them to view the relevant graphic introduction. Obviously, in the context of integrating a huge amount of TCM knowledge, this way of presenting information and popularizing science is relatively inefficient.

At present, there is only one application with the highest download volume of 22,000, and most of the top-ranked applications have a download volume of less than 500, and the most common comments are: "The explanations are very specific, but it is troublesome to operate them", "I want to understand, but I feel it is a little bit boring", "Learning for a period of time feels very sleepy", "The content is so much and complicated, it is a bit boring to use", etc. It can be seen that the popularization of this type of application and the learning mechanism is very easy to cause fatigue in learning, and it is difficult to arouse the users' interest in learning.

2.3 Gamification Design

A common definition of gamification is the use of game design elements in non-game situations [8]. Through gamification design, gamification elements and mechanisms can be added to non-game scenarios to create a game-like experience and stimulate users' behavioral engagement [9]. The goal of gamification, as defined by Huotari and Hamari, is "a process that enhances the gaming experience as a service to support the overall value creation of the user" [10], which is based on the service experience perspective that the purpose of gamification is to enhance the user experience by using gamification mechanisms to help create user value. Nowadays, gamification has become an interdisciplinary research field, and its related research has covered a variety of fields, including health [11], education [12, 13], public service [14], environmental protection [15] and so on. [16] Assumptions about gamification seek to increase user engagement in tasks and promote user behavior. Gee's study highlights the potential application of gamification to the cognitive learning process [17]; Medius, a gamification-based digital application, provides targeted and effective learning for children with autism [18]; and Dymora's study specifies that gamification may be beneficial for children with dyslexia [19]; and a study by [20] specified that gamified lessons are more motivating than traditional lessons. The above studies prove the positive effects of gamification in enhancing learning and cognition.

Secondly, gamification may also be beneficial in shaping positive learning emotions; a study by [21] found that students with high positive emotions were more motivated and willing to strive for academic achievement. When faced with more complex learning tasks, pleasurable emotions can make the learning process smoother and lead to excellent learning efficiency. Pleasant experiences and emotions are exactly what gamification can provide.

Gamification Design Elements. Kevin Werbach proposed the gamification DMC design structure [22], also known as the gamification pyramid structure model, as shown in Fig. 1. The model divides the gamification elements into three structural levels from top to bottom: Dynamics, Mechanics, and Components [22], and each level contains subdivided gamification elements. Dynamics are the macro forces that promote gamification behavior; Mechanics to advance the game process and user participation; Components are the most basic gamification elements, which are the instantiated forms of dynamics and mechanics. Component-level gamification elements are formed into rules by the framework and process of the mechanics layer, and then combined with the intrinsic drive of the dynamics layer to form a complete game function and system.

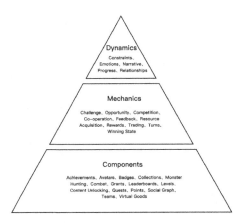

Fig. 1. Gamification DMC Pyramid Model

2.4 Gamification of Mobile Learning

Based on the previous analysis, it can be concluded that the core of gamification lies in applying gamification elements to non-game scenarios by using gamification mechanisms to promote users' intrinsic motivation, help solve problems and achieve goals. The immersive experience and good user behavioral drivers brought by gamification can promote the improvement of learning-oriented tasks in terms of effectiveness and user experience. However, there is less literature on the effectiveness of gamification elements in TCM learning. Therefore, the research goal of this paper is to utilize gamification design mechanisms to incorporate extracted gamification elements into a TCM learning mobile application so that it can function as a learning incentive [23]. The results of this study will provide useful assistance to enhance users' efficacy and learning experience in learning TCM knowledge. In this paper, we will use the TCM learning game we designed as a test tool, and three experiments and user interview method will be used to study the usability of the system, the effectiveness of gamification on TCM learning, and the tendency of users to use the emotional experience.

3 Methodology

3.1 Construction of a Gamified Mobile Application for Learning Chinese Medicine

In this paper, we designed a gamified TCM learning application and actionable prototype kinematics with the entry point of learning about Chinese medicine herbs, which were used to test whether the user's learning outcomes could be improved, and the user experience related to usability. The designers included the instructor and a graduate student. The design team referred to a large number of gamification design methodology literature, and chose the most downloaded software in the Apple App Store–"Chinese Medicine Think Tank" as the theoretical and basic prototype reference, combined with the DMC pyramid model theory, constructed the game flow and framework through a combination of gamification elements and mechanisms, and completed the prototype with gamification features. We have completed the interface design and interactive prototype development of a TCM learning mobile application with gamification features, named "AIYI", which can be operated by mobile devices through an interactive platform. Currently "AIYI" has been fully utilized and experienced by more than 70 users and received positive feedback.

The design of "AIYI" extracts several game component elements such as achievements, badges, leaderboards, content unlocking, tasks, points, virtual goods, and several mechanisms such as challenges, resource acquisition, rewards, trading, and winning status to form a gameplay framework through a reasonable organization, and then optimizes the visual effects and outputs the interface rendering.

Figure 2(a) shows the start interface of the game; Fig. 2(b) shows the introduction story of a game, leading the player into the game and the role; Fig. 2(c) shows the learning process of TCM knowledge divided into several chapters; the game adopts the challenge mode of level unlocking, where the player searches for and identifies herbs in the map; Fig. 3 shows the break-in interface for identifying herbs; Fig. 4(a), (b) shows the herbs deposited into the herb bank after successful unlocking, and provides the user with a display of information on rewards and level changes; and the gold coins accumulated during the process can be used for trading, purchasing more herbs and expanding the herb library, and more new gameplay can be unlocked by reaching a certain level (Fig. 5).

3.2 Experiment 1: System Usability Testing

Test Tool. Usability is usually defined as the effectiveness, efficiency, and subjective user satisfaction that a product can be used by a particular user for a particular purpose in a particular context of use, and a standardized scale is a reliable assessment tool for

(a) Game Launch Interface

(b) Game Description

(c) Game Chapters

Fig. 2. Game Start Interface

Fig. 3. Identify Herbs Level Interface

(a) Herb Unlocking Success

(b) Honor Level Upgrade

Fig. 4. Rewards for successful herb unlocking and player honor level change interface.

testing system usability. The System Usability Scale (SUS Scale) was originally created by John Brooke in 1986 [24]. It is now widely used. The SUS Scale consists of 10 items, with odd-numbered items being positive statements and even-numbered items being negative statements, and each item consists of a 5-point scale ranging from Strongly Agree (1 point) to Strongly Disagree (5 points) [24]. The SUS Scale can be used to evaluate existing systems for ease of use, learnability, efficiency, and satisfaction [25].

Fig. 5. Entrance screen for more gameplay such as Herbal Depot and Buying Supplies.

In order to obtain the result of SUS scale, the score of each topic needs to be converted. For odd-numbered items, "original score minus 1" should be adopted, and for even-numbered items, "original score minus 5" should be adopted. The score range of each topic is "0–4". After adding up the converted replies of each user, the total score is multiplied by 2.5 to obtain the total score of percentile SUS.

SUS scores are interpreted on a percentile basis, with 68 as the score threshold, with a score above 68 indicating good acceptability and below 68 indicating below average [26].

The SUS scores are calculated as follows:

$$\left[\sum (X - 1) + \sum (5 - Y)\right] \times 2.5 = SUS\ score \tag{1}$$

where X = score for odd-numbered question items; Y = score for even-numbered question items.

The SUS scores reflect the overall usability and Fig. 6 shows the interpretation and meaning of the SUS scores [27].

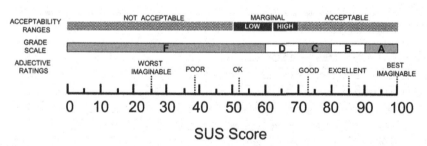

Fig. 6. A comparison of the adjective ratings, acceptability scores, and school grading scales, in relation to the average SUS score.

Table 1 is the SUS scoring benchmark showing the SUS ranks and corresponding percentile rankings summarized in the database [28].

The original SUS questionnaire was used for this test, with minor modifications and adjustments: the word "system" in SUS was replaced by "application". The scoring system of the questionnaire remained unchanged.

Participants. Seventy-six randomly recruited users between the ages of 18 and 45 were recruited via the Internet to test the usability of "AIYI". The subjects participated

Table 1. SUS scores, grades, and percentile ranks.

Grade	SUS	Percentile Range
A+	84.1–100	96–100
A	80.8–84.0	90–95
A−	78.9–80.7	85–89
B+	77.2–78.8	80–84
B	74.1–77.1	70–79
B−	72.6–74.0	65–69
C+	71.1–72.5	60–64
C	65.0–71.0	41–59
C−	62.7–64.9	35–40
D	51.7–62.6	15–34

independently, were in good health prior to the test, and it was the first time that they had been exposed to "AIYI".

Experimental Procedure. Participants opened the demonstrable interaction prototype on their mobile devices and started using it. For the participants who were confused in the use, the enumerator provided them with a brief explanatory note and after the use, the subjects were provided with the SUS questionnaire as shown in Fig. 7. Finally, the data collected from the completed questionnaires were entered into the SPSS software.

Guidelines:
This is an anonymous questionnaire about using AIYI. You may mark your answer choices to the right of each question in the questionnaire. In this case, Strongly Agree = 5 points, Agree = 4 points General = 3 points, Disagree = 2 points, Strongly Disagree = 1 point.
Thank you for your cooperation!

	1	2	3	4	5
1. I think that I would like to use this application frequently.					
2. I found the application unnecessarily complex.					
3. I thought the application was easy to use.					
4. I think that I would need the support of a technical person to be able to use this application.					
5. I found the various functions in this application were well integrated.					
6. I thought there was too much inconsistency in this application.					
7. I would imagine that most people would learn to use this application very quickly.					
8. I found the application very cumbersome to use.					
9. I felt very confident using the application.					
10. I needed to learn a lot of things before I could get going with this application.					

Fig. 7. "AIYI" Usability scale questionnaire

3.3 Experiment 2: Testing the Learning Effectiveness of Gamified Chinese Medicine Learning App

Theoretical Testing Tool. In order to quantitatively test whether the use of a gamification-based mobile application for learning TCM can enhance users' knowledge of TCM to a certain extent, a theoretical test on the knowledge of Chinese medicinal herbs was formulated, which was extracted from the "Chinese Medicine Wisdom Bank" application, which is the most downloaded application in the Apple App Store. The questions are compiled by experts in the field and have a certain degree of authority and reliability. The selected questions are all related to TCM herbs that users will come into contact with in the course of using "AIYI", and are well-targeted, making it feasible to quantitatively test users' learning outcomes.

Experiment Sample. The theoretical test experiment was set up as a control experiment, and two kinds of apps were used. The sample used by the experimental group was a mobile app for learning TCM based on gamification design, which is "AIYI", while the app used by the control group could also be interacted with on the mobile device, only the elements and mechanisms of gamification were removed, and only the original interface information was retained, which is common to the two kinds of apps, and the two kinds of apps are completely consistent with each other in the rest of the interface information presentation.

Participants. In this experiment, 20 persons aged 18–30 were invited as experimental subjects, divided into 10 in the experimental group and 10 in the control group. All of them are ordinary users, and through the pre-survey, it can be determined that the participants have no obvious a priori knowledge of TCM herbs, and can almost exclude the factor of having contacted or learned about some TCM herbs due to illness. Each subject participated in the experiment independently, was a first-time user of "AIYI", and was not one of the participants in the aforementioned usability test.

Experimental Equipment. In the experiment, each subject was equipped with a cell phone with access to the Internet, with good network quality, in a quiet and interference-free experimental environment, and the subject first used the cell phone to operate the application and then continued to use the device to complete the test questions.

Experimental Procedure. The experiment was conducted in two groups, and the people in each group participated in the experiment independently. In the preparation phase, subjects entered the prepared experimental environment and debugged the equipment and network, in the experimental phase, subjects opened the interactive prototype of the application and started to operate it, after the first complete use, they took a 10-s break and continued with the second one, and after the second use, subjects exited the application and completed the theoretical test. The procedure was the same for both sets of experiments. At the end of the experiment, the time spent on the test and the answers of each subject were recorded in the background, and this information was presented in an anonymized form to be used for subsequent data processing and analysis.

3.4 Experiment 3: Emotional Experience Measurement and Experimental Interviews

After the theoretical testing experiment was completed, an emotional experience questionnaire was provided to the 10 subjects in the experimental group and they were interviewed, the purpose of the interview was to analyze the experience and the details of the subjects' use of the gamification application and to record the subjective feelings of the subjects. The content of the questionnaire is shown in Fig. 8.

Guideline:
    This is an anonymous questionnaire about using AIYI. Please mark your answer choices below each question in the questionnaire based on the experience you have just had with the app. Thank you for your co–operation!

Select the following options according to your situation:

		emotion	-4	-3	-2	-1	0	1	2	3	4	emotion
Q1	angry											lively
Q2	alert											sleepy
Q3	controlled											dominated
Q4	friendly											pejorative
Q5	still											Excited
Q6	ruling											compliant
Q7	painful											cheerful
Q8	interested											relaxed
Q9	guided											proactive
Q10	excited											Irritated
Q11	Relaxed											hopeful
Q12	influential											affected

Fig. 8. Questionnaire for measuring the emotional experience of users in the experimental group.

This emotional experience questionnaire is based on the PAD emotion scale corresponding to the PAD emotion model proposed by psychologists Mehrabian et al. [29, 30], in which the user's emotional state is categorized into three dimensions, namely pleasure (P), activation (A) and dominance (D). Based on this, researchers proposed a simplified Chinese version of the PAD Emotion Scale [31], which has been shown to have good structural validity and applicability. The scale consists of 12 items, with 4 items for each of the three dimensions of P, A, and D, and scores ranging from "−4" to "4 ". After further research, a reference table of baseline PAD values for 14 basic emotions was obtained [32] (Table 2).

PAD affective tendency was measured by the spatial coordinate distance "L" between the measured affective state and the 14 basic emotions, and the magnitude of "L" indicated the degree of tendency to the 14 basic emotions. The smallest L-value corresponds to the basic emotional state that is the emotional state being measured. This scale was used to form a questionnaire to test the emotional tendency of users in the experimental group in the process of using "AIYI" (Fig. 8).

Table 2. Reference table for PAD values of 14 basic emotions.

Serial number	Emotional type	P-value	A-value	D-value
1	Happy	2.77	1.21	1.42
2	Optimistic	2.48	1.05	1.75
3	Relaxed	2.19	−0.66	1.05
4	Amazed	1.72	1.71	0.22
5	Mild	1.57	−0.79	0.38
6	Dependent	0.39	−0.81	−1.48
7	Idle	−0.53	−1.25	−0.84
8	Sad	−0.89	0.17	−0.70
9	Scared	−0.93	1.30	−0.64
10	Anxious	−0.95	0.32	−0.63
11	Supercilious	−1.58	0.32	1.02
12	Nasty	−1.80	0.40	0.67
13	Perturbed	−1.98	1.10	0.60
14	Hostile	−2.08	1.00	1.12

4   Results and Discussion

4.1   Experiment 1: System Availability Test Results

Reliability and Validity of the Questionnaire. In this study, usability testing was completed in the first step and a total of 76 users completed the usability questionnaire. In order to test the reliability and validity of the questionnaire data, a reliability test analysis was completed based on SPSS software with ten questions as evaluation indicators. The results of the analysis are tabulated below (Tables 3 and 4):

Table 3. Questionnaire Reliability Analysis Results

Type of question	Cronbach's Alpha	Item count
Positive question	0.826	5
Negative question	0.830	5

From the reliability statistics in Table 2, the Cronbach alph values for both forward and reverse questions are greater than 0.8. Table 3 demonstrates that the KMO values for forward questions are greater than 0.8 and KMO values for reverse questions are greater than 0.7, which suggests that the questionnaire data are sufficiently reliable and valid and the results of the analyses based on the questionnaire data will be meaningful.

Table 4. Questionnaire Validity Analysis Results

Type of question	KMO and Bartlet test	Bartlett Sphericity Check	
		Approximate chi-square	Sig.
Positive question	0.819	126.601	<.001
Negative question	0.753	154.842	<.001

Analysis of Questionnaire Results. A total of 76 sets of data were collected in this experiment, and the data were organized using Excel, and the SUS scores of the 76 sets of data were calculated according to the SUS score formula, as well as the usability of its sub-dimension question items 4 and 10 and the learnability scores of the remaining eight items [33]. The results are shown in Table 5.

Table 5. SUS Score Results

SUS Score	75
Usability Score	75
Learnability Score	71

The results show that the total SUS score of "AIYI" is 75, and according to Fig. 6, the average score of users who rated it as "Good" is 71, and the test score is greater than this score, indicating that the perceived usability experience of "AIYI" is good. The sub-dimension usability score calculated individually is 75, which proves that "AIYI" has good usability. The learnability score calculated based on the sub-dimensions is 71, which is lower compared to the other two, which may be related to the fact that the knowledge of TCM herbs is relatively obscure to learn. According to the SUS benchmark (Table 1), "AIYI" has a SUS score of 75, which corresponds to a percentile rating [28] of "B" and a percentile rank [28] of about 73, indicating that "AIYI" has better usability than 73% of the products in the database. In summary, "AIYI", a mobile application for learning TCM that incorporates gamification design, reports better system usability, which indicates that the addition of gamification elements is reasonable and useful, and to a certain extent improves the experience of using this type of application to learn the more obscure knowledge of TCM, making it more usable and easy to use, reducing the difficulty of use, which will favor more user engagement and continuous learning.

4.2   Theoretical Test Results

There were a total of 20 data from the theory test experiment, 10 from the control group and 10 from the experimental group, and the final recorded and counted data were summarized and organized into two categories: test scores and time spent on answering the questions, and the data results are demonstrated in Table 6:

Table 6. Theoretical Test Score Results

Serial number	Experimental group		Control group	
	Score	Time	Score	Time
1	72	110 s	54	91 s
2	100	47 s	79	87 s
3	100	128 s	26	44 s
4	54	81 s	72	71 s
5	63	60 s	66	140 s
6	54	47 s	39	74 s
7	42	61 s	41	104 s
8	66	44 s	70	131 s
9	91	117 s	80	83 s
10	84	33 s	57	91 s
average value	73	73 s	58	92 s

It can be seen that the theoretical test score of the experimental group (73) is higher than that of the control group (58), while the average time taken by the experimental group (73s) is smaller than the average time taken by the control group (92s), and the highest score of the experimental group (100) is greater than the highest score of the control group (80). The data indicate that the experimental group had better learning outcomes than the control group, which means that using an application that incorporates a gamified design to learn TCM knowledge can be helpful in enhancing users' learning outcomes compared to using an ordinary TCM learning application. The gamified use experience may make the knowledge more quickly accepted and remembered by users, which has positive significance in enhancing the effectiveness of users' learning of TCM knowledge and reaching a more efficient dissemination of TCM knowledge.

4.3 Experiment 3: Results of the Emotional Experience Questionnaire

Based on the study of [31], the P, A, and D values are taken as the mean of the total scores of the four groups of emotion words corresponding to each of them, and based on the results of the scale scoring, the P, A, and D values of the 10 groups of data are calculated as follows: P = 1.63, A = −0.35, and D = 0.40, respectively. The data presented in Table 7 are the spatial coordinate distances "L" between the tested user's affective states and the 14 basic emotions [32] as derived by the Euclidean distance algorithm, and it can be seen that the smallest value is 0.44, which corresponds to the "mild" emotional state. In addition, the spatial distance to "relaxation" is 0.91, which is the closest to 0.44, indicating that the user's affective tendency includes both "mild" and "relaxation".

The positive P-value of this sentiment measure indicates that the overall sentiment of users is positive during the process of using AIYI, which also indicates that the usability of the application is better; however, the negative A-value indicates that the emotional

Table 7. User Emotion Measurement Results

Emotional type	L-value
Happy	2.18
Optimistic	2.12
Relaxed	0.91
amazed	2.07
mild	0.44
dependent	1.71
idle	2.65
sad	2.80
scared	3.22
anxious	2.86
supercilious	3.34
nasty	3.52
perturbed	3.90
hostile	4.01

arousal of users is relatively low, which may be related to the unfamiliarity of users when they are exposed to the game-based TCM learning application for the first time; A positive value of D indicates that the user's emotions are more under his/her active control during the process of using the application, which means that "AIYI" has a high ease of use, and the cognitive load of the user is small, which is also consistent with the results obtained from the usability test. Overall, the emotional tendency of "mild" and "relaxed" indicates that the gamified TCM learning application brings positive emotional experience to users, and users feel relaxed about it. This suggests that gamification is effective, and that relaxed and positive emotions can promote user motivation and make the learning process more enjoyable, which is meaningful for users to continue to participate in learning TCM knowledge.

Results of the Interviews. Finally, this study completed the statistics of the interview results of the experimental group (Table 8). The results show that users like and agree with the gamified TCM learning app, and the sense of achievement and pleasure brought by gamification to users will be an important factor to promote their continuous learning motivation. Most of the users responded that the gamified application made the learning process of TCM knowledge, which was originally boring and difficult to understand, more relaxing and interesting, and enhanced the user experience to a greater extent. Meanwhile, the game tasks and the barrier mechanism prompted the curiosity of the users, and the users were happy to continue to advance the game and participate in the learning tasks, which is of great significance in promoting the learning of TCM knowledge.

Table 8. Analysis of User Interview Results

Interview questions	Interview results
1. Do you find the story and player characters of this mini-game interesting and engaging?	Yes; It's interesting and Intriguing
2. Have the challenges and tasks you complete in the game made you feel more curious about Chinese herbs?	Yes; It's great to arouse curiosity and learn useful knowledge in playing
3. Do the achievements and rewards you get in the game keep you wanting to unlock more herbs to learn more about them?	Yes; Expanding Achievements
4. Do you like the rewards you get in the game and the badges that symbolise your status?	Yes; Sense of achievement
5. Will you gain some interest and motivation in learning Chinese medicine through this mini game?	Yes; Want to Learn More

5 Conclusion

In this paper, we found that adding gamification elements to TCM learning apps is effective in enhancing users' learning outcomes, and that gamification can optimize users' experience in using such apps to learn more complex knowledge about TCM herbs and has better usability, making the originally boring and difficult-to-understand apps more usable and easy to use, and making the more obscure learning process interesting and enjoyable. At the same time, gamification also promotes the generation of user motivation, the user's mood is more positive and positive, and the relaxing and enjoyable experience and curiosity increase the user's participation in learning TCM knowledge. This also provides a feasible direction to guide the inheritance, learning and dissemination of TCM. The research in this paper has some limitations, firstly, the sample size of the experiments cannot cover a wide range of user groups, and secondly, the research of the experiments is not deep enough, future research can continue to explore the influence and usefulness of specific gamification elements and mechanisms on the learning of Chinese medicine. Expanding more possibilities for the learning and dissemination of TCM.

References

1. Jingyu, Y., Duanchang, L., Chenjin, W.: Reflections and explorations on gamification of traditional Chinese medicine-taking the development and design of materia medica spiritual orchid record as an example. Comp. Res. Cult. Innov. **6**(23), 98–101 (2022). (in Chinese)
2. China Internet Network Information Centre releases the 52nd "Statistical Report on Internet Development in China". Nat. Libr. J. **32**(05), 13 (2023). (in Chinese)
3. Taowei, J., Rongwei, L., Lili, H.: Reflections on the application of gamification-based mobile learning in higher colleges of traditional Chinese medicine-taking "Apricot Grove Kui Shou"

independent learning platform as an example. Mod. Distance Educ. Chin. Med. China **18**(13), 168–170 (2020). (in Chinese)

4. Jin, Y.: Research of one mobile learning system. In: Proceedings of the International Conference on Wireless Networks and Information Systems, Shanghai, China, pp. 162–165. IEEE (2009)

5. Yang, Y., Tian, D., Ling, W.: Influence analysis of mobile learning research on modern distance education. In: Proceedings of the 2nd IEEE International Conference on Computer and Communications, Chengdu, China, pp. 883–886. IEEE (2016)

6. Jiugen, Y., Ruonan, X.: Mobile terminal based mobile learning system design. In: Proceedings of the 11th International Conference on Computer Science & Education, Nagoya, Japan, pp. 699–703. IEEE (2016). https://doi.org/10.1109/ICCSE.2016.7581664

7. Taowei, J., Lili, H.: Design and application of Chinese medicine self-learning platform based on gamification concept under the threshold of mobile internet. Wirel. Connect. Technol. **20**(01), 48–50 (2023). (in Chinese)

8. Deterding, S., Dixon, D., Khaled, R., Nacke, L.: From game design elements to gamefulness: defining gamification. In: Proceedings of the 15th International Academic MindTrek Conference: Envisioning Future Media Environments, pp. 9–15. ACM, New York (2011)

9. Palmquist, A.: A product to gamify other products; implementing gamification in existing software. In: 11th International Conference on Virtual Worlds and Games for Serious Applications, Vienna, Austria, pp. 1–8. IEEE (2019)

10. Huotari, K., Hamari, J.: Defining gamification: a service marketing perspective. In: Proceeding of the 16th International Academic MindTrek Conference, pp. 17–22. Association for Computing Machinery, New York, NY, USA (2012)

11. Kamada, M., et al.: Large-scale fandom-based gamification intervention to increase physical activity: a quasi-experimental study. Med. Sci. Sports Exerc. **54**(1), 181–188 (2022)

12. Hamari, J., Shernoff, D.J., Rowe, E., et al.: Challenging games help students learn: an empirical study on engagement, flow and immersion in game-based learning. Comput. Hum. Behav. **54**, 170–179 (2016)

13. Mat, R.C., Kazunori, M., Rahman, A.A.: The development of mobile Japanese halal gamification (MJHG). Int. J. Interact. Mob. Technol. **14**(17), 113–129 (2020)

14. The Speed Camera Lottery. TheFunTheory. http://www.thefuntheory.com/speed-camera-lot tery-0. Accessed 7 July 2015

15. Lidia, A.C., Julio, R.T., Petra, D.S.P., Rafael, P.J.: How to encourage recycling behaviour? The case of WasteApp: a gamified mobile application. Sustainability **10**(5), 20 (2018)

16. Simões, J., Redondo, R.D., Vilasand, A.F.: A social gamification framework for a K-6 learning platform. Comput. Hum. Behav. **2**(29), 345–353 (2012)

17. Gee, J.P.: What video games have to teach us about learning and literacy. Comput. Entertain. (CIE) **1**(1), 20 (2003)

18. Daouadji Amina, K., Fatima, B.: MEDIUS: a serious game for autistic children based on decision system. Simul. Gaming **49**(4), 430–440 (2018)

19. Dymora, P., Niemiec, K.: Gamification as a supportive tool for school children with Dyslexia. Informatics **6**(4), 48 (2019)

20. Chapman, J.R., Rich, P.J.: Does educational gamification improve students' motivation? If so, which game elements work best? J. Educ. Bus. **93**(7), 315–322 (2018)

21. Serdar Erdogan, B., Baykose, N.: Examination of the relationship between mood and achievement goal orientations of the students studying at Faculty of Sports Sciences. Asian J. Educ. Training **7**(1), 46–50 (2021)

22. Werbach, K., Hunter, D.: For the Win: How Game Thinking Can Revolutionize Your Business. Wharton Digital Press, Philadelphia (2012)

23. Kamunya, S., Maina, E., Oboko, R.: A gamification model for e-learning platforms. In: 2019 IST-Africa Week Conference (IST-Africa), Nairobi, Kenya, pp. 1–9. IEEE (2019). https://doi.org/10.23919/ISTAFRICA.2019.8764879

24. Brooke, J.: SUS - a quick and dirty usability scale. Usability Eval. Ind. **189**(194), 4–7 (1996)

25. Arain, A.A., Hussain, Z., Rizvi, W.H., Vighio, M.S.: Evaluating usability of m-learning application in the context of higher education institute. In: Zaphiris, P., Ioannou, A. (eds.) Learning and Collaboration Technologies, LCT 2016. LNCS, vol. 9753, pp. 259–268. Springer, Cham (2016). https://doi.org/10.1007/978-3-319-39483-1_24

26. Sauro, J.: Measuring usability with System Usability Scale (SUS) (2011). https://measuringu.com/sus/. Accessed 3 Feb 2011

27. Lewis, J.R., Sauro, J.: Item benchmarks for the system usability scale. J. Usability Stud. **13**(03), 158–167 (2018)

28. Sauro, J.: Interpreting single items from the SUS. https://measuringu.com/sus-items/. Accessed 11 July 2018

29. Mehrabian, A.: Pleasure-arousal-dominance: a general framework for describing and measuring individual differences in temperament. Curr. Psychol. (New Brunswick N.J.) **14**(4), 261–292 (1996)

30. Mehrabian, A.: Emotional correlates of preferences for situation-activity combinations in everyday life. Genet. Soc. Gen. Psychol. Monogr. **123**(4), 461–477 (1997)

31. Xiaoming, L., Xiaolan, F., Guofeng, D.: A preliminary trial of the simplified Chinese version of the PAD Mood Scale among university students in Beijing. Chin. J. Ment. Health **22**(5), 327–329 (2008)

32. Xiaoming, L.: PAD 3D Emotional Modelling. Computer world (2007). (in Chinese)

33. Lewis, J.R., Sauro, J.: The factor structure of the system usability scale. In: Kurosu, M. (ed.) HCD 2009. LNCS, vol. 5619, pp. 94–103. Springer, Heidelberg (2009). https://doi.org/10.1007/978-3-642-02806-9_12

Accuracy Evaluation of AR Navigation in Partial Nephrectomy

Toshihiro Magaribuchi[1], Masanao Koeda[2], Kimihiko Masui[1], Takashi Kobayashi[1], and Atsuro Sawada[3]([✉])

[1] Department of Urology, Graduate School of Medicine, Kyoto University, Kyoto, Japan
[2] Department of Human Information Engineering, Okayama Prefectural University, Okayama, Japan
[3] Department of Urology, Faculty of Medicine, Miyazaki University, Miyazaki, Japan
atsurou_sawada@med.miyazaki-u.ac.jp

Abstract. The standard treatment for small renal cell carcinoma is a "partial nephrectomy", which is the surgical removal of a tumor from the kidney. A significant challenge in this surgery is the difficulty in locating tumors that are embedded within the kidney. To address this issue, research has been conducted on Augmented Reality (AR) navigation, which involves projecting a kidney model created from preoperative CT scans onto the intraoperative field. However, adapting this navigation to the kidney's deformation during surgery is challenging, and the accuracy is insufficient. In our approach, we resolved this problem by limiting the application to scenarios where there is minimal organ deformation during surgery. This strategy enabled the realization of a high-accuracy AR navigation system. This study reports the objective accuracy evaluation of this navigation system, conducted using a 3D printer model.

1 Introduction

1.1 Navigation in Partial Nephrectomy

The Standard treatment for small renal cell carcinoma is "partial nephrectomy (PN)", which entails removing the tumor from the kidney. PN requires not only the complete removal of the lesion but also the preservation of renal function by minimizing damage to normal kidney tissue. The reduction of normal renal parenchyma, including nephrons, is known to be associated with worsened cancer-specific mortality and decreased renal function [1]. Considering this, the tumor must be appropriately excised, which necessitates accurate localization of the tumor. However, tumor localization can be challenging when the tumor is embedded within the kidney.

Intraoperative ultrasound is commonly used to locate tumors during partial PN [2], but it can be particularly difficult to identify embedded tumors. As a solution to this problem, navigation using Augmented Reality (AR) that projects a preoperatively created kidney model onto the intraoperative screen is being researched [3]. This method allows the surgeon to visualize the 3D models of the kidney and tumor on the surgical monitor, helping to determine the tumor location and the depth of excision required.

M. Kurosu and A. Hashizume (Eds.): HCII 2024, LNCS 14686, pp. 194–202, 2024.
https://doi.org/10.1007/978-3-031-60428-7_14

1.2   Achievements and Challenges of AR Navigation

The first experience of AR navigation in actual partial nephrectomy surgery was reported in 2008. Since then, numerous clinical experiences have been reported, and a systematic review in 2022 confirmed that it reduces the risk of perioperative complications. However, there are significant challenges in intraoperative navigation for partial nephrectomy. During surgery, the kidney deforms and moves, meaning that the shape of the kidney during surgery is not the same as that captured in the CT. Therefore, achieving high-precision navigation is difficult, and the accuracy remains insufficient. Various studies have been conducted to address organ deformation and movement, but the issue has not yet been resolved.

1.3   Our Development of a Highly Accurate Navigation System

As a solution to this problem, we opted for a method that limits navigation to scenarios with minimal organ deformation. If the organ deformation is minimal, the shape of the kidney during surgery approximates that in the CT, allowing for highly accurate navigation and lowering the technical barrier. For surgeons, even temporary but accurate localization of the tumor offers significant benefits, even if they cannot respond to real-time organ deformation during surgery. The existing method, which roughly aligns the 3D kidney model with the 2D surgical screen, was common since it was difficult to precisely match the CT kidney with the intraoperative kidney. However, by limiting to scenarios with minimal organ deformation, a navigation system that projects the 3D kidney model onto a three-dimensional point cloud viewed stereoscopically from a stereo camera became feasible. The two 3D models are rigid bodies, and their point clouds are registered using Iterative Closest Point (ICP). This study evaluates the accuracy of this navigation system.

2   Accuracy Evaluation of the Navigation System

2.1   Accuracy Evaluation Using Fiducial Markers

Generally, in intraoperative navigation, fiducial markers are placed on fixed parts of the body, and these markers are used as references for registering the body with CT or MRI imaging data. This method allows for an objective accuracy assessment. It is commonly used in surgical areas like head and neck surgery, where the target organ does not deform significantly during the operation. Our navigation involves registering two rigid 3D models, and we conducted an accuracy evaluation using these fiducial markers.

2.2   Creation of a Kidney Model with Fiducial Markers

We created two types of kidney models: an original kidney model that simulates a human kidney and a 3D-printed kidney model output from a 3D printer. Both kidney models were created using common fiducial markers.

The original kidney model was created by referencing the size and shape of the human kidney, as previously described [7]. Blender, a 3D modeling application, was used to create the original kidney model. For the fiducial markers, red, blue, yellow, green, purple, and pink-colored arbitrary vertices were used for distinction. The data used for registration required vertex color information; therefore, we prepared it in PLY format.

We used the original kidney model output in STL format to create a 3D-printed kidney model. The 3D printer used was SnapMaker F350 (Snapmaker Technologies, Inc. China), and the filament used was an iSANMATE Marble-Like PLA+ (iSANMATE Technologies, Ltd. Taiwan), which has a marble-like pattern that facilitates the capture of feature points using a camera. Using Blender, we indented the vertices with fiducial markers on the original kidney model and filled them with the corresponding colored clay to create the fiducial markers. Therefore, we created two kidney models with common fiducial markers. Furthermore, we captured this 3D-printed kidney model using the stereo camera of the surgical support robot da Vinci Xi (Intuitive Surgical Inc. USA) and plotted a 3D point cloud. In our imaging system, the left and right camera images of the da Vinci Xi are each output at 960 × 1080 pixels. However, considering the aspect ratio and processing speed, we reduced them to 960 × 540 pixels. A series of flows is shown in Fig. 1.

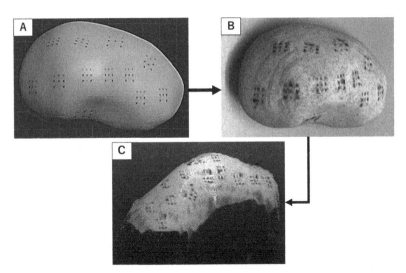

Fig. 1. A: Original kidney model. B: 3D-printed kidney model. C: 3D point cloud created by capturing the 3D-printed kidney model using a stereo camera.

2.3   Generating a 3D Point Cloud of the Kidney via Stereo Matching

To generate a 3D point cloud, it is necessary to first determine the disparity image from the images captured from the left and right sides by the stereo camera. In this study, stereo matching was performed using semi-global block matching (SGBM) implemented in OpenCV [8]. The SGBM searches for the corresponding points between the left and right images and calculates the distance between them. The disparity image represents the calculated distance in terms of color and brightness. To generate a 3D point cloud from the obtained disparity image, the following transformation was performed:

$$\begin{pmatrix} X \\ Y \\ Z \end{pmatrix} = \frac{1}{d/B} \begin{pmatrix} u - c_x \\ v - c_y \\ f \end{pmatrix} \qquad (1)$$

where X, Y, and Z are the coordinates of the 3D point cloud, u and v are the coordinates of the disparity image, d is the disparity, cx and cy are the coordinates of the intersection of the optical axis and imaging surface of the left camera, f is the focal distance, and B is the baseline distance of the stereo camera. An example of a disparity image generated from intraoperative stereo camera images is shown in Fig. 2.

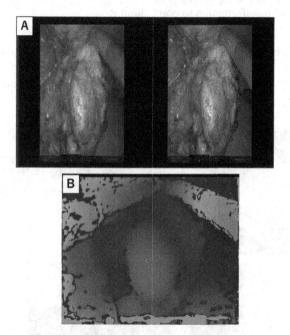

Fig. 2. A: Stereo image pair. B: Disparity image.

The camera and 3D-printed kidney model were photographed at intervals of 1 cm, and considering the surgical operation range in laparoscopic surgery, the distance between the camera and kidney model was set to a maximum of 15 cm.

2.4 Registration of Point Clouds Derived from CT and Stereo Cameras

Registration of the original kidney model and point cloud generated by stereo matching was performed using point-to-plane iterative closest point (ICP) algorithm [9]. The fiducial marker of each 3D point cloud required color information; therefore, the PLY format was used.

The point-to-plane ICP algorithm is a computational method that minimizes the difference in distance between two point clouds for registration. The main goal was to determine the best rigid transformation (translation or rotation) to align the two point clouds. The algorithm proceeds as follows:

1. For each point in the point cloud P, search for the nearest point in the point cloud Q.
2. The rigid transformation that minimizes the error function is calculated as follows.

$$E(T) = \sum_{i=1}^{N}((TP_i - Q_i) \cdot n_i)^2 \tag{2}$$

Here Pi, Qi are the corresponding points in the point clouds P, Q; T is the rigid transformation matrix; ni is the normal vector obtained from the plane near Pi; and N is the number of corresponding points.
3. Apply the rigid transformation to point cloud P.
4. Repeat until convergence.

The distance between the common fiducial markers was measured in the registered point cloud using ICP. The distance measurements between the two points were performed using CloudCompare. The distance indicated in CloudCompare was calculated as $9 = 1$ cm (Fig. 3).

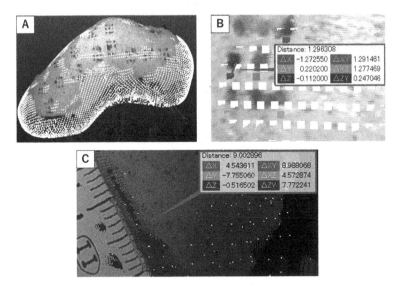

Fig. 3. A: Registered point clouds. B: Accuracy assessment conducted by measuring the distance between the fiducial markers. C: In CloudCompare, the displayed distance was treated as 9 units equivalent to 1 cm.

2.5   Result of the Accuracy Evaluation

The closer the distance between the camera and 3D-printed kidney model, the smoother the 3D point cloud depicted by stereo matching (Fig. 4).

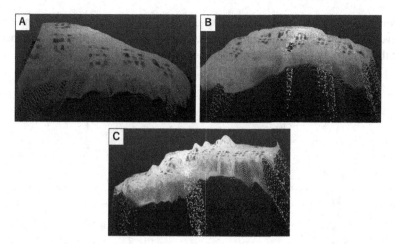

Fig. 4. A: Point cloud when the distance between the camera and the model is 5 cm. B: Point cloud when the distance between the camera and the model is 10 cm. C: Point cloud when the distance between the camera and the model is 15 cm.

The closer the distance between the camera and the model, the higher the matching rate of the fiducial markers; conversely, the further the distance, the lower the matching rate. Particularly, when the distance between the two was 7 cm or less, the misalignment between the original kidney model and the 3D-printed kidney model was less than 2 mm for 75% of the observations, and 100% were less than 4 mm excluding outliers. Stereo vision was impossible when the distance between the camera and kidney model was 2 cm or less (Fig. 5).

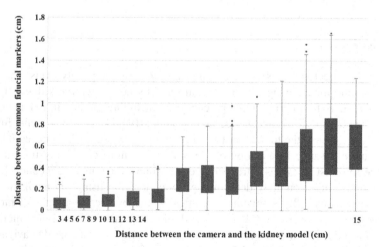

Fig. 5. Figure 5 was created using a box-and-whisker plot. The closer the distance between the camera and the kidney model, the lesser the discrepancy observed between fiducial markers.

However, the closer the distance between the camera and the kidney model, the narrower the field of view captured by the camera; and the further the distance, the wider the field of view captured by the camera (Fig. 6).

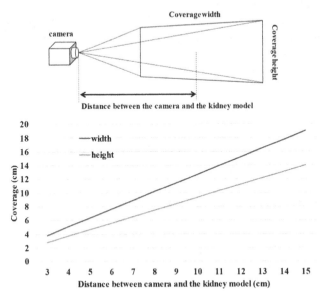

Fig. 6. Top: Image diagram of the distance between the camera and kidney model, and the height and width of the field of view. Bottom: As the distance between the stereo camera and the kidney model decreases, the field of view of the camera correspondingly narrows.

3 Discussion

In Partial Nephrectomy (PN), it is required not only to completely excise the lesion but also to minimize damage to the normal renal tissue to preserve kidney function. Indeed, a reduction in normal renal parenchyma, including glomeruli, is known to be associated with worsened cancer-specific mortality [10] and a decline in renal function [1]. Considering this, the tumor must be appropriately excised, which necessitates the most accurate possible localization of the tumor. The most commonly used imaging technique to assist in this is intraoperative ultrasound for tumor delineation [2], but research into more accurately determining tumor location using 3D navigation with Augmented Reality (AR) is ongoing. Specifically, this involves creating a 3D model of the kidney from preoperative CT images and reflecting this on the surgical monitor to clearly indicate the tumor location to the surgeon. Studies conducting 3D navigation in actual PN have been reported and demonstrated its effectiveness. However, in surgeries like PN where the target organ moves during operation, there is a problem in directly registering the preoperative CT-derived 3D model. In head and neck surgery, where the target organ barely moves during surgery, a common method involves placing fiducial markers on the body surface and registering these with CT or MR images. However, in PN, the changing positional relationship between the fiducial markers and the kidney makes this method ineffective. The continual movement and deformation of the target organ during surgery is the greatest challenge to precise surgical navigation.

We devised a method for high-precision AR navigation in PN by deliberately limiting the timing of navigation. In surgical areas where the target organ moves and deforms, the kidney comparatively undergoes less organ deformation. Therefore, there are moments during surgery when the shape of the kidney is almost unchanged from the CT image, allowing for high-precision AR navigation at these times. For surgeons, accurately understanding the relationship between the tumor and the kidney, even for this limited period, offers significant benefits. Previous AR navigation in PN involved overlaying a 3D kidney model on a 2D surgical screen, but our method transforms the surgical environment into 3D, allowing for registration with the 3D kidney model, thus enabling more precise AR navigation.

It is known that the accuracy of 3D navigation in surgical areas like head and neck surgery, where the target organ does not deform, is within 1 mm [6]. On the other hand, in gastrointestinal surgery where the target organ deforms during surgery and fiducial markers are fixed on the body surface for AR navigation, one study reported an average accuracy displacement of 19.4 mm. No such accuracy assessment using this method has been reported in clinical PN AR navigation. In our experiments using fiducial markers, we confirmed that if the camera and target distance are within 7 cm, 75% of cases had an error of 2 mm or less, indicating relatively high-precision navigation is possible. This study evaluated the accuracy of 3D navigation using a kidney model created with a 3D printer. This method allows for experiments in many cases without worrying about invasiveness to the patient. While placing fiducial markers on the kidney requires invasive embedding [11], this was not a concern in our study.

In our experiments, the closer the distance between the stereo camera and the subject, the more accurate the point cloud generated and the higher the registration accuracy, which is a reasonable outcome considering the principles of stereo matching. Namely, the closer the distance, the less ambiguity in texture, more pixels covering the object making feature identification easier, and larger disparity making it easier to find matching points. An important point in our results is that when using a stereo camera for robotic surgery and employing stereo matching, high-precision navigation is possible at distances required for surgery of organ sizes handled in surgery. This is the first study to report an objective accuracy assessment of PN AR navigation using fiducial markers. Additionally, while the closer the distance between the camera and the subject, the more precise it is, there is a trade-off as the field of view captured by the camera narrows. Conversely, the further the distance, the wider the field of view, but the lower the accuracy. How this narrowing field of view affects surgeons is something that needs to be confirmed in clinical trials.

The method of registering rigid 3D models with ICP, as conducted in this study, has been researched in the past [12]. However, these reports were not practices in actual PN but studies using surgical recording videos, and no objective indicators were established to evaluate their accuracy. Reports on practicing the method of registering 3D models with ICP in actual PN surgeries do not yet exist. This study confirms that our AR navigation method can be realized with high precision based on objective indicators, and we plan to evaluate its effectiveness in clinical trials.

Disclosure of Interests. The authors have no competing interests to declare that are relevant to the content of this article.

References

1. Bertolo, R., Zargar, H., Autorino, R., et al.: Estimated glomerular filtration rate, renal scan and volumetric assessment of the kidney before and after partial nephrectomy: a review of the current literature. Minerva Urol. Nefrol. **69**, 539–547 (2017)
2. Qin, B., Hu, H., Lu, Y., et al.: Intraoperative ultrasonography in laparoscopic partial nephrectomy for intrarenal tumors. PLoS ONE **13**, e0195911 (2018)
3. Dubrovin, V., Egoshin, A., Rozhentsov, A., et al.: Virtual simulation, preoperative planning and intraoperative navigation during laparoscopic partial nephrectomy. Cent. Eur. J. Urol. **72**(3), 247–251 (2019)
4. Ukimura, O., Gill, S.: Imaging-assisted endoscopic surgery: Cleveland Clinic experience. J. Endourol. **22**, 803–810 (2008)
5. Piramide, F., Kowalewski, K., Cacciamani, G., et al.: Three-dimensional model-assisted minimally invasive partial nephrectomy: a systematic review with meta-analysis of comparative studies. Eur. Urol. Oncol. **5**, 640–650 (2022)
6. Tzelnick, S., et al.: Skull-base surgery- a narrative review on current approaches and future developments in surgical navigation. J. Clin. Med. **12**, 2706 (2023)
7. Glodny, B., et al.: Normal kidney size and its influencing factors – a 64-slice MDCT study of 1.040 asymptomatic patients. BMC Urol. **9**, 19 (2009)
8. Hirschmuller, H.: Stereo processing by semiglobal matching and mutual information. IEEE Trans. Pattern Anal. Mach. Intell. **30**(2), 328–341 (2008)
9. Chen, Y., Medioni, G.G.: Object modeling by registration of multiple range images. Image Vis. Comput. **10**(3), 145–155 (1992)
10. Antonelli, A., Minervini, A., Sandri, M., et al.: Below safety limits, every unit of glomerular filtration rate counts: assessing the relationship between renal function and cancer-specific mortality in renal cell carcinoma. Eur. Urol. **74**, 661–667 (2018)
11. Kong, S.H., Haouchine, N., Soares, R., et al.: Robust augmented reality registration method for localization of solid organs' tumors using CT-derived virtual biomechanical model and fluorescent fiducials. Surg. Endosc. **31**, 2863–2871 (2017)
12. Su, L.M., Vagvolgyi, B.P., Agarwal, R., Reiley, C.E., Taylor, R.H., Hager, G.D.: Augmented reality during robot-assisted laparoscopic partial nephrectomy: toward real-time 3D-CT to stereoscopic video registration. Urology **73**, 896–900 (2009)

An Investigation into the Rise of Wearable Technologies in the Healthcare Sector

Abhishek Sharma[1]([✉])[iD], Kunnumpurath Bijo[1], Shisir Prasad Manandhar[1], and Lakshmi Sharma[2]

[1] Institute of Health and Management, Melbourne, Australia
sharmaabhishek570@gmail.com, bijo@hcigroup.com.au,
shisir@healthcareers.edu.au
[2] Amity University, Noida, India

Abstract. Wearable technologies and self-tracking healthcare apps are becoming increasingly popular among people all over the world. Moreover, with the rapid increase in technological advancements, studies on the ease of use and intent to adopt wearable devices have gained prominence in the aftermath of the Covid-19 Pandemic. More specifically, fitness wearables have grown in popularity as health consciousness among the younger and older populations has grown, allowing them to track and monitor their heart rate, calories, sleep, and steps taken throughout the day. These wearable technologies are considered to have a wide range of applications ranging from the workplace to recreational activities. Several studies have shown how the emergence of wearable technology will benefit society, but fewer studies have integrated the practical implementations of wearable technologies and wearable devices which is utilised for personalised healthcare applications. As a result, the current study employs a bibliometric approach using Scopus databases to refine articles related to health tracking applications, remote patient monitoring, chronic disease management, and infectious disease prevention. In doing so, the findings of the study are portrayed in conjunction with VOSviewer, which showcases the key clusters and studies that are related to wearable technologies and their applications as physiological and biometric sensors. More specifically, the findings show that most studies emphasise on how wearable technologies are concentrated as physiological sensors to track important information about an individual's health, as well as how wearable technologies are widely adopted among older populations and can track critical diseases, enabling effective remote patient monitoring in healthcare fields. Finally, the paper concludes by acknowledging the risks and privacy concerns of using wearable technologies within the healthcare sector.

Keywords: Wearable Technologies · Healthcare · Remote patient monitoring · chronic disease management · Electrocardiography (ECG) · Electroencephalography (EEG) · Electromyography (EMG) and Photoplethysmography (PPG) · Electrocardiography (ECG) · Electroencephalography (EEG)

M. Kurosu and A. Hashizume (Eds.): HCII 2024, LNCS 14686, pp. 203–220, 2024.
https://doi.org/10.1007/978-3-031-60428-7_15

1 Introduction

Wearable technology is a growing field of research that has received a lot of attention in recent years due to its ease of use and benefits for real-time monitoring (Awotunde et al., 2024; Bianchi et al., 2023; Kazanskiy et al., 2024; Osama et al., 2023; Sivani & Mishra, 2022). Moreover, there has been a significant increase in the adoption of wearable technologies across various industries, with the healthcare sector being at the forefront of this revolution (Aekanth & Tillinghast, 2023; Malwade et al., 2018; Sivani & Mishra, 2022). Wearable technologies in the healthcare sector are broadly classified as fitness wearables and medical wearables (Aekanth & Tillinghast, 2023; Devi et al., 2023). Medical wearables, on the other hand, are devices that enable the tracking and continuity of health services for patients who have various chronic diseases and needs attention (Devi et al., 2023; Zhang et al., 2020). Wearable devices, which were once primarily used for personal communication and fitness tracking, have evolved into powerful tools that are completely changing the way healthcare is administered and managed (Bayoumy et al., 2021; Nazaret et al., 2023). These technologies are embedded with sensors and are enabled with wireless connectivity features that allows individuals to track their activity (i.e., heart rate, calories, sleep, and steps) taken within the whole day (Cheung et al., 2021; Shei et al., 2022; VandeBunte et al., 2022).

More precisely, wearable technology has been widely adopted by older adults as it enables telemonitoring of people suffering from chronic diseases or exhibiting multiple symptoms of an ongoing disease (Lui et al., 2022; Mattison et al., 2022). Additionally, the COVID-19 pandemic has accelerated the adoption in wearable devices, leading to an immediate urgency among researchers to understand the drivers (Binyamin & Hoque, 2020), engagement level (Oh & Kang, 2021), user friendliness (Schmidt et al., 2022), and adoption potential of wearable devices among a wide range of population (Bianchi et al., 2023; Sharma, 2021). According to recent market reports, the wearable devices market will grow at a compounded annual rate of nearly 20% until 2026, with the Asia-Pacific region experiencing the fastest growth (Research-and-Markets, 2023). As a result, it is of higher importance to understand how these wearable technologies have benefited a diverse range of populations in the domains of chronic disease management and remote patient monitoring techniques. Hence, the current study seeks to address this gap by (a) conducting a bibliometric analysis on Scopus databases to refine articles relevant to health tracking applications, remote patient monitoring, chronic disease management, and infectious disease prevention, (b) utilising VOSviewer to investigate thematic representations of common themes and their relationships.

2 Background of the Study

Wearable devices are a subset of the Internet of Things (IoT) that are primarily designed as portable devices that can accumulate health-related information for individuals on a daily basis (Subhan et al., 2023; Talaat & El-Balka, 2023). These IoT-based wearables are intelligent devices that can be worn with additional accessories, affixed to the skin, implanted in the body, or embedded in clothing (Hickey et al., 2021; Prakashan et al., 2023). On these notions, Sivani and Mishra (2022) showcased the various wearable devices and how these devices are utilised by individuals as health tracking devices (See Fig. 1).

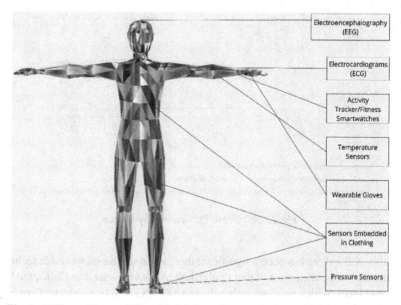

Fig. 1. Different Types of Wearable Devices. Source- Author's Own Representation

These wearable technologies consist of various devices ranging from smartwatches, sociometric badges, headbands till sensors that are embedded in clothing that offer valuable insights into one's health and overall wellness (Aekanth & Tillinghast, 2023). Moreover, adoption of these wearable devices allows individuals to track their vital health metrics from the comfort of their own homes, allowing for early detection of health issues and more proactive management of chronic conditions. Furthermore, the real-time feedback and personalized insights allows individuals to adopt healthier habits and adhere to treatment plans more effectively (Azizan et al., 2023; Sivani & Mishra, 2022). For example, fitness trackers encourage users to increase their physical activity levels and meet their exercise goals, while smartwatches can remind individuals to take their medications on time. As a result, given the growing importance of wearable technologies in healthcare domains, the following sub-section will showcase a trend analysis of wearable technology adoption since the Covid-19 pandemic.

2.1   Trend Analysis

Based on the data gathered from Scopus database, it can be stated that the top five major sources of publications within the field of wearable technologies and its implementation in patient monitoring are from Sensors, IEEE Access, Lecture Notes in Computer

Science, Sensors Switzerland and International Journal of Environmental Research and Public Health (See Fig. 2). Moreover, it can be asserted from Fig. 2 below that Sensors had the highest number of publications since 2020 (i.e., 303) with a dramatic increase in studies that are pertaining to wearable technology in healthcare fields.

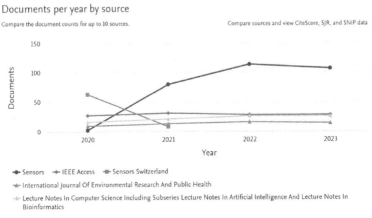

Fig. 2. Number of Publications by Source

Additionally, there has been a significant increase in studies on wearable technology in healthcare fields, with most of them published by countries such as China, the United States, and India, which were severely affected by the Covid-19 pandemic (See Fig. 3).

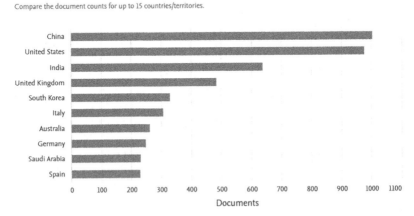

Fig. 3. Number of Studies Published on Wearable Technology by Countries

3   Research Methodology

The methodology covered in this section showcases how various wearable devices have been implemented within the healthcare sectors. Additionally, based on the papers extracted and reviewed from the bibliometric analysis, it can be asserted that wearables devices are mostly utilised for remote monitoring for patients who are related to various chronic diseases and needs attention (See Table 1). Moreover, the bibliometric analysis is conducted on Scopus databases and showcases that the literature published in 2021 (833 studies), 2022 (2314 studies), 2023 (1708 studies) and 2024 (100 studies) depicts the growth in studies on adoption of wearable technology in healthcare applications. Additionally, a detail analysis of the various clusters of studies that have utilised the wearable technologies in healthcare applications are showcased in the upcoming sub-sections.

Table 1. Keyword Search Query on Scopus Database

Keywords	Scopus
("AI" OR "Artificial intelligence" OR "IOT") AND ("Wearables" OR "Wearable technologies") AND ("Healthcare") AND PUBYEAR > 2019 AND PUBYEAR < 2025 AND (LIMIT-TO (DOCTYPE, "ar")) AND (LIMIT-TO (LANGUAGE, "English"))	4955

4   Findings

Based on the search results gathered from the Scopus database, VOSviewer is utilised in this study to analyse the cluster analysis and network visualisation of how wearable technologies have been used within the domains of healthcare industries.

4.1   Cluster Analysis

Based on the search results gathered from Scopus database, a co-occurrence analysis is conducted on Vosviewer which generated five major clusters (i.e., Red, Green, Blue, Yellow, and Purple) which showcases studies that are related to wearable technologies and its applications as physiological and biometric sensors. More specifically, the red clusters show how wearable technologies are used as physiological sensors to track important information about an individual's health. Furthermore, the green cluster demonstrates how wearable technologies are widely adopted among older populations and can track critical diseases. Additionally, the blue clusters demonstrate how wearable technology is well integrated with IoT to enable effective remote patient monitoring in healthcare fields. Finally, the yellow and purple clusters show studies on wearable devices such as smartwatches, which can help with pattern recognition for a variety of human activity health parameters (Table 2).

Table 2. Clusters and Occurrence of Keywords

Keywords	Links	Total Link Strength	Occurrences
Cluster 1 (22 Items)- Red			
Atrial Fibrillation		268	52
Breathing Rate		156	31
Electrocardiography		706	148
Electroencephalography		301	73
Electromyography		113	31
Emotion Recognition		85	33
Machine Learning		1584	546
Photoplethysmography		306	65
Sleep		145	43
Cluster 2 (21 Items)-Green			
Aged		578	182
Depression		126	32
Exercise		235	69
Mental Health		172	69
Parkinson Disease		168	47
Physical Activity		355	123
Technology Adoption		102	70
Cluster 3 (19 Items)- Blue			
Healthcare		895	317
Internet of Things		1401	621
Patient Monitoring		549	131
Wearable Technology		1867	767
Cluster 4 (6 Items)-Yellow			
Deep Learning		1333	429
Fall Detection		125	39
Pattern Recognition		495	161
Wearable Sensors		1193	491
Cluster 5 (4 Items)-Purple			
Diseases		639	149
Smartwatch		130	47
Total (72 Items)	1768	13562	

The comprehensive review demonstrates that wearable technologies have primarily been used as physiological sensors such as Electrocardiography (ECG), Electroencephalography (EEG), Electromyography (EMG) and Photoplethysmography (PPG). In detail, Electrocardiography (ECG) is useful in monitoring heartbeat rhythms and various cardiac conditions, whereas Electroencephalography (EEG) is utilized to detect and monitor brain signals that are associated with an individual's physical and cognitive activity. Moreover, Electromyography (EMG) deals with the real-time tracking of muscular and neuron cells that are involved in an individual's movement and Photoplethysmography (PPG) examines the variations in blood volume within tissues to determine the mental health (i.e., stress/depression/anxiety) of an individual.

On these lines of discussions, the Table 3 below showcases the key literatures that related to wearable technology and are identified within the network visualization stage of the analysis (See Fig. 4). Moreover, density visualisation showcases that majority of the studies on wearable technology were linked to IoT, machine learning, sleep tracking, patient monitoring, fitness management, stress management and the various physiological sensors (such as ECG, EEG, EMG, PPG) (See Fig. 5).

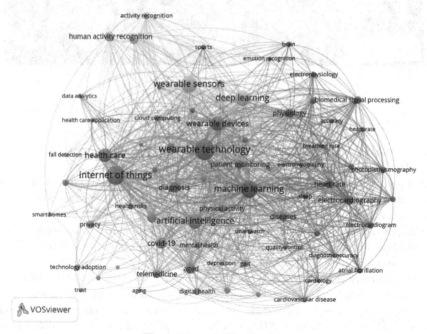

Fig. 4. Network Visualization

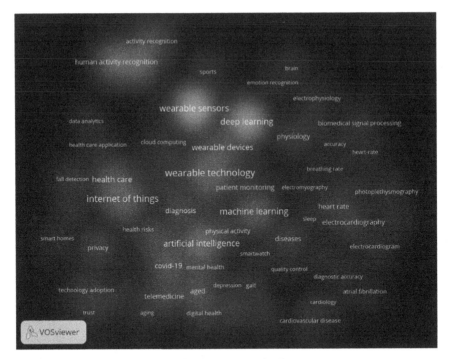

Fig. 5. Density Visualization

4.2 Different Types of Smart Wearable Technologies

Aside from remote patient monitoring techniques, IoT-based wearable technologies are transforming the way healthcare professionals provide care to patients. While remote monitoring capabilities allow clinicians to monitor patients' health status in real-time, medical wearables are critical in providing critical health-related information of patients and intervene promptly if any issues arise. This not only improves the efficiency of healthcare delivery but also enables more proactive and personalized care. Some of these applications are used for heart health, cardiovascular disease, blood pressure monitoring, and a variety of other purposes, as shown in Table 4.

Additionally, wearable devices are facilitating medical research and innovation by generating vast amounts of data that can be analysed to gain insights into various health conditions and trends. Some of these key wearable devices are smart watch (Samyoun et al., 2021; Sivani & Mishra, 2022; Subhan et al., 2023), smart glasses (Subhan et al., 2023), smart mask (Selvadass et al., 2022; Subhan et al., 2023), smart ring (Santhiya et al., 2023), smart belt (Kumar & Mufti, 2021; Piuzzi et al., 2020); Subhan et al. (2023), smart gloves (Caeiro-Rodríguez et al., 2021; Ozioko & Dahiya, 2022; Subhan et al., 2023) and smart thermometer (Panunzio et al., 2021; Subhan et al., 2023) that are utilised by individuals to track key health information, improve diagnostic methods, and enhance overall healthcare practices.

Table 3. Studies Related to Applications of Wearable Technology in Healthcare

Applications of Wearable Technology	Related Studies
Electrocardiography	Alshamrani (2022); Baklouti and Othmen (2022); Bhattarai et al. (2022); John et al. (2021); Sivani and Mishra (2022); Sowmya and Jose (2023); Zhang et al. (2021)
Electroencephalography	Cannard et al. (2021); Elmalaki et al. (2021); Imtiaz (2021); Sawan et al. (2024); Zanetti et al. (2021)
Electromyography	Al-Ayyad et al. (2023); He et al. (2023); Prange et al. (2021); Wang and Wang (2023)
Photoplethysmography	Fioravanti et al. (2024); Kim and Baek (2023); Lee et al. (2021); Namvari et al. (2022); Sirkiä et al. (2024)
Atrial Fibrillation	Fioravanti et al. (2024); Han et al. (2023); Ma et al. (2023); Mäkynen et al. (2022); Sun et al. (2024); Wang et al. (2022)
Breathing Rate Recognition	Janik et al. (2022); Martillano et al. (2022); Pineda-Alpizar et al. (2023); Ritsert et al. (2022)
Emotion Recognition	Feng et al. (2020); Shu et al. (2020); Wijasena et al. (2021)
Brain Activity, Sleep Tracking	Anupama et al. (2022); Anusha et al. (2022); Cook et al. (2022); Edgley et al. (2023); Rostaminia et al. (2022)
Fitness Management & Tracking/Exercise/Physical Activity/Human Activity Recognition	Ash et al. (2021); Barricelli et al. (2020); Bhatia et al. (2021); Garg et al. (2022); Hannan et al. (2021); Nazaret et al. (2023)
Stress/Depression/Mental Health	Abd-Alrazaq et al. (2023); Booth et al. (2022); Dai et al. (2022); Hickey et al. (2021); Kang and Chai (2022); Kishimoto et al. (2022); Talaat and El-Balka (2023); Tanwar et al. (2024)
Parkison's Disease	Bagrodia et al. (2022); Castelli Gattinara Di Zubiena et al. (2022); Chen et al. (2023); Jansi Rani et al. (2022); B. Yang et al. (2022)
Technology Adoption	Eckhaus and Sheaffer (2022); Hayat et al. (2022); Mitra et al. (2022); Nayak et al. (2022); Pathania et al. (2022); Q. Yang et al. (2022)
Sleep Apnea	Gupta et al. (2021); Imtiaz (2021); Lujan et al. (2021); Tran et al. (2023); Yoon and Choi (2023)

(continued)

Table 3. (*continued*)

Applications of Wearable Technology	Related Studies
Elderly Care Monitoring	Kulurkar et al. (2023); Liu et al. (2019); Olmedo-Aguirre et al. (2022); Teixeira et al. (2021); Tun et al. (2021)
Fall Detection	González-Cañete and Casilari (2021); Kulurkar et al. (2023); Subramaniam et al. (2022); Tanwar et al. (2022)
Seizure Detection	Garção et al. (2023); Li et al. (2022); Tang et al. (2021)
Stroke Prediction	Edgley et al. (2023); Han et al. (2023); Islam et al. (2022); Postolache et al. (2020); Razfar et al. (2023)
Covid-19	Babu et al. (2024); Chatterjee et al. (2023); Chiu et al. (2023); Peng et al. (2022)
Internet of Things/Machine Learning	Adi and Park (2023); Al-Atawi et al. (2023); Braun et al. (2024); D'Aniello et al. (2024); Diaz-Ramos et al. (2023); Fioravanti et al. (2024); Hou et al. (2023); Khan et al. (2023); Mani et al. (2023); Nair and Sakthivel (2022); Sirkiä et al. (2024); Zhao et al. (2024)

Table 4. IoT Based Applications Used for Personalised Monitoring

IoT-Based Application Used for Personalised Monitoring	Related Studies
Electrocardiogram (ECG)	Alshamrani (2022); Baklouti and Othmen (2022); Bhattarai et al. (2022); John et al. (2021); Sivani and Mishra (2022); Sowmya and Jose (2023); Zhang et al. (2021)
Glucose Level	Alshamrani (2022); Rodriguez-León et al. (2021); Subhan et al. (2023)
Blood Pressure	Alshamrani (2022); Kumar et al. (2024); Subhan et al. (2023)
Body Temperature	Alshamrani (2022); Patel et al. (2022); M. Seçkin et al. (2023); Subhan et al. (2023)
Oxygen Level	Alshamrani (2022); Mirjalali et al. (2022); A. Ç. Seçkin et al. (2023); Subhan et al. (2023)
Rehabilitation system	Alshamrani (2022); De Fazio et al. (2023); Subhan et al. (2023); Toh et al. (2023)
Essential Healthcare Services	Alshamrani (2022); Okazaki et al. (2022); Serhani et al. (2020); Subhan et al. (2023)

5 Conclusion

With the widespread adoption of wearable technologies in healthcare, there are several challenges, particularly those related to data privacy and security. Some of these key issues include those wearable devices should be friendly so that skin damages do not occur on an individual's body (Iqbal et al., 2021; Ling et al., 2020; Subhan et al., 2023). Furthermore, as the majority of wearables run on rechargeable batteries, it should be ensured that these batteries are of low consumption and have higher efficiency when wearable devices are used by patients (Jiang et al., 2015; Park & Jayaraman, 2021; Subhan et al., 2023). Lastly, as it understood that wearable devices collect sensitive health information, it is crucial to ensure that proper safeguards are in place to protect patient confidentiality and comply with regulatory requirements (Sivani & Mishra, 2022; Subhan et al., 2023).

References

Abd-Alrazaq, A., AlSaad, R., Shuweihdi, F., Ahmed, A., Aziz, S., Sheikh, J.: Systematic review and meta-analysis of performance of wearable artificial intelligence in detecting and predicting depression. NPJ Digit. Med. **6**(1), 84 (2023)

Adi, G.S., Park, I.: Emerging machine learning in wearable healthcare sensors. J. Sens. Sci. Technol. **32**(6), 378–385 (2023)

Aekanth, S.G., Tillinghast, D.J.: The emergence of wearable technologies in healthcare: a systematic review. In: Human-Automation Interaction, pp. 43–59

Al-Atawi, A.A., et al.: Stress monitoring using machine learning, IoT wearable sensors. Sensors **23**(21), 8875 (2023)

Al-Ayyad, M., Owida, H.A., De Fazio, R., Al-Naami, B., Visconti, P.: Electromyography monitoring systems in rehabilitation: a review of clinical applications, wearable devices and signal acquisition methodologies. Electronics **12**(7), 1520 (2023)

Alshamrani, M.: IoT and artificial intelligence implementations for remote healthcare monitoring systems: a survey. J. King Saud Univ.-Comput. Inf. Sci. **34**(8), 4687–4701 (2022)

Anupama, C., Sivaram, M., Lydia, E.L., Gupta, D., Shankar, K.: Synergic deep learning model–based automated detection and classification of brain intracranial hemorrhage images in wearable networks. Pers. Ubiquit. Comput. **26**, 1–10 (2022)

Anusha, A., Preejith, S., Akl, T.J., Sivaprakasam, M.: Electrodermal activity based autonomic sleep staging using wrist wearable. Biomed. Signal Process. Control **75**, 103562 (2022)

Ash, G.I., et al.: Establishing a global standard for wearable devices in sport and exercise medicine: perspectives from academic and industry stakeholders. Sports Med. **51**(11), 2237–2250 (2021)

Awotunde, J.B., et al.: AIoMT enabling real-time monitoring of healthcare systems: security and privacy considerations. In: Handbook of Security and Privacy of AI-Enabled Healthcare Systems and Internet of Medical Things, pp. 97–133 (2024)

Azizan, A., Ahmed, W., Razak, A.H.A.: Sensing health: a bibliometric analysis of wearable sensors in healthcare. Health Technol. **14**, 1–20 (2023)

Babu, M.V., Ramya, V., Murugan, V.S.: A proposed high efficient current control technique for home based upper limb rehabilitation and health monitoring system during post Covid-19. Int. J. Intell. Syst. Appl. Eng. **12**(2s), 600–607 (2024)

Bagrodia, V., Holla, V.V., Kamble, N.L., Pal, P.K., Yadav, R.: Parkinson's disease and wearable technology: an Indian perspective. Ann. Indian Acad. Neurol. **25**(5), 817 (2022)

Baklouti, M., Othmen, F.: E-safe: smart ECG-based authentication on-wrist healthcare wearable system. Eng. Lett. **30**(4), 1327 (2022)

Barricelli, B.R., Casiraghi, E., Gliozzo, J., Petrini, A., Valtolina, S.: Human digital twin for fitness management. IEEE Access **8**, 26637–26664 (2020)

Bayoumy, K., et al.: Smart wearable devices in cardiovascular care: where we are and how to move forward. Nat. Rev. Cardiol. **18**(8), 581–599 (2021)

Bhatia, D., Jo, S.H., Ryu, Y., Kim, Y., Kim, D.H., Park, H.-S.: Wearable triboelectric nanogenerator based exercise system for upper limb rehabilitation post neurological injuries. Nano Energy **80**, 105508 (2021)

Bhattarai, A., Peng, D., Payne, J., Sharif, H.: Adaptive partition of ECG diagnosis between cloud and wearable sensor net using open-loop and closed-loop switch mode. IEEE Access **10**, 63684–63697 (2022)

Bianchi, C., Tuzovic, S., Kuppelwieser, V.G.: Investigating the drivers of wearable technology adoption for healthcare in South America. Inf. Technol. People **36**(2), 916–939 (2023)

Binyamin, S.S., Hoque, M.R.: Understanding the drivers of wearable health monitoring technology: an extension of the unified theory of acceptance and use of technology. Sustainability **12**(22), 9605 (2020)

Booth, B.M., Vrzakova, H., Mattingly, S.M., Martinez, G.J., Faust, L., D'Mello, S.K.: Toward robust stress prediction in the age of wearables: modeling perceived stress in a longitudinal study with information workers. IEEE Trans. Affect. Comput. **13**(4), 2201–2217 (2022)

Braun, B.J., et al.: Wearable activity data can predict functional recovery after musculoskeletal injury: feasibility of a machine learning approach. Injury **55**(2), 111254 (2024)

Caeiro-Rodríguez, M., Otero-González, I., Mikic-Fonte, F.A., Llamas-Nistal, M.: A systematic review of commercial smart gloves: current status and applications. Sensors **21**(8), 2667 (2021)

Cannard, C., Wahbeh, H., Delorme, A.: Electroencephalography correlates of well-being using a low-cost wearable system. Front. Hum. Neurosci. **15**, 745135 (2021)

Di Zubiena, C.G., et al.: Machine learning and wearable sensors for the early detection of balance disorders in Parkinson's disease. Sensors **22**(24), 9903 (2022)

Chatterjee, A., Prinz, A., Riegler, M.A., Das, J.: A systematic review and knowledge mapping on ICT-based remote and automatic COVID-19 patient monitoring and care. BMC Health Serv. Res. **23**(1), 1047 (2023)

Chen, M., Sun, Z., Xin, T., Bu, D., Chen, Y., Su, F.: An interpretable deep learning optimized wearable daily detection system for Parkinson's disease. IEEE Trans. Neural Syst. Rehabil. Eng. **31**, 3937–3946 (2023)

Cheung, M.L., Leung, W.K., Chan, H.: Driving healthcare wearable technology adoption for Generation Z consumers in Hong Kong. Young Consum. **22**(1), 10–27 (2021)

Chiu, P.-C., et al.: Development and testing of the smart healthcare prototype system through COVID-19 patient innovation. Healthcare **11**, 847 (2023)

Cook, D.J., Strickland, M., Schmitter-Edgecombe, M.: Detecting smartwatch-based behavior change in response to a multi-domain brain health intervention. ACM Trans. Comput. Healthc. (HEALTH) **3**(3), 1–18 (2022)

D'Aniello, G., Gaeta, M., Gravina, R., Li, Q., Rehman, Z.U., Fortino, G.: Situation identification in smart wearable computing systems based on machine learning and Context Space Theory. Inf. Fusion **104**, 102197 (2024)

Dai, R., Kannampallil, T., Zhang, J., Lv, N., Ma, J., Lu, C.: Multi-task learning for randomized controlled trials: a case study on predicting depression with wearable data. Proc. ACM Interact. Mob. Wearable Ubiquit. Technol. **6**(2), 1–23 (2022)

De Fazio, R., Mastronardi, V.M., De Vittorio, M., Visconti, P.: Wearable sensors and smart devices to monitor rehabilitation parameters and sports performance: an overview. Sensors **23**(4), 1856 (2023)

Devi, D.H., et al.: 5G technology in healthcare and wearable devices: a review. Sensors **23**(5), 2519 (2023)

Diaz-Ramos, R.E., Noriega, I., Trejo, L.A., Stroulia, E., Cao, B.: Using wearable devices and speech data for personalized machine learning in early detection of mental disorders: protocol for a participatory research study. JMIR Res. Protoc. 12(1), e48210 (2023)

Eckhaus, E., Sheaffer, Z.: Adoption of wearable technology: risk and success factors. Fashion Style Popular Culture 9(4), 457–481 (2022)

Edgley, K., Chun, H.-Y.Y., Whiteley, W.N., Tsanas, A.: New insights into stroke from continuous passively collected temperature and sleep data using wrist-worn wearables. Sensors 23(3), 1069 (2023)

Elmalaki, S., Demirel, B.U., Taherisadr, M., Stern-Nezer, S., Lin, J.J., Al Faruque, M.A.: Towards internet-of-things for wearable neurotechnology. In: 2021 22nd International Symposium on Quality Electronic Design (ISQED) (2021)

Feng, X., Lu, X., Li, Z., Zhang, M., Li, J., Zhang, D.: Investigating the physiological correlates of daily well-being: a PERMA model-based study. Open Psychol. J. 13(1), 169–180 (2020)

Fioravanti, V.B., et al.: Machine learning framework for Inter-Beat Interval estimation using wearable Photoplethysmography sensors. Biomed. Signal Process. Control 88, 105689 (2024)

Garção, V.M., et al.: A novel approach to automatic seizure detection using computer vision and independent component analysis. Epilepsia 64(9), 2472–2483 (2023)

Garg, H., Sharma, B., Shekhar, S., Agarwal, R.: Spoofing detection system for e-health digital twin using EfficientNet Convolution Neural Network. Multimedia Tools Appl. 81(19), 26873–26888 (2022)

González-Cañete, F.J., Casilari, E.: A feasibility study of the use of smartwatches in wearable fall detection systems. Sensors 21(6), 2254 (2021)

Gupta, D., Kayode, O., Bhatt, S., Gupta, M., Tosun, A.S.: Hierarchical federated learning based anomaly detection using digital twins for smart healthcare. In: 2021 IEEE 7th International Conference on Collaboration and Internet Computing (CIC) (2021)

Han, D., et al.: A smartwatch system for continuous monitoring of atrial fibrillation in older adults after stroke or transient Ischemic attack: application design study. JMIR Cardio 7, e41691 (2023)

Hannan, A., Shafiq, M.Z., Hussain, F., Pires, I.M.: A portable smart fitness suite for real-time exercise monitoring and posture correction. Sensors 21(19), 6692 (2021)

Hayat, N., Salameh, A.A., Malik, H.A., Yaacob, M.R.: Exploring the adoption of wearable health-care devices among the Pakistani adults with dual analysis techniques. Technol. Soc. 70, 102015 (2022)

He, J., Niu, X., Zhao, P., Lin, C., Jiang, N.: From forearm to wrist: deep learning for surface electromyography-based gesture recognition. IEEE Trans. Neural Syst. Rehabil. Eng. 32, 102–111 (2023)

Hickey, B.A., et al.: Smart devices and wearable technologies to detect and monitor mental health conditions and stress: a systematic review. Sensors 21(10), 3461 (2021)

Hou, Y., et al.: 3D printed conformal strain and humidity sensors for human motion prediction and health monitoring via machine learning. Adv. Sci. 10(36), 2304132 (2023)

Imtiaz, S.A.: A systematic review of sensing technologies for wearable sleep staging. Sensors 21(5), 1562 (2021)

Iqbal, S.M., Mahgoub, I., Du, E., Leavitt, M.A., Asghar, W.: Advances in healthcare wearable devices. NPJ Flexible Electron. 5(1), 9 (2021)

Islam, M.S., Hussain, I., Rahman, M.M., Park, S.J., Hossain, M.A.: Explainable artificial intelligence model for stroke prediction using EEG signal. Sensors 22(24), 9859 (2022)

Janik, P., Janik, M.A., Pielka, M.: Monitoring breathing and heart rate using episodic broadcast data transmission. Sensors 22(16), 6019 (2022)

Jansi Rani, S., Chandran, K.S., Ranganathan, A., Chandrasekharan, M., Janani, B., Deepsheka, G.: Smart wearable model for predicting heart disease using machine learning: wearable to predict heart risk. J. Ambient. Intell. Humaniz. Comput. 13(9), 4321–4332 (2022)

Jiang, H., Chen, X., Zhang, S., Zhang, X., Kong, W., Zhang, T.: Software for wearable devices: challenges and opportunities. In: 2015 IEEE 39th Annual Computer Software and Applications Conference (2015)

John, A., Redmond, S.J., Cardiff, B., John, D.: A multimodal data fusion technique for heartbeat detection in wearable IoT sensors. IEEE Internet Things J. **9**(3), 2071–2082 (2021)

Kang, M., Chai, K.: Wearable sensing systems for monitoring mental health. Sensors **22**(3), 994 (2022)

Kazanskiy, N.L., Khonina, S.N., Butt, M.A.: A review on flexible wearables-recent developments in non-invasive continuous health monitoring. Sens. Actuators A: Phys. 114993 (2024)

Khan, R., Ghani, A., Chelloug, S.A., Amin, M., Saeed, A., Teo, J.: Machine learning-enabled communication approach for the Internet of Medical Things. Comput. Mater. Continua **76**(2), 1569–1584 (2023)

Kim, K.B., Baek, H.J.: Photoplethysmography in wearable devices: a comprehensive review of technological advances, current challenges, and future directions. Electronics **12**(13), 2923 (2023)

Kishimoto, T., et al.: Development of medical device software for the screening and assessment of depression severity using data collected from a wristband-type wearable device: SWIFT study protocol. Front. Psych. **13**, 1025517 (2022)

Kulurkar, P., Kumar Dixit, C., Bharathi, V., Monikavishnuvarthini, A., Dhakne, A., Preethi, P.: AI based elderly fall prediction system using wearable sensors: a smart home-care technology with IOT. Meas. Sens. **25**, 100614 (2023)

Kumar, D., Mufti, T.: Impact of coronavirus on global cloud based wearable tracking devices. In: 2021 9th International Conference on Reliability, Infocom Technologies and Optimization (Trends and Future Directions) (ICRITO) (2021)

Kumar, S., Yadav, S., Kumar, A.: Blood pressure measurement techniques, standards, technologies, and the latest futuristic wearable cuff-less know-how. Sens. Diagn. **3**, 181–202 (2024)

Lee, I., Park, N., Lee, H., Hwang, C., Kim, J.H., Park, S.: Systematic review on human skin-compatible wearable photoplethysmography sensors. Appl. Sci. **11**(5), 2313 (2021)

Li, C., Lammie, C., Dong, X., Amirsoleimani, A., Azghadi, M.R., Genov, R.: Seizure detection and prediction by parallel memristive convolutional neural networks. IEEE Trans. Biomed. Circuits Syst. **16**(4), 609–625 (2022)

Ling, Y., An, T., Yap, L.W., Zhu, B., Gong, S., Cheng, W.: Disruptive, soft, wearable sensors. Adv. Mater. **32**(18), 1904664 (2020)

Liu, Y., et al.: A novel cloud-based framework for the elderly healthcare services using digital twin. IEEE Access **7**, 49088–49101 (2019)

Lui, G.Y., Loughnane, D., Polley, C., Jayarathna, T., Breen, P.P.: The apple watch for monitoring mental health–related physiological symptoms: literature review. JMIR Mental Health **9**(9), e37354 (2022)

Lujan, M.R., Perez-Pozuelo, I., Grandner, M.A.: Past, present, and future of multisensory wearable technology to monitor sleep and circadian rhythms. Front. Digit. Health **3**, 721919 (2021)

Ma, Z., et al.: FlexiPulse: a machine-learning-enabled flexible pulse sensor for cardiovascular disease diagnostics. Cell Rep. Phys. Sci. **4**(12), 101690 (2023)

Mäkynen, M., Ng, G.A., Li, X., Schlindwein, F.S.: Wearable devices combined with artificial intelligence—a future technology for atrial fibrillation detection? Sensors **22**(22), 8588 (2022)

Malwade, S., et al.: Mobile and wearable technologies in healthcare for the ageing population. Comput. Methods Programs Biomed. **161**, 233–237 (2018)

Mani, N., Haridoss, P., George, B.: Smart suspenders with sensors and machine learning for human activity monitoring. IEEE Sens. J. **23**, 10159–10167 (2023)

Martillano, D.A., Iligan, M.C., Ramos, A.R.R., Daraman Jr, A., Abadines, M.F.H.: Wearable tool for breathing pattern recognition and exacerbation monitoring for COPD patients via a Device-to-Cloud communication model. J. Commun. **17**(6), 423–433 (2022)

Mattison, G., et al.: The influence of wearables on health care outcomes in chronic disease: systematic review. J. Med. Internet Res. **24**(7), e36690 (2022)

Mirjalali, S., Peng, S., Fang, Z., Wang, C.H., Wu, S.: Wearable sensors for remote health monitoring: potential applications for early diagnosis of Covid-19. Adv. Mater. Technol. **7**(1), 2100545 (2022)

Mitra, S., Singh, A., Rajendran Deepam, S., Asthana, M.K.: Information and communication technology adoption among the older people: a qualitative approach. Health Soc. Care Community **30**(6), e6428–e6437 (2022)

Nair, B.B., Sakthivel, N.: An upper limb rehabilitation exercise status identification system based on machine learning and IoT. Arab. J. Sci. Eng. **47**(2), 2095–2121 (2022)

Namvari, M., et al.: Photoplethysmography enabled wearable devices and stress detection: a scoping review. J. Personalized Med. **12**(11), 1792 (2022)

Nayak, B., Bhattacharyya, S.S., Kumar, S., Jumnani, R.K.: Exploring the factors influencing adoption of health-care wearables among generation Z consumers in India. J. Inf. Commun. Ethics Soc. **20**(1), 150–174 (2022)

Nazaret, A., Tonekaboni, S., Darnell, G., Ren, S.Y., Sapiro, G., Miller, A.C.: Modeling personalized heart rate response to exercise and environmental factors with wearables data. NPJ Digit. Med. **6**(1), 207 (2023)

Oh, J., Kang, H.: User engagement with smart wearables: four defining factors and a process model. Mob. Media Commun. **9**(2), 314–335 (2021)

Okazaki, K., Okazaki, K., Uesugi, M., Matsusima, T., Hataya, H.: Evaluation of the accuracy of a non-invasive hemoglobin-monitoring device in schoolchildren. Pediatr. Neonatol. **63**(1), 19–24 (2022)

Olmedo-Aguirre, J.O., Reyes-Campos, J., Alor-Hernández, G., Machorro-Cano, I., Rodríguez-Mazahua, L., Sánchez-Cervantes, J.L.: Remote healthcare for elderly people using wearables: a review. Biosensors **12**(2), 73 (2022)

Osama, M., et al.: Internet of medical things and healthcare 4.0: trends, requirements, challenges, and research directions. Sensors **23**(17), 7435 (2023)

Ozioko, O., Dahiya, R.: Smart tactile gloves for haptic interaction, communication, and rehabilitation. Adv. Intell. Syst. **4**(2), 2100091 (2022)

Panunzio, N., Bianco, G.M., Occhiuzzi, C., Marrocco, G.: RFID sensors for the monitoring of body temperature and respiratory function: a pandemic prospect. In: 2021 6th International Conference on Smart and Sustainable Technologies (SpliTech) (2021)

Park, S., Jayaraman, S.: Wearables: fundamentals, advancements, and a roadmap for the future. In: Wearable Sensors, pp. 3–27. Elsevier (2021)

Patel, V., Chesmore, A., Legner, C.M., Pandey, S.: Trends in workplace wearable technologies and connected-worker solutions for next-generation occupational safety, health, and productivity. Adv. Intell. Syst. **4**(1), 2100099 (2022)

Pathania, A., Dixit, S., Rasool, G.: 'Are online reviews the new shepherd?'–examining herd behaviour in wearable technology adoption for personal healthcare. J. Market. Commun. 1–27 (2022)

Peng, X., Menhas, R., Dai, J., Younas, M.: The COVID-19 pandemic and overall wellbeing: mediating role of virtual reality fitness for physical-psychological health and physical activity. Psychol. Res. Behav. Manage. **15**, 1741–1756 (2022)

Pineda-Alpizar, F., Arriola-Valverde, S., Vado-Chacón, M., Sossa-Rojas, D., Liu, H., Zheng, D.: Real-time evaluation of time-domain pulse rate variability parameters in different postures and breathing patterns using wireless photoplethysmography sensor: towards remote healthcare in low-resource communities. Sensors **23**(9), 4246 (2023)

Piuzzi, E., Pisa, S., Pittella, E., Podestà, L., Sangiovanni, S.: Wearable belt with built-in textile electrodes for cardio—respiratory monitoring. Sensors **20**(16), 4500 (2020)

Postolache, O., Hemanth, D.J., Alexandre, R., Gupta, D., Geman, O., Khanna, A.: Remote monitoring of physical rehabilitation of stroke patients using IoT and virtual reality. IEEE J. Sel. Areas Commun. **39**(2), 562–573 (2020)

Prakashan, D., Ramya, P.R., Gandhi, S.: A systematic review on the advanced techniques of wearable point-of-care devices and their futuristic applications. Diagnostics **13**(5), 916 (2023)

Prange, S., Mayer, S., Bittl, M.-L., Hassib, M., Alt, F.: Investigating user perceptions towards wearable mobile electromyography. In: Ardito, C., et al. (eds.) Human-Computer Interaction–INTERACT 2021: 18th IFIP TC 13 International Conference, Bari, Italy, 30 August–3 September 2021, Proceedings, Part IV 18. Springer, Cham (2021). https://doi.org/10.1007/978-3-030-85610-6_20

Razfar, N., Kashef, R., Mohammadi, F.: An Artificial Intelligence model for smart post-stroke assessment using wearable sensors. Decis. Analytics J. **7**, 100218 (2023)

Research-and-Markets. Smart Wearable Market - Growth, Trends, COVID-19 Impact, and Forecasts (2023–2028) (2023). https://www.researchandmarkets.com/reports/4769754/smart-wearable-market-growth-trends-covid-19?utm_source5BW&utm_medium5PressRelease&utm_

Ritsert, F., Elgendi, M., Galli, V., Menon, C.: Heart and breathing rate variations as biomarkers for anxiety detection. Bioengineering **9**(11), 711 (2022)

Rodriguez-León, C., Villalonga, C., Munoz-Torres, M., Ruiz, J.R., Banos, O.: Mobile and wearable technology for the monitoring of diabetes-related parameters: systematic review. JMIR Mhealth Uhealth **9**(6), e25138 (2021)

Rostaminia, S., Homayounfar, S.Z., Kiaghadi, A., Andrew, T., Ganesan, D.: PhyMask: robust sensing of brain activity and physiological signals during sleep with an all-textile eye mask. ACM Trans. Comput. Healthc. (HEALTH) **3**(3), 1–35 (2022)

Samyoun, S., Shubha, S.S., Mondol, M.A.S., Stankovic, J.A.: IWash: a smartwatch handwashing quality assessment and reminder system with real-time feedback in the context of infectious disease. Smart Health **19**, 100171 (2021)

Santhiya, S., Jayadharshini, P., Abinaya, N., Vasugi, M., Nallamangai, K.S.: Enrichment of human life through intelligent wearable technology. In: Artificial Intelligence and Machine Learning, pp. 26–36. CRC Press (2023)

Sawan, A., Awad, M., Qasrawi, R., Sowan, M.: Hybrid deep learning and metaheuristic model-based stroke diagnosis system using electroencephalogram (EEG). Biomed. Signal Process. Control **87**, 105454 (2024)

Schmidt, L.I., Jansen, C.-P., Depenbusch, J., Gabrian, M., Sieverding, M., Wahl, H.-W.: Using wearables to promote physical activity in old age: feasibility, benefits, and user friendliness. Z. Gerontol. Geriat. **55**(5), 388–393 (2022)

Seçkin, A.Ç., Ateş, B., Seçkin, M.: Review on wearable technology in sports: concepts challenges and opportunities. Appl. Sci. **13**(18), 10399 (2023)

Seçkin, M., Seçkin, A.Ç., Gençer, Ç.: Biomedical sensors and applications of wearable technologies on arm and hand. Biomed. Mater. Devices **1**(1), 443–455 (2023)

Selvadass, S., Paul, J.J., Bella Mary, I.T., Packiavathy, I.S.V., Gautam, S.: IoT-enabled smart mask to detect COVID19 outbreak. Health Technol. **12**(5), 1025–1036 (2022)

Serhani, M.A., El Kassabi, H., Ismail, H., Nujum Navaz, A.: ECG monitoring systems: review, architecture, processes, and key challenges. Sensors **20**(6), 1796 (2020)

Sharma, A.: The role of IoT in the fight against Covid-19 to restructure the economy. In: Stephanidis, C., et al. (eds.) HCI International 2021 - Late Breaking Papers: HCI Applications in Health, Transport, and Industry, vol. 13097, pp. 140–156. Springer, Cham (2021). https://doi.org/10.1007/978-3-030-90966-6_11

Shei, R.-J., Holder, I.G., Oumsang, A.S., Paris, B.A., Paris, H.L.: Wearable activity trackers–advanced technology or advanced marketing? Eur. J. Appl. Physiol. **122**(9), 1975–1990 (2022)

Shu, L., et al.: Wearable emotion recognition using heart rate data from a smart bracelet. Sensors **20**(3), 718 (2020)

Sirkiä, J.-P., Panula, T., Kaisti, M.: Wearable edge machine learning with synthetic photoplethys-mograms. Expert Syst. Appl. **238**, 121523 (2024)

Sivani, T., Mishra, S.: Wearable devices: evolution and usage in remote patient monitoring system. In: Mishra, S., González-Briones, A., Bhoi, A.K., Mallick, P.K., Corchado, J.M. (eds.) Connected e-Health. Studies in Computational Intelligence, vol. 1021, pp. 311–332. Springer, Cham (2022). https://doi.org/10.1007/978-3-030-97929-4_14

Sowmya, S., Jose, D.: Detecting anomalies in fetal electrocardiogram records using deep learning models. J. Intell. Fuzzy Syst. **45**, 1–18 (2023)

Subhan, F., et al.: AI-enabled wearable medical internet of things in healthcare system: a survey. Appl. Sci. **13**(3), 1394 (2023)

Subramaniam, S., Faisal, A.I., Deen, M.J.: Wearable sensor systems for fall risk assessment: a review. Front. Digit. Health **4**, 921506 (2022)

Sun, Y., Shen, J., Jiang, Y., Huang, Z., Hao, M., Zhang, X.: MMA-RNN: a multi-level multi-task attention-based recurrent neural network for discrimination and localization of atrial fibrillation. Biomed. Signal Process. Control **89**, 105747 (2024)

Talaat, F.M., El-Balka, R.M.: Stress monitoring using wearable sensors: IoT techniques in medical field. Neural Comput. Appl. **35**, 1–14 (2023)

Tang, J., et al.: Seizure detection using wearable sensors and machine learning: setting a benchmark. Epilepsia **62**(8), 1807–1819 (2021)

Tanwar, R., Nandal, N., Zamani, M., Manaf, A.A.: Pathway of trends and technologies in fall detection: a systematic review. Healthcare **10**, 172 (2022)

Tanwar, R., Phukan, O.C., Singh, G., Pal, P.K., Tiwari, S.: Attention based hybrid deep learning model for wearable based stress recognition. Eng. Appl. Artif. Intell. **127**, 107391 (2024)

Teixeira, E., et al.: Wearable devices for physical activity and healthcare monitoring in elderly people: a critical review. Geriatrics **6**(2), 38 (2021)

Toh, S.F.M., Fong, K.N., Gonzalez, P.C., Tang, Y.M.: Application of home-based wearable technologies in physical rehabilitation for stroke: a scoping review. IEEE Trans. Neural Syst. Rehabil. Eng. **31**, 1614–1623 (2023)

Tran, N.T., Tran, H.N., Mai, A.T.: A wearable device for at-home obstructive sleep apnea assessment: state-of-the-art and research challenges. Front. Neurol. **14**, 1123227 (2023)

Tun, S.Y.Y., Madanian, S., Mirza, F.: Internet of Things (IoT) applications for elderly care: a reflective review. Aging Clin. Exp. Res. **33**, 855–867 (2021)

VandeBunte, A., et al.: Physical activity measurement in older adults: wearables versus self-report. Front. Digit. Health **4**, 869790 (2022)

Wang, Y.-C., et al.: Current advancement in diagnosing atrial fibrillation by utilizing wearable devices and artificial intelligence: a review study. Diagnostics **12**(3), 689 (2022)

Wang, Y., Wang, Y.: A high-bandwidth wireless wearable armband based on surface electromyography. In: 2023 IEEE 6th International Conference on Pattern Recognition and Artificial Intelligence (PRAI) (2023)

Wijasena, H.Z., Ferdiana, R., Wibirama, S.: A survey of emotion recognition using physiological signal in wearable devices. In: 2021 International Conference on Artificial Intelligence and Mechatronics Systems (AIMS) (2021)

Yang, B., et al.: Intelligent wearable system with accurate detection of abnormal gait and timely cueing for mobility enhancement of people with Parkinson's disease. Wearable Technol. **3**, e12 (2022)

Yang, Q., Al Mamun, A., Hayat, N., Jingzu, G., Hoque, M.E., Salameh, A.A.: Modeling the intention and adoption of wearable fitness devices: a study using SEM-PLS analysis. Front. Public Health **10**, 918989 (2022)

Yoon, H., Choi, S.H.: Technologies for sleep monitoring at home: wearables and nearables. Biomed. Eng. Lett. **13**(3), 313–327 (2023)

Zanetti, R., Arza, A., Aminifar, A., Atienza, D.: Real-time EEG-based cognitive workload monitoring on wearable devices. IEEE Trans. Biomed. Eng. **69**(1), 265–277 (2021)

Zhang, X., Jiang, M., Wu, W., de Albuquerque, V.H.C.: Hybrid feature fusion for classification optimization of short ECG segment in IoT based intelligent healthcare system. Neural Comput. Appl. 1–15 (2021)

Zhang, Y., Chen, G., Du, H., Yuan, X., Kadoch, M., Cheriet, M.: Real-time remote health monitoring system driven by 5G MEC-IoT. Electronics **9**(11), 1753 (2020)

Zhao, Z., et al.: Machine learning-assisted wearable sensing for high-sensitivity gesture recognition. Sens. Actuators, A **365**, 114877 (2024)

Study of a Method for Reducing VR Sickness Using the Tunnel Effect

Kaito Watanabe[1]([✉]), Katsuhiko Onishi[1], Masanao Koeda[2], Morihiro Tsujishita[3], and Hiroshi Noborio[1]

[1] Osaka Electro-Communication University, Shijonawate, Osaka, Japan
`ht20a117@oecu.jp`
[2] Okayama Prefectural University, Soja, Okayama, Japan
[3] Naragakuen University, Nara, Nara, Japan

Abstract. VR technology is used for a variety of content. However, using VR causes a symptom called VR sickness. There are various methods to reduce VR sickness, and we focused on methods to reduce it from the field of vision. However, methods of reducing VR sickness that affect vision have the problem of impeding the immersive experience. So, this time, we focused on the tunnel effect. The tunnel effect is a technique to reduce VR sickness by darkening or blurring the periphery of the visual field. The tunneling effect was used to study methods that do not interfere with the immersive experience. There are also still problems with the way VR sickness is measured. Therefore, we wanted to measure VR sickness using eye movements and fingertip temperature in this study. In addition to eye movements and fingertip temperature, we attempted to measure VR sickness using EEG and SSQ questionnaires.

Keywords: VR sickness · Tunnel effect · Saccade · EEG

1 Introduction

Virtual reality (VR) technology has been increasingly used in various fields. However, on the other hand, various problems have occurred due to the use of VR. One of them is VR sickness. This VR sickness is also called VIMS or simulator sickness and is considered to be a type of motion sickness. Symptoms such as headache, nausea, vertigo, vomiting, and upset stomach often appear along with a sense of discomfort. The occurrence of VR sickness varies from person to person. Although there are various theories on the conditions that cause VR sickness, it is said that the main cause is a discrepancy in the information sent to the brain. Therefore, to reduce VR sickness without compromising the quality of the VR experience, there are many methods, such as teleportation of movement and methods to reduce acceleration/deceleration of movement speed. One such approach is to the field of view, such as the tunnel effect that hides or blurs the peripheral vision of the person experiencing VR or the cockpit effect that places the driver's seat of a car or the cockpit of a robot around the screen. Both of these methods limit the peripheral vision and suppress the occurrence of vection to avoid information mismatch, which is considered a contributing factor to VR sickness. However, this method may reduce the sense of presence and immersion because of the restricted viewing angle. To maintain a

M. Kurosu and A. Hashizume (Eds.): HCII 2024, LNCS 14686, pp. 221–235, 2024.
https://doi.org/10.1007/978-3-031-60428-7_16

sense of presence, a blurring process is applied to the peripheral field of view to create a vignette effect. However, it has been pointed out that this method is less effective in reducing VR sickness than the method that restricts the field of view [1].

Therefore, in this study, we conducted a comparison experiment of several visual presentation methods to investigate a presentation method that can maintain a sense of presence while maintaining the effectiveness of the VR sickness reduction effect. Specifically, in addition to blur processing, we compared two methods: the placement of objects that produce a cockpit effect and the movement of blur processing linked to the movement of the visual field. In parallel with verifying this method, we also verified the real-time measurement of VR sickness. In many studies, VR sickness is often compared before and after the experiment, making it difficult to confirm when it occurred. For this reason, many validations have been conducted using the physiological indices of the subjects during the experiment [2, 3]. However, many studies use extensive facilities and expensive equipment, and reproducibility in general studies is also problematic. Therefore, we used inexpensive and highly reproducible temperature acquisition in this study to perform real-time measurements of eye movements and the terminal nervous system.

2   Tunnel Effect Expression Method

In pursuit of a display methodology that significantly mitigates VR sickness while preserving the integrity of the virtual reality experience, this study examines an approach that integrates blur processing with the cockpit effect for rendering peripheral vision. The experiment systematically evaluates four distinct conditions associated with peripheral vision, delineated in the subsequent sections.

Fig. 1. HMD images when there is none.

2.1 Displayed Image Without Nothing (Condition 1)

This condition was defined as a scenario without incorporating additional elements into the displayed image. Figure 1 shows an example image of the field of view under this condition.

2.2 Displayed Image with Blur on the Edge of View (Condition 2)

This condition was defined as a scenario with applied blur to the image within the field of view. The blur was explicitly configured to appear at the edges of the field of view. Figure 2 shows an example image of the field of view under this condition.

Fig. 2. Blurred view at the edge of the HMD's field of view.

2.3 Displayed Image with Blur and Immobile Objects at the Edge of View (Condition 3)

This condition was defined as a scenario where blur is applied to an image with a motionless object in the field of view. The blur was set to be noticeable at the edge of the field of view, like Condition 2. Figure 3 shows an example image of the field of view under this condition. Figure 4 also displays the motionless object within the field of view. The object was shaped like a pair of monocular glasses to consider the effect on both eyes when viewing moving images.

Fig. 3. Blur and immobile objects at the edge of view.

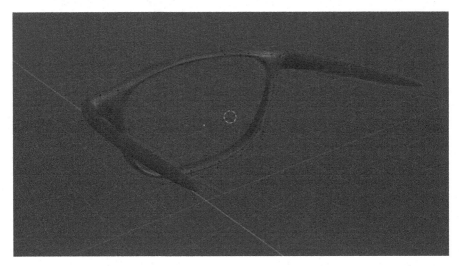

Fig. 4. Motionless objects placed in view.

2.4 Displayed Image with Blur Moving with the Gaze (Condition 4)

This condition involves applying a line-of-sight moving blur to the image in view. The blur is centered around the point of gaze but appears off-center in the field of view. Figure 5 shows the field of view under these conditions. In this figure, the view is captured as the eye looks to the right; the building on the right is in focus, while the rest of the scene is blurred.

Fig. 5. Blurred vision on the right and other parts of the eye at gaze.

3 Comparative Evaluation Experiment

Basic experiments were conducted to compare the characteristics of the four tunneling effect methods described previously. Physiological indices were used as objective measures for this evaluation. These indices included eye movements, fingertip temperature, and electroencephalogram (EEG) data. For continuous real-time monitoring of VR sickness, eye movement and fingertip temperature data were constantly acquired throughout the experiment. As for the subjective index, the Simulator Sickness Questionnaire (SSQ), which is widely used in research, was employed.

3.1 Experiment Outline

In the experimental setup, EEG, a thermometer, and an eye-tracking device are initially calibrated. Subsequently, participants are asked to watch a 5-min walk-through video in a 3D environment via an HMD (Head-Mounted Display). Following this, EEG measurements are taken. The walk-through video includes the four types of tunneling effects mentioned earlier. Additionally, participants were informed beforehand that the experiment was related to VR sickness and consent was obtained prior to the experiment.

Figure 6 shows a scene from the created experiment environment. In this system, the participant automatically navigates through a cityscape, with the speed of movement varying based on the slope's angle. This variability in speed, which can cause acceleration and deceleration, is likely to induce VR sickness. We introduced variable speeds to categorize sections where VR sickness is less likely from those where it is more probable. This approach aids in the real-time assessment of VR sickness.

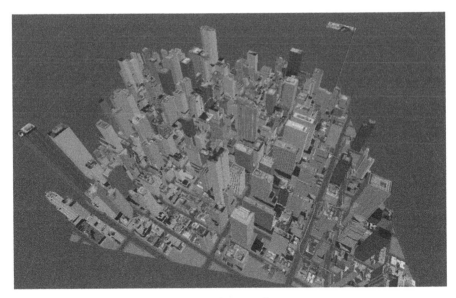

Fig. 6. Experiment environment

3.2 Eye Movement

Eye movements were utilized as a key physiological indicator. Eye tracking data was collected using the Vive Pro Eye HMD's built-in eye tracking feature. This function captures various details such as blinking, gaze direction, and focus. Notably, we focused on pupil position, which previous research [4] has suggested as a reliable metric for real-time measurement of VR sickness. Earlier studies have calculated pupil position in terms of dispersion. However, we noted that dispersion can increase if the subject consistently looks towards the edge of the field of view. Therefore, in this study, we chose to measure the frequency of saccades, rapid eye movements, as an indicator.

Saccades, or impulsive eye movements, are quick and occur during shifts in gaze. It has been proposed that VR sickness can be mitigated by providing a fixed point of gaze in the image [5]. This mitigation is attributed to 'continuous gazing at a specific object' [6].

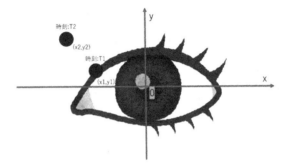

Fig. 7. Acquiring angular velocity using the pupil.

On the contrary, frequent saccades, resulting from shifting gaze between multiple objects, may contribute to VR sickness. A high correlation has been observed between eye strain from excessive eye use and VR sickness [7], with saccades potentially contributing to this strain. Based on these insights, we inferred that the frequency of saccades could be an effective measure for VR sickness and included it in our study.

The measurement method was designed based on the gaze analysis system described in [8]. Saccades typically occur three times per second and are characterized by eye movements with an instantaneous angular velocity of 100 degrees/second or more [9]. Our analysis system, as illustrated in Fig. 6, calculates the angular velocity of each saccade using Eq. (1). Any saccade with an angular velocity exceeding 100 degrees/second was counted, and the total number of such saccades was recorded throughout the experiment (Fig. 7).

$$\omega = \sqrt{(x_2 - x_1)^2 + (y_2 - y_1)^2} \times 90/t_2 - t_1 \tag{1}$$

3.3 Fingertip Temperature

VR sickness elicits a mental stress response in individuals, leading to various physiological symptoms due to the effect on the autonomic nervous system. One such symptom is a decrease in peripheral skin temperature, resulting from changes in blood flow. This temperature change is most pronounced in the nasal area. The nasal area is rich in arteriovenous anastomoses (AVAs) and venous anastomoses (peripheral cutaneous vessels), which regulate capillary blood flow and are more densely concentrated there than in other parts of the body. Additionally, these vessels in the nasal area run through a narrow space between the skin and the nasal bone, unlike in other body parts where they lie beneath a layer of fat. Since skin temperature reflects changes in blood flow, the psychological state induced by emotional stress is significantly manifested in the skin temperature of the nasal area [10]. Thus, nasal skin temperature has been proposed as an effective indicator for immediate detection of VR sickness [11]. However, placing a thermometer on the nasal area might interfere with the immersive experience in VR.

Therefore, in this study, we opted to measure fingertip temperature, which is easier to obtain and also exhibits a stress-induced decrease in skin temperature similar to the nasal area. Fingertip temperature was recorded using a thermistor thermometer (Murata NXFT15XH103FA2B). This choice was made considering the accessibility and less intrusive nature of measuring fingertip temperature compared to nasal temperature.

3.4 EEG

The electroencephalogram (EEG) is a comprehensive recording from the cranial surface of the brain of the minute changes in electrical currents produced by working nerve cells in the brain. EEG is divided into five types according to frequency range: δ waves (0.5–3 Hz), θ waves (4–7 Hz), α waves (8–13 Hz), β waves (14–30 Hz) and γ waves (30–100 Hz). The characteristics are described below [12].

δ waves: appear during deep sleep and rarely occur during wakefulness.

θ waves: appear in states of mental concentration, such as meditation or slumber.

α waves: appear in a relaxed state and occur most predominantly during arousal.

β waves: occur under physical and mental strain and occur in states of tension and intoxication.

γ waves: They occur in states of happiness and learning, and often appear together with theta waves. They also increase during deep sleep.

In this study, δ waves, which do not occur during wakefulness, and γ waves, which often appear in combination with θ waves, were excluded from the measurement in this experiment. During EEG measurements, artifacts (population noise), which are

ID

The Simulator Sickness Questionnaire (SSQ)

評価日 :

氏名 :

No.	Symptom (症状)	Score (点数)			
		0 (none)	1 (slight)	2 (moderate)	3 (severe)
1	General discomfort(全般的に気分が悪い)	まったくない	少しある	中程度にある	大いにある
2	Fatigue(疲労感がある)	まったくない	少しある	中程度にある	大いにある
3	Headache(頭痛がする)	まったくない	少しある	中程度にある	大いにある
4	Eyestrain(目の疲れを感じる)	まったくない	少しある	中程度にある	大いにある
5	Difficulty focusing(目の焦点が合わせにくい)	まったくない	少しある	中程度にある	大いにある
6	Increased salivation(唾液がよく出る)	まったくない	少しある	中程度にある	大いにある
7	Sweating(冷や汗が出る)	まったくない	少しある	中程度にある	大いにある
8	Nausea(吐き気がする)	まったくない	少しある	中程度にある	大いにある
9	Difficulty concentrating(注意集中が困難である)	まったくない	少しある	中程度にある	大いにある
10	Fullness of head(頭重感がする)	まったくない	少しある	中程度にある	大いにある
11	Blurred vision(視界がぼやける)	まったくない	少しある	中程度にある	大いにある
12	Dizzy<eye open>(開眼で身体がふらつく)	まったくない	少しある	中程度にある	大いにある
13	Dizzy<eye closed>(閉眼で身体がふらつく)	まったくない	少しある	中程度にある	大いにある
14	Vertigo(回転性のめまいがする)	まったくない	少しある	中程度にある	大いにある
15	Stomach awareness(胃重感がする)	まったくない	少しある	中程度にある	大いにある
16	Burping(ゲップが出る)	まったくない	少しある	中程度にある	大いにある

【採点方法】 score

Nausea (N 悪心)	: 1,6,7,8,9,15,16の合計×9.54	
Oculomotor (O 眼精疲労)	: 1,2,3,4,5,9,11の合計×7.58	
Disorientation (D 失見当識)	: 5,8,10,11,12,13,14の合計×13.92	
Total Severity (TS 総合スコア)	: 全ての合計×3.74	

Kennedy RS,et al:Simulator Sickness Questionnaire: An Enhanced Method for Quantifying Simulator Sickness,Int.J.Aviat.Psychol 3,203-220,1993.
平柳 要: 乗り物酔い(動揺病)研究の現状と今後の展望, 人間工学 42(3), 2006

Fig. 8. SSQ questionnaire

potentials generated from sources other than the brain, are likely to be mixed in. For this reason, one minute of artefact removal was carried out before measuring the EEG.

As an evaluation index for this experiment, the integrated value of the β-wave content rate at the start and end of the experiment is used to make a judgment. The difference in the numerical value of the content rate at the end of the experiment from the content rate at the start was determined, and the presence or absence of the VR sickness reduction effect was judged from a comparison of the amount of change.

3.5 SSQ Questionnaire

The SSQ questionnaire can determine three sub-indices (nausea, eye strain, and disorientation) and an overall score by answering 16 questions in four levels. Because it is possible to quantify the degree of VR sickness by using this, it has been used in many papers. In this study, by comparing with the above conditions, we thought of confirming the reliability of the evaluation indices and making judgments through comparison. The questionnaire used in this experiment is shown in Fig. 8.

4 Results

The experiment was carried out with the cooperation of seven adult participants, both men and women. This section provides a summary of the results obtained from the measurements of eye movements, fingertip temperature, EEG data, and SSQ questionnaires.

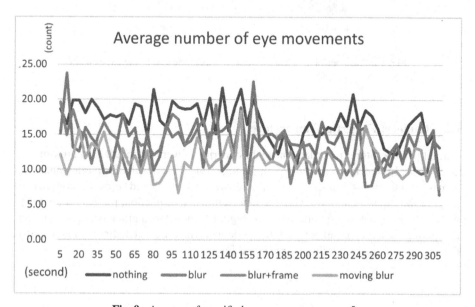

Fig. 9. Average of specified eye movements every 5 s

4.1 Results of Eye Movement

During the experiment, the frequency of specific eye movements made by the participants was systematically recorded and summarized at intervals of every five seconds. These data were subsequently plotted on a graph for detailed analysis. The study involved a total of fourteen participants, consisting of seven men and seven women, each labeled A through G. Figure 9 shows the average frequency of these particular eye movements for each participant across conditions 1–4. Furthermore, Fig. 10 presents the overall average count of eye movements observed at the end of the experiment.

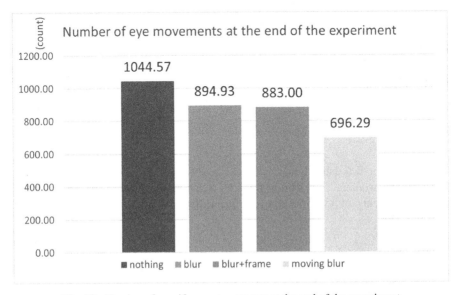

Fig. 10. Number of specific eye movements at the end of the experiment

4.2 Results of Fingertip Temperature

Fingertip temperatures recorded during the experiment were summarized approximately every 0.2 s. Figure 11 presents a graph summarizing these results for participants A-G across conditions 1–4. Fingertip temperatures were also measured before the commencement of the experiment. However, due to a technical malfunction, pre-experiment data were only available for conditions 2 to 4. Figure 12 provides a graphical representation comparing the mean pre-experiment temperatures with the mean temperatures recorded during the experiment for these three conditions.

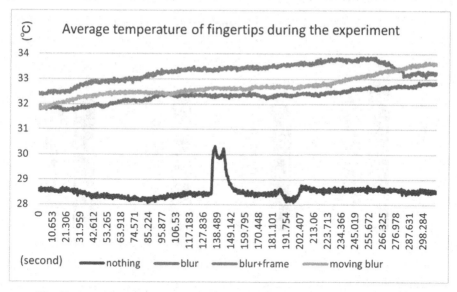

Fig. 11. Average fingertip temperature of all experimenters during the experiment.

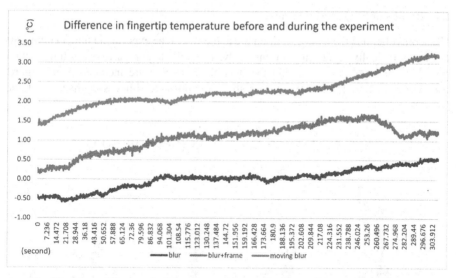

Fig. 12. Mean difference in fingertip temperatures before and during the experiment.

4.3 Results of EEG

A graphical comparison of EEG data before and after the experiment is presented. Figure 13 shows a comparison of the average values, calculated from the integrated β-wave content, before and after the experiment.

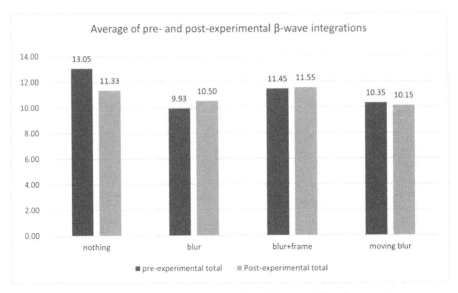

Fig. 13. Average of integrated β-wave values before and after the experiment

4.4 Results of SSQ Questionnaire

The scores obtained from the questionnaire at the end of the experiment under conditions 1–4 are graphically represented in this study. To facilitate comparisons with the ocular data, both the eye strain data and the overall SSQ score are included in the figure. For conditions 2 to 4, an additional question was introduced to assess discomfort and

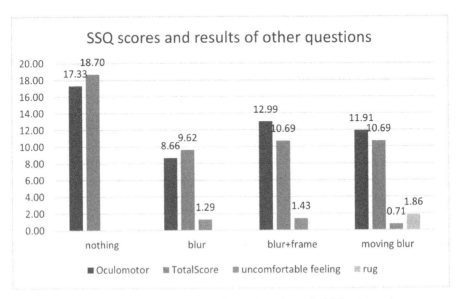

Fig. 14. Average of results from SSQ questionnaire and additional questions

ensure that the VR experience retained its realism. Moreover, for Condition 4, a question regarding lag was added, as this condition experienced more video lag compared to Conditions 1 to 3. Figure 14 shows these results.

5 Discussion

In the current study, changes were specifically set to occur at four downhill sites: 175–195 s, 205–215 s, 255–265 s, and 270–280 s. These sites were identified as being most likely affected by the change. According to Fig. 9, a slight association was observed between the duration of descent and eye movements at the 175–195 and 270–280 s intervals. However, no such association was evident at the other two intervals. The intervals where this association was found shared a longer downhill duration in common, suggesting that this may be an effective method to measure areas prone to prolonged VR sickness. The two intervals with observed commonalities showed a decrease in frequency in later conditions compared to Condition 1, indicating that the VR sickness reduction effect might be highest in Condition 4. Additionally, in all four conditions, including the downhill sections, there were intervals where eye movement frequency increased, occurring around 55, 75, 115, 150, 160, and 240 s. The characteristics of these points are as follows: the 55-s point involves a curved path beside an obstacle, the 75-s point has a brief upward viewpoint shift, the 115-s point features a slight incline, the 150-s point marks the first steep ascent, the 160-s point is near the top of the first ascent, and the 240-s point is near the top of the second ascent. These results suggest that eye movement at these points may be more likely to cause eyestrain, as the eye receives more information during gentle upward movements compared to rapid downward movements. Figure 12 shows that despite some noise-like variations, no significant fluctuations in fingertip temperature were observed at the downhill locations. Additionally, no other correlations were found in the eye movements observed in the other conditions, making it challenging to confirm the measurement of VR sickness using fingertip temperature in this study.

Next, the study examines the implications of the number of eye movements. Figure 10 shows that, in comparison to Condition 1, Conditions 2 and 3 exhibited a decrease of approximately 100 eye movements, while Condition 4 showed a reduction of around 300 eye movements. Figure 14 reveals that oculomotor activity was lower in Conditions 2, 3, and 4 than in Condition 1, suggesting that VR sickness is less likely in these conditions. An analysis of the data in Fig. 14 implies a potential decrease in VR sickness in the order of Condition 2, followed by Condition 4, and then Condition 3. However, it is noteworthy that participant C recorded the highest eye movement values in Conditions 1 and 4. It is postulated that participant C, who is more susceptible to VR sickness, experienced greater discomfort, and disturbance from the moving blur in these conditions, particularly due to image lag. This suggests that reducing image lag might alleviate discomfort, thereby potentially making these conditions less conducive to VR sickness. Consequently, Condition 4, despite the higher values recorded by participant C, may have the potential to reduce VR sickness more effectively compared to the other conditions.

Thirdly, the study assessed fingertip temperature. It was determined that real-time measurement of fingertip temperature is challenging, as no significant changes were observed at specific points during the experiment. Figure 12 indicates an unexpected increase in fingertip temperature in Conditions 2 to 4. This increase is thought to be caused by heat accumulation due to the thermometer attached to the fingertip and the bandage used to secure it. The experiment was conducted during winter, and the room was heated. Therefore, it is possible that fluctuations in room temperature affected the results. Consequently, fingertip temperature was deemed an unsuitable indicator for this study.

Fourthly, the EEG data, specifically β wave values, were analyzed. The integrated values shown in Fig. 13 reveal variations in β wave values before and after the experiment. This fluctuation is thought to have occurred because the values were initially high due to pre-experiment tension. However, after the experiment, the tension appeared to have increased compared to the initial levels, possibly because the subjects became more accustomed to the experiment over time. The change in integrated β-wave values was +0.57 for Condition 2, +1.00 for Condition 3, and −0.20 for Condition 4, while for Condition 1, it was −1.72. Based solely on these values, Condition 1 seems to have had the most significant reduction effect. However, when considering the totalized value at the end of the experiment, the lowest value was observed in Condition 4. Given that the integrated β wave value is derived from the content rate, Condition 4 had the lowest β waves at the end of the session overall. This suggests that Condition 4 might be the most effective in reducing VR sickness, according to EEG data.

Finally, the results of the Simulator Sickness Questionnaire (SSQ) are discussed. As illustrated in Fig. 14, the SSQ scores show that Conditions 2, 4, and 3, in that order, had the lowest incidence of VR sickness. This outcome aligns with the earlier observation of higher scores for participant C in Condition 4. The discomfort scores, in descending order, were highest for Condition 4, followed by Condition 2, and then Condition 3. This suggests that the immersive VR experience was least compromised in Condition 4. Additionally, the score for the lag-related question in Condition 4 was 1.86, close to 2, indicating that while Condition 4 may be most effective in reducing VR sickness according to the SSQ, it also resulted in considerable discomfort due to image lag.

6 Conclusion

In this study, experiments were conducted to explore the reduction of VR sickness and its real-time measurement. The findings suggest that Condition 4 may be the most effective in reducing sickness compared to Condition 1. The correlation with the Simulator Sickness Questionnaire (SSQ) indicated that the results of specific eye movements could be used to measure VR sickness. However, an increase in frequency was often observed on gentle uphill slopes, indicating potential challenges in responding to rapid movements. The temperature at the fingertips was found to be influenced by the installation location and room temperature, suggesting that more attention should be paid to measuring temperature under the nose in future experiments. Implementing strict room temperature controls could enhance the accuracy of such measurements. While EEG data were compared before and after the experiment, examining the content rate could provide an indicator of VR sickness. However, the observed increases and decreases in values warrant further scrutiny. Based on these insights, it is deemed necessary to carefully control room temperature and location during experiments for accurate temperature acquisition and to thoroughly examine EEG data. In future experiments, we aim to improve the accuracy of temperature and EEG data acquisition, striving to develop another simple, real-time index for measuring VR sickness.

References

1. Groth, C., Tausche, J.-P., Heesen, N., Castillo, S., Magnor, M.: Visual techniques to reduce cybersickness in virtual reality. In: 2021 IEEE Conference on Virtual Reality and 3D User Interfaces Abstracts and Workshops (VRW), pp. 486–487. IEEE (2021)
2. Watanabe, K, Onishi, K.: Study of the effectiveness of cockpit effects in reducing VR sickness. In: Proceedings of the 85th National Conference of the Information Processing Society of Japan, 2ZE-06, pp.4–83–4–84, March 2023
3. Tanaka, R., Fukushima, S., Hautasaari, A., Naemura, N.T.: Proposal of a peripheral luminance contrast suppressing method for reducing VR sickness. In: Proceedings of the 27th Virtual Reality Society of Japan Conference, 3D5-3, September 2023
4. Watanabe, K., Onishi, K.: Study of the occurrence of VR motion sickness using physiological indices. In: Proceedings of the 28th Virtual Reality Society of Japan Conference. 3C1-01, September 2023
5. Webb, N.A., Griffin, M.J.: Optokinetic stimuli: motion sickness, visual acuity, and eye movements. Aviation Space Environ. Med. 73(4), 351–358 (2002)
6. Miura, N., Ujike, H., Ohkura, M.: Influence of fixation point movement on visually induced motion sickness suppression effect. In: International Conference on Applied Human Factors and Ergonomics, pp. 277–288. Springer, Cham (2018)
7. Ono, K., Oyama, Y., Yoshizawa, N., Sano, N., Hirate, K.: Considerations on VR sickness for weariness and physiological responses. J. Environ. Eng. AIJ 70(594), 77–83 (2005)
8. Anzai, R.: Design of gaze analysis systems in VR environments, Hiraishi Laboratory. https://hiralab.jp/hiralab/research/2020/B/S17010.pdf
9. Mimura, Y., Inagaki, T., Noda, K., Ogino, H.: A study on structuring of traffic safety indicator by eye movement view point of community road, J. Civil Eng. Plann. Res. Proc. 42, CD-ROM (2011)
10. Zenju, H., Nozawa, A., Tanaka, H., Ide, H.: Estimation of unpleasant and pleasant states by nasal thermogram. Trans. Inst. Electr. Eng. Japan, C (J. Electron. Inf. Syst. Div.) 124(1), 213–214 (2004)
11. Yanaka, S., Kosaka, T.: Detection of visually induced motion sickness while watching a video using variation in autonomic nervous activity. In: Entertainment Computing Symposium, November 2016
12. Hitomi, T., Ikeda, A.: Basic knowledge of brain waves. Clin. Neurophysiol. 42(6), 365–370 (2014)

Research on User Experience Design of Artificial Intelligence (AI) Medical Consultation System

Min Yang and Yongyan Guo[✉]

East China University of Science and Technology, Xuhui District, Shanghai, China
2633474125@qq.com

Abstract. The introduction of online consultations has played a positive role in alleviating the current pressure on healthcare resources, especially the emerging AI consultation technology is more capable of alleviating the shortage of healthcare personnel and providing patients with more convenient online consultation services. To optimize users' emotional experience when interacting with AI to make them more relaxed and comfortable with AI consultation, we recruited 20 participants for the experiment. In the experiment, we tested the impact of the AI consultation system on the pragmatic and hedonic qualities of users using button interaction and free text interaction mechanisms, respectively, and conducted in-depth interviews with the participants after the experiment. The findings show that the button interaction mechanism significantly improves the utility of the AI interrogation system compared to the free text interaction mechanism. However, the free text interaction mechanism did not significantly improve the hedonic quality of the AI questioning system compared to the button interaction mechanism. When making AI inquiries, users preferred to use the button interaction mechanism as opposed to free text interaction. This trend suggests that the use of button interactions with predefined answers is more in line with users' tendencies in the design of AI questioning systems. It is suggested that future AI consultation systems should adopt an integrated design of multiple interaction mechanisms to meet the dual needs of users in terms of practicality and emotional needs. Such a design solution will better balance users' expectations for professionalism and convenience, thus enhancing the overall user experience.

Keywords: AI interrogation · User experience · Interaction mechanisms · Pragmatic and hedonic quality

1 Background

Nowadays, in many countries and regions, due to the scarcity and unbalanced distribution of medical resources and the imbalance between supply and demand, the medical needs of a large number of patients cannot be met, while the healthcare system also carries a huge medical pressure [1]. Therefore, many patients began to choose online medical consultation online self-diagnosis, and other methods [2]. However, there are many problems with these methods, including online doctors responding to untimely information, inadequate communication, misleading patients with inaccurate information [3],

M. Kurosu and A. Hashizume (Eds.): HCII 2024, LNCS 14686, pp. 236–252, 2024.
https://doi.org/10.1007/978-3-031-60428-7_17

charging for advertisements when asking for medical advice, privacy not being guaranteed, and many other problems. Therefore, Artificial Intelligence (AI) consultation (also known as health chatbot) provides a better way of online consultation [4].

Artificial Intelligence (AI) technology plays an important role in healthcare, where AI uses technologies such as natural language processing combined with machine learning and medically relevant knowledge bases to provide online health counseling to patients [5, 6]. However, existing research on Artificial Intelligence (AI) consultation focuses on user acceptability of technology for AI consultation [7], perceived utility [8], and uncertainty theory [9]. Many current healthcare AIs are usually task-oriented to achieve user-specific goals, and the effectiveness and usability of AI questioning are mainly considered. Although some papers have studied the user experience of chatbots [10], there is a lack of user research on medical AI questioning from the perspective of emotional experience.

The interaction mechanism chosen and used by the user during the online consultation process is crucial for accurately expressing symptoms and effectively communicating with the diagnostic system, which is important for enhancing the user's emotional experience. Due to a lack of medical expertise, many users may feel confused when faced with online consultations and do not know how to answer consultation questions [3]. In contrast, many people prefer face-to-face doctor consultations because real doctors can understand the patient's feelings, recognize the patient's natural language expressions, and guide him/her to answer relevant questions, thus reducing communication barriers and improving consultation efficiency. Nowadays, there are many ways of interaction mechanisms for communicating with AI, including button interaction with predefined answers, voice interaction, free text interaction [11], and even gesture interaction. The common interaction mechanisms in AI consultation are button interaction and free-text interaction. Button interaction can give the user a preset answer in the consultation process, and the user can make his/her own choices [12], and the efficient interaction can also make the patient feel that the whole consultation process is smooth and pleasant.

AI consultation systems with free text interaction mechanisms enable users to make consultations in natural language, and the system processes user input to recognize their language, thus making the consultation process more flexible and increasing user engagement [13]. This move further increases the anthropomorphic nature of the system. Although users are more concerned with the pragmatic quality of their consultations, it is also crucial to focus on the quality of their emotional enjoyment as a healthcare system [14]. Therefore, we are interested in the relationship between free text interaction and pragmatic-hedonic quality in AI consultation systems.

Therefore, the purpose of this study is for users to be able to easily and comfortably engage in health consultations with the AI consultation system, thereby increasing their trust in the AI consultation system and optimizing the user experience. Understanding the user experience and psychological responses when using AI consultation can optimize the technology and provide better healthcare services to patients. Analyzing the impact of interaction mechanisms (free text interaction and button interaction) during AI consultations on the pragmatic and hedonic quality of the user experience. Therefore, this paper is based on Hassenzahl's [15] pragmatic-hedonic modeling framework to study the user experience of AI consultation systems.

Structure of this paper: the Sect. 1 is the research background. The Sect. 2 reviews the relevant literature and summarizes the user experience framework in the context of artificial intelligence (AI) questioning. The Sect. 3 introduces the research methodology of the article. The Sect. 4 presents the results and discussion. The Sect. 5 enhances the AI questioning user experience by making recommendations and discusses the research implications and limitations of the article.

2 Literature Review

2.1 User Experience of the Whole Process of AI Consultation

According to related literature, when conducting online health consultation, users experience three stages before, during, and after the consultation, involving emotions, behaviors, preferences, beliefs, perceptions, and reactions before, during, and after using the interactive system [16]. It is important to study the user's consultation experience throughout the process to more comprehensively improve and enhance the efficiency and pleasantness of the user's consultation. Table 1 lists the positive and negative factors affecting the user experience before, during, and after the consultation in some previous literature studies. Some of these factors are cross-cutting in nature, with both or all three stages present.

Pre-questioning: a study by Nadarzynski [8] and others showed that user acceptance of AI technology affects the use of health chatbots. Designers need to be user-centered and consider users' motivations, perspectives, etc. to address users' concerns and enhance the user experience. Diffusion of innovation theory then states that the adoption of new technology is a process in which the key factors include people's broad awareness, deep understanding, and effective utilization of the technology [17]. Only when users accept and trust AI consultation will they effectively go on to use the AI consultation system [8].

In diagnosis: Fan et al. [18] used a case study to get the questions asked by the AI before the user exits the diagnosis or gives a negative evaluation, including six categories: demographic information, physiological data, transition problems, symptoms, medical history, and type of disease. Chen et al. [19] got that the factors that the user gave positive evaluation in mHealth APP diagnosis are easy operation, high efficiency of consultation, safety and convenience, high professionalism, and ease of interaction, and the factors that gave negative evaluation were difficult operation and low consultation efficiency.

Post-diagnosis: Fan et al. [18] concluded that the diagnostic report given by AI contains many medical terms and specialized knowledge leading to difficult or inaccurate understanding for users with low health literacy and knowledge, and users' information needs are not met, which tends to lead to negative evaluations from the users, and more actionable medical information should be provided to the users after the diagnosis. Shi et al. [20] concluded that several Good follow-up services after mHealth diagnosis and the availability of diagnosis-related health insurance services tend to result in positive user evaluations.

Table 1. Positive and negative factors of the online consultation process

Consultation process	Positive psychology	Negative psychology
Pre-consultation (Psychology of choosing software)	Technical acceptability; credibility	
During consultation	Simple operation; high consulting efficiency; safe and convenient; professional; easy to interact	Transition questions (such as questions that prompt the user to answer the question again, often resulting in the termination of the chatbot's use); Symptoms (Questions related to symptoms are often difficult to answer and can easily overwhelm or even confuse users, making them unsure of what input to provide and ultimately causing them to terminate the conversation); Type of disease (milder symptoms, privacy, and social stigma issues, such as sexually transmitted diseases); Medical Records; Physiological data; Demographic information; Difficult operation; Low consulting efficiency
After the visit - the return visit	Health insurance availability; Follow-up service	The diagnostic report was difficult to understand; Inaccuracy of diagnosis

In summary, AI consultation is a new form of healthcare, few researchers have studied users' experiences and psychological responses when performing AI consultation, and most of the previous literature has focused on studying the effectiveness and usability of the whole process of AI consultation, focusing on the diagnostic ability of AI, and lack of studies on the psychological and emotional experience of users from the perspective of psychological and emotional experience as well as interaction mechanisms for AI consultation systems that are mainly task-oriented to achieve user-specific behavioral goals. Emotional experience perspective as well as the interaction mechanism to study the users of medical AI consultation. Although some papers have studied the user experience of chatbots by adopting Hassenzahl's pragmatic-hedonic model [10], there is no more in-depth research on specific AI consultation-based chatbots. Therefore, the purpose of this study is for users to be able to easily and comfortably conduct health consultations with AI consultation systems, to increase users' trust in AI consultation systems, and to optimize the user experience.

2.2 Characterization of the Product: Practical-Hedonic Attributes

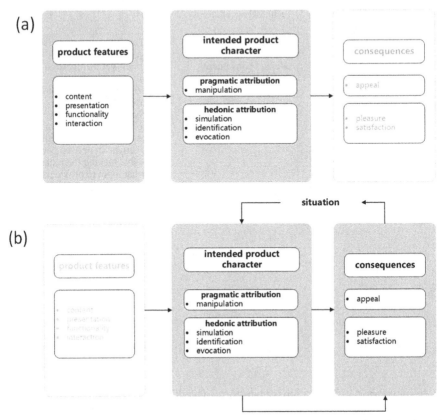

Fig. 1. Overview of the interactive system user experience model from the designer's and user's perspectives

Hassenzahl [15] outlined some of the key elements of a user experience model for interactive systems from both the designer and user perspectives (see Fig. 1), where the user experience model is divided into two perspectives, designer and user:

1. Each product has specific product characteristics, i.e., content, presentation style, functionality, and interaction style, which are selected by the product designer to be combined to communicate the designer's intended product characteristics, and the product characteristics made by the designer are subjective and only what the designer expects, and there is no guarantee that the user will perceive and appreciate the product in the way the designer expects. Therefore, a proper design process must ensure that appropriate product features are selected and that these features are correctly communicated to the user to avoid deviations between the user and the designer's intent.

2. When users come into contact with a product, they will first perceive various features of the product. On this basis, each person will construct a personal version of the product features - the epiphenomenal product features, and these epiphenomenal product features include clusters of attributes such as utility attributes and hedonic attributes. These epiphenomenal product features have certain behavioral consequences (e.g., increased product usage time), affective consequences (e.g., feeling satisfied, happy), and appealing judgmental consequences (e.g., "it's good/bad") for the user. These consequences are subjective views and perceptions of the product formed by the user after perceiving the product's external features. In our AI consultation user experience study, we focus on the user-centered, emotional experience of these product features (product epiphenomena), i.e., utility-hedonic attributes that bring the user an easy, pleasurable, and effective product experience.

Practical and hedonic attributes are exogenous product characteristics.

1. Utility attributes relate to the operation of a product in its environment, including the associated functionality (utility) and the means of accessing that functionality (usability). Common utility attributes for software products are "useful", "clear", "controllable", and "supported". Products with utility attributes are primarily instrumental and can be used to accomplish internally and externally generated behavioral goals. Users tend to value utility attributes when using functional products.
2. Hedonic attributes, with the three properties of stimulation, identity conveyance, and memory arousal, Hassenzahl categorizes all other remaining attributes of a product as hedonic attributes. Common hedonic attributes are "impressive", "interesting" and "exciting". Hedonic attributes include emotional needs such as curiosity and identification. It is an attribute that focuses on the user's mental health.

Products can be considered utilitarian because they provide an effective and efficient means of operating the environment, or hedonic because they provide stimulation, communicate identity, or evoke memories. For example, the utility attribute of a shopping application ensures that users complete their shopping tasks efficiently, such as clear categorization and easy-to-use shopping carts, while the hedonic attribute stimulates the user's interest in shopping by suggesting new products and personalizing the experience while conveying a unique identity and taste.

2.3 Attrak Diff Questionnaire

In this study, we build on Hassenzahl's [15] pragmatic-hedonic model of user experience, and use the AttrakDiff2 questionnaire tool from Hassenzahl et al. [21] to test the pragmatic and hedonic qualities of the AI consultation system. The AttrakDiff [21] consists of 28 pairs of semantically opposite words (e.g., "confusing-clear", "professional-amateur") and measures pragmatic quality on a 7-point scale. (PQ), hedonic quality (HQ including HQ-I and HQ-S) and attractiveness (ATT). For example, "Confusion-Clarity" on a scale of 1 to 7, with higher scores indicating that the product is clearer in some aspects of its design. Kathleen et al. [13] used the AttrakDiff2 questionnaire in their study of customer service chatbots, removing three items that did not match the environment, for a total of 18 items that were rationally adapted to measure the utility-hedonic quality of the customer service chatbots. Adapted to measure the pragmatic-hedonic quality of customer service chatbots. Deleting the items that do not match the measurement environment in the experiment makes the questionnaire more compatible with the measurement environment, which leads to more accurate measurement results.

2.4 Interaction Mechanisms

The interaction mechanism between the user and the AI can involve a variety of ways, depending on the design and functionality of the AI. When a user encounters an unexpected situation, intelligent voice assistants can convert and recognize information dictated by the user into text using speech recognition technology, thus providing real-time voice guidance to laypersons and assisting them in effectively performing emergency assistance operations such as CPR [22]. Many self-driving cars give commands to in-vehicle intelligent systems through gestures [23]. Many chatbots interact through emoticons to increase user satisfaction with services [24]. Interaction mechanisms such as quick replies, persistent menus, buttons, and free-text interactions are often used to effectively interact with the user when engaging in dialogic communication activities with AI [25].

Nowadays, free text interaction and button interaction are the two main methods used in AI consultation systems [25, 26]. Although free text interaction has high requirements for the AI's natural language recognition technology, this type of interaction allows users to express their thoughts freely, and at the same time enhances the user's perception of the AI's human similarity [13]. Button interactions, while reducing the human similarity of the AI, allow for simpler and faster communication to quickly solve the user's problem [12]. The impact of these two interaction mechanisms on pragmatic and hedonic quality is something we are curious about. Therefore we will also focus on the impact of the interaction mechanisms used (free text interaction and button interaction) on the pragmatic-hedonic quality of AI questioning. We propose the following two hypotheses:

- H1: The button interaction mechanism improves the pragmatic quality of the AI interrogation system compared to the free text interaction mechanism.
- H2: The free text interaction mechanism improves the hedonic quality of the AI questioning system compared to the button interaction mechanism.
- H3: The button interaction mechanism is preferred over the free text interaction for AI questioning.

2.5 AI Ask the Doctor User Experience Framework

Synthesizing the current literature research and combining the user experience model of interactive systems outlined by Hassenzahl [15] from both designer and user perspectives, we formulated the user experience modeling framework of AI interrogation for this study (see Fig. 2). Based on this research framework, we will conduct further research and analysis.

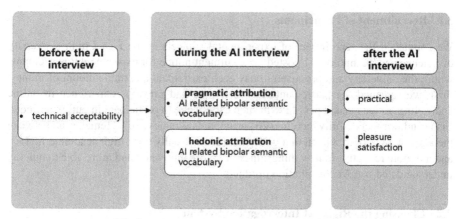

Fig. 2. User experience model of AI consultation

3 Method

In this paper, we use Hassenzahl's [15] pragmatic-hedonic modeling framework as a basis to study the user experience of an AI questioning system. To analyze the effect of interaction mechanisms (free text interaction and button interaction) on the pragmatic and hedonic quality of user experience during AI consultation, we used a multivariate experimental design, where the independent variables are button interaction and free text interaction, and the dependent variables are pragmatic and hedonic quality. There were 20 participants to experiment, and the final data were subjected to a paired-sample t-test; a t-test effect size is required for significant differences, and this metric is not affected by sample size. We adopted a combination of qualitative and quantitative methods, the specific research methods and steps are as follows:

1. Recruitment of subjects, recruitment of subjects who have used the online consultation, balance between men and women, and collection of basic information about the subjects.
2. Choosing the appropriate experimental tools, we chose two small programs on WeChat, one is the button interaction program of AI Ask and the other is the free text interaction program of AI Ask, and they have roughly the same overall style except for the different interaction mechanisms.
3. Experimental procedure: before the experiment the subjects, were interviewed and three pre-experimental questions were collected. The experimental subjects are required to fill out the AttrakDiff questionnaire once after using one kind of applet each time. The experimental participant subjects were required to conduct a final interview after using two small programs and filling out the relevant questionnaires. The interview included asking them to compare the similarities and differences between online and AI consultations. As well as some of the problems and feelings encountered in the AI consultation. And which interaction form they prefer, and which interaction mechanism they like most in the AI consultation process.
4. Collect data and process it.

3.1 Recruitment of Participants

We conducted the recruitment of experimental subjects at the East China University of Science and Technology. I posted a recruitment notice for experimental participants within the university and promised to pay each participant a certain amount of money. First, we screened the participants to see if they had previous experience in online counseling, as we needed people with such experience to participate in our experiment. In the end, we successfully recruited 20 participants, 8 males and 12 females, all between the ages of 18 and 25. Given that college students usually have high academic literacy and are more receptive to new things, they are more motivated and more able to quickly understand and use AI consultation products.

3.2 Choosing the Right AI Interrogation System

The two AI consultation systems used in this study are small programs in WeChat, without the need for participants to download any APP, which is "Extreme Diagnosis AI Intelligent Self-Diagnosis" and "Left Hand Doctor".

The interaction mechanism of the "Extreme Diagnosis AI Intelligent Self-Diagnosis" applet is a push-button interaction mechanism, which is characterized by the collection of basic information about the patient, and the user's further interaction by selecting pre-defined answer options.

The interaction mechanism of the "Left Hand Doctor" app is free text interaction, which also collects basic information about the patient first, and the main feature is that the patient can use the free text interaction form to carry out the consultation operation.

In addition to the different interaction mechanisms, the two AI consultation applets have roughly the same interface design and consultation method. Both will ask the user's age and gender and other basic information before the consultation and after several rounds of questions and answers, the final diagnostic results and recommendations will be given.

Screenshots of the interfaces of the two consultation applets are shown in Figs. 3 and 4.

3.3 Experimental Process

After describing the procedure and the two mini-procedures of the experiment, and with the consent of the participants, researcher personnel administered a pre-survey to the participants before the experiment began. Participants were asked to complete a questionnaire consisting of three questions. The questionnaire can be viewed in Appendix 1. All participants then began the experiment. Due to time and other constraints, we let each participant set a topic to experiment, such as describing to the AI the last time they had a cold and fever, or the last time they were sick and had diarrhea. An adapted 7-point AttrakDiff2 scale was completed after each use of an applet. Before data collection, the AttrakDiff2 scale was adapted by removing 10 items and is a 7-point semantic bipolar scale with a total of 11 items to apply to the AI questioning environment of our study. After completing the two mini-programs and filling out the questionnaires, a final

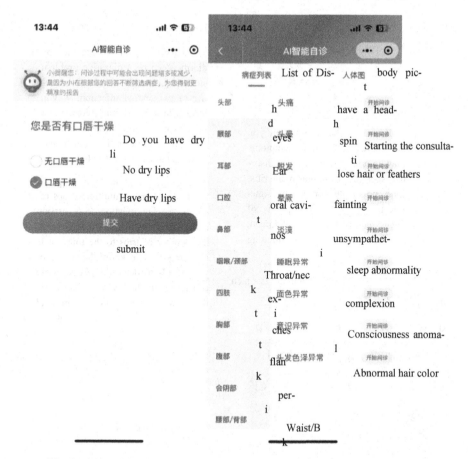

Fig. 3. Screenshot of "Extreme Diagnosis AI Intelligent Self-diagnosis" applet

interview was conducted with the participants. The questionnaire and interview items for all measurement instruments can be viewed in Appendix 1.

Throughout the experiment a research facilitator moderated and one person took notes, and the process was summarized as follows.

1. Participants completed two pre-survey questions
2. Participants used the first applet, "Extreme Diagnosis AI Intelligent Self-Diagnosis" (button interaction mechanism) to ask for a consultation.
3. Completion of the first applet's questionnaire scale
4. Participants use the second applet "Left Hand Doctor" (free-text interaction mechanism) to ask for a consultation.
5. Completion of the questionnaire for the second applet
6. Final interviews
7. Data collection and organization

Each participant was asked to use the two AI programs and to conduct interviews and questionnaires, and the data collection process lasted one week. Data processing was

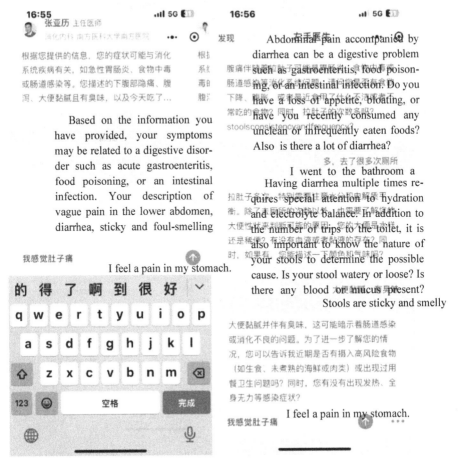

Fig. 4. Screenshot of "Dr. Left Hand" applet

done using SPSS version 26, with paired samples t-tests to test hypothesized outcomes and to calculate effect sizes.

4 Results and Discussion

In this section, we detail the results of our experiments and some interesting findings on the effect of interaction mechanisms on the quality of practical hedonic enjoyment. The results of the hypothesis testing presented earlier are presented, summarizing some of the meaningful results we obtained based on our interviews.

4.1 Participants' Attitudes Towards AI Interrogation

Before the experiment, we conducted a pre-survey, asking the participants whether they had used AI consultation-related systems and whether they trusted AI consultation, and the content of the questionnaire is shown in Appendix 1. Only 6 out of 20 people used AI consultation systems, and the rest used online real-life consultation. 8 people felt distrustful of AI consultation in this way, and the main reasons for distrust were fear of misdiagnosis due to the lack of maturity of AI technology (7); fear of misdiagnosis due to the lack of looking and hearing (3); more convenient to communicate directly with the doctor (5); and fear of leaking privacy (2).

We observed a generally positive attitude towards AI consultations. Most people expressed a willingness to try this new and emerging way of asking for medical advice, however, some people were also skeptical. This skepticism stems mainly from the differences between AI and real doctors, including but not limited to anthropomorphic shortcomings, convenience, and privacy. In addition to technological enhancements, the user experience of AI consultations is also affected by the emotional experience it brings, i.e., whether it can make the user feel relaxed and at ease.

4.2 Impact of AI Interrogation Interaction Mechanisms on Pragmatic and Hedonic Quality

Table 2 shows the results of the paired samples t-tests for all independent and dependent variables and also includes the effect sizes. In the table, we can see that the button interaction mechanism improves the utility quality of the AI questioning system compared to the free text interaction mechanism. The type of button interaction mechanism has a significant effect on utility quality. Where the effect size $d = 1.08 > 0.8$, the estimated effect size for this difference is larger. This is consistent with our hypothesis H1.

However, from the data results, free text interaction did not significantly improve the hedonic quality of the AI questioning system compared to button interaction during AI questioning, and button interaction also scored higher than free text interaction during AI questioning. Where the effect size $d = 0.4, 0.20 < d < 0.50$, the estimated effect size for this difference is small. Hypothesis H2 does not hold.

Table 2 shows the results of the paired samples t-test data Effect size: $d < 0.20$: too small effect; $0.20 < d < 0.50$: small effect; $0.50 < d < 0.80$: large effect; $d > 0.80$: large effect.

Table 2. Paired samples t-test results

	Interaction mechanism	Mean	SD	t	df	Sig(2-tailed)	Effect size (d)
Pragmatic quality	Buttons	21.60	3.02	3.86	19	<0.05	1.08
	Free text	17.70	4.122				
Hedonic quality	Buttons	32.80	5.44	1.56	19	0.134	0.40
	Free text	30.20	7.47				

At the end of the interview, we asked the participants which interaction mechanism they preferred during the consultation, 14 people chose the button interaction and only 6 chose the free-text interaction. The button interaction mechanism was preferred over the free-text interaction during the AI consultation. Consistent with Hypothesis H3. Subsequently, we also conducted short interviews with the experimenters about the user experience of these two types of interrogation interactions.

4.3 Users' Perceptions of AI Interrogation Interaction Mechanisms

Post-interview participants answered questions about their experiences and feelings about the two AI questioning systems, see Appendix 1.

For the participants who preferred the button interaction method (14) of the AI questioning system, the following are the findings and summaries of their post-interviews:

1. In urgent situations where rapid self-diagnosis is required, the push-button interaction demonstrated significant efficiency in completing the initial diagnosis by simply selecting the preset options.
2. (Button interactions excelled in the important step of diagnosis, namely, identifying and narrowing down the physiological parts of the body that were experiencing discomfort, step by step. The clarity of its delineation far exceeded the way participants freely described it in free text, and this approach led to a more accurate diagnosis.
3. The push-button interactive AI consultation system provided an easier and more accurate way to express themselves to participants who often have difficulty organizing their language.
4. Compared to free text interaction, the AI uses some specialized medical terms when asking participants about their symptoms, which often bothers participants because, in free text, it is difficult for participants to express their feelings clearly, which leads to the problem of misdiagnosis.
5. Many colloquial expressions may cause the AI to misinterpret the patient's symptoms, which in turn bothers the user. The normalization of button interactions is expected to solve this problem.

For the participants of the AI interrogation system who preferred the free-text interaction approach (6), the following findings and summaries were drawn from their interviews:

1. The free-text interaction style of questioning allows participants to answer freely and feel a free and comfortable atmosphere that enables them to express their situation with ease and comfort.
2. Free-text interaction is suitable for individuals who have subjective opinions and are keen to express their views, as it allows for unlimited input of personally thought-out answers.
3. When using the button interaction AI questioning system, one may sometimes be faced with the option of not being able to accurately express a symptom, which can lead to difficulties in answering.
4. Button interaction sets up a framework for answers, giving the impression that the flexibility of the questioning is limited and that the answers feel pre-determined.

5. The button interaction approach makes it difficult for participants to perceive that an AI questioning is taking place, and is more like a multiple-choice interaction with a mechanical robot, which may lower participants' expectations.

These findings highlight the different experiences triggered by free text interaction modalities and button interaction modalities in AI questioning, further providing insights into our understanding of users' attitudes towards different questioning modalities. Participants also expressed their expectations for realizing the combination of diverse interaction mechanisms in AI questioning systems. In particular, they would like to use button interactions for questions involving specific body parts or containing specialized medical terminology, and free-text interactions for questions exploring aspects such as user feelings. This feedback reveals a possible strategy for adapting to users' response preferences for different types of questions by flexibly combining button interactions and free-text interactions. This variety of interaction mechanisms is expected to improve the flexibility and accuracy of the AI questioning system, while reducing the burden on the patient and creating a more enjoyable user experience. This innovative interaction design is expected to provide a useful direction for improving the acceptance and effectiveness of AI consultation systems.

5 Conclusion

In this paper, we explore the impact of different interaction mechanisms of artificial intelligence (AI) questioning systems on pragmatic and hedonic quality. By gaining insights into users' experiences and psychological responses when using AI questioning systems with different interaction mechanisms, we find that button interactions affect both utility and hedonic quality, while free text interactions do not significantly enhance hedonic quality in AI questioning. The results suggest that the button interaction mechanism improves the utility of the AI consultation system compared to free text interaction; however, free text interaction does not significantly improve the hedonic quality of the AI consultation system compared to button interaction. Based on the results of the study, we propose the following recommendations to make it easier for users to use the AI consultation system: when designing future AI consultation systems, a combination of free text interaction and button interaction can be used for consultation. Button interaction can be used for consultations involving specialized medical terminology or mechanical questions, while free text interaction can be used for questions that require patients to give real answers about their personal feelings.

Although our questions and experiments provide useful help and suggestions for the user experience of AI questioning, especially in terms of interaction mechanisms, this study still has some limitations. First, the experimental subjects were small in scope and insufficiently randomized, and were recruited only in schools, which involved too homogeneous a sample and failed to comprehensively reflect the feelings of different populations about the use of different AI questioning interaction mechanisms. Future research can study the feelings of different populations on the user experience of AI consultation by conducting experiments on different populations. Second, the sample size of the study is small, although 20 research samples have been collected, the interview results show that a larger sample size is needed to obtain more results and novel perspectives. Therefore, the sample size should be increased for a more accurate study in future research on the impact of hybrid interaction mechanisms on the emotional experience of AI consultation users.

Finally, the research on the design of the emotional experience of AI interrogation users has not been comprehensive enough, and has been limited by focusing only on the impact of interaction mechanisms on the pragmatic and hedonic qualities of AI interrogation. Future research could delve deeper into the impact of hybrid interaction mechanisms on the user experience of AI interrogation systems and investigate the full impact of multiple AI interrogation system dimensions on pragmatic and hedonic qualities.

Appendix

The following questionnaire items and interview questions were used in this study.

Questionnaire Items. The questionnaire items included instruments to measure both pragmatic and hedonic quality.

Pragmatic Quality	Hedonic quality
Impractical – Practical Confusing – Clearly structured Cumbersome – Straightforward Complicated – Simple	lame – captivating Ordinary – Novel Conservative – Innovative Cautious – Bold Unpresentable – Presentable Cheap – Premium Tacky – Stylish
Adapted from Hassenzahl, Burmester and Koller (2003)	Adapted from Hassenzahl, Burmester and Koller (2003)

Interview Questions. The interview questions are as follows, 1–3 are pre-experiment pre-survey questions and 4–6 are post-experiment interview questions with participants

(1) Now that AI technology is gradually developing, have you used the AI Artificial Intelligence Consultation System?

   – Have used it - Have not used it

(2) Do you trust AI to diagnose your condition?

   – Trust - Don't trust

(3) Why don't you trust AI for diagnosis?

   – Fear that AI technology is not mature enough to misdiagnose
   – Fear of misdiagnosis due to the lack of diagnosis and diagnosis

– It is more convenient to communicate with doctors directly
– Fear of leaking privacy

(4) Which interaction method do you think you prefer for consultation and why?
(5) Please tell us how you feel when you use the AI consultation system with button interaction.
(6) Please tell us your feelings about using an AI consultation system with free text interaction.

References

1. Ye, Q., Deng, Z., Chen, Y., Liao, J., Li, G., Lu, Y.: How resource scarcity and accessibility affect patients' usage of mobile health in China: resource competition perspective. JMIR Mhealth Uhealth **7**(8), e13491 (2019)
2. Xiaojuan, M., Xinning, G., Jiayue, F., Mingqian, Z., Yunan, C., Kai, Z.: Professional medical advice at your fingertips: an empirical study of an online "Ask the Doctor" platform. ACM Hum.-Comput. Interact. **2**(10), 1–22 (2018)
3. Swire-Thompson, B., Lazer, D.: Public health and online misinformation: Challenges and recommendations. Annu. Rev. Public Health **41**(2), 433–451 (2020)
4. Denis, H., Mario, R., Servaas, A.M., Dipak, K.: Artificial intelligence: power for civilisation – and for better healthcare. Public Health Genomics **22**(5–6), 145–161 (2020)
5. Shah, W.S., Elkhwesky, Z., Jasim, K.M., et al.: Artificial intelligence in healthcare services: past, present and future research directions. Rev. Manag. Sci. **18**, 941–963 (2023)
6. He, J., Baxter, S.L., Xu, J., et al.: The practical implementation of artificial intelligence technologies in medicine. Nat. Med. **25**(1), 30–36 (2019)
7. Wutz, M., Hermes, M., Winter, V., Köberlein-Neu, J.: Factors influencing the acceptability, acceptance, and adoption of conversational agents in health care: integrative review. J. Med. Internet Res. **25**, e46548 (2023)
8. Nadarzynski, T., Miles, O., Cowie, A., Ridge, D.: Acceptability of artificial intelligence (AI)-led chatbot services in healthcare: a mixed-methods study. Digit. Health **5**, 205520761987180 (2019)
9. Seoni, S., Jahmunah, V., Salvi, M., Barua, P.D., Molinari, F., Acharya, U.R.: Application of uncertainty quantification to artificial intelligence in healthcare: a review of last decade (2013–2023). Comput. Biol. Med. **165**, 107441 (2023)
10. Følstad, A., Brandtzaeg, P.B.: Users' experiences with chatbots: findings from a questionnaire study. Quality User Experience **5**, 3 (2020)
11. Jain, M., Kumar, P., Kota, R., Patel, S.N.: Evaluating and informing the design of chatbots. In: Proceedings of the Designing Interactive Systems Conference, pp. 895–906 (2018)
12. Jain, M., Kumar, P., Kota, R., Patel, N.S.: Evaluating and informing the design of chatbots. In: Proceedings of the 2018 Designing Interactive Systems Conference (DIS 2018), pp. 895–906 (2018)
13. Kathleen, I., Følstad, A., Cameron T., Bjørkli, C.A.: Understanding the user experience of customer service chatbots: an experimental study of chatbot interaction design. Int. J. Hum.-Comput. Stud. **161**, 102788 (2022)
14. Kvale, K., Sell, O., Hodnebrog, S., Følstad, A.: Improving conversations: lessons learnt from manual analysis of chatbot dialogues. In: Følstad, A., et al. (eds.) CONVERSATIONS 2019. LNCS, vol. 11970, pp. 187–200. Springer, Cham (2020). https://doi.org/10.1007/978-3-030-39540-7_13

15. Hassenzahl, M.: The Thing and I: understanding the relationship between user and product. In: Blythe, M., Monk, A. (eds.) Funology 2. HIS, pp. 301–313. Springer, Cham (2018). https://doi.org/10.1007/978-3-319-68213-6_19

16. ISO 2019 Certification. ISO. Ergonomics of human-computer interaction - Part 210: Human-centered interaction system design. The international Organization for Standardization (ISO) (2019)

17. Laufer, R.: The social acceptability of AI systems. Artif. Intell. Crit. Concept. **6**, 197–220 (1992)

18. Fan, X., Chao, D., Zhang, Z., Wang, D., Li, X., Tian, F.: Utilization of self-diagnosis health chatbots in real-world settings: case study. J. Med. Internet Res. **23**(1), e19928 (2021)

19. Chen, L., Xiao, Y., Huang, L.: The research on the user experience of consultation designed by China's medical mobile media platforms under the background of COVID-19. In: Stephanidis, C., et al. (eds.) HCII 2021. LNCS, vol. 13094, pp. 509–521. Springer, Cham (2021). https://doi.org/10.1007/978-3-030-90238-4_36

20. Shi, V.Y., Komiak, S., Komiak, P.: Are you willing to see doctors on mobile devices? A content analysis of user reviews of virtual consultation apps. In: Nah, F.H., Tan, C.H. (eds.) HCI in Business, Government and Organizations. Interacting with Information Systems, vol. 10293, pp. 224–238. Springer, Cham (2017). https://doi.org/10.1007/978-3-319-58481-2_18

21. Hassenzahl, M., Burmester, M., Koller, F.: AttrakDiff: Ein Fragebogen zur Messung wahrgenommener hedonischer und pragmatischer Qualität. Mensch & Computer 2003. Berichte des German Chapter of the ACM, vol. 57, pp. 187–196 (2003)

22. Otero-Agra, M., et al.: Can a voice assistant help bystanders save lives? A feasibility pilot study chatbot in beta version to assist OHCA bystanders. Am. J. Emerg. Med. **1**, 169–174 (2022)

23. Shaotran, E., Cruz, J.J., Reddi, V.J.: Gesture learning for self-driving cars. In: 2021 IEEE International Conference on Autonomous Systems (ICAS), pp. 1–5 (2021)

24. Shubin, Y., Luming, Z.: Emojifying chatbot interactions: an exploration of emoji utilization in human-chatbot communications. Telematics Inform. **86**, 102071 (2024)

25. Valério, F.A.M., Tatiane, G.G., Raquel, O.P., Heloisa, C.: Comparing users' perception of different chatbot interaction paradigms: a case study. In: Proceedings of the 19th Brazilian Symposium on Human Factors in Computing Systems (IHC 2020). Association for Computing Machinery, New York, NY, USA, Article 11, pp. 1–10 (2020)

26. Chi-Hsun, L., Su-Fang, Y., Tang-Jie, C., Meng-Hsuan, T., Ken, C., Yung-Ju, C.: A conversation analysis of non-progress and coping strategies with a banking task-oriented chatbot. In: Proceedings of the 2020 CHI Conference on Human Factors in Computing Systems (CHI 2020), pp. 1–12 (2020)

Measurement and Evaluation of Organ Shifts in Real-Life Surgery

Daiki Yano[1], Masanao Koeda[2], Miho Asano[3], Takahiro Kunii[4], and Hiroshi Noborio[5]([✉])

[1] denLabo LLC., Abeno, Osaka, Japan
d.yano+paper2024@denlabo.co.jp
[2] Okayama Prefectural University, Soja, Okayama, Japan
[3] Osaka International University, Moriguchi, Osaka, Japan
[4] Takamatsu, Kagawa, Japan
[5] Osaka Electro-Communication University, Shijonawate, Osaka, Japan
nobori@osakac.ac.jp

Abstract. The author has already proposed an algorithm to perform depth image generation directly from Digital Imaging and Communications in Medicine (DICOM) on a Graphics Processing Unit (GPU) and an algorithm to perform Depth-Depth-Matching (DDM) on a GPU. The author has already proposed an algorithm to perform depth image generation directly from DICOM on a GPU and a DDM on a GPU. Here, the speed of the position and pose estimation is evaluated from actual liver surgery images to determine how fast it is necessary to obtain the required response speed during the procedure. The response speed of the liver surgery support system is evaluated based on actual liver surgery videos to determine how fast the position and posture estimation should be performed to obtain the required response speed during the surgery. The response speed of the liver surgery support system was evaluated based on actual liver surgery videos.

Keywords: real-life surgery · measurement of organ shifts · GPU's speed up

1 Introduction

Liver surgery is complicated by the complexity of the vascular system. Surgeons refer to preoperative imaging diagnosis using computed tomography (CT) and magnetic resonance imaging (MRI) to confirm the location of tumors and blood vessels. Preoperative imaging diagnosis uses MPR (Multi-Planer Reconstruction), which enables observation of the internal state of organs from multiple cross-sections, and volume rendering, which provides an image representation of the internal state of organs. However, it is not easy to grasp the internal structures of organs during surgery, as the position and posture of organs differ from those before surgery.

Therefore, commercial surgical systems are used to grasp the internal structures of organs during surgery [1–4]. These systems can provide real-time navigation of the

Takahiro Kunii—Freelance SE

© The Author(s), under exclusive license to Springer Nature Switzerland AG 2024
M. Kurosu and A. Hashizume (Eds.): HCII 2024, LNCS 14686, pp. 253–263, 2024.
https://doi.org/10.1007/978-3-031-60428-7_18

three-dimensional positioning of the tumor and surgical instruments using tomographic images taken before surgery. These navigation systems require landmark markers to be fixed. Stereotactic surgery is therefore suitable and used in orthopedic and neurosurgery. Soft, flexible, or deformable organs cannot be used as they cannot be marked. This is because it is not possible to mark the organs. We are therefore developing a surgical support system for organs that are difficult to mark and are soft and therefore deformable during surgery.

A surgical support system has been developed to prevent surgical accidents during laparotomy. The system aims to prevent intraoperative vessel amputation accidents by calculating the distance between the hepatic vessels and the scalpel tip position during surgery. As it is difficult to directly measure the distance between the hepatic vessels and scalpel tip during surgery, the system uses several estimation methods to calculate the distance between the hepatic vessels and scalpel tip during surgery.

First, a scalpel tip position estimation algorithm was created to estimate the position of the scalpel tip during surgery using a marker-based optical 3D position tracker, and the position estimation accuracy was evaluated using several markers. For the evaluation, a plastic pseudo-scalpel modelled with a 3D printer was used to assess the possibility of estimating the scalpel tip position. The results showed that the estimation error of the scalpel tip position could be estimated to be 2 mm. However, due to the low accuracy of the plastic pseudo-scalpel modelled with a 3D printer, a high estimation accuracy could not be achieved in this paper [5].

Next, to improve the estimation accuracy of the scalpel tip position, a pseudo-scalpel with a hard steel rod with a pointed tip was fabricated, the design of the marker to be attached was changed and the position estimation accuracy was evaluated using multiple markers. The results showed that the position estimation error of the scalpel tip position was 0.3 mm, which met the surgical requirements, and concluded that the proposed algorithm had reasonable performance to be incorporated into a liver surgery support system [6].

The author also proposed a wired intelligent surgical scalpel with LED level meter for liver surgery ('intelligent scalpel') as a method to provide feedback to the surgeon on the estimated scalpel tip position during surgery. In the proposed method, the LED level meter gradually lights up to alert the surgeon when the scalpel approaches a site that should not be cut. The effectiveness of the proposed method's intelligent scalpel for surgeon navigation was evaluated using a simulated task in which a subject traced an invisible circle on a table. The results showed that navigation to the subject could be performed with a maximum error of 14 mm [7].

However, due to the low availability and high price of optical 3D position trackers, a wireless surgical scalpel attachment ('smart scalpel') was developed that uses an inexpensive USB camera and ArUco markers to navigate the surgeon. The Smart Scalpel is smaller than the Intelligent Scalpel and can provide feedback to the surgeon on the position of the scalpel tip and the location of target vessels and tumors via wireless communication A quasi-task was conducted to evaluate the performance of ArUco markers and surgeon navigation, and the proposed method was comparable to a position tracker Optical 3D navigation accuracy was evaluated [8].

Then, after these premise studies on scalpel tip position estimation, the author embarked on a study to incorporate the proposed scalpel tip position estimation algorithm into a liver surgery support system. The liver surgery support system uses a liver position estimation system to estimate the position of the liver during surgery, and in order to assess the accuracy of the two systems when combined, the liver position estimation system created a real model with flexible holes (hereafter, simulated liver) and a cubic STL with holes, and annealing methods were The system was evaluated by estimating the position and posture using the hole formed in the simulated liver was used as a simulated blood vessel, and the distance accuracy when the scalpel tip was in contact with the simulated blood vessel on the surface of the simulated liver was evaluated and estimated with an average error of 5.76 mm. However, according to liver surgeons, the diameter of blood vessels that can be thermostatically stopped by electrocautery is less than 5 mm, and this paper did not meet the required accuracy and conditions [9, 10].

Subsequently, in a study on scalpel tip position estimation, it was decided to focus on a liver position and orientation estimation system, since the accuracy of the tip position estimation met the surgical requirements. Next, to estimate the positional orientation of the liver intraoperatively, the 3D camera is used to capture the shape of the liver surface intraoperatively and depth images are acquired. The DICOM of the liver taken preoperatively and the Z-buffer generated from the depth images taken by the 3D camera are used to estimate the positional posture of the liver. The estimation of the positional orientation of the liver uses a depth-depth matching algorithm that compares the depth images and minimizes the score of the evaluation function using an annealing-based algorithm. This algorithm treats the measurement information as a point cloud and can estimate the position-posture at a lower computational cost than 3D camera positioning [11, 12].

Finally, the estimated position and orientation of the liver and the scalpel tip are sent to the liver simulator, which estimates the distance to the vessel. The liver simulator uses a stereolithographic (STL) model generated by preoperative DICOM segmentation. This model consists of the liver STL, artery group STL, vein group STL and portal vein group STL, and the 3D polygonal model of the liver is sliced and deformed according to the surgery. The calculated distances to vessels and tumors are sent to the intelligent surgical scalpel and are visually displayed on an LED level meter. In this way, several estimation systems can be used to calculate the distance from the tip of the surgical scalpel to the vessel or tumor.

Between CPU-based and GPGPU-based depth matching algorithms, the GPU-based depth matching algorithm can complete operations five times faster, and the DICOM for the process of generating depth images directly from the DICOM and comparing them with depth images from the 3D camera of the GPGPU improved the number of operations [13, 14]. In addition, as the real-time estimation of intraoperative liver position and posture requires a huge amount of computation, the GPGPU is used to speed up the process by computing the comparison between images in parallel.

When the liver moves at high speed during surgery, the number of calculations for position and posture estimation is insufficient and it takes time for the simulator to reflect the actual position and posture, resulting in errors. Therefore, it is necessary to improve the accuracy by estimating the position and posture in real-time according to the intraoperative situation [15].

In this paper, the movement speed of the liver during an actual laparotomy is evaluated from actual surgical images. The response speed required for the liver position and posture estimation system is evaluated by determining the speed of liver movement and the number of moving frames during surgery. The results confirm that our GPU-based fast organ tracking algorithm is fast enough to handle organ movement in actual surgery.

In this paper, the responsiveness and algorithm optimization required for actual surgery are first described in Sect. 2, where measurement experiments in the operating theatre are described. Then, in Sect. 3, the amount of organ movement during actual surgical procedures is evaluated. The study is then summarized in Sect. 4.

2 Measurement Experiments in the Operating Theatre

To evaluate the response speed of the liver surgery support system, the amount of organ movement during surgery was evaluated from surgical images taken with a color camera in a real operating theatre in 2012.

The surgical images were captured by a camera attached to a contrast-free light installed above the operating table. The experimental measurement environment in the actual operating theatre is shown in Fig. 1. The surgeon performs the operation and proceeds with the resection while moving the organ during the operation, as shown in Fig. 2.

Fig. 1. Experimental measurement environment in an actual operating theatre.

Fig. 2. Organs undergoing laparotomy.

3   Organ Mobility Assessment

The speed of movement of the intraoperative organs was evaluated based on the surgical video. To determine the location of the intraoperative organs, the location was estimated using NCC template matching. As conditions for estimation, the target area for matching was set to the laparotomy area shown in Fig. 3, and the area shown in Fig. 4 was set as the template.

The changes in organ positions during surgery estimated by template matching are shown in Fig. 5. The major movements of the organs during surgery were measured as the movement during resection with the scalpel and the movement to change the orientation of the organs. As there were frames during surgery where template matching could not be performed well due to the surgical instruments and the surgeon's hands, the range of continuous movement was visually confirmed from the estimation results and the video. Typical surgical situations and frames of the estimated organ positions are shown in Table 1. Furthermore, the matching status of each frame is shown in Figs. 6, 7, 8, 9, 10, 11, 12 and 13.

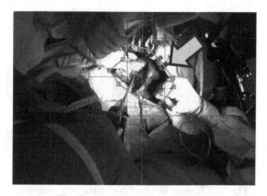

Fig. 3. Target area for matching.

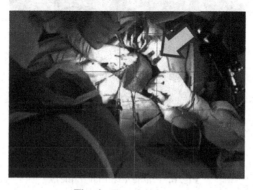

Fig. 4. Template area.

Table 1. Frames of surgical situation and estimated organ location.

Frame	Surgical situation	Estimated position X-coordinate	Estimated position Y-coordinate	Relative position X-coordinate	Relative position Y-coordinate
1	Initial state	249.216	128.507	-	-
60	Before transfer with surgical instruments	250.634	130.141	-1.418	-1.634
71	During transport with surgical tools	251.252	129.248	-2.036	-0.741
121	After transfer by surgical instruments	249.724	128.423	-0.508	0.084
840	Intraoperative suction	250.738	130.265	-1.522	-1.758
889	Before organ transfer due to change of surgical field	257.356	145.262	-8.140	-16.755
905	During organ transfer due to change of surgical field	264.624	145.117	-15.408	-16.610
925	During organ transfer due to change of surgical field	264.611	151.974	-15.395	-23.467

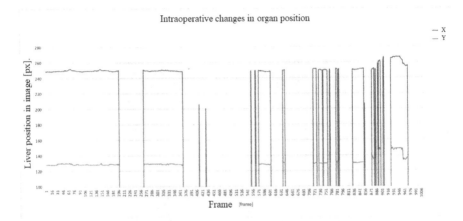

Fig. 5. Changes in organ position during surgery.

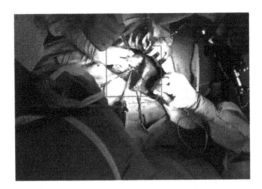

Fig. 6. Frame 1 (initial frame).

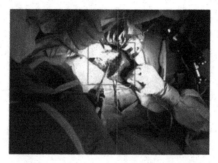

Fig. 7. Frame 60 (before movement with surgical instrument.

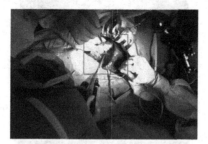

Fig. 8. Frame 71 (during movement by surgical instrument).

Fig. 9. Frame 121 (after movement with surgical instrument).

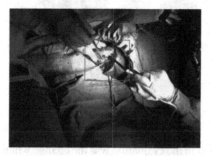

Fig. 10. Frame 840 (intraoperative suction).

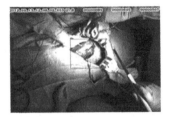

Fig. 11. Frame 889 (before organ transfer due to change of surgical field).

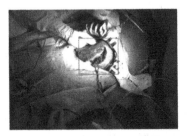

Fig. 12. Frame 905 (during organ transfer due to change of surgical field)

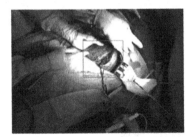

Fig. 13. Frame 925 (during organ transfer due to change of surgical field).

Fig. 14. Reference surgeon's thumb (19.5 pixels).

The fastest movement in the evaluation was the change when the organ was lifted and moved by the surgeon to change the operating field. To calculate the movement speed, the pixel size was converted based on the 19.5 pixels of the surgeon's thumb shown in Fig. 14. When the thumb size is 21 [mm], the pixel resolution per pixel is 1.077 [mm/pixel] and the frame rate is 21 fps. Table 2 shows the speed of movement between frames, where each is converted into the speed of movement. The fastest movement speed was 10.276 [mm/s] when moving organs by changing the operating field.

Table 2. Organ estimated travel speed with initial state.

interframe	Number of frames	Elapsed time $[s]$	X-axis travel $[mm]$	Y-axis travel $[mm]$	Vector amount $[mm]$	Movement speed $[mm/s]$
60 - 71	11	0.524	-0.618	0.893	1.086	2.233
889 - 905	16	0.762	-7.268	0.145	7.269	10.276
889 - 925	36	1.714	-7.255	-6.712	9.884	6.209

4   Conclusions

In the previous work [15], to improve the response speed of the liver surgery support system, a GPU-based method for generating virtual depth images from DICOM was proposed and evaluated. A method for generating depth images directly from DICOM was developed, and it was confirmed that depth images could be generated in 5.1 ms (about 200 times/s) on average. Furthermore, we succeeded in improving the response speed by a factor of 5 compared to the CPU by using a GPU to process the matching process between the actual liver surface shape measured by the depth camera and the depth image generated from the 3D model, which had been a bottleneck in response speed.

Finally, the response speed of the liver surgery support system was evaluated based on actual liver surgery videos to determine how fast the position and posture estimation should be to obtain the required response speed during surgery. As a result, the fastest movement speed was 10.276 [mm/s], approximately $10 \, mm/200 = 0.05$ mm/times, when the organ was moved by changing the surgical field, and it can be concluded that a human can confirm the movement of the organ at the fastest movement during surgery, which was obtained in the evaluation.

Acknowledgments. This study is partly supported by 2014–2017 Grants-in-Aid for Scientific Research (B) (No. 26289069) from the Ministry of Education, Culture, Sports, Science, and Technology, Japan. Further support was provided by the 2022 Cooperation Research Fund B from the Graduate School at Osaka Electro-Communication University.

Disclosure of Interests. All authors declare that they have no competing interests.

References

1. Cranial Navigation - Brainlab. https://www.brainlab.com/ja/surgery-products/overview-neurosurgery-products/cranial-navigation/. Accessed 3 Feb 2021
2. Navix - ClaroNav. https://www.claronav.com/navix/. Accessed 3 Feb 2021
3. Surgical Navigation Systems - StealthStation—Medtronic. https://www.medtronic.com/us-en/healthcare-professionals/products/neurological/surgicalnavigation-systems/stealthstation.html. Accessed 4 Feb 2021
4. Plan and Navigate - Surgical Theater. https://surgicaltheater.net/plan-navigate/. Accessed 3 Feb 2021
5. Doi, M., et al.: Knife tip position estimation using multiple markers for liver surgery support. In: Proceedings of the 6th International Conference on Advanced Mechatronics (ICAM2015), Nishiwaseda Campus of Waseda University, Tokyo Japan, 1A2-08, pp. 74–75, 5–8 December 2015
6. Koeda, M., Yano, D., Doi, M., Onishi, K., Noborio, H.: Calibration of surgical knife-tip position with marker-based optical tracking camera and precise evaluation of its measurement accuracy. Int. J. Bioinform. Neurosci. (JBINS) 4(1), 155–159 (2018)
7. Yano, D., Koeda, M., Onishi, K., Noborio, H.: Development of a surgical knife attachment with proximity indicators. In: Marcus, A., Wang, W. (eds.) HCI (19). Design, User Experience, and Usability: Designing Pleasurable Experiences, DUXU 2017. LNCS, vol. 10289, pp. 608–618. Springer, Cham (2017). https://doi.org/10.1007/978-3-319-58637-3_48, Print ISBN: 978-3-319-58636-6, Online ISBN: 978-3-319-58637-3
8. Koeda, M., Yano, D., Shintaku, N., Onishi, K., Noborio, H.: Development of wireless surgical knife attachment with proximity indicators using ArUco marker. In: Kurosu M. (eds.) Human-Computer Interaction. Interaction in Context, HCI 2018. LNCS, vol. 10902, pp.14–26. Springer, Cham (2018). https://doi.org/10.1007/978-3-319-91244-8_2, Print ISBN 978-3-319-91243-1, Online ISBN 978-3-319-91244-8
9. Yano, D., et al.: Verification of accuracy of knife tip position estimation in liver surgery support system. In: Proceedings of the 2017 International Conference on Intelligent Informatics and Biomedical Sciences (ICIIBMS), November 2017, pp. 284–285 (2017). https://doi.org/10.1109/ICIIBMS.2017.8279688
10. Yano, D., et al.: Accuracy verification of knife tip positioning with position and orientation estimation of the actual liver for liver surgery support system. J. Bioinform. Neurosci. 3(3), 79–84 (2017). e-ISSN: 2432-5422, p-ISSN: 2188-8116
11. Watanabe, K., Yoshida, S., Yano, D., Koeda, M., Noborio, H.: A new organ-following algorithm based on depth-depth matching and simulated annealing, and its experimental evaluation. In: Marcus, A., Wang, W. (eds.) HCI (19). Design, User Experience, and Usability: Designing Pleasurable Experiences. DUXU 2017. LNCS, vol. 10289, pp. 594–607. Springer, Cham (2017). https://doi.org/10.1007/978-3-319-58637-3_47, Print ISBN: 978-3-319-58636-6, Online ISBN: 978-3-319-58637-3
12. Noborio, H., Yoshida, S., Watanabe, K., Yano, D., Koeda, M.: Comparative study of depth-image matching with steepest descendent and simulated annealing algorithms. In: Proceedings of the 11th International Joint Conference on Biomedical Engineering Systems and Technologies (BIOSTEC 2018) - Volume 1: BIODEVICES, pp. 77–87, Funchal, Madeira-Portugal, 19–21 January 2018. ISBN: 978-989-758-277-6
13. Numata, S., et al.: A novel liver surgical navigation system using polyhedrons with STL-Format. In: Kurosu, M. (eds.) Human-Computer Interaction. Interaction in Context. HCI 2018. LNCS, vol. 10902, pp. 53–63. Springer, Cham (2018). https://doi.org/10.1007/978-3-319-91244-8_5, Print ISBN 978-3-319-91243-1, Online ISBN 978-3-319-91244-8

14. Koeda, M., Yano, D., Mori, T., Onishi, K., Noborio, H.: DICOM depth image generation using GPGPU for fast position and orientation estimation on liver surgery support system. In: Proceedings of IEEE TENCON 2019 Technologies for Smart Nation (TENCON2019), pp. 354–358, October 2019

15. Yano, D., Koeda, M., Noborio, H., Onishi, K.: Evaluation of depth-depth-matching speed of depth image generated from DICOM by GPGPU. In: Kurosu, M. (eds.) Human-Computer Interaction. Interaction Techniques and Novel Applications. HCII 2021. LNCS, vol. 12763, pp. 644–655. Springer, Cham (2021). https://doi.org/10.1007/978-3-030-78465-2_46

Author Index

A

Asano, Miho 253
Ashrafi, Navid 3
Ayanoğlu, Hande 63
Azad, Md. Tariquzzaman 163

B

Bijo, Kunnumpurath 203
Boldi, Arianna 99
Bukht, Baidar 22

C

Chan, Gerry 117

F

Fellmann, Michael 22
Friday, Aniefiok 117
Fu, Rongrong 177

G

Gao, Tanhao 41
Gensichen, Jochen 133
Grunert, Hannes 22
Guo, Yongyan 177, 236

H

Hernández Ramírez, Rodrigo 63
Hossain, Md. Farhad 163

I

Ikonomi, Tedi 133

K

Kobayashi, Takashi 194
Koeda, Masanao 51, 149, 194, 221, 253
Krcmar, Helmut 133
Kunii, Takahiro 253

M

Magaribuchi, Toshihiro 194
Manandhar, Shisir Prasad 203
Masui, Kimihiko 194
Mishra, Deepti 87
Morgado, Mafalda 63
Munderia, Rageshwari 78

N

Nachenahalli Bhuthegowda, Bhavana 87
Neuhaus, Vanessa 3
Ning, Jin 41
Noborio, Hiroshi 51, 149, 221, 253

O

Onishi, Katsuhiko 51, 149, 221
Orji, Rita 117

P

Pande, Akshara 87
Peperkorn, Nicolina Laura 3
Prommegger, Barbara 133

Q

Qiao, Yue 41

R

Rahman, Safin 163
Rapp, Amon 99
Reen, Jaisheen Kour 117
Reindl-Spanner, Philipp 133

S

Sawada, Atsuro 194
Schmidt, Angelina Clara 22
Sharma, Abhishek 203
Sharma, Lakshmi 203
Shiban, Youssef 3
Shidujaman, Mohammad 163
Singh, Rajbala 78

M. Kurosu and A. Hashizume (Eds.): HCII 2024, LNCS 14686, pp. 265–266, 2024.
https://doi.org/10.1007/978-3-031-60428-7

T
Tsujishita, Morihiro   149, 221
Tsukuda, Yoshio   51

V
Voigt-Antons, Jan-Niklas   3
Vona, Francesco   3

W
Watanabe, Kaito   221

X
Xue, Mengru   163

Y
Yang, Mengshi   41
Yang, Min   236
Yano, Daiki   253

Z
Zhou, Hongtao   41

Printed in the United States
by Baker & Taylor Publisher Services